Sugar Confectionery and Chocolate Manufacture

Sugar Confectionery
and
Chocolate Manufacture

R LEES   E B JACKSON

LEONARD HILL BOOKS
AN INTERTEXT PUBLISHER

Published by
Leonard Hill Books
a division of
International Textbook Company Limited
24 Market Square, Aylesbury, Bucks HP20 1TL

First published 1973

ISBN 0 249 44120 9

Printed in Great Britain by
Clarke, Doble & Brendon Ltd. Plymouth

Contents

List of Figures

List of Plates

Preface

The authors had five objectives in preparing this book: (i) to bring together relevant information on many raw materials used in the manufacture of sweets and chocolate; (ii) to describe the principles involved and to relate them to production with maximum economy but maintaining high quality; (iii) to describe both traditional and modern production processes, in particular those continuous methods which are finding increasing application; (iv) to give basic recipes and methods, set out in a form for easy reference, for producing a large variety of sweets, and capable of easy modification to suit the raw materials and plant available; (v) to explain the elementary calculations most likely to be required.

The various check lists and charts, showing the more likely faults and how to eliminate them, reflect the fact that art still plays no small part in this industry.

To help users all over the world, whatever units they employ, most formulations are given in *parts by weight*, but tables of conversion factors are provided at the end of the book.

There also will be found a collection of other general reference data in tabular form; while the Glossary explains a number of technical terms, many of them peculiar to the industry.

This is a time of world-wide change in the structure of the sugar confectionery and chocolate industry. It is experiencing consolidation with a general movement towards larger manufacturing units employing less labour with higher investment and capital costs in automatic and continuous high-output production lines.

Many old-established factories have been closed because of mergers or takeovers or changing market pressures. But new, small vigorous companies have been formed to manufacture lines which the larger firms are finding uneconomic to produce in batch quantities. Confectionery packs offered under the retailer's own label are accelerating the change to more efficient production to cope with the lower profit margins generally associated with this trade. New firms entering the industry have high sales potential provided a good product is offered, effectively packaged and efficiently marketed. Sales of confectionery products in the United Kingdom are considerable, as the following figures for 1971 show.

	Producers £	United Kingdom Imports £	Exports £
Chocolate and chocolate confectionery	182 169 000	4 197 000	16 984 000
Chocolate crumb, cocoa butter and other cocoa products	12 402 000	20 136 000	3 666 000
Chocolate couverture and similar products	12 163 000	63 000	472 000
Medicated confectionery	1 810 000	—	187 000
Sugar confectionery	108 248 000	3 208 000	14 610 000

(Source: *Business Monitor*, June 1972, HMSO.)

Sales by United States manufacturers during 1970 were 1925 million dollars of which 770 million dollars were direct sales to retailers (Source: US Industrial Outlook, US Department of Commerce).

Sales of sugar confectionery and chocolate in 1968 in the EEC (the original 6) were £244 million and £388 million respectively (Economist Intelligence Unit Reports 95, 98, 101, 113).

Both authors acknowledge the help and encouragement of many friends and colleagues: to Alan Maiden who has given considerable encouragement and assistance over several years and especially of their wives for their patience and tact during the writing. Ronald Lees wishes to thank Mr. Frank Cruden, Editor of *Confectionery Production*, for permission to reproduce tables from his articles in that journal under the nom de plume John F. Ingleton. The following individuals most kindly gave information and permission to reproduce illustrations:

Dr. J. Buckle, H.P. Bulmer Co. Ltd., Hereford, England.

Mr. B. W. Minifie, Knechtel Laboratories Ltd., Saltford, Bristol, England.

Mr. J. W. Mansvelt, Lenderink Co., N.V., Schiedam, Holland.

Dr. A. M. Maiden, CPC (United Kingdom) Ltd., Esher, Surrey, England.

Mr. P. Fawcett, CPC (United Kingdom) Ltd., Esher, Surrey, England.

Mr. J. Reid, E. T. Oakes Ltd., Macclesfield, England.

G. A. Steele, Baker Perkins Ltd., Peterborough, England.

Mr. C. Warren, Confectionery Development Ltd., Hemel Hempstead, Hertfordshire, England.

The directors and staff of CPC (United Kingdom) Ltd., Manchester and Esher, England.

Information, illustrations and/or photographs on machinery and manufacturing process are warmly acknowledged also from the following companies:

Bramigk and Co. Ltd., London, E.3.
Cadbury Schweppes Ltd., Bournville, Birmingham.
Otto Hansel GmbH, Hannover, Germany.
Hamac Hansella, GmbH, Viersen, Germany.
R. Simons and Sons Ltd., Basford, Nottingham.
Norman Bartleet Ltd., London W14.
Gebr. er Braak N.V., Rotterdam, Holland.
Justus Theegarten, Koln, Germany.
Winkler Dunnebier, Neuwied/Rhein, Germany.
Sollich OHG, Bad Salzuflen, Germany.
Lenderink Co. N.V., Schiedam, Holland.
Bulmer Co. Ltd., Hereford, England.
E. T. Oakes Ltd., Macclesfield, England.
G. A. Steele, Baker Perkins Ltd., Peterborough, England.
Confectionery Development Ltd., Hemel Hempstead, Herts, England.

1

Basic Technical Considerations

1.1 INTRODUCTION

Some understanding of the chemical and other scientific properties of sugar confectionery and chocolate is important for the technologist; notably in overcoming faults that may have developed in the product; in the preparation of matching recipes; for detecting wrong blending of ingredients or incorrect processing conditions; and in the maintenance of high standards of quality.

Throughout the book reference is made to such general scientific concepts as moisture content, pH, etc. This introductory chapter is intended to describe briefly the more important of these and their significance to the properties of confectionery.

1.2 MOISTURE AND TOTAL SOLIDS CONTENT

The amount of water left in a sugar confectionery product depends on the type of raw materials used and on the extent of the processing during manufacture. When water is heated under normal atmospheric conditions it will boil at 100° C (212° F); but this boiling temperature is increased when sugar is present in solution. For a fixed concentration of sugar, under standard conditions of atmospheric pressure, a solution will always boil at the same temperature. Conversely if a sugar solution is boiled to a fixed temperature under standard conditions the remaining liquor will always contain the same percentage concentration of sugar and water. The increase in boiling temperature for varying concentrations of sucrose is shown in Table 1.

The effect of other sugars (which are described in Chapter 2) in raising the boiling point is shown in Table 2 and the effect of boiling under vacuum in Table 3.

Before the general availability of thermometers, a number of crude tests were used to determine boiling level. To enable the reader to use older recipes, these are set out in Table 4.

1

TABLE 1.   Boiling Point of Sucrose (Cane or Beet Sugar) Solutions

Sucrose Concentration %	Boiling Point	
	°C	°F
40	101·4	214·5
50	102	215·5
60	103	217·5
70	105·5	222
75	108	227
80	111	232
85	116	241
90	122	252
95	130	266

The presence of other raw materials, such as fats, non-sugar milk solids, starch etc., does not significantly affect the boiling temperature. It is therefore possible to determine the boiling points used in the manufacture of a competitor's confection through a knowledge of the composition and, in particular, the water content (see also §17.10).

A knowledge of the water (moisture) content of a raw material is important in developing confectionery recipes. In the United Kingdom it is necessary to incorporate more than 4% butterfat in any sweet which contains in its title the word 'butter'. If the weight of butter added was divided by the batch weight after processing, an erroneous value for the percentage butter content would be calculated, for butter contains some water and this must be taken into account when developing recipes which contain this ingredient (see also §17.2).

The water left in a confection can also influence its storage behaviour in a number of ways: e.g. whether or not the product will dry out or pick up moisture in store, and the extent of crystallisation occurring during its expected shelf life. Boiled sweets which contain more than 4·0% moisture will normally crystallise (grain) while in store. Average moisture content for a range of sugar confectionery products and raw materials is shown in Table 5.

TABLE 3.   Effect of Boiling under Vacuum

Approximate Total Solids Value %	Open Boil Temp.		Vacuum Cooking		
	°C	°F	Boiling Temp. °C	°F	Vacuum lb/in²
96	143·4	290	129·5	265	25
97	150	302	135	275	27
98	160·1	320	140·6	285	28

TABLE 2. Boiling Temperatures of Glucose Syrup and Invert Sugar Syrups and Mixtures thereof

Temperature		Glucose Syrup Concentration %	Glucose Syrup Solids / Invert Sugar Ratio					Invert Sugar Concentration %
°C	°F		4:1	2:1	1:1	1:2	1:4	
105·5	222	81·0	79·2	78·0	76·5	75·0	73·8	72·0
111·1	232	85·6	83·8	82·7	81·2	79·7	77·6	76·8
116·1	241	89·3	87·8	86·7	85·5	84·2	83·1	81·6
122·2	252	92·7	91·6	90·9	90·0	89·1	88·4	87·3
130·0	266	97·8	96·9	96·2	95·5	94·7	94·0	93·1

TABLE 4. Traditional Degrees of Sugar Boiling

Name	Test	Observation	Approx. Temp. °C	°F
Thread (gloss)	A	Thin strands	103	215
Large Thread (large gloss)	A	Stronger and more strands	104	219
Small Pearl	B	Forms small droplets	105	220
Large Pearl	B	Forms large droplets	106	222
Blow (soufflé)	C	Bubbles set on syrup	110	230
Feather	B	Forms feathery hard strands	111	232
Small Ball	B	Syrup forms soft ball	116	240
Large Ball	B	Syrup forms hard ball	120	248
Light Crack	B	Forms thin sheet	129	264
Medium Crack	B	Sheet forms, slightly brittle	133	271
Hard Crack	B	Rapidly formed sheet	143	289
Extra Hard Crack	B	Sheet shows signs of browning	168	334
Caramel	B	Brown brittle sheet forms	180	356

Tests: A. Place sample of cooked syrup between two wetted fingers and open. B. Dip finger or spatula (above 110° C) in water, then in portion of boil, return to cold water. C. Blow on spatula dipped in syrup.

1.3   TOTAL SOLIDS AND TOTAL SOLUBLE SOLIDS

The total solids content of a sweetmeat includes all the solid matter in the ingredients used for the recipe. Total soluble solids content includes only those components which are soluble in water. It is therefore mainly composed of the added sugars and as such is a useful guide as to whether the product is liable to ferment on store or whether correct processing conditions have been used. A sufficiently accurate determination of total soluble solids content can be made during manufacture of jellies and similar products using a pocket sugar refractometer.

1.4   SUGARS AND SUGAR SOLUBILITY

A range of sugar ingredients are used in the manufacture of sweets and chocolates. These include cane and beet sugar, glucose syrups, high sugar content syrups such as treacle and honey, invert sugar syrups, dextrose,

TABLE 5. Typical Percentage Moisture Content of Sugar Confectionery, Chocolate and Various Raw Materials

Sugar Confectionery and Chocolate

Sweet	Moisture %	Sweet	Moisture %
Agar Jellies	24·0	Jellies Gelatine	22·0
(High) Boiled Sweets	2·0	Jellies Pectin	22·0
Butterscotch	3·5	Jellies Table	25·0
Candied Fruit	20·0	Liquorice Paste	18·0
Caramels	8·0	Lozenges	1·5
Chocolate	1·0	Marshmallow grained	12·0
Creams	14·0	Marshmallow cast	18·0
Cream Paste	6·0	Nougat	8·0
Fondant	12·0	Pectin Jellies	22·0
Fudge	7·0	(Compressed) Tablets	1·0
Gelatine Jellies	22·0	Turkish Delight	20·0
Jellies Agar	24·0		

Raw Materials

Component	Moisture %	Component	Moisture %
Agar	16·0	Maltose	16·7
Block Liquorice Juice	18·7	Enzyme	16·7
Brown Sugar	2·9	Golden Syrup	16·7
Butter	13·8	Granulated Sugar	0·01
Candied Peel	20·0	Gum Arabic	9·9
Chocolate	1·0	Gum Tragacanth	9·9
Chocolate Crumb	1·0	Honey	18·0
Citric Acid, Hydrate	8·3	Icing Sugar	0·01
Condensed Milk	27·0	Invert Sugar	28·0
Cornflour	12·3	Lactose	0·1
Dates	24·8	Milk Powder	22·9
Dextrose Hydrate	9·1	Nuts	2·0
Fruit Pulp	39·8	Sorbitol	30·0
Gelatine	12·3	Soya Flour	7·4
Glucose Syrup		Starch	10·7
Low DE*	19·4	Tartaric Acid	1·0
Regular	18·7	Treacle	18·8
High DE	18·0	Wheat Flour	13·8

*DE=dextrose equivalent (see §2.3)

fructose and lactose. Cane or beet sugar (sucrose), dextrose (sometimes called glucose), fructose (sometimes called laevulose) and lactose (sometimes called milk sugar) are single sugars; all others are mixtures of sugars. Glucose syrup contains dextrose, maltose and a range of complex sugars while invert sugar is a mixture of dextrose and fructose. Properties of various types of confectionery sugars are considered in more detail in Chapter 2.

Sugar confections which contain high concentrations of cane or beet sugar (sucrose) may crystallise (grain) during manufacture or while on store. Although this may be desired for certain products, e.g. fondants, fudge, in other cases it is a quality defect. If the level of sucrose is lowered to under 75% in a confection, such as a jelly, to lessen the danger of graining, then the product becomes liable to mould and yeast growth. Both defects can be cured by the addition of the so called 'doctor-sugars', usually glucose syrup and invert sugar syrup (see §2.3 and §2.9), which inhibit crystallisation and raise the overall level of sugars in solution.

Doctor sugars have the ability to break down certain types of complex chemical compounds; because of this they are said to have reducing properties. Various analytical techniques are used to determine reducing sugar content usually based on breaking down compounds containing copper [see R. LEES, *Laboratory Handbook of Methods of Food Analysis*, 1971, Leonard Hill Books]. Practically all the solid matter present in an invert sugar syrup is made up of reducing sugars but only a part of the glucose syrup solids are of this type. Determinations on glucose syrup are carried out as though the only reducing sugar present is dextrose. For comparative purposes a dextrose equivalent (DE) value is quoted for this sugar mixture which indicates the equivalent amount of dextrose present in the dried syrup that would give the same chemical behaviour during analysis. The amount of reducing sugars in a sugar confection is important in indicating how well the recipe has been balanced (Chapter 17).

Table 6 shows that at 20° C a pure saturated solution of sucrose (cane or beet sugar) can only hold 67% of solids but that progressive additions of invert sugar increases this figure. This increase in total solids content produces improved non-crystallising characteristics and builds up a resistance to microbiological attack. As the amount of invert sugar is increased, the syrup becomes saturated with respect to dextrose (a component of invert sugar).

The effect obtained using invert sugar to increase syrup concentration is limited: Table 7 shows that beyond 52% invert syrup, the solids content decreases although crystallisation may still remain acceptable.

The most effective method of 'doctoring' is to use glucose syrup (see

TABLE 6.   Concentration of Sucrose/Invert Sugar Syrups Saturated with respect to Sucrose

Solids Present		Solids Content of Solutions just Saturated with Sucrose at 20° C (68° F) % by weight
Sucrose %	Invert Sugar %	
100	0	67·1
78·6	21·4	70·0
67·6	32·4	72·0
57·6	42·4	74·0
48·8	51·2	76·0

TABLE 7. Concentration of Sucrose/Invert Sugar Syrups Saturated with respect to Invert Sugar

Solids Present		Solids Content of Solutions just Saturated with Dextrose at 20° C (68°F) % by weight
Sucrose %	Invert Sugar %	
47·5	52·5	76·1
40·0	60·0	73·6
30·0	70·0	70·5
20·0	80·0	67·7

TABLE 8. Concentration of Sucrose/Glucose Syrups Saturated with respect to Sucrose

Solids Present		Solids Content of Solutions just Saturated with Sucrose at 20° C (68° F) % by weight
Sucrose %	42 DE Glucose Syrup Solids %	
100	0	67·1
78·6	21·4	70·0
67·6	32·4	72·0
57·6	42·4	74·0
48·8	51·2	76·0
40·9	59·1	78·0
34·1	65·9	80·0
28·4	71·6	82·0
23·7	76·3	84·0

§2.3). Table 8 shows that a syrup solids content of 84% can be achieved using a mixture of sucrose and 42 DE glucose syrup without sucrose or dextrose crystallisation taking place.

In practice the situation is complicated by the fact that whilst sucrose crystallises fairly readily from solution, dextrose monohydrate does not. A certain amount of dextrose supersaturation can exist indefinitely provided that no dextrose monohydrate is present to initiate crystallisation (or 'seed' the solution). Dextrose will not crystallise from unseeded solutions until the concentration is over 150% higher than that of the solubility value.

1.5 EQUILIBRIUM RELATIVE HUMIDITY

The amount of moisture present in air is indicated by the *relative humidity* value. This relates the amount of water present in the air with the total amount of moisture that could be held if the air was fully saturated under the same conditions. The moisture in the air contributes a measurable pressure to the total air pressure and a comparative value, known as the *relative vapour pressure* (r v p), can be derived by relating the determined value to the maximum value known for moisture-saturated air under the same conditions.

The temperature at which moisture condensation from the air occurs is known as the *dew point*. An examination of the relative humidity and temperature will enable an accurate prediction to be made of the point at which moisture formation will occur. Moisture deposition is particularly likely to occur for instance when chocolates leave the cooling tunnels after coating. This deposited moisture can leach out some of the sugar present in the chocolate coating, which later crystallises causing 'sugar bloom'.

The moisture in a sweetmeat will exert a vapour pressure on the atmosphere which immediately surrounds the confection. A value relating the amount of moisture present in the surrounding air to fully saturated air can be calculated. When this value known as the *Equilibrium Relative Humidity* (e r h), is equal to the relative humidity of the air, the product neither gains nor loses moisture. If the e r h is below this the confection will gain moisture and if above, will lose it.

Confections with high equilibrium relative humidities, over 70%, when packed in sealed containers give rise to conditions which encourage mould growth during storage. Changes in temperature result firstly in moisture loss from the confection and later deposition on the surface. Leaching of sugars occur and the weak sugar syrup will permit the growth of mould. A number of methods for the theoretical calculation of e r h (or r v p) have been suggested [J. W. GROVER, 1947, *J. Soc. Chem. Ind.*, *66*, 201–5], [A. E. POUNCY, B. C. L. SUMMERS, 1939, *J. Soc. Chem. Ind.*, *58*, 162], [PROCTOR LANDROCK, 1951, *Food Tech.*, *5*, 332–7], [E. G. GILES, 1955, *Confectionery Production*, (1), 61] and practical methods for their determination developed [J. W. GROVER, 1947, *J. Soc. Chem. Ind.*, *66*, 201], [J. KELLEHER, 1955, *Int. Sugar J.*, *57*, 36–38], [R. W. MONEY, R. BORN, 1951, *J. Sci. Fd. Agric.*, April 180], [R. S. NORRISH, 1964, *Confectionery Production*, *30* (10), 769–771, 808], [G. D'ALTON, 1962, *Confectionery Manufacture*, 8], [W. POERSCH, 1963, *Starké*, *15*, (11), 405–12].

TABLE 9. Typical Equilibrium Relative Humidity Values of Sugar Confections

Confection	Equilibrium Relative Humidity %
(High) Boiled Sweets	less than 30
Caramels	45–50
Creams	80–85
Fondant	75–80
Fudge	65–75
Jellies	60–76
Liquorice	57–65
Marshmallow	64–72
Turkish Delight	60–70

1.6 ACID CONTENT

Five acids are commonly used in sugar confectionery products: citric, malic, tartaric, lactic, and acetic acids. The first four are said to be 'weak' acids and they are used for flavouring. In laboratory reports, the analyst for convenience commonly indicates the percentage of acid as if it were citric. Additional tests are necessary to identify the particular acid used. As a general rule confections with a mild fruit flavour should contain 0·5% acid, those sold as fruit confections need 1·0% acid and those sold as acid drops should have an acid content of between 1·5%–2·0%.

1.7 pH

A knowledge of the amount of acid present although helpful, is not indicative of the real acid strength of the product. A solution of 1% sulphuric acid has quite different chemical acidic properties from a 1% solution of citric acid.

The strength of an acid is related to the amount of dissociated hydrogen ions in solution. Pure water, H_2O can in simple terms be thought of as dissociating into hydrogen H+ and hydroxyl OH− ions. When acids are present they cause a greater dissociation and therefore increase the number of hydrogen ions present. Alkalis cause reassociation thereby lowering the amount of free hydrogen ions. Different acids cause different levels of dissociation. The full scientific explanation is more complex.

A scale has been devised—pH—which gives comparable whole values for indicating the acidity or alkalinity of a wide range of products. This scale expresses the logarithm of one, *divided* by the hydrogen ion concentration, so that the 'pH value' is lower, the more acid the solution. The method was suggested by Sorensen in 1909 and has been widely adopted in the food industry. pH is easily measured either by colour matching changes in dyes under particular acid or alkaline conditions or, more usually, by measuring changes in electrical conductivity.

A neutral solution has a pH of 7·0, lower values indicate an acid solution, higher values an alkaline solution. A 0·6% solution of nitric acid, a strong acid, has a pH of 1·0 while the same concentration of weak acetic acid has a pH of 2·9; such variations are indicated in Table 10.

The pH scale runs from 0 to 14; it is possible only under exceptional conditions to get pH values as low at 1·5 and as high as 14. Below pH 1 and above pH 13 the determined values are inaccurate. In sugar confectionery manufacture the scale readings lie mainly between pH 2 and pH 8.

To stabilise the acidity of a product, use is made of so-called buffer-salts, compounds produced from strong alkalis and weak acids; notably sodium citrate. In the presence of extra acid, the citrate ion re-combines to form

TABLE 10. Variation in Acid Content to achieve Constant pH.

R. HEISS, L. SCHACHINGER, W. BARTUSCH, 1953, *Manufacturing Confectioner, 33* (8), 9.]

Acid	pH	Concentration %
Hydrochloric	2·0	0·0315
Tartaric	2·0	2·265
Citric	2·0	2·44
Lactic	2·0	1·912
Acetic	2·0	1·95

TABLE 11. Typical pH Values of Sugar Confections and their Constituent Raw Materials

Material	pH	Material	pH
Boiled Sweets	(*Acid*) 2·2	Gelatine (lime produced)	5·1
Apple Pulp	2·5	Glucose Syrup	5·2
Lactic Acid (buffered)	3·0	Alginate Jellies	5·3
Pectin Jelly	3·1	Marzipan	6·0
Honey (dependent on source)	3·4–6·0	Cream	6·2
Table Jellies	3·8	Cocoa	6·3
Pineapple Pulp	3·8	Milk, Evaporated	6·4
Lactose	3·9	Liquid Sugars	6·4
Creams	4·2	Cocoa Butter	6·6
Gelatine (acid produced)	4·2	Milk Powder	6·6
Gelatine Jellies	4·4	Butter	6·7
Fondant	4·4	Pure deionised Water	(*Neutral*) 7·0
Egg Albumin	4·7	Sodium Alginate	(*Alkaline*) 7·7
Gum tragacanth	5·0		

the weak citric acid, thus 'buffering' the effect of the acid. Sodium citrate is used in the manufacture of confectionery jellies, e.g. of pectin jellies.

The rate of inversion of the more complex sugars into the simpler sugars is dependent on the pH of the solution. In particular, the breakdown of sucrose into an invert sugar mixture is pH dependent. Work carried out by Heiss and co-workers (loc cit) has shown the efficiency in the production of invert sugar is in the order of effectiveness—hydrochloric, tartaric, citric, lactic, acetic and cream of tartar. The effect of pH on inversion of sucrose has been shown by ATKINSON *et al.* [F. E. ATKINSON, C. C. STRACHAN, A. W. MOYLE, J. A. KESTON, *Food Techn.*, 1952, *6*, 1431] and is shown in Table 12.

Variation in product pH can considerably effect the gel strength of jellies and the whipping power of the certain raw materials. These changes are discussed in greater detail in the chapters concerning these ingredients.

Gelatine, agar, starch, pectin, wheat flour and alginates are variously used as gelling agents in the manufacture of sweets. To compare the strength of the jellies produced with these ingredients and between com-

TABLE 12. Rate of Inversion of Sucrose Solutions with Increasing pH (50%
Sucrose Solution, 7 days inversion at 120° F)

pH	Conversion %
3·00	79
3·50	38
3·75	26
4·00	15
4·50	7

1.8   GELLING AGENTS

petitive products a number of different test methods are used. Three main
types of results are quoted under the appropriate ingredient and product
sections, these are bloom, jelly strength and gel strength determined
respectively on the bloom gelometer, British Food Manufacturing Industries Research Association FIRA tester and the Corn Industries Research
Foundation tester.

These instruments depend on the depression resulting from the application of weight applied from above, or the force needed to turn a blade
inserted into the jelly.

1.9   VISCOSITY

Viscosity is a measure of the drag or friction of a liquid in movement.
If two adjacent layers, equal in area, move at different speeds, then a
force or stress will be needed to maintain this difference. The relationship
between the differing speeds of the layers is known as the *rate of shear*.

According to Newton, when twice the stress is applied at a fixed temperature then the liquid layers will move with twice the difference in speed.
'Newtonian' liquids, such as water, sucrose solutions, and oil, behave in
this way: viscosity remains constant irrespective of rate of shear. Molten
chocolate, which is a multiphase system containing liquid and solid fat,
sugar syrup, sugar crystals and cocoa particles: is 'non-Newtonian' since
its viscosity changes with rate of shear. The determination of the viscosity
and yield values must therefore be carried out over a range of rates of
shear to give an accurate prediction of behaviour during enrobing and
depositing (see §8.11 and §8.13).

A non-Newtonian product requires a minimum shear stress to be exerted
before the liquid commences to move. The point at which this stress is just
exceeded is known as the *Yield Value*. The flow properties of chocolate
are best measured by the *Casson Viscosity*, derived from the linear plot
of the square roots of stress and rate of shear; from this information the
viscosity at any rate of shear and the yield value can be calculated.

Variations in the viscosity of sugar confectionery and chocolate can be
achieved in various ways, including: (1) varying the moisture content,

(2) controlling the extent of crystallisation, (3) varying the crystal size of the solid fraction, (4) mechanically working the mix, (5) varying the amount and ratio of fat-to-non-fat components, (6) adding viscosity reducing or thickening agents, (7) varying the temperature of the mix, (8) varying the amount of contained air, (9) heat treatment and (10) ageing.

Instruments used for measuring viscosity include the MacMichael, BFMIRA Brookfield, Rotovisco, Bayer, Brabender Plastograph, Emila, Dragé and Ferranti Viscometers. 'Degrees MacMichael', commonly quoted in the United States of America relate plastic viscosity and yield value; in general 'Casson Viscosity' values are quoted in the United Kingdom. Adaptions to the Brookfield Viscometer now enables correlations to be made with the MacMichael instrument. Most viscometers work on the principle of holding the chocolate in a cup and measuring the force needed to rotate an inserted cylinder.

Considerable research on the determination of the viscosity of chocolate and its rheological properties has been carried out by E. H. STEINER [E. H. STEINER, 1959, *Rheology of Disperse Systems,* (Pergamon Press), 1972, *Manuf. Conf., 52,* (9), 24–8, 66, 71].

1.10   TEXTURE

The terms which can be used to describe the texture of sugar confections fall into five main classes, which are listed in Table 13.

TABLE 13.   Terminology for the Texture of Sugar Confections

| | | Class | | |
A	B	C	D	E
Brittle	Chewy	Chalky	Crumbly	Dry
Crisp	Fluffy	Coarse	Doughy	Greasy
Crunchy	Hard	Crystalline	Fibrous	Moist
Flaky	Light	Lumpy	Floury	Oily
	Short	Powdery	Gooey	Sticky
	Soft	Rough	Mushy	Tacky
	Spongy	Sandy	Pasty	Treacly
	Springy	Smooth	Spongy	Waxy
	Stiff		Stringy	Wet
	Tender			
	Tough			

Texture differences are extremely important in the overall assessment of the quality of a sweetmeat. In carrying out comparison tests on similar products, a four-stage approach should be adopted: (1) characteristics noted prior to eating; (2) initial chew; (3) rating during chewing; (4) overall assessment.

Changes made necessary because of adverse assessments can be achieved by adopting one or more of the following procedures: (*a*) vary the moisture content; (*b*) vary the content, type and strength of the gelling/foaming agent; (*c*) vary the sucrose:glucose syrup ratio; (*d*) vary the sucrose: invert sugar solids ratio; (*e*) vary pH; (*f*) alter the process temperature conditions; (*g*) vary the milk protein content; (*h*) seed the batch with fondant or icing sugar; (*i*) change the required level of total sugars; (*j*) alter processing conditions to vary particle size; (*k*) alter the incorporated air content.

1.11 CRYSTALLISATION

There are seven basic forms into which crystals can be grouped. Sucrose is a member of the 'monoclinic' class and its crystal form is illustrated in Fig. 1.

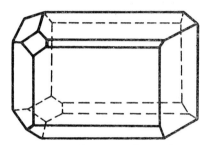

FIGURE 1. Basic crystal shape of sucrose.

In monoclinic crystals all the axial lengths are unequal. It is unlikely that the crystals of sucrose present in sugar confectionery products take on the exact shape of Fig. 1: the presence of other sugars and raw materials disrupt the shape, and faces may be absent.

A solution which holds more than its saturation level of sucrose may spontaneously form crystals. Crystallisation can also occur because the solution has been 'seeded' with fine sucrose crystals or because foreign particles such as dust have acted as a grain. Seeding is particularly important in the manufacture of sugar confections and the extent to which crystallisation occurs is dependent both on the degree of supersaturation and on the proportion of seed, that has been added. The larger the proportion of seed, the smaller the crystals that will be produced. Supersaturation is defined as

$$S = \frac{\text{gr sucrose}/100 \text{ gr water at temperature}}{\text{gr sucrose}/100 \text{ gr water when saturated at temperature}}$$

W. OSTWALD [1897, *Z. Phys. Chem.*, **22**, 289] has suggested that undisturbed solutions pass through a series of zones during cooling. These zones are listed in Table 14.

In sugar manufacture it is common to boil to the metastable zone to give a closer control of crystallisation. These zone limits are altered when other materials are present in solution. During crystallisation, heat is liberated and the temperature rises: this is particularly noticeable during the tempering of chocolate when cocoa butter crystallises.

Crystal growth takes place through the molecules of the compound being progressively laid down across the surface of the crystal in layers. Different faces grow at different rates; if the solution is not saturated the layers will recede correspondingly. The characteristic crystal shape is achieved by slow growth in an undisturbed solution; it is affected by concentration, temperature, purity and agitation of the solution.

TABLE 14. Crystallisation Zones of Supersaturated Solutions

Supersaturation	Sucrose Concentrn. %	Zone	Occurrence
S 1·3 and over	73	Labile	Spontaneous crystallisation
S 1·2–1·3	70	False Grain	Rapid growth of crystals when external seeding takes place
S 1·0–1·3	67–70	Metastable	No spontaneous crystallisation but crystal growth can occur
S 1·0 and below	67	Stable	No crystallisation

This last affects crystal form, crystal size, number of crystals and the rate of crystallisation. Graining on the surface of sugar confections is invariably of a 'spherulitic' type, that is, a number of crystals radiating out from a central point.

2

Sugars and Related Materials

The term sugar is used loosely in the sweet industry to indicate sucrose, the chemical term for sugar extracted from sugar cane or beet. 'Sugar' is a generic term which is taken to mean any form of carbohydrate suitable for use as a sweetener. All recipes in this book are given as cane or beet sugar, and quoted in the analyses as 'sucrose'.

Cane Sugar

Mature sugar canes contain a hard outer shell with a high sucrose content fibre; they grow to a height of 12 ft or more and are best harvested by hand cutting. Yields vary widely from 3 tons to 8 tons per acre (about 7–20 tonnes per hectare). At the processing factory, the canes are shredded and then passed through squeezing rollers to express the sugar liquor under hydraulic pressure; at this stage it contains 13–14% sucrose.

Beet Sugar

Sugar beets are sown in spring and harvested during autumn and winter. The beets are first washed, then sliced and passed into the diffusing unit, where progressively stronger sucrose liquor flows over the material.

Crude Refining

Both types of raw juice are heated and milk of lime added. The mix is carbonated and the precipitated chalk, which holds the impurities, removed. The resultant liquor is concentrated in multiple evaporators. Final concentration is carried out in vacuum evaporators. Crude sugar is obtained by spinning off the sucrose crystals from this *massecuite* in high speed centrifuges.

Purification

At the processing factory, the raw sugar is mixed with syrup obtained from later stages in processing to form a magma. The syrup mix is then concentrated under vacuum on an automatic cycling basis to a high solids content. Crystallised sugar is removed by centrifuging at speeds of

1200 rev/min or higher; the raw liquor discharged from the centrifuges is used to form the magma. The crystals in the centrifuge are washed with hot water and redissolved. Milk of lime is added, followed by carbonation. This liquor is then pressure filtered, and decolourised with active carbon. Following concentration to the supersaturation level, the liquor is seeded with milled sugar held in isopropanol; the proportion of seed added affects the crystal size of sugar produced. Brown sugar is prepared by drawing off the sugar at earlier stages, or by adding caramelised sugar to the white sugar.

Cane or beet sugar should be purchased on the basis of a nine point examination of the supplier's sample: (1) basic colour; (2) reducing sugar content; (3) turbidity in alcohol; (4) level of nitrogenous impurities; (5) ash content; (6) water content; (7) colour; (8) effect of heating a 50% solution; (9) bacteriological purity.

Typical analyses of cane or beet sugars are:

	White Sugar %	Brown Sugar %
Purity (sucrose)	99·8	92·0
Moisture	0·1	3·5
Reducing sugars, as invert sugar	0·05	4·0
Ash	0·02	0·5
Impurities	0·005	0·01

Abnormally high ash contents can be found in some sugars particularly those extracted from beet. These impurities can affect crystal size and shape, boiling properties and the extent to which inversion occurs during processing. High mineral matter may cause a buffering effect in sugar boils which can cause difficulties when the production of doctor-sugars is based on in-process inversion using cream of tartar.

Carry-over of trace flavours in the sugars into the manufactured sweets can arise, and it is advisable to use routine taste tests on sugars being delivered from new sources of supply.

Physical Properties of Sucrose are as follows

Solubility:

Temperature °C	°F	Solubility %
20	68	67·1
50	122	72·4
100	212	84·1

Specific Heat: (67% solution)

Temperature °C	°F	Specific Heat Btu/lb/°C
20	68	0·63
100	212	0·72

(sucrose crystal 0.3)

Equilibrium Rel. Humidity: Approximately 60%
crushed 'damp' crystals—80%

Boiling Point Rise: 67·1% solution boils at 105°C (221°F)
(see also Table 1, §1.2)

Optical Rotation: +66·5 degrees ($^d{}_{20}{}°_c$)

Specific Gravity: (67·1% solution)	*Temperature*		*Specific Gravity*
	°C	°F	
	20	68	1·33
	60	140	1·29

Specific Gravity: (74·0% solution)	*Temperature*		*Specific Gravity*
	°C	°F	
	20	68	1·37
	60	140	1·33

Bulk Density: 47 to 55 lb/ft³ (varying according to packing)

Comparative Sweetness: Varies with test method, but approximates to:
Sucrose   one
Dextrose   two-thirds
Glucose syrup (42 DE)   one-third
Glucose syrup (63 DE)   one-half
Fructose   two

(For relation of concentration of sucrose to degrees Baumé see Table 71.)

The *colour* developed by sucrose solutions on boiling varies according to the type and quantity of impurities present and to the degree of boiling. Impurities are themselves affected by the acidity of the mix and by varying oxidation arising through agitation. Additions of bisulphite inhibit colour formation but increase the amount of inversion occurring during processing.

The small traces of impurities which are present in sucrose include amino acids, mineral salts, arabin, xylan and dextran. During the development of the sucrose crystals, these impurities become entrapped in the inclusions in the growth of the crystal layers by the successive deposition of the sucrose molecules. Low crystal sizes therefore are less likely to contain high levels of impurities.

Concreting (damping or caking) of sugar on store is due to humidity and to the level of the inclusions of syrup in the crystal. This is most likely to occur when the relative humidity of the air exceeds 70%. The speed at which the crystals have been dried can affect the amount of included moisture. Water contents vary greatly; large crystals can be found containing up to 0·2% moisture while small crystals can hold as little as 0·01% contained water. Variations in included water result in variable relative vapour pressure contents for different samples of cane and beet sugar, with consequent differences in properties on store. The nearer the inclusion of water or syrup and impurities are to the surface, the more probable it is that the crystals have been rapidly dried. Syrup migration occurs under adverse conditions, the released liquor collecting at the points of crystal contact. Drying then occurs and the crystals 'cake' together.

Sucrose is best stored at temperatures above that normally maintained in production departments namely 30°–35° C (86°–95° F) and at relative humidities under 60%. Nevertheless, storage temperature should not vary more than 5° C (9° F) from that at which it is discharged from the sugar tanker. Storage hoppers should have sides at angles of 60–80 degrees from one another. These silos can be constructed of plywood but need an inner liner of aluminium or stainless steel. Transportation of the sugar to other points in the factory is best achieved by the use of screw conveyors or belts. Pneumatic conveying may be used but attrition occurs and gloss will be lost from the crystal. It is therefore necessary to use low pressures and low feed rates, with rotary valves for proportioning and mixing.

The presence of other sugars in solution can affect sucrose *solubility*. Larger quantities of some salts, such as occur in molasses, can make the sugar partially or wholly uncrystallisable. The presence of invert sugar can, at its maximum effect, raise the total solubility to 76% at 20° C while dextrose as the second sugar alone, will only raise the value to 68%.

Icing sugar is prepared by milling white cane or beet sugar to a low particle size (0·001 in). The colour of the sugar is influenced by the average size of the milled crystals and the distribution of the various crystal sizes. A typical size distribution for commercial icing sugar is given in Table 15. The properties of the icing sugar on store can vary as to whether it is produced from the waste from cube sugar, or directly from granulated sugar. The former tends to produce icing sugars with higher water contents. The smaller the particle size of the icing sugar, the more likely will it be to cake while on store.

TABLE 15. Weight Distribution of Icing Sugar Particles

Size Microns	10 and below	11 to 20	21 to 30	31 to 40	41 to 60	61 to 80	81 to 100
Weight %	9·3	24·1	21·2	10·7	19·7	10·5	4·5

Icing sugar can be produced in a pulverisation mill which consists of rotating arms, revolving at 300–400 rev/min held in a cylinder which at the bottom consists of a sieve. The arms break up the sugar entrapped between blades and the cylinder walls. The icing sugar so produced is hot through friction and tends to cling due to the presence of static electricity.

Up to 1·5% of *anticaking agents* are normally added to commercial grades of pulverised or milled sugar. These agents can hold up to 4 times their own weight of moisture without greatly affecting the flow properties of the sugar. Suitable anticaking agents are tricalcium phosphate, magnesium carbonate, magnesium trisilicate and calcium silicate. Of these, tricalcium phosphate is probably the most effective. It can be blended into factory-produced pulverised sugar in a dry mixer running at 30–40 rev/min. Icing sugar added to turkish delight packs to improve keeping qualities must contain an anticaking agent. It is not advisable to use icing sugar which contains starch (added to improve flow properties) for this purpose.

Explosion Risk

The risk of sugar dust explosion is dependent on four factors: (1) concentration of sugar dust; (2) source of ignition; (3) amount of oxygen present; (4) rate of pressure increase after ignition.

These factors have been reviewed by SCHNEIDER and SCHLIEPHAKE [1961, *Zucker*, *14*, 569–79]. The danger is greatly lessened once the particle size exceeds 100μ. There is both a minimum and maximum concentration of sugar dust that will lead to an explosion. Specific surface area is much more significant in assessing the explosibility of ground sugar than is particle size. Disturbed deposits of sugar dust on hot steam pipes may ignite spontaneously.

The lower limit for the concentration of dust in the atmosphere likely to give rise to an explosion is considered to be as little as $0.02 \text{ oz}/\text{ft}^3$. A number of differing temperatures have been suggested as the likely ignition point of a dust explosion. These approximate to 400° C. Both conditions for concentration of dust and ignition temperature can be found in confectionery plants which are not practising good factory housekeeping. Danger areas are indicated below

Dust	*High Temperatures*
(a) Fragments of sugar dust arising during delivery or conveying.	(a) Sparking in motors, lighting units, etc.
(b) Sugar dust generated during milling.	(b) Presence of metallic fragments and stones in grinding units.
(c) Progressive build-up of dust on girders, top of machines, stores, etc.	(c) Bad earthing.
(d) Filter units in starch-drying plants.	

Effective filter traps should be built into all shaker and grinding units. Pressure relief vents must be an integral part of all grinding or sieving plant to permit the escape of the explosive gases. Suppressant fire-fighting equipment may also be built into plant, and can be designed to be triggered off by the rise in pressure which occurs immediately before the dust explosion.

The storage properties of *brown sugar* are similar to invert sugar when the reducing sugar content (see §1.4) exceeds 12%. It is extremely difficult to get the invert sugar contained in brown sugar to crystallise. These sugars therefore always tend to be moist in texture and have a high absorbing capacity for moisture from the atmosphere. Depending on the method of preparation, the reducing sugar content of brown sugars can vary between 2% and 12%.

A *substitute* for cane or beet sugar can be prepared by dissolving 500 gr of saccharin in 1 l of hot water and adding 250 gr of sodium bicarbonate. This solution should then be diluted to 15 l. Of this diluted solution, 25 cm³ has a sweetness equivalent to 2·5 kg of cane or beet sugar (about 5 lb). Ammoniated glycerhizin is fifty times sweeter than sucrose but more expensive to use than saccharin.

2.2   HONEY

Honey was once widely used for the manufacture of sugar confectionery products but is now only present in recipes of certain speciality sweet products. It is best purchased on the basis of analytical composition as the components in honey vary according to source. Other factors influencing composition include the season of the year at which it is gathered and the weather at the time of collection.

An average composition for honey is:

Moisture		17%
Dry Solids		83%
Laevulose	38%	
Dextrose	34%	
Maltose	7%	
Sucrose	6%	
Resins, etc.	5%	
Undetermined matter	3%	
Dextrin	2%	
Higher sugars	2%	
Acidity as gluconic	1·2%	
Ash	0·2%	
Nitrogen	0·1%	
Reducing sugars as dextrose		77%
Optical rotation		−5° to −10°

This analysis is based on the work of [J. W. WHITE, et al., US Dept. of Agric., 1962, T.B. 1261], [J. W. WHITE, et al., *Food Tech.*, 1964, *18*, (4), 153–6], [F. N. HOWES, 1949, *Food*, *18*, 106], [K. C. KIRKWOOD, T. J. MITCHELL, D. SMITH, *Analyst*, 1960, 412] and [R. LEES, under J. F. INGLETON, 1970, *Confectionery Production*].

In addition to the components listed above, honey contains traces of flavouring materials, fibrous matter, bee hairs, pollen seeds and various enzymes. Other sugars that are present include raffinose and isomaltose and acids such as gluconic, acetic, citric, formic, lactic, and malic. Honey varies in pH from 3·4–6·1 but English honeys tend to fall within a more limited pH range of 3·6–4·3. It is thought that upwards of 10 compounds contribute towards the overall flavour of honey and the relative proportions and presence vary according to the collection area visited by the bees. Identification of the type of honey is usually by means of a microscopic examination of the traces of pollen that can be detected in the syrup.

Following the collection and transportation of the nectar (a weak sugar liquor) by the bees to the hive, the water evaporates thereby raising the total solids content from a low 14% to between 75%–80%. Sugar conversion occurs through the action of the enzymes that have become entrapped in the honey. The combs are removed from the hive and transferred to rotary centrifuges which throw off the honey by a low speed spinning action. After straining a heating process may be given in which the temperature is raised to 70° C (158° F). This is thought to reduce the danger of excessive crystallisation on storage. Adulteration can take place at this stage and is usually carried out by the addition of invert sugar syrup. Detection is difficult and depends on methods for the identification of hydroxymethylfurfural, a trace component present in invert sugar.

Honey normally contains a crystal phase, dextrose, and a mixed sugar/syrup phase. Clear honeys, which contain no crystal phase, are available but have no advantage to the confectioner. Texture is dependent both on the total solids content and on the relative proportions of the syrup and crystal phases. The relationship of the two phases is dependent on the type and amount of sugars present and on the water content. Crystallised honey will be found to vary in composition throughout the depth held in a container. The extent of the variation depends on the degree of settling. When using honey which has been on store for a long period it is therefore essential to gently reheat and stir before weighing out batch quantities. The probability that graining will occur in a batch of honey increases as the sucrose and dextrose content rises and decreases when more of the higher sugars are present.

The viscosity of honey cannot be used as an indication of sugar content as it is affected by the presence of nitrogenous material. Viscosity is important in that it will affect the speed of weighing and the efficiency of blending with other components. The amount of honey that should be incorporated in a sweet should preferably be held under 20%. A 10% addition is sufficient to achieve a satisfactory contribution to the flavour of the product without adversely affecting storage properties. The confections that are produced using honey will have a softer texture and be more yellow in colour. Grained honeys should replace an equivalent weight based on 2:1 sucrose:glucose syrup proportion while clear honeys should replace a 1:2 ratio of these sugars. Over-use of honey gives rise to stickiness and shortened shelf life.

Honey is best stored in bulk at 15° C in sealed drums. During prolonged storage, the ratio of the sugars with each other will vary and the acid content will rise.

2.3   GLUCOSE SYRUP

The industrial production of glucose syrup consists of two basic processes—starch hydrolysis followed by the refining of the hydrolysate. In the manufacture of dextrose monohydrate from the hydrolysate, a further process of crystallisation is required. The most widely used method of starch hydrolysis is that using a mineral acid in a batch system. This is now being supplemented by enzyme hydrolysis and by the use of continuous processing systems. Manufacture of glucose syrup by enzyme or by dual/ enzyme hydrolysis enables products to be made having widely differing constitutions and properties. Continuous production, especially in a system which is highly automated, has assumed increasing importance.

Hydrolysis of Starch By Acid

Starch consists of anhydro glucose polymers, present in two distinct molecular forms, known as amylose and amylopectin. Amylose, which is linear in character, comprises about 30% of maize starch and is composed of units linked in the 1–4 position. Various degrees of polymerisation have been ascribed to this fraction with chain lengths falling within the range of 100–1000 units.

Amylopectin, on the other hand, contains 1–6α glucosidic linkages, as well as the 1–4α type. Thus, amylopectin consists of chains which, although essentially linear, exhibit branching at the 1–6α position. The degree of polymerisation is much greater than with amylose and presents a highly ramified molecule.

Hydrolysis of starch with an acid catalyst, therefore, chiefly involves the scission of both 1–4α and 1–6α linkages to yield fragments of lower molecular weight. In glucose syrup only partial hydrolysis is carried out, the resulting hydrolysate being a mixture of fragments ranging from dextrose, maltose and higher sugars, through to more complex molecules of a dextrinous character. The composition of a hydrolysate will vary according to the extent to which the reaction is allowed to proceed. This degree of hydrolysis is indicated by the dextrose equivalent (DE) which is defined as the total reducing power expressed as dextrose, calculated to a dry basis. The relationship between dextrose equivalent and the composition of acid hydrolised glucose syrup is shown in Table 16.

The hydrolysis reaction with an acid catalyst is of necessity carried out in commercial processes at elevated temperatures. This produces certain undesirable side reactions, in addition to the scission of glucosidic linkages. The most important side effects result from the reaction of the acid upon the constituent dextrose molecule. In this case, dehydration occurs within the molecule, giving rise initially to 5–hydroxymethyl furfuraldehyde, with

TABLE 16.   Carbohydrate Composition of Acid-converted Glucose Syrups of
Varying Dextrose Equivalent
(Technical Advisory Committee, Corn Industries Research Foundation Inc.)

Dextrose Equivalent	SUGAR TYPE							
	Mono	Di	Tri	Tetra	Penta	Hexa	Hepta	Higher
10	2·3	2·8	2·9	3·0	3·0	2·2	2·1	81·7
15	3·7	4·4	4·4	4·5	4·3	3·3	3·0	72·4
20	5·5	5·9	5·8	5·8	5·5	4·3	3·9	63·3
25	7·7	7·5	7·2	7·2	6·5	5·2	4·6	54·1
30	10·4	9·3	8·6	8·2	7·2	6·0	5·2	45·1
35	13·4	11·3	10·0	9·1	7·8	6·5	5·5	36·4
40	16·9	13·2	11·2	9·7	8·3	6·7	5·7	28·3
45	21·0	14·9	12·2	10·1	8·4	6·5	5·6	21·3
50	25·8	16·6	12·9	10·0	7·9	5·9	5·0	15·9

further transformation taking place to yield levulinic acid or polymers of hydroxymethyl furfuraldehyde. A recombination of dextrose also occurs to form disaccharides having 1–6α and 1–6β linkages. This reaction assumes some importance in the commercial manufacture of dextrose, but has less significance with glucose syrup.

Degradation products are undesirable, because on the one hand they represent a loss in yield to the producer and on the other a loss in quality. The rate of formation of degradation products increases with strength of acid, concentration of starch and reaction temperature. For economic reasons, a sufficiently high concentration of starch has to be used to avoid the removal of large quantities of water at a later stage. Similarly, acidity and temperature must also be sufficiently high for the reaction to proceed quickly, otherwise production would be slow and costly. On a commercial scale, the conditions of hydrolysis are inevitably a compromise in which costs, yields and level of degradation products are carefully balanced.

Although, theoretically, any mineral acid would be suitable as a catalyst for starch hydrolysis, in fact hydrochloric acid is the one most commonly used. Phosphoric acid and sulphuric acid have been proposed and, indeed, the latter is known to have been applied commercially. However, it has the disadvantage in hard water districts of causing a haze in the finished product by precipitation of calcium sulphate.

Glucose syrup manufacture is shown diagramatically in Fig. 2. The starch is generally available as an aqueous slurry from the wet milling of corn. Ideally, it should be free from impurities such as oil, protein and fibre. Typical characteristics of starch slurry milled for glucose refining are:

Baumé at 15·5°C (60°F)	25·0°
Starch % by weight	44·4
Total Protein % (DE)	0.34
Soluble Protein %	0·02
pH	3·9
Solubles %	0·10
Fibre ppm	600

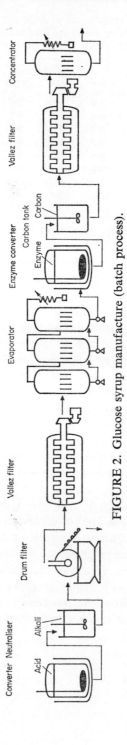

FIGURE 2. Glucose syrup manufacture (batch process).

Batch acid conversion is conventionally carried out in 2000 gallon capacity autoclaves heated by injections of live steam.

The starch slurry is *acidified* to pH 1·8–2·0 and transferred into the autoclave as steam pressure is applied. The slurry must be added slowly to avoid the formation of lumps of partially gelatinised starch. For glucose syrup conversion a steam pressure of 30–35 lb is employed, equivalent to a temperature of about 136° C. The total conversion time is in the region of 25 minutes, although only a few minutes are at full steam pressure. *Neutralisation* which follows has a two-fold effect. Primarily it causes the conversion to cease, and for this reason is carried out as quickly as possible after hydrolysis. Secondly, raising the pH has resulted in the precipitation of impurities, such as fatty acid and proteins. Removal of the latter is of prime importance and it is usual to neutralise the liquor to the isoelectric point of the proteins (that point at which any positive or negative charges in the structure are equally balanced) to ensure maximum precipitation. The usual type of neutraliser is a wooden vat equipped with an agitator to permit intimate mixing-in of the alkali. In practice, 16° Baumé sodium carbonate solution is added to adjust the pH within the range 4·9–5·2. An addition of activated carbon is sometimes made prior to neutralisation to assist in the flocculation of the precipitated material and facilitates its removal at the *precoat filter stage* which follows.

In this operation a rotary drum filter is used, upon the surface of which is deposited a 3 in cake of kieselguht or diatomaceous earth. The neutraliser liquor is drawn through the cake by an internally applied vacuum. Clogging is minimised by the rotation of the drum and the removal of the top surface of the cake by a doctor blade. The clarified filtrate is collected in a holding tank pending refining with activated carbon or bone char.

Most of the colour bodies are negatively charged and therefore greater decolourisation is obtained under acid conditions. Soluble proteins are most effectively removed at their iso-electric point; the amount of proteins remaining after neutralisation and carbon treatment is half that originally present. Activated carbon also has a beneficial effect in removing any hydroxymethylfurfural. During treatment a greater absorbency of the impurities is achieved at elevated temperatures and by the intimate contact of the carbon with the liquor.

Refining may be carried out by either allowing the liquor to percolate through a bed of carbon or, more usually, by batch contact in which the liquor is agitated with slightly less than 1% of activated carbon at 76·7° C (170° F) for 20 minutes. Provided sufficient carbon is used there is no tendency for the absorbed particles to be redischarged into the liquor. When refining is complete the carbon is separated from the liquor by filtration through a leaf press. In a typical press (Vallez type) the refined filtrate is discharged from a hollow central shaft leaving behind the carbon evenly distributed over the surface of the leaves. The main carbon treatment is reserved for liquor which has already had the in-place treatment together with some concentration to increase the soluble solids content.

Concentration of the process liquor is normally carried out under vacuum to avoid heat degradation. Multiple effect evaporators are preferred which are so linked that the discharged vapours are used to heat the next stage. Typically a triple effect evaporator will raise the soluble solids content of a liquor from 40% to around 55% and it is after this concentration that the main carbon refining is given.

The refining process at this point is substantially complete, although it is considered beneficial to filter the liquor through a bed of diatomaceous earth. This process exerts a polishing effect, producing a sparkle and improved clarity in the finished glucose syrup.

Final concentration now takes place in which the total solids of the glucose syrup are raised to 75–85%. This is carried out in single effect units. During concentration a small quantity of sodium bisulphite is drawn into the evaporator such that, even allowing for a slight loss from vaporisation, approximately 400 ppm of sulphur dioxide is left in the glucose syrup.

Acid–Enzyme Hydrolysis

Under the conditions conventionally applied in glucose syrup manufacture, the level of reversion products formed is tolerable for low and medium conversion syrups to a DE of about 50. However, with highly converted syrups in the range 60–65 DE the formation of degradation products is rapid and production using full acid hydrolysis is not acceptable. For this type of syrup, it has been found more practicable to employ a dual acid/enzyme process. Enzymes can best be described as organic catalysts, complex compounds of protein-like character, and are commonly of bacterial, malt or fungal origin. Starch is hydrolysed principally by the diastatic enzymes α and β amylase, each having a slightly different action in the breakdown. α amylase attacks both amylose and amylopectin randomly at $1-4\alpha$ linkages, thus causing their scission.

β amylase attacks linear chains, either amylose or branching chains of amylopectin from the non-reducing ending of the molecule. By this endwise action the chain is progressively broken down at $1-4\alpha$ linkages and always in groups of two glucose units (maltose). Unlike catalysis using acid neither α or β amylase attack the $1-6\alpha$ linkages. A more significant result of this specificity of enzymes is that no intramolecular reaction occurs thereby forming no colour bodies or bitter tasting degradation products. Enzyme reaction proceeds relatively slowly and has critical temperature and pH requirements for optimum activity. α and β amylase differ as to their optimum reaction conditions and where diastatic conversion is carried out a compromise has to be made.

High conversion syrups are manufactured by a dual acid/enzyme process on a batch system, requiring little modification of the normal acid method. Acid hydrolysis is first carried out to give a DE of 48. This is then followed by neutralisation, initial carbon treatment, and triple-effect concentration to 55% soluble solids.

TABLE 17. Enzyme Conversion of Acid Hydrolysate at pH 5·0, 54° C (134° F) and 0·015% Enzyme

Time (hours)	Hydrolysate DE (%)
Start	48·0
10	50·0
20	52·0
40	55·6
60	58·6
80	61·0
100	62·8
120	63·6
140	64·0

The liquor at this point is ready to receive the enzyme treatment.

Enzyme conversion is undertaken in large stainless steel vessels, equipped with agitators and controlled temperature heating coils. After transfer to the enzyme converter, the liquor is adjusted to pH 5·0 and a temperature of 54·4° C (130° F). Concentrations of between 0·012–0·017% of enzymes are added, depending on the desired time cycle. Under the conditions described the final degree of conversion will be attained in between 5 and 7 days. Table 17 shows the relationship of reaction time and dextrose equivalent for a typical enzymic conversion. Main carbon treatment is then given as described under acid conversion and the batch evaporated to the required soluble solids content in the normal way.

Continuous Conversion

Production of glucose syrup using continuous methods differs principally from batch processing in the procedures used for hydrolysis, neutralisation and final concentration.

Hydrolysis is most easily accomplished by passing an acidulated starch slurry first through a pre-paster and then a holding coil. The pre-paster consists of four stages, each containing a bank of cupro-nickel tubes connected in parallel and enclosed in a tubular steel shell. Rapid liquefaction of the starch paste is essential in order to avoid blockage of the tubes and heat is provided by injection of steam at 150 lb/in² into the tubular shell. The holding coil comprises a single bore tube, insulated to maintain the temperature of the liquor passing through it and acts mainly as a fine control in the hydrolysis. The regulation of conversion is achieved by varying the flow rate through the coil. The discharged liquor is rapidly neutralised by pumping in alkali through an injection nozzle, thereby obtaining an intimate mixing. The liquor is then passed into a flash chamber to permit its reduction to atmospheric pressure and to allow the escape of carbon dioxide formed during the neutralisation. The injection of alkali, and hence pH, is automatically controlled. From here on, the flow follows the course of the batch process in respect of pre-coat filtration, carbon treatment and preliminary concentration of solids. Evaporation to final solids content may be carried out either in multiple effect or continuous plate evaporators.

Batch Enzyme—Enzyme Process

It is possible to produce glucose syrups by wholly enzyme conversion. The syrups which are obtained have a different distribution of carbohydrates from those obtained using acid or acid/enzyme processes. Furthermore, degradation products resulting from the intramolecular action of acid are not formed in a total enzyme conversion. The use of α and β amylase, free from glucoamylase, will yield a product with a high maltose content, in which dextrose is almost absent.

In the manufacture of double enzyme converted syrups an initial starch liquefaction with α amylase is carried out. An enzyme of high activity and good thermal stability is used to liquefy a starch slurry of 35–40% concentration. The presence of calcium ions has been found to promote this reaction and are added during the adjustment of pH to its optimum value.

α amylase of good thermal stability is mixed with the starch slurry which has been pH adjusted, and then transferred to the converter. Normally a conversion time of approximately one hour under specified conditions is sufficient to produce adequate liquefaction.

At this stage filtration can only be carried out with difficulty and is deferred until the second enzyme treatment has been completed. This requires different conditions, β amylase action for instance, necessitates a lowering of temperature and pH to below 60° C (140° F) and 5·0 respectively. It is important that this second enzyme treatment should follow rapidly in order to arrest the retrogradation of the liquefied starch. Retrograded starch is virtually immune from attack by β amylase. On completion of hydrolysis, further action is prevented by raising the temperature of the batch. Under these conditions the thermolabile β amylase is inactivated.

Production of Spray Dried Glucose Syrup

For ease in handling it is sometimes convenient to use powdered glucose syrup. This can be produced by reducing the moisture content of glucose syrup to under 3%. A variety of methods has been used to remove the water: thin film evaporation, roll drying and, most satisfactorily, spray drying. A fine spray of glucose syrup is introduced into a high temperature atmosphere giving a very rapid evaporation of moisture. The high degree of liquid dispersion required in this process is obtained by pumping the syrup under high pressure through a fine atomising nozzle or through slotted high-speed centrifugal discs.

The drying air is heated and filtered before its introduction into the chamber, to prevent contamination by atmospheric dust. The hot air inlets are positioned at the sides of the chamber and around the atomiser and are so directed as to give intimate mixing of hot air and spray. Under these conditions, with air at an inlet temperature of about 149° C (300° F), drying is instantaneous. Total holding time in the spray dryer is usually less than one minute.

The bottom section of the dryer is in the form of an inverted cone, which causes spiral flow of the hot gases and forces the dried particles down into a packaging unit. Spray dried glucose is hygroscopic and packaging is in polythene bags or paper bags lined or sprayed with polythene. Filling is preferably carried out in an air-conditioned room.

Composition, Properties and use of Glucose Syrup

The composition of the generally available types of glucose syrup is shown in Table 18. The properties of these syrups are listed in Table 19 and recommendations for their use in Table 20.

Production of Dextrose Monohydrate

Acid hydrolysis–dextrose is produced from starch by allowing the hydrolysis reaction used for the preparation of glucose syrup to proceed to completion. In practice and using acid catalysts, this is never fully achieved, due to side reactions, of which the rates increase markedly during the final stages of hydrolysis when substantial quantities of dextrose have been formed.

To increase the conversion rate it is necessary to use lower concentration

TABLE 19. Glucose Syrups: Dextrose Equivalent for various functions

Function	DE-Type Lower	Higher	Function	DE-Type Lower	Higher
Bodying Agent	*		Hygroscopicity		*
Browning Reaction		*	Vapour Pressure		
Control of Crystal-			Increase	*	
lisation	*		Fermentability Rate		*
Cohesiveness	*		Foam Stabiliser	*	
Sweetness		*	Nutritive Value	*	*
Colour Increase on			Sheen Producer	*	*
Boiling		*	Thickening Agent	*	
Emulsion Stabiliser	*		Prevention of Sugar		
Binder	*		Crystal	*	
Humectancy	*	*	Osmotic Pressure		*

TABLE 18. Types of Glucose Syrup

Type	Low DE	Low DE	Regular DE	Intermediate DE	High DE	High Maltose
Specific Gravity (deg. Baumé)	41·2°	43·2°	43·2°	43·2°	43·2°	43·2°
Total Solids content (%) (by RI method)	75·97	80·67	80·67	81·55	82·03	80·67
Dextrose Equivalent (%)	26	38	42	55	64	42
Ash	0·3	0·3	0·3	0·3	0·3	0·3
Monosaccharides (dextrose) (%) DB	8·0	15·0	19·3	30·8	37·0	5·9
Disaccharides (maltose)	7·5	12·5	14·3	18·1	31·5	44·4
Trisaccharides	7·5	11·0	11·8	13·2	11·0	12·7
Tetrasaccharides	7·0	9·0	10·0	9·5	5·0	3·3
Pentasaccharides	6·5	8·0	8·4	7·2	4·0	1·3
Hexasaccharides	5·0	7·0	6·6	5·1	3·0	1·5
Heptasaccharides	4·5	5·0	5·6	4·2	2·0	1·0
Octasaccharides and high mol. weight sugars (or dextrines)	54·0	32·5	24·0	11·9	6·5	29·4
Viscosity, Cp, at 16° C (60° F)	500 000	360 000	340 000	220 000	130 000	340 000
Processing	acid conv.	acid conv.	acid conv.	acid conv. or enzyme	Enzyme conv.	Enzyme conv.

starch slurries (12° Bé) compared to those used in the manufacture of glucose syrup (25° Bé). With converter pressures of 45 lb/in² a maximum DE of 90 is quickly attained. Attempts to increase the DE value by prolonging the hydrolysis produce a gradual falling away from the peak conversion. The treatment of the converted mix closely follows the process described for glucose syrup. The final stages in processing are concentration to 39·5° Bé (equivalent to 76·5% soluble solids content), cooling and crystallisation.

Dextrose is available in two forms—the monohydrate, and anhydrous powder. Anhydrous dextrose can exist as α and β isomers. At temperatures above 50° C the anhydrous form crystallises from solution. Lower solution temperatures result in the crystallisation of dextrose monohydrate. Crystallisation can be considered as a two-fold process requiring first the formation of crystal nuclei, and then their growth into crystals. Although the two stages proceed simultaneously it is necessary in dextrose production to curb the unrestricted formation of nuclei, in order to control crystal size and thereby prevent later difficulties during washing.

The degree of supersaturation is the significant factor in the control of crystallisation. If the solution is too concentrated, then too many new nuclei will be formed. Should the supersaturation fall unduly, the crystallisation rate falls and may even yield no new crystals or produce growth. If the concentration falls under supersaturation then dissolution of the crystal layers may occur.

In commercial practice, supersaturation conditions are usually held around the middle of the metastable zone, which gives crystal growth and very little fresh nucleation. Ample growth centres are provided by the practice of seeding, that is the carry-over of part of the crystal crop in the crystalliser to serve as nuclei for the following cycle. Controlled cooling forms an integral part of the process. By the gradual lowering of the solution temperature, the desired degree of dextrose supersaturation can be maintained and kept in balance with the removal of crystals from the solution.

Gentle agitation is applied during crystallisation to increase the rate of crystal growth, facilitate heat transfer and keeps the smaller crystals in solution.

Crystallisers in common use have about 8000 gallon working capacity and are constructed of mild steel lined with stainless steel. They are essentially cylindrical tanks, mounted horizontally, and are equipped with double shell cooling jacket and coil. The coil rotates during operation at approximately 20 rev/hr. The process liquor from the cooling tank is transferred to the crystalliser at about 52° C (125° F), being added to residual seed from the previous cycle, representing 15% of the total charge. Before the cooling cycle is commenced, the liquor and seed are gently mixed for several hours, during which time the temperature is reduced by 9° C (16° F).

The cooling cycle proper is then started and an adequate degree of supersaturation is obtained by automatically lowering the temperature of the mass by 0·5° F per hour. As crystallisation progresses, the liquor becomes more exhausted and the viscosity of the massecuite increases. In the process described, cooling is carried out to a temperature of about 21° C (70° F) and is achieved within an overall crystallisation time of 90–100 hours. The crystallisers are emptied, leaving behind 15% as residual seed and the massecuite transferred to a temporary holding vessel known as a mingler box.

The dextrose crystals are separated from the mother liquor by centrifugal force produced by high speed rotation of a batch of massecuite around a central point. The basket of the centrifuge is filled with the massecuite

TABLE 20. Proportions of Glucose Syrup as Percentage
of Total Sweeteners

Type of Confection	Glucose Syrup % Range	Type of Glucose Syrup Most Suitable
High Boilings—General	30–70	Regular
Plastic	40–60	Regular or High Maltose
Deposited	40–60	High Maltose or Regular
Rock (Pulled)	30–60	Low DE or Regular
Caramels—General	30–70	Regular
Deposited—Chocolate Covered	20–60	High DE or Regular
Slab—Unwrapped	30–60	Low DE or High Maltose
Toffees	30–70	Regular or Low DE
Fudge—General	20–40	Regular or High Maltose
Fudge—Slab	20–40	Regular or High Maltose
Fudge—Deposited	30–50	High DE or Regular
Fondant—Direct	10–30	Regular or Intermediate
Fondant—Remelt Syrup	30–50	High DE or Regular
Gum Arabic Gums	15–40	Regular or High DE
Starch Jellies	55–65	Regular or Intermediate
Starch Gums	50–70	Regular or Intermediate
Gelatine Jellies	30–70	Regular Intermediate or High DE
Agar Jellies	30–50	Regular or Intermediate
Pectin Jellies	40–60	Regular or High DE
Marshmallow	40–80	High DE or Intermediate
Nougat	40–60	Regular, High Maltose or Low DE
Liquorice Dough	30–50	Regular or High DE
Cream Pastes	20–40	Intermediate or High DE
Tablets—Lozenge	5–15	Regular
Tablets—Compressed	2–5	Regular or Low DE
Marzipan	5–15	Low DE or Regular
Soft Panning	25–80	Low DE or Regular
Chewing Gum	40–70	Regular or Low DE 45 Be
Liqueur	20–40	High DE

while operating at a slowly rotating speed. When filling is completed, the spinning cycle is commenced and carried out on an automatic basis. An 8 minute purging is carried out at high speed, of the order of 1500 rev/min, to remove most of the mother liquor contained in the massecuite.

Dextrose monohydrate sold in the United Kingdom usually conforms to the specification of the British Pharmacopoeia, and to achieve this purity a further washing of some 2 or 3 minutes is given to eliminate all traces of mother liquor. The water is sprayed over the spinning sugar mass through fine nozzles, but this wash is kept as short as is compatible with the requirements of purity; unnecessary extension leads to a loss in yield by the dissolution of crystals in the wash water. A further spin of some 7 minutes is then given for de-watering, at this point the moisture content of the product is about 14 or 15%. The batch-wise operation of a battery of centrifuge is used to maintain a continuous flow of crystals to the drier.

Dextrose monohydrate has a theoretical water of crystallisation content of 9·1%, and drying is carried out to reduce the moisture content of the hydrous crystals obtained from the centrifuges to this value. It is carried out in horizontal rotary dryers consisting of cylindrical vessels equipped with 'flights' running longitudinally along their length. A regulated stream of hot air (heated by passage through steam coils) both reduces the moisture content of the crystals and assists in transportation through the system. A temperature of approximately 140° C (284° F) is sufficient. The discharged crystals are passed through vibratory sifters to remove coarse material and agglomerates before being packed, usually in multiwall paper sacks.

Acid/Enzyme Process

A wholly acid conversion of starch to dextrose suffers from the inherent disadvantages of colour and flavour development, coupled with loss of yield. A more satisfactory process is one in which the hydrolysis is achieved by means of enzymes. Conventionally, the enzyme conversion follows a mild acid treatment, given chiefly as a means of solubilising the starch. This stage is carried out in the usual converters, processing starch slurries of 16° Baumé, to a dextrose equivalent of about 15%.

The liquor is neutralised by the addition of sodium carbonate solution and after precoat filtration, transferred to enzyme converters of some 30 000 gallons capacity. A mixture consisting principally of glucoamylase (dextrose producing) enzyme of fungal origin is employed for this process. Its addition is made during the filling of the enzyme converter vessels, with sufficient agitation to ensure its dispersion. Thermostatic controls maintain a temperature slightly below 60°C (140°F), over some 72 hours. The hydrolysate at this point can be expected to have a DE in excess of 95%, although it is more convenient to crystallise at 90% DE. This reduction in dextrose equivalent is carried out by blending 'hydrol' (mother liquor from crystallisation) and wash water. The subsequent refining and crystallisation follows the processes described for the acid converted product.

2.4   STARCH HYDROLYSATES

These hydrolysates are dried conversion products available in a powdered form. Up to 20 DE they are normally referred to as malto-dextrins or hydrolised cereal solids. Above 20 DE they are more commonly termed spray dried glucose syrup solids. They differ in the method and extent of their conversion and three typical examples are given below:

TABLE 20A.   Starch Hydrolysates: Typical Specifications

Properties	Type A	Type B	Type C
Moisture Content	5% maximum	5% maximum	5% maximum
Dextrose Equivalent	17–20%	26–32%	40·5–43·5%
pH	4·5–5·5	4·5–5·5	4·5–5·5
Sulphur Dioxide	40 ppm max.	40 ppm max.	40 ppm max.
Solution Clarity (50% w/v)	Clear	Clear	Clear

Carbohydrate Composition (Based on Dry Weight)

	Type A %	Type B %	Type C %
Dextrose	3·0	9·0	5·5
Maltose	7·0	8·4	42·0
Maltotriose	5·0	7·9	15·0
Maltotetrose	6·0	7·7	5·0
Maltopentose	7·0	6·8	3·0
Maltohexose	11·0	5·6	3·0
Higher Saccharides	61·0	54·6	26·5
	100·0	100·0	100·0

Analytical Composition

	Type A	Type B	Type C
Ash (SO$_2$)	0·40%	0·40%	0·40%
Sodium Chloride	0·30%	0·30%	0·30%
Protein (N × 6·25)	0·03%	0·03%	0·03%
Iron	2 ppm	2 ppm	2 ppm
Copper	1 ppm	1 ppm	1 ppm
Lead	Less than 1 ppm	Less than 1 ppm	Less than 1 ppm
Arsenic	Less than 0·5 ppm	Less than 0·5 ppm	Less than 0·5 ppm
Bulk Density (lb/ft^3)	30	32	35
Form	White amorphous powder	White amorphous powder	White amorphous powder

Properties

The properties depend mainly upon the degree of conversion which is expressed as the dextrose equivalent (DE). In Table 21, direction of arrow indicates increasing effect upon the particular property.

TABLE 21.   Relationship of Dextrose Equivalent to
Functional Properties of Starch Hydrolysates

Property	DE 15...................45
Sweetness	—————————→
Viscosity	←—————————
Moisture Pick-up	—————————→
Film Forming	←—————————
Crystallisation Prevention	←—————————
Browning	—————————→
Freezing Point Depression	—————————→

Type A malto-dextrin at 20 DE provides an unusual combination of properties—fully soluble carbohydrate material of low bulk density, which is virtually non-sweet. Types B and C glucose syrup solids offer the functional properties of liquid glucose syrup, coupled with the convenience of a low moisture content.

Applications

Spray dried hydrolysates find application in a wide range of processed and convenience foods, principally as filler/carrier and sweetness reducer. To some extent the products are interchangeable and ultimate choice depends upon the emphasis desired on specific functional properties (Table 21). They are ideally suited for blending into powdered formulations, and serve the following purposes. As filler/carrier, they can (1) reduce loss of volume in contents on storage or in transit; (2) absorb fats and oils to retain free-flowing properties; (3) aid dispersion during make-down; (4) standardise the quality of products prepared from variable natural sources (spice mixes, flavours); (5) dilute concentrated or expensive ingredients (flavours, flavour enhancers); (6) save cost by partial replacement of lactose and milk powder in certain applications, such as in the manufacture of tablets.

In marshmallow based on egg albumen, useful cost saving may be derived by its partial replacement by malto-dextrin. Up to 15% of the albumen by weight may be replaced with no change in marshmallow quality or processing.

Many products can be made more acceptable by lowering their level of sweetness. In most cases it is essential to achieve this without reducing the total solids content. Reformulating, using low conversion hydrolysates, achieves this reduction without greatly affecting other properties. Malto-dextrin is, weight for weight, the most effective, possessing only a fraction of the sweetening power of sugar. It can be employed to reduce sweetness of foods containing high sugar concentration (preserves, fondants, fillings), or to offset the sweetening effect of invertase (chocolate cream centres).

New Developments

Glucose syrup manufacturers are now employing other conversion pro-cesses to produce a wide range of new products. These new processes have increased the range of glucose syrups by varying the carbohydrate com-position. They make use of specific acting enzymes to produce the desired characteristics, in particular for preparing glucose syrup with high disaccharide contents or with enhanced levels of trisaccharides. It is ex-pected that high laevulose bearing syrups will soon be available which will have enhanced sweetening properties.

2.5 LIQUID SUCROSE AND MIXED SUGAR SYRUPS

Liquid sugar, a solution of sucrose in water, can be purchased for use in those industries which can employ a sucrose syrup of 66·5° Brix or less in their processes. Mixtures of sugars are also available for purchase in syrup form, these are also offered under the group name of liquid sugar. A balanced liquid mixture of sucrose, glucose syrup and invert sugar can be of value to the sugar confectioner in that the weighing out of the individual components is replaced by simple metering to the pans.

Following the extraction or preparation of the individual syrup compon-ents, individual sugar blends are prepared to customer requirements. Other sweeteners such as honey and treacle can be added during the blending.

To use liquid sugar mixtures effectively, bulk handling installations must be installed; only large users of syrup can justify the outlay on such equipment. Liquid sugars are subject to microbiological spoilage and hence the syrups have a limited life; a high throughput is therefore essential.

Two storage tanks are needed, each capable of receiving one tanker load; of around 2500–3000 gallons. The rate of usage governs the fre-quency rather than the size of deliveries. The tanks are filled and alter-nately completely drained and sterilised before each re-filling. The tanks should be sited in non-productive areas; their capacity depending on the relative heights of the tanks and points of use. Delivery to the process areas can be either by pump or gravity. Tanks must be completely self-draining. Both stainless steel and resin lined mild steel give the highly polished internal surfaces vital for cleanliness. On a firm flooring, tubular steel legs should be fitted; or gussetted brackets may be used to suspend tanks from overhead steelwork.

To avoid surface dilution of liquid by condensation, a small blower should be fitted in the tank lid which draws air through a labyrinth filter and passes it through the tank to a well-protected vent. This slight pressurisation with clean air removes any water vapour and will give trouble-free storage.

Liquid sugar mixtures have comparatively low viscosities and can be pumped over long distances. Positive rotary type pumps (but not centrifugal) manufactured from stainless steel, zinc-free phosphor bronze or high nickel content cast iron should be used. These pumps should be designed for easy sterlisation and hold the minimum of liquid. They should not be oversize so that 'slipping' and gland leakage occurs, nor should they cause 'cavitation' which invariably results in aeration.

With liquid mixtures it is essential to obtain accurate measurement in the process units. Modern pipeline meters are normally accurate to within 0·5% and can be calibrated to give either weight or volume. An integrating device may be incorporated to record total consumption, for stock control or to check on the adherence to recipe.

Liquid sugar mixtures should be used within one week in summer or two weeks in winter. Deliveries should be used in order of receipt. Once emptied, a liquid sugar storage tank and its associated pipework should be sterilised before each reloading; if this is impracticable at not less than weekly intervals.

Two ways are available for sterilising; by steaming or by flushing with a sterilant. Before either process, the empty tank and associated pipelines should be rinsed with warm water until the drained liquor is free of sugar. If the sterilisation is with steam, then sufficient live steam should be passed into the system to produce a temperature on the interior surfaces of 100°C (212°F); this should be held for at least 30 minutes. Alternatively, after washing with hot water, a hot solution of sterilising agent should be held in contact with the internal surfaces of the tanks and pipes for a minimum of 30 minutes, after which the whole is flushed with potable water. A sterilising agent solution can be used more than once, but dilution by flush water will lessen its effect.

2.6 DEXTROSE

Dextrose can be used (1) to promote crystallisation; (2) to lower the overall crystal size present in the solid phase; (3) to tenderise the sweet, or (4) to create a 'cooling' taste in the mouth.

Sweets which include dextrose have different eating qualities to those made with sucrose and glucose syrup alone. Recipes should be balanced so that the sucrose to dextrose ratio achieves the required product texture. The incorporation of dextrose will increase the likelihood that crystallisation will occur either on store or during manufacture. Replacement usage levels for dextrose normally lie between 5% and 15% of the sucrose content. Dextrose can be prepared in three crystal forms which are given in Table 22.

TABLE 22.   Crystalline Forms of Dextrose

Type of Dextrose	Crystal Formation	Moisture Content %
αDextrose Hydrate	from solutions held below 50° C	8·5–9·5
αDextrose Anhydrous	from solutions held between 50°–115° C	0·3
βDextrose Anhydrous	from solutions at above 115° C	0·2

Dextrose is normally supplied to the confectionery industry in the hydrated form. All three forms come into equilibrium with each other when dissolved in water and although different forms may crystallise during sweet manufacture, they quickly revert to an equilibrium mix. Solubility values vary according to the type of dextrose being examined but once in solution the value rises or falls to that of the equilibrium mix.

TABLE 23.   Solubility in Water of Dextrose and Sucrose

Temperature °C	°F	Dextrose Solubility % w/v	Sucrose Solubility % w/v
20	68	47·7	67·1
30	77	51·2	68·0
40	104	61·8	70·8

It will be seen from Table 23 that dextrose is less soluble than sucrose. Mixtures of dextrose and sucrose have a greater total solubility than those of dextrose and sucrose alone, but individual solubilities are depressed. Dextrose is only slightly soluble in alcohol (0·1%). At all equivalent concentrations, dextrose solutions are less viscous than sucrose concentrations.

Boiling characteristics of dextrose solutions, compared to the equivalent strength sucrose solutions, are shown in Table 24.

The boiling properties of dextrose solutions held under vacuum are of a similar pattern to those quoted for open pan boiling, but the difference from

TABLE 24.   Boiling Characteristics of Dextrose and Sucrose Solutions

Concentration %	Sucrose		Dextrose	
	°C	°F	°C	°F
40	101·4	215	102·0	216
50	102·0	216	103·2	218
60	103·0	218	105·1	221
70	105·5	222	107·2	225

sucrose is less marked. Dextrose solutions slowly darken on boiling particularly when the pH is between 5·0 and 6·0; this effect is increased by any nitrogenous impurities.

Other properties of dextrose of relevance to the sugar confectioner are:

Optical rotation, at equilibrium	$52 \cdot 5° - 52 \cdot 8°\,^{d}\,_{20°C}$
Ash	not more than $0 \cdot 05 \%$
Sulphur dioxide	not more than 75 ppm
Melting point	
Anhydrous	$110°$ C $(230°$ F)
Hydrate	$83°$ C $(181°$ F)—redissolves in the released water of crystallisation

Commercial dextrose should be packed to give protection against moisture in multilayered paper or plastic sacks. Caking occurs through inadequate packing, bad storage or inadequate drying. The method of manufacture of dextrose has been described earlier (§2.3) and is summarised in Fig. 3.

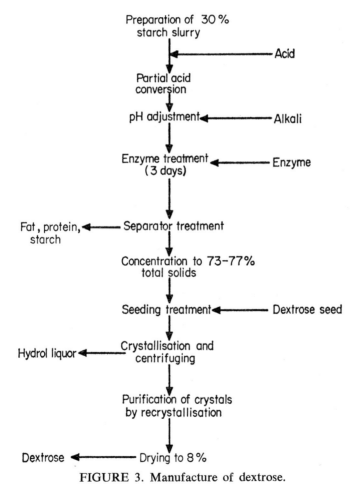

FIGURE 3. Manufacture of dextrose.

2.7   FRUCTOSE

The use of fructose (laevulose) in the manufacture of sugar confectionery became possible with the development in Finland in 1969 of commercial methods for the extraction of this sugar. Fructose (fruit sugar) can be added to (a) give diabetic properties to the product; (b) increase the sweetness level; (c) inhibit crystallisation; (d) enhance fruit flavour; (e) act as a humectant. It is also claimed that there is less danger of tooth decay when using fructose to replace cane or beet sugar.

Fructose is available as stable anhydrous crystals which melt at between 102°–104° C (216°–219° F). When dissolved in water at 20° C (68° F) it forms a 78·9% w/v solution. Solutions of fructose are difficult to crystallise and are approximately twice as sweet to taste as similar concentrations of sucrose. They are also less viscous.

A partial replacement of sucrose (10%) by fructose usefully raises the sweetness levels of high acid content confections, and may also be used to lower the total solids of a confection while retaining the same sweetness. The use of fructose in sweets will inhibit crystallisation and improve moisture retention, thereby slowing hardening while on store; but it increases the tendency to pick up moisture from the atmosphere unless adequately protected by packaging. At low levels of usage fructose may be used without any modification to the original recipe. Higher replacement levels (5% or more) require a reduction in the amount of glucose syrup solids or sucrose, depending on whether or not the confection is expected to contain a crystal phase.

Grades of glucose syrup are available which contain upwards of 40% of fructose.

2.8   MALTOSE

Maltose is not commercially produced for use as a confectionery ingredient. It is however present in significant amounts in glucose syrup and malt extract. It is a relatively soluble sugar, a saturated solution at 20° C (68° F) having a solubility of over 40%. The solubility rises rapidly with increasing temperature and at approximately 90° C (194° F) is equal to that of sucrose. Further increases in temperature produce higher concentration solutions than can be achieved with sucrose. The reducing power of maltose is theoretically just over half that of dextrose. However, when used with copper reagents in the Fehling test for reducing sugars, the determined reducing power is about 62% that of dextrose. A 10% solution of maltose has a relative sweetness equivalent to about 46% of that similar concentration of sucrose.

By selective processing, glucose syrups can be manufactured which contain a high percentage of maltose. The properties and possible uses of maltose for the manufacture of sugar confectionery will become more known as the uses of these special high maltose glucose syrups are investigated.

2.9 INVERT SUGAR

Dextrose and Fructose (Laevulose) are the components of 'invert sugar' which is produced from the inversion (breakdown) of sucrose. They are isomers, i.e. they have the same chemical formula, but a different molecular arrangement.

Invert sugar syrups contain a nearly equal proportion of the two sugars. These syrups can be commercially purchased at 70%, 75% and 80% concentrations, or produced on site by the inversion of sucrose. A 66% sucrose solution is processed at 75° C (167° F) for 1 hour with the addition of a 1% level of hydrochloric acid. The syrup should then be neutralised and filtered. Inversion can also be achieved using invertase, the prepared syrups having a better colour and consistency; but this lengthens the inversion period to 7 days.

Under unfavourable conditions, considerable amounts of invert sugars may be produced in sugar confections. A high invert sugar sweet is more likely to attract moisture from the atmosphere than those containing equivalent amounts of other confectionery sugars.

2.10 INVERTASE

Invertase is an enzyme which may be used to convert sucrose (cane or beet sugar) to 'invert sugar' in creams and syrups. It is extracted from baker's or brewer's yeast or from moulds and is normally supplied to confectioners in solutions of glycerol or sorbitol. The enzyme is known alternatively as sucrase or as saccharase. Solutions of invertase should be colourless and odourless.

The effectiveness of invertase in converting sucrose to the simpler sugars is influenced by (i) temperature at time of addition of invertase and in subsequent holding period; (ii) pH of mix at these respective times; (iii) type of other ingredients present; (iv) level of usage of invertase; (v) strength of invertase solution; (vi) length of time stored after addition of invertase; and (vii) storage conditions of treated material.

Invertase is best added to sugar confectionery materials at a level of 0·125% of the final batch weight. The temperature at the time of addition should be in the range 60°–70° C (140°–158° F) and the pH in the range 3·8–5·2. High temperatures and strongly acid conditions will destroy the activity of invertase. Certain dyestuffs have an effect on this process though not in general at the level used in confectionery. The major part of the conversion occurs within seven days.

Invertase should be stored, away from light, in cool conditions and in tightly sealed amber-coloured bottles, and used in strict order of purchase.

2.11   LACTOSE

Lactose is the natural sugar occurring in milk and is sometimes referred to as 'milk sugar'. It can be a useful additive for grained sugar confections such as fudge. The sugar is extracted from whey and, when pure, has the following composition

	%
Lactose	99·0
Moisture	0·4
Proteinous matter	0·3
Mineral matter	0·3

The lactose molecule contains two simpler sugars—dextrose and galactose, which are strongly linked and this linkage, unlike that present in sucrose, is difficult to break. It exists in two forms termed α and β, and solutions of lactose in water are equilibrium mixtures of both forms (approx. two parts α to one part β). Lactose is not very soluble, at 20° C (68° F) the solution concentration is only 16% increasing to 60% at 90° C (194° F). If lactose graining is not required in a sugar confection the milk sugar content must be held to under 4%.

Lactose is slow to crystallise from solutions unless seeded, and the resultant crystals are large and coarse. The main application for mono-hydrate lactose is as a diluent and granulating product in the preparation of pharmaceutical tablets. Great care should be exercised when using lactose in confectionery, to avoid coarse textures developing during storage.

A. J. NIELSEN [*Candy Ind*. 1963, *120*, (8), 40–2] has found that the complete replacement of milk solids by lactose gave caramels which were colourless, more viscous and more elastic. Only if albumen was added did the typical colour and flavour of caramel develop. Caramels with high casein content were very soft when compared to those manufactured with the usual milk solids mixture present in condensed milk.

2.12   CARAMEL

Caramel is produced in its simplest form when sugar is burnt. It can be prepared from various sources of sugar but some of the highest purity grades are manufactured from dextrose monohydrate. It is essentially a brown colouring material, universally permitted; its contribution to flavour is small.

Modern methods for the production of caramel consist of heating solutions of reducing sugars under controlled conditions with ammonia or sodium hydroxide. The main sources of sugar for manufacture are invert sugar, glucose syrup and dextrose-hydrate, these often being interchangeable. The caramelisation temperature must be strictly controlled; heating should be rapid, and followed by rapid cooling. Over-caramelisation can cause the development of a very harsh flavour. The degree of caramelisation gives the finished caramel its final colour or 'tinctorial value'.

At the end of the reaction, water is added to dilute the caramel into a handlable product. Caramels are very corrosive substances and must therefore be produced in stainless steel equipment or in specially treated plant.

The type of caramel selected should be suitable for the manufacture of sugar confectionery, as to colour value (For Tinctorial EBC Numbers, see European Brewing Convention: 'Analytical method for determining tinctorial colour value using EBC slides or colour discs.' *Analytica*, 2nd Edn., p. 20), flavour and stability.

General Characteristics and Uses of Liquid Caramels

EBC Colour Value	Solids Content % w/w	Characteristics and Use
56 000	65·5	Very high tinctorial value. Used where no critical stability required, for example liquorice doughs or pastes.
48 000	71·6	High tinctorial values. Stable in salt solution or acid solution. Used in glazes, fruit pastes and toffee.
32 500	76·2	Soft flavoured caramel for fillings and caramel products.
23 000	77·3	Resistant to vegetable extracts, also acids. Stable in ethyl and isopropyl alcohol up to 70%. For flavouring essences.
17 000	69·6	Stable to alcohol up to 80%; specially for whisky, rum and spirit liquors.

2.13   SPRAY DRIED CARAMEL

Recent advances in spray drying techniques have resulted in the manufacture of caramel powders, derived from liquid caramel and dried on a starch dextrin base. Two main types are available which differ in their tinctorial value and in certain aspects of stability. Some caramels are sensitive to calcium ions and salt, and in hard water districts can give rise to haze. This can be overcome by the addition to the caramel of 20% of its weight of anhydrous hydrogen orthophosphate. Caramel powders are quite hygroscopic and containers must be re-sealed after use.

Caramel powders overcome the difficulties of dispensing liquid caramel in small percentage, and are convenient for addition to dry-mix products, for weighing and handling. Typical specifications for caramel powders are given below.

	Unstable in Salt Solution	Stable to Salt
Colour—°EBC	54 000°–58 000°	42 000°–46 000°
pH (50% w/w solution)	4·4–5·6	4·4–5·6

A particle size analysis for these caramel powders would be determined by sieving through various sizes of silks; the following range would be typical:

Residue on 8 silk	Trace
Residue on 10 silk	5% maximum
Residue on 12 silk	10% maximum
Residue on 16 silk	50% maximum

2.14   SORBITOL

Sorbitol occurs widely in nature particularly in seaweed and in fruit berries. Much of the sorbitol used in sweet manufacture is produced synthetically and frequently contains smaller amounts of sugars, particularly mannitol. Preparation methods vary but basically depend on heating of dextrose with alkaline earths, with subsequent neutralisation and hydrogenation under raised temperature and pressure in the presence of nickel as catalyst.

Sorbitol is a polyhydric alcohol related to sugar; glycerol (glycerine) is also an alcohol but simpler in composition. This explains the similarity in the effects of sorbitol or glycerol in a sugar confectionery recipe. Sorbitol is extremely stable to acids, enzymes and to temperatures up to 140° C (248° F). It is produced in a number of different forms for sale to sweet manufacturers. Anhydrous sorbitol (containing about 1% of water) melts at 110° C (230° F), the crystalline form at 98° C (208° F). Both are white, non-volatile, odourless powders which tend to pick up water from the air. Sorbitol can also be purchased as a 70% solution which has a refractive index of 1·46, a specific gravity of 1·30 and boils at 105° C (221° F). Powdered sorbitol is very readily soluble and can form solutions which contain over 80% of the alcohol. Supersaturated solutions of sorbitol may be prepared. At equivalent concentrations sorbitol solutions are more viscous than glycerol but less than regular grade glucose syrups. Solutions of sorbitol are neutral.

Sorbitol, like dextrose, produces a cooling taste on the tongue, due to its negative heat of solution. Although varying results can be obtained by changing the test concentration level, it is possible to generalise that sorbitol has only half the sweetness of sucrose. The optical rotation of pure sorbitol is $-1·99$ (a^d $_{20°}$ C) (see glossary) and the powder density, depending on particle size, is between 1·3 and 1·4.

Sorbitol is a good conditioning agent slowing down the loss of moisture from the confection to air—in this, it comes midway between glycerol, the most, and invert sugar, the least, effective. It is also freely metabolised by the human body.

The addition of sorbitol to confections will cause them to become softer in texture though not very perceptibly until 5%. For 5–15% additions the boiling temperature should be raised by 1°–3° C (2°–6° F). Once a usage level of 5% has been exceeded an equal amount of glucose syrup solids must be omitted. Boils which contain sorbitol are less viscous and this can influence both crystallising and whipping properties.

Five to ten per cent levels of sorbitol are suitable for soft textured products such as cream paste, fudge and nougat. The freshness of dessicated coconut and other nuts can be improved by holding the nuts in a 10% syrup of sorbitol which contains 0·5% of salt, for 30 minutes prior to adding to the confectionery batch. The addition of 5% sorbitol to candied fruit syrup is thought to improve syrup penetration. Sorbitol increases the gloss on fudge and can be used to produce 'sugar free' boiled sweets.

Some syrups of sorbitol contain between 5–8% mannitol. This is claimed by some sweet manufacturers to be advantageous in that the mixed syrup is less liable to crystallisation.

2.15   GLYCERINE

Glycerine can be added to recipes for its value as a conditioner and to prevent moisture loss. It is a viscous, clear, non-crystallising liquid that is compatible with other confectionery ingredients, and under the conditions used for the manufacture of sweets, is non-volatile.

Glycerine can be purchased at concentration levels of 95% and 99% which have specific gravities of 1·25 and 1·26 respectively. It is less viscous than sorbitol at an equivalent 70% concentration which has a specific gravity of 1·185. The freezing point of pure glycerine is slightly below room temperature, 18° C (64° F), but the presence of even small traces of water greatly depress this value.

The sweetness of glycerine depends on concentration: at 95% concentration it has two-thirds the sweetening power of cane or beet sugar, at 70% concentration only one-half.

When incorporated at a 3% level in coconut confections it reduces moisture loss and the resultant product has a fresher taste. Additions of $2\frac{1}{2}$% to the final glaze used on glacé fruits will lengthen the period before white spots of crystallised sucrose develop. The addition of 2% glycerine to marshmallow, jelly and gum batches assists in the retention of softness. It can also be added to cream and French paste to lower the rate of moisture loss while on store.

C

2.16   MALT EXTRACT

Malt extract produced by the treatment of barley grain, may be used in caramel manufacture as a flavouring. The quantities used are much greater than those of other flavouring agents and adjustments are necessary in the weights of the other ingredients. An average composition for malt extract is:

	%
Total solids	88
Moisture	22
Sucrose	4
Maltose	55
Dextrose and fructose	2
Dextrins	13
Proteins	3
Mineral ash	1

3

Cocoa Beans

3.1 GROWTH

The cocoa bean is the fruit of *Theobroma cacao* Linn. Flowers, and later, the pods holding the bean, develop on the trunk of the trees and on the main stems in clusters. Dependent on the variety, the tree will start to bear fruit after 4–8 years. Successful cultivation depends on high humidity, around 90–100%; temperatures in the range 25°–27° C; adequate water supply; good soil conditions, and space for growth. Cocoa flourishes at the lower altitudes of tropical climates. Wind is one of the greatest enemies of the cocoa tree and shelter is therefore normally provided by planting surrounding trees of larger species; but this shading effect generally results in lower yields [R. K. CUNNINGHAM, P. W. ARNOLD, 1961, Agricultural Group, Society of Chemical Industry Symposium]. Growth in full sun necessitates greater care, with frequent watering. Yields of cocoa beans per acre vary from 200 lb (91 kg) to upwards of 700 lb (318 kg). With careful crop treatment yields could exceed 1000 lb (454 kg) and for some of the stronger varieties up to 5000 lb (2268 kg)/acre.

3.2 TYPES

It was originally considered that there were two commercial categories of cocoa bean, Criollo and Forastero. The use of these basic gradings have been considerably devalued by cross breeding. Criollo gives a finer cocoa flavour but accounts for only 5–8% of the world production. The fall in its availability largely arises from failure to control disease and insect attack, and lack of knowledge on the use of fertilisers. West African beans, the main source in use in Britain, and Brazilian beans, extensively used in the USA, are both of the more common Forastero type.

Trinitario beans are a cross between Criollo and Amazonian Forastero varieties and are considered 'fine grade' as regards flavour.

3.3 Sources

Sources of cocoa beans are shown in Tables 25 and 26 and world production statistics in Table 27. In producing a recipe for chocolates, the beans should be blended to give a characteristic aroma and flavour. Costa Rica, Brazil or West Africa beans are best used as the 'bulk' or 'basic' bean with smaller proportions of Samoa, Trinidad or Venezuela beans added to improve the flavour. See also Table 38 in Chapter 8.

3.4 Cocoa Fruit

Each mature pod weighs between 400–500 gr and has an inner weight of beans of about 140–150 gr. The pods, which measure 6–8 in (15–20 mm) contain 30–40 beans. Each bean after drying weighs on average 1·1–1·3 gr. The seed consists of a shell, a thin skin and an inner cotyledon containing the germ rootlet. At the time of harvesting the skin of the bean accounts for one-eighth the total weight of the seed. The shell, skin and germ rootlet are mostly removed during later processing and normally do not account for more than 2% of the bean used for the manufacture of chocolate. The characteristics of the basic types of beans are shown in Table 28.

TABLE 25. Commercial Descriptions and Origins of Cocoa Beans

Common Name	Country
Accra	Ghana
Arriba	Ecuador
Bahia	Brazil
Caracas	Venezuela
Guayaquil	Ecuador
Lagos	Nigeria
Machala	Ecuador
Maracaibo	Venezuela
Maripipi	Philippines
Puerto Cabello	Venezuela
Sanchez	Dominican Republic
Vandeloo	Congo

TABLE 26. Main Sources and Characteristics of Cocoa Beans

Source	Characteristics
Brazil	Good, well-processed general bean but acidic nature dictates care in use.
British Guiana	Occasional off-flavours noted.
Cameroons	A Forastero bean with a good average flavour.
Ceylon	Quality varying, between fine to basic.

TABLE 26—*continued*

Source	Characteristics
Congo	A Forastero bean with a full but rather astringent flavour.
Costa Rica	A mild-flavoured bean of Criollo type.
Dominican Republic	A good bean but subject to uneven processing.
Ecuador	Variable quality according to season—a good general bean with a satisfactory flavour.
Ghana	Normally well processed but lacking in distinctive flavour—a good 'bulk' bean.
Grenada	A Forastero bean with a good flavour.
Ivory Coast	A good quality bean.
Java	A Criollo bean with some hybridisation; good aroma with a weak flavour.
Mexico	Uneven processing leads to variable quality.
New Guinea	A fine grade aroma bean; quality varies considerably between estates.
Nigeria	Good well-processed bean but somewhat lacking in flavour.
Samoa	A hybrid bean with mild but good flavour.
San Thomé	Good quality Forastero bean.
Trinidad	A good quality bean; some particularly fine flavours.
Tobago	Mixed bean quality.
Venezuela	Some good quality Criollo with fine flavour, but other crops of lower grade.

TABLE 27. World Cocoa Production

Country	Production in kilo tons 1970–71	1971–72 (forecasted)
Ghana	386	455
Nigeria	303	248
Brazil	179	157
Ivory Coast	177	219
Cameroon	110	126
Ecuador	60	58
Guinea	32	20
New Guinea	29	28
Mexico	27	27
Dominican Republic	25	40
Colombia	21	22
Venezuela	18	19
Others	115	114
World Total	1482	1533

(Ref. Gill and Duffus (London) Market Report dated August 1972.)

TABLE 28. Differences between Criollo and Forastero Beans

Characteristic		Criollo	Forastero
Pod	Colour:	Red–yellow	Yellow–orange
	Shape:	Tapered	Plump
	Wall:	Indented surface, soft	Smoother surface, hard
Bean	Colour:	Cream–pale purple	Rose–dark red
	Skin:	Thin	Thicker than Criollo
	Shape:	Oval and flat	Flattened

As has been stated earlier (§3.2) the difference between the varieties has been considerably affected by hybridisation and the characteristics could well differ from those for the basic bean shown in the Table 28. The pH of the bean varies according to the source as well as the season. Some typical pH values are

Accra	5·6
Bahia	5·2
Sanchez	5·8
Arriba	5·4
Trinidad	5·0

In the pod the beans are arranged around a central placenta. They are surrounded by a mucilaginous pulp which has an essential function in the later processing.

If unripe beans are harvested they tend to be small, flat, have a poor colour, are hard, have low fat contents and bitter off-flavours. This type of bean should not be used in chocolate manufacture. In particular flat beans are difficult to roast giving rise to uneven processing. During ripening the tannin content rises and this contributes to the astringency of the beans. Beans which have started to germinate will cause difficulty in manufacture. They are considerably more susceptible to mould, are less resistent to insect attack and differ chemically from the ripe ungerminated bean; this gives rise to change in flavour characteristics.

During ripening the sugar content increases, though never so much as to significantly affect any subsequent analysis of chocolate. There is also a change in fat content, and to some extent of the composition of the natural fat (cocoa butter) during ripening. Fat, like weight of shell, is dependent on harvesting season: the cocoa butter content can range in one growing area from 52–58% depending on the time of harvesting. The major chemical components of cocoa beans are given below

Organic acids	Citric, lactic, acetic, possibly malic and tartaric acids. The content and relationship between the acids vary according to season and source. Values for the free volatile acid—mainly acetic—are around 0·20% and for non-volatile acids 1–2%.

Sugars	Glucose, sucrose and fructose with lesser quantities of raffinose, melibiose, stachyrose and other higher sugars.
Amino acids and proteins	Principal amino acids are glutamic and aspartic acids; proteins include albumin, globulin and glutamin. About one-seventh of the solid matter in cocoa beans at this stage is nitrogenous matter.
Other major components	Caeffine, theobromine and a wide range of trace elements including manganese, iron, copper and zinc.

Two types of cells can be detected in the structure of cocoa beans. Around 90% are colourless and contain the fat, starch, sugar and enzymes. The others are pigment cells and contain tannin, colour pigments and theobromine.

3.5 HARVESTING

As the pods ripen they change colour; when ripe, they are carefully cut from the tree by a machette or a similar type of knife, to avoid damaging the tree or pods. Diseased pods are separated, and those suitable for chocolate manufacture, stacked and transported to the fermentation areas. This must be carried out promptly, or fermentation will commence. The pods are opened by hand and the beans scooped out on to drying mats; a skilled operative can open 250–300 pods each hour. Mechanical breaking machines have been developed, to operate at around 1000 pods per hour [G. R. WOOD, 1968, *Cocoa Growers Bulletin*, (11), 25–26] but the quality of the beans obtained is lower. The introduction of an intermediate husk removal and rapid wash has however produced beans of similar quality to those from manually broken pods. The temperature must not exceed 60°–65° C (140°–149° F) during drying if flavour and colour are not to be impaired [V. C. QUESNEL, K. JUGMOHUNSINGH, 1970, *J. Sci. Fd. Agric.*, *21*, 537–41].

3.6 PULP

The pulp in the cocoa pod consists principally of water (80–90%), various sugars, proteins, starch, acids and various inorganic salts. Glucose and sucrose are predominant among the sugars. The acidic nature is mainly caused by citric acid. The sugar and acid content increases considerably during ripening. Successful fermentation of cocoa beans is dependent on a high sugar content and therefore harvesting should only be carried out when the pod and its contents have fully matured.

3.7 FERMENTATION

Fermentation is necessary to produce a bean which, on processing, will have a good cocoa flavour, is even in colour, is brittle and will break easily during winnowing. Chemical, biochemical and enzymic changes occur and germinating properties of the bean are killed. The process can be carried out by a number of different methods, the beans being either placed in a hole in the ground, piled in heaps, or held in baskets, non-metallic boxes, or trays. The most inefficient method used is placing the beans in a leaf-lined hole in the ground covering with more leaves, for this precludes the essential aeration. The most widely used method is to heap the extracted beans and pulp on to broad leaves (such as banana) and to cover with more leaves or canvas sheeting. Alternatively the beans are placed in wicker or similar open-structured baskets which are then covered with large leaves. Non-metallic boxes or tanks, used on the larger estates, hold 1000 kg of beans. Holes in the sides of the tank give aeration and permit drainage. Tray fermentation has recently been proposed, in which the beans are heaped on stacked wooden trays.

The fermentation period needed varies according to area and country of growth, harvesting season, type and size of bean and quantity of beans. If too many beans are used, the fermentation rate falls due to the lack of aeration. If too small a weight is taken, the heat loss is too great and fermentation is inefficient. Long periods can give rise to mould development and loss of flavouring components. Because of the variation in conditions it is difficult to specify an average fermentation period, but Criollo beans usually take from 2 to 4 days and Forastero from 6 to 10.

The weight of beans falls to one-half during fermentation, and temperatures up to 50°–60° C (122°–140° F) can occur; an optimum temperature of 45° C (113° F) is usual.

Changes occur during fermentation in both the pulp and the bean. These are associated with enzymic action, yeast fermentation and bacteriological growth. Sugar is first converted into alcohol in the pulp liquor and subsequently into various acids. Enzymic action takes place within the bean and the pigment cells break down releasing the contents into the main cotyledon mass. At this stage there is some loss of theobromine and tannins. Changes occur in the protein and the amount of soluble nitrogen component rises [O. F. KADEN, *Zucker u Susswaren-Wirts*, 1952, *5*, 479–81]. Primary oxidation products are formed which develop into flavour components during later processing. With the breakdown of pigment cells, there is the destruction of the germinating power of the seed. This occurs partly because of the high temperatures but mainly due to the increased quantities of acetic acid formed in the pulp [V. C. QUESNEL, *J. Sci. Fd. Agric.*, 1965, *16*, 441–7].

At least one day at the raised temperature is needed to destroy the germinating power. The beans swell during fermentation, internal fissures appear in their structure and they become more brittle.

The end of fermentation is normally assessed by the colour of the beans on cutting, the length of time and the odour. Beans which have had a long fermentation period are changed in colour, are more brittle and have secondary ammoniacal aroma. Fermenting beans too quickly develops an off-flavour in the chocolate after processing.

3.8 DRYING

This reduces the moisture content of the fermented cocoa beans from 60% to the dispatch level of 7%; a secondary effect is the oxidation of certain of the flavour precursors of chocolate. Three quarters of the acid formed in the fermentation stage is also lost by drying.

Cocoa beans may be dried by one of four basic methods: (i) *sun drying*, in which the beans are heaped on mats and left in the sun to dry; (ii) *tray drying*, in which they are evenly spread on trays and then stacked to permit drying; (iii) *storing*, in which trays of beans are transferred to hot rooms; and (iv) *mechanical drying* by rotary hot air dryers.

The use of drying rooms reduce the processing period from 5 to 10 days to 2 days or less. Chocolate flavour developed in beans which have been stove-dried is not of the same high quality as with the sun dried. Rotary drum drying reduces processing time even further to 1 day but again flavour quality is reduced. Balanced sun and mechanical drying periods can be given, to utilise the best of both procedures. In rotary drying some of the skin is removed during processing and the beans are partly polished. The temperature of rotary dryers should not exceed 90° C (194° F) [DE VOS: *Bull. Landb. Proefstn, Surinam* 1956, 73].

An intermediate wash can be inserted midway in the drying period. The thickness of the bean layers on trays or mats must be reduced towards the end of drying to ensure an even release of internal moisture; most of the water released in the early stages is that held near the surface.

During drying, the pH value of the bean rises, probably as a result of the release of acetic acid. The reduction in size as moisture is lost is helpful in the subsequent removal of the shell.

If more than 8% water is left in the beans they will develop mould growth during transportation. Protection from rain is needed during drying. Beans which are partially dried, wetted and then redried will be of inferior quality. The amount of water left in the beans before roasting is claimed by W. MOHR [*Fette Seifen AnstrM*, 1970, 72, (8) 695–703] to be of importance in the subsequent development of cocoa aroma.

3.9 DISEASES OF COCOA

Many growing areas have been badly afflicted by disease of either the tree or the pod. Strict control, the selective use of insecticides and the burning of infected trees have considerably reduced the threat of devastation of complete areas. The major diseases and pests affecting cocoa are:

Black Pod: A fungus disease in which the pod blackens and the beans and pulp become affected. It causes low yields of beans and lowers the sugar content of the pulp, important for fermentation. This disease particularly occurs in wet weather.

Swollen Shoot: A virus disease in which swellings occur on the shoots and branches. The leaves change colour and fall, the tree becomes bare and dies. The virus is transferred by mealy bugs.

Witches Broom: A fungus disease particularly occurring in South America and Trinidad. The pod is attacked while in growth and its attendant shoots thicken.

Cocoa Thrips: These insects feed on the sap of the tree; the leaves darken and eventually fall.

A number of other pests and diseases cause severe local difficulties; while some insect pests affect the beans once they have been processed. These are discussed below (§3.11).

3.10   STORAGE OF COCOA BEANS

Cocoa beans can be stored in sacks or in silos. They should not be allowed to fall unimpeded on to other beans or on the silo or hopper walls, as damaged beans are more liable to mould growth. The beans from sacks or from bulk deliveries should be discharged gradually down sloping chutes to produce a final fall of no more than a few inches. Beans which contain more than 8% moisture are more liable to go mouldy. Adequate air circulation through the silos will extend shelf life which, under satisfactory conditions, will be nine to twelve months.

The walls and floors of storage areas should be completely smooth with no crevices or girders to harbour insects. Any grids or air vents should be meshed to prevent the entry of rodents. Sacks of cocoa beans should be stacked away from walls and should be held on pallets to allow an adequate circulation of air.

The equilibrium relative humidity of cocoa beans is low at 22%. This rises on roasting to between 26% and 36%, but falls to around 30% when made into cocoa liquor. To prevent condensation on the beans the temperature of silos or stores should not be allowed to fall below 16° C (61° F).

3.11   STORAGE PESTS

Three in particular are found troublesome: the tropical warehouse moth, the Indian meal moth and the warehouse moth. Others include the cigarette beetle and rust-red flour beetle.

A wide choice of control measures are available to reduce infestation, including aerosol insecticide sprays, Malathion spray, DDT spray, valpona strips, lindane smoke generator and fumigation with methyl bromide, ethylene oxide or with pyrethrins held in oil. (See also *Infestation Control in the Cocoa, Chocolate and Confectionery Industry*: Cocoa, Chocolate and Confectionery Alliance, 1970.)

The choice of control procedure should be dictated by prevailing legislation which varies considerably from country to country.

3.12 CHOCOLATE FLAVOUR AND AROMA

The characteristic flavour and aroma of chocolate is developed during the fermentation and roasting of cocoa beans. Chocolate which is produced from beans which have not been fermented has little or no characteristic taste of cocoa. Similarly unroasted beans make little contribution to chocolate flavour. No other process in chocolate making has been found to have the same effect on cocoa flavour and aroma.

Research has indicated that it is the presence of acetic acid in the fermentation process which plays a significant part in the development of flavour precursors in the cocoa bean. Over 200 possible flavour components, volatile and non-volatile, have been identified in trace amounts in cocoa beans. Those compounds however which play a significant contribution to chocolate flavour and aroma are iso-valeraldehyde, dimethyl disulphide, valine, leucine and epicatechin, normally in association with natural sugars.

To achieve a satisfactory blend of flavour and aroma it is essential to balance the varieties of cocoa beans used in a recipe (see §8.4 Chocolate Recipes). The flavour of chocolate is not fully developed on manufacture but can take several months to reach its full quality. Chocolate flavour falls in strength after some twelve months storage.

Fuller information on the research into flavour components of chocolate has been documented by T. A. ROHAN in *Food Proc. and Marketing*, 1969, (1), 12–17 and in *Gordian*, 1969, 443–590; and by A. LOPEY & V. C. QUESNEL in *J. Sci. Fd. Agric.* 1971, *26*, (i), 19–20, 2–4.

3.13 BEAN QUALITY

Bean quality may be judged on analytical characteristics and by visual examination. In particular, samples of beans should be assessed for (i) germinated beans (ii) insect and worm affected beans (iii) even fermentation (iv) presence of mould spores (v) broken beans (vi) flat beans (vii) slaty or violet beans; and (viii) uniformity of size.

When examining cocoa beans the cut test should be used [C. DEL BOCA, *Int. Choc. Rev.*, 1962, *17*, (5), 218–223]. A specified number of beans (say 50) should be cut open and their interior appearance examined. Slaty and purple beans arise because of the presence of anthocyanin, which is normally destroyed during fermentation when the contents of the individual cells present are diffused throughout the bean. Faulty beans can cause off-flavours to develop. Common causes of these flavours are listed below:

Astringent: Beans poorly fermented, with too high a proportion of purple beans.
Bitter: Excessive amount of tannins and prurines.
Low Flavour Level: Lacking in flavour beans, or flavour beans badly fermented.
Musty: Mould on beans.
Off-flavours: Sour milk: overfermented beans. Smoky: flavour contamination during drying. Ham-like: peak fermentation temperature too low.

The range of terms used world-wide for grading cocoa beans has been listed elsewhere [ANON, *Gordian*, 1961, *61*, 1454–8].

4

Fats and Related Ingredients

4.1 GENERAL

Fats and oils are constituted from the glycerol molecule in which the various hydroxyl endings have been substituted with different fatty acids. Both the type and substitution position of the fatty acids will influence the properties of the fat. The various endings of the glycerol molecule are not necessarily occupied by the same type of fatty acids in a particular fat. Some of the fatty acids have linkages which are chemically satisfied, i.e. saturated, while others are still capable of further linkage, i.e. unsaturated. Generally the fats which contain higher proportions of unsaturated acids are more likely to deteriorate on store.

Fats are extracted either by expellation in which oil seeds or nuts, after cleaning, are pressed to rupture the cells, or by removal with a solvent. Expelled oil is extracted by treatment with steam and expelling in tapering screw presses followed by filtration before refining. Hexane is the most frequently used solvent, the oil or fat being recovered by distillation. Refining is a four-stage process in which the oil is neutralised with an alkali, centrifuged or filtered to remove any insoluble salts, bleached with Fuller's Earth and finally deodorised with supersaturated steam.

Fats can be hydrogenated to raise the level of saturated fatty acids. This is usually carried out by treating the refined heated oil with hydrogen under pressure in the presence of a catalyst such as treated nickel. A range of treated fats can be produced by the careful control of the processing conditions. As the saturation level rises the melting point of the fat will increase.

Fats can be bulk delivered by tanker and stored in stainless steel or coated iron or mild steel tanks, the capacity of which should be no greater than one tanker load. The tanks should be jacketed and be capable of being heated either by steam or electricity. When fats are supplied by drum they should be stored in a cool dark area and used in strict order of delivery. Drum melters should be used where required to automatically meter the liquid fat into the processing pans. Heating can be carried out

57

by wrapping electrical heater tapes round the drums or by progressively lowering steam coils into the fat.

4.2   Borneo Illipé (Illipé-Butter, Borneo Tallow)

Borneo illipé fat is extracted from nuts of the *shorea* tree found in the forests of Borneo. Following collection the nuts are dried before shipment to the processing plant.

The colour varies from white to pale green. It has properties which closely resemble those of cocoa butter, completely melting at 37°–38° C (99°–100° F). The fatty acid composition is very simple, consisting of stearic, oleic and palmitic acids. On cooling, the fat crystals form at a lower temperature than those which form in cocoa butter treated under similar conditions. Borneo illipé is harder than cocoa butter and the fat can be used to improve the handling properties of chocolate products such as Easter eggs. The incorporation of Borneo illipé in chocolate raises the melting point and improves the storage resistance, particularly when manufactured for the tropics.

The temperature range used for tempering chocolate should be raised if illipé butter is incorporated.

4.3   Coconut Oil

Coconut oil is extracted from the fruit of the coconut palm grown in West Africa, India, Ceylon and the Philippines. After drying, the oil is extracted from the flesh of the nut. The composition of the oil varies according to the processing method.

The fat has a brittle texture and may vary from cream to deep yellow brown in colour. It has a clear melting point at 25° C (77° F). Refining removes much of the colouring matter and most of the coconut flavour present in the raw material.

Coconut oil can be selectively hydrogenated to raise the melting point and stability of the fat. Completely hydrogenated coconut oil melts at 35° C (95° F).

4.4   Groundnut Oil (Peanut Oil, Earthnut Oil)

This is extracted from the nuts removed from the pods of the groundnut plant. The oil content of the groundnut is 45–48% depending on source: the extracted unrefined oil varies in colour from yellow to brown and is nutty in taste.

The extractable fatty material, after refining, sets at 0° C. As the temperature approaches freezing point, a crystalline sediment of stearines develop in the oil. The fatty acid composition of the oil varies according to source, the major acids being oleic and linoleic. Groundnut oil is quite stable and resistant to oxidation. Hydrogenation may be used to raise the melting point.

4.5 PALM OIL

The fruit of the oil palm has a high oil content, up to 55%, which can be extracted and processed to produce a food grade fat. The colour of the unrefined oil varies from yellowish brown to pale orange red. Untreated palm oil can vary in melting point from 35°–40° C (95°–104° F).

Refined palm oil is a soft fat whose main fatty acids are palmitic and oleic. Hydrogenation raises the melting point to give a range of fats which have a maximum melting point of 58° C (136° F). Palm oil which has been hydrogenated is harder than the untreated oil.

4.6 PALM KERNEL OIL

This oil is extracted from the kernel of the palm fruit, which contains up to 50% of extractable oil. Palm oil is yellowish in colour but is whitened by refining.

The refined oil melts at 28°–29° C (82°–84° F) and contains lauric, myristic and oleic acids as the major fatty acids.

Palm kernel oil can be readily hydrogenated to develop a range of high melting fats. Completely hydrogenated palm kernel oil melts at 48° C (118° F). *Hydrogenated palm kernel oil*, more commonly known as HPKO, is the most commonly used fat for sweet manufacture. The product used is the partially hydrogenated fat which melts at around 32° C (90° F).

The constituent glycerides in palm kernel oil can be separated and certain of the stearines have properties similar to those of cocoa butter. Stearine mixtures are the basis of many of the commercial substitutes for cocoa butter.

4.7 BUTTER

Butter is produced by the continuous beating of cream. During the churning process the emulsion of fat in water is broken. Subsequent kneading causes the fat globules to recombine and crystallise to form butter. Excess water is exuded during the final stages of the manufacturing process.

A typical analysis of butter is:

	%
Butterfat	82·0
Water	15·5
Salt	1·5
Lactose	0·5
Casein	0·3
Albumen	0·1
Calcium Phosphate	0·1

The level of salt concentration in butter varies from 0·5% to 1·5% depending on source. English butters contain the higher levels of salt. Salt not only enhances the flavour of the butter but reduces danger from mould growth on the exposed surfaces. Water is distributed throughout the butter as fine droplets. Excessive water levels are indicated by the appearance of water droplets on the blade of an inserted spatula or similar equipment used during batching up the butter for confectionery recipes. The exuding of water may also be brought about by ineffective processing methods during manufacture.

A small proportion of the butterfat, up to 10%, may be present as liquid fat but the major part is dispersed throughout the product in a fine crystalline form.

Many of the commercial butters offered to the sweet manufacturers are blends and not single source products. Blends are produced by kneading together various imported and local butters and increasing the salt concentration. Blends have advantages over single source butters in that a more consistent quality can be maintained and the properties more easily matched to the purchaser's requirements.

Butter texture is relatable to the type and amount of fats present, the method of production, the crystal form of the fats and the storage temperature.

Butter is more likely to undergo oxidation than the vegetable fats. This type of rancidity, due to butyric acid, can be minimised by the use of anti-oxidants. Trimethylamine formed from the breakdown of butter lecithin causes unpleasant fishy odours in the fat. Caramels containing high amounts of butter are liable to develop off-flavours. The butterfat at the surface of the confection is particularly liable to become rancid. Control procedures include the use of caramel wrappers which contain small traces of anti-oxidants, and packing in tight sealed foil wrappers. Small traces of iron, copper and chromium can accelerate the development of rancidity.

The colour of butter is dependent on the presence of fat-soluble pigments, the level of which falls during the winter months as the animals find less fresh grass. Diacetyl is mainly responsible for the characteristic butter flavour and the synthetic product can be used to boost the butter flavour of the confection. Many other trace flavouring materials present in butter are of the carbonyl, ketonic and aldehydic groups.

Sugar confections need strongly flavoured butters to overcome the flavour losses which occur due to heat treatment. Other off-flavours can occur in addition to those arising from rancid butter, particularly through bacteriological deterioration. Cheesiness is normally due to the breakdown of the protein components of the butter. High acid content butters are caused by poor processing and these can lead to excessive inversion occurring during the boiling of sugar confectionery mixes.

Quality checks on incoming deliveries of butter should include: acidity as lactic; appearance; blend quality; colour; flavour; microscopic appearance; protein; surface quality; texture; and water.

4.8 OFF-FLAVOURS IN FATS

The main causes of development of off-flavours are:

Oxidative rancidity: Unsaturated fatty acids present in the fat take up oxygen from the atmosphere.

Hydrolytic rancidity: Part of the fatty acid chains present in the fat splits away producing a soapy flavour.

Reversion: The fat redevelops the natural flavour of the base product which had been removed during refining.

Hydrolytic rancidity is caused by enzymes which break down the fatty acid chains; the presence of glycerol inhibits this type of deterioration. This kind of rancidity in nut-containing products is best controlled by keeping the water content of the nuts to a minimum. Oxidative rancidity is not immediately detectable and a time delay—the induction period—occurs during which the peroxide level rises sufficiently for the product to develop a rancid taste. This can be measured in weeks or months depending on the composition of the fat, the storage conditions and presence of catalytic compounds. Traces of metals will strongly accelerate the rate at which oxidative rancidity develops, particularly copper, iron and manganese. Fat tanks must be regularly cleaned out to prevent residual rancidity affecting subsequent batches.

4.9 ANTIOXIDANTS

These compounds lengthen the induction period and thereby delay the appearance of the characteristic rancid taste. It is thought that antioxidants work by cancelling the electrical charges that occur in the chemical reactions involved in oxidation and that they mask the products which promote oxidative rancidity. Among suggested antioxidants for food products are *n*–propyl gallate, *n*–octyl gallate, butylated hydroxyanisole (BHA), butylated hydroxytoluene (BHT).

The regulations controlling the addition of antioxidants vary from country to country and checks should be made as to the current legislation. Commercial lecithin has antioxidant properties though it is not as effective as the synthetic products described above.

There is little value in adding antioxidants to products containing hardened vegetable oils or cocoa butter alone. These fats are very stable and deterioration only occurs under very adverse conditions. Nuts are particularly prone to rancidity and the incorporation of 100 ppm of BHA (based on the nut content) improves keeping properties. Confections containing butter and full cream milk products can develop oxidative rancidity and the addition of traces of an antioxidant will extend shelf life.

4.10   OILSEED LECITHINS

These may be used in the manufacture of sugar confectionery as inexpensive emulsifiers or for reducing the viscosity of chocolate instead of adding extra cocoa butter.

Three lecithins are available to the confectioner. These are extracted from soyabean, groundnut and cottonseed. Only soyabean lecithin is widely available though limited supplies of the other two materials are offered from time to time. The composition of the three lecithins are given in Table 29.

TABLE 29.   Composition of Oilseed Lecithins

Lecithin Type	Soyabean	Groundnut	Cottonseed
Moisture, %	1·2	1·3	1·0
Acetone Solubles %	33·7	27·1	46·1
Acetone Insolubles %	64·4	71·9	52·9
Phosphorus, %	2·4	2·5	1·9
Choline	2·5	3·0	2·0
Consistency	fluid	viscous liquid	viscous liquid
Colour	deep yellow	deep brown	black

Although composition figures are widely quoted for purchasing, they bear little relation to the desired properties required from lecithin. The amount of commercial lecithin incorporated into caramel recipes is normally so great as not to be affected by minor differences between supplies. Lecithins from different sources and even from the same source can produce significantly different viscosity changes in chocolate. Samples of lecithin should be compared by addition to a standard chocolate in a fixed amount and examined for viscosity reduction under specified test conditions. Commercial lecithin will reduce viscosity up to a peak addition of around 0·5%: further additions give a falling off in viscosity reducing power.

A major disadvantage in using oilseed lecithin arises from the development of reversion products which produce a flavour taint in chocolate though this is not generally detectable in caramels or fudge.

4.11   LECITHIN YN AND OTHER SYNTHETIC VISCOSITY REDUCING AGENTS

Lecithin YN is a synthetic viscosity reducing agent developed in the Cadbury Bros. Laboratory (British Patent 1 032 485) to overcome the problem of flavour tainting from oilseed lecithins. The additive is produced by glycerolysis of rapeseed oil at raised pressure and temperature; it is phosphorylated with phosphorus pentoxide, neutralised, and screened to size. The commercial material available to the confectioner consists mainly of ammonium salts of phosphatidic salts of mono-, bi- and triglyceride held in a carrier oil and containing a small amount of natural phospholipids. The properties of lecithin YN are similar to those exhibited by soyabean lecithin, though the viscosity reducing behaviour continues to increase with additions of more than 0·5% to chocolate. Maximum viscosity reduction occurs in the addition range 0·2% and 0·4%.

Sodium salts of phosphatidic acid materials and polyglyceryl polyrincinoleate are commercially prepared for use as substitutes for commercial lecithin in chocolate manufacture.

4.12   GLYCERYL MONOSTEARATE

Glyceryl monostearate (GMS) is a substituted mono-diglyceride produced by the inter-esterification of fats, such as lard or tallow, with glycerol. A typical commercial product contains 35–45% of the monoester, 30–40% of the diester and 10–20% of the triester.

The product can be produced at varying levels of purity and composition. Vacuum distillation can be used to raise the level of the monosubstituted glyceride to 95% or over. The type of fatty acid present will vary according to the fat used during manufacture. The product normally offered to the confectionery industry contains predominantly stearic acid and, to a lesser extent, palmitic acid.

The action of glyceryl monostearate is that the non-esterified hydroxyl portion is associated with the sugar, water or syrup droplets while the remaining part of the molecule is held in the fat. This differing association ensures that GMS is a good stabiliser for the type of emulsions that are present in caramels or toffees. It is claimed that the addition of GMS improves the cutting performance of the guillotine knives. The presence of an emulsifier in any confection which contains a fat will improve the dispersion of that fat, lower the globule size and, provided it is not used in excess, improve the flavour quality. GMS when added to viscous confections improves the flow properties. It should not be added to whipped confections as it acts as an antifoaming agent. Glyceryl monostearate should be added to caramel and toffee batches at a rate of 0·3–0·4% of the final batch weight.

GMS melts at around 59° C (138° F) compared with 42° C (108° F) for polyoxyethylene sorbitan monostearate ('Tween') and 53° C (127° F) for sorbitan tristearate ('Span'), both alternative emulsifiers. Lactic and citric acid esters of the monoglycerides are also available for use as emulsifiers but at a raised product cost (see also §4.13).

4.13   'SPAN' AND 'TWEEN' ESTERS

Sorbitan esters of lauric and palmitic acids are generally available under the trade name of 'Span', the polyoxyethylene esters of the same acids being called 'Tween' (both are proprietary emulsifiers manufactured by Honeywell-Atlas Ltd.). 'Span' esters are good emulsifiers for oil in water emulsions, being predominantly soluble in the fat. 'Tween' esters are soluble in aquaeous solutions. 'Span 60' may also be added, at a 1% level, to chocolate couverature as a means of inhibiting the formation of bloom (see also chocolate enrobing, §8.12).

4.14   RELEASE AGENTS

Release agents are used to grease equipment used for manufacturing certain types of sugar confectionery to promote easy removal of the sweet. The most commonly available material suitable for all sweet manufacturing purposes is purified high-viscosity mineral oil, which is neutral in taste and has little odour. It should be used carefully: there is a legal limit of 0·2% in the United Kingdom.

Acetylated monoglycerides (see below) have excellent release properties. A number of alternatives based on vegetable oil are available, but difficulty arises with these materials from the development of rancidity on the film surface on the sweets during storage.

4.15   ACETOGLYCERIDES

Acetoglycerides are fat derivatives which are prepared by acetylation using acetic anhydride. The properties are dependent on the type of fatty acids used and the amount of acetic anhydride used in the reaction. They can be used to form a stable film on the surface of confections, which significantly reduces shrinking, hardening through moisture loss, fat degradation and the danger of mould growth.

Solid food grade acetoglycerides soften between 30°–32° C (86°–90° F) and 42°–46° C (108°–115° F). A film of acetoglycerides can be sprayed continuously onto the confections on a moving band. No drying period is needed. One to a half per cent level of the material should be used for this purpose.

Acetoglycerides have excellent release properties and can be used for boiled sweet manufacture and in liquorice production. They can be sprayed on to equipment thereby having an advantage over other release agents for continuous methods of manufacture.

4.16 WAXES

Waxes are used in the sweet industry as polishes for panned confectionery and as constituents of release agents. Four chief waxes in decreasing order of hardness, are *Carnauba wax, Candellia wax, Beeswax* and *Paraffin wax.*

One of the most widely used is beeswax which varies in composition but has the following general properties.

	°C		°C
Melting point	63–65	Ester value	72–78
Acid value	17–21	Sap value	87–95

The thermal conductivity of beeswax is 96×10^{-6}. [T. C. HELVEY, 1954, *Food Research, 19,* 282–92.] Pure beeswax is white, the characteristic yellow colour being due to impurities derived from plants and brought into the hive by bees.

Carnauba wax is extracted from the leaves of the carnauba palm and then purified by treating the extracted wax with caustic soda followed after neutralising, by separating and purifying.

5

Milk and Milk Products

5.1 MILK

Milk from the cow, after pasteurisation, is not satisfactory as an ingredient for the manufacture of sugar confectionery and chocolate, because of its high water content. This lengthens processing time and the enhanced danger from inversion (see §2.9) outweighs the advantage gained from lower cost of the milk. Typical composition of cow milk is given below

		%
Water	87·4	
Fat	3·7	
Solids, not fat.	8·9	
Lactose		4·9
Casein		3·0
Other proteins		0·5
Acidity as lactic		0·14

Both the 'fat' and 'milk solids not fat' values will vary according to the season of the year.

If it is necessary to use liquid milk for the manufacture of the sweets then the recipe ingredients containing high levels of reducing sugars (see §1.4) should be reduced. It is also advisable to reduce the quantity of water present for blending or dissolving the other raw materials. Conditions giving fast boiling should always be used.

Storage of liquid milk and other milk products should be in aluminium or glass lined steel or plastic coated steel vessels. Cleaning is carried out by a hot solution of a calcium sequestrating agent followed by a hot alkaline detergent solution containing a quaternary ammonium sterilant.

5.2 CONDENSED MILK

Condensed milk is produced for the manufacture of sugar confectionery either sweetened or unsweetened. The former is preferable as the sugar has a preserving action and the product a reduced water content, which is of considerable advantage in lowering boiling time. The amount of milk solids

66

present does not greatly depend on whether the product is sweetened (28–35%) or unsweetened (27–33%).

Average compositions of three types of condensed milk are:

	Sweetened full cream %	Sweetened skimmed %	Unsweetened full cream (evaporated) %
Water	25·0	27·0	67·0
Fat	9·5	0·4	9·2
Protein	8·5	9·4	9·0
Milk Solids	33·0	26·3	33·5
Total Carbohydrate	55·0	61·0	13·0
Including:			
Sucrose	42·0	46·5	—
Lactose	13·0	14·5	13·0
Mineral Components	2·0	2·3	2·0
Acidity, as Lactic Acid	0·3	0·3	0·3

Condensed milk can be purchased as full cream, containing around 9% milk fat, or as skimmed, in which the milk fat is under 1%.

The amount and type of milk protein present is of particular importance in the manufacture of caramels and fudge. Variations in shrinkage rate and toughness of caramels are relatable to this factor. Three major proteins are present in condensed milk—casein, albumen and globin. Increasing the casein content will result in toughening of the confections. A high albumen content produces a sweetmeat which is soft and lacks body. Above 120° C (248° F) casein becomes progressively insoluble and the protein eventually coagulates.

Two major sugars are present in sweetened condensed milk—added sucrose, and lactose (milk sugar), the latter both in solution and in a crystalline form. The solubility of lactose is considerably lower than sucrose (§2.11) and it has only one-fifth to one-sixth of that sugar's sweetening power. The presence of lactose will depress the solubility of sucrose, while increasing the overall sugar solubility value. Heat causes lactose to brown and subsequently caramelise.

Condensed milks contain some natural lecithin, but not sufficient to act as the sole emulsifier in sweet manufacture. Milk lecithin degrades under the high temperatures involved in processing confectionery. An emulsifier is necessary to maintain the fine dispersed fat globule size which gives the required quality to the milk and to the caramel.

Lipase may also be present in condensed milk. This enzyme is responsible for the development of tallow flavours; it is destroyed by high temperatures.

The stages in the manufacture of condensed milk are shown in Fig. 4. Preheating is necessary to destroy the enzyme lipase; to prevent subsequent thickening on store; to remove some of the moisture, and to sterilise the

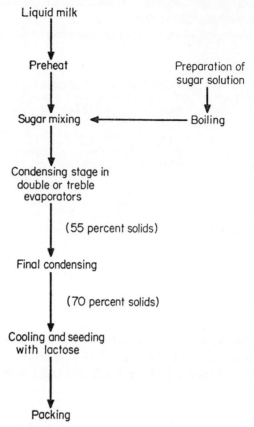

FIGURE 4. Production of sweetened condensed milk.

milk. Moisture continues to be lost after the evaporation process has been completed and the milk has been discharged. It is therefore usual for the milk to be concentrated to a slightly lower solids content to allow for this loss. Lactose is present in a supersaturated state and slow crystallisation on store can produce large crystals which give a gritty taste. To prevent this a fine lactose seed is added to the boil. Crystal sizes achieved are dependent on the amount of crystal seed added, the temperature of the mix and the amount of agitation applied. Under adverse storage conditions, lactose crystallisation continues, and in addition protein changes may result in the gelation of the product. Storage conditions are preferably from 5°–10° C (41°–50° F) in a darkened store. Under these conditions sealed containers should keep for up to 6 months. Condensed milk discolours, taking on a brownish tint, if it is stored in warm conditions or if traces of iron are present. In hot weather, covering the drums with wet sacks will keep them cooler.

Condensed milks and other milk products should not be pumped through conventional plastic hoses, which can be affected by contact with them.

5.3   CONDENSED WHEY

The use of condensed whey is an inexpensive means of introducing milk solids into low-priced caramels and fudge. An average composition of sweetened condensed whey is:

		%
Water	25·0	
Fat	0·5	
Protein	5·5	
Milk Solids		33·0
Total Carbohydrate	76·0	
Including:		
Sucrose		40·0
Lactose		26·0
Mineral Components	2·0	

Whey is produced from the liquor remaining after casein has been removed from milk, in the manufacture of cheese. The protein composition of whey differs from condensed milk and therefore the texture of the sweets which are produced will differ.

Whey can be used as a complete substitute for the milk solids in condensed milk or on a 50:50 or 75:25 basis. The high lactose content may result in crystallisation while on store. But whey gives better browning during manufacture.

Suitably packed condensed whey will store for 3 to 4 months.

5.4   DRIED MILK POWDERS

The composition of dried milk is as follows

	Whole Milk Powder %		Skimmed Milk Powder %	
Lactose	28		52	
Fat	27		1	
Protein	26		36	
Minerals	6		7	
Milk Solids, not fat		70		95
Water	3		4	

The whole of the sugar content is present as lactose. As a general guide, lactose exhibits one-sixth the sweetness of sucrose. Should the milk powder become damp the lactose will partially redissolve and then crystallise in a different form to that induced during manufacture, causing lumping of the milk powder.

The merits and demerits of using dried milk as a substitute for sweetened condensed milks are listed in Table 30.

Three basic types of milk powder are produced whose properties differ because of the processes used for manufacture: (*a*) roller dried milk; (*b*) spray dried milk; and (*c*) 'instant' milk.

TABLE 30. Powdered Milks: Advantages and Disadvantages

Advantages	Disadvantages
1. Less water content reduces processing costs and boiling times.	1. Product quality is lower when powdered milks are used.
2. Less storage space required: handling and weighing simplified.	2. A reconstitution process necessary, increasing the overall cost of raw material.
3. Deteriorates more slowly than condensed milk, if well packed.	3. Powdered milks can produce a gritty texture unless used correctly.
4. Variations in product composition can be achieved more easily.	

Roller dried milk is prepared by spraying or drip feeding liquid milk on to heated rollers. The moisture is flashed off, the dried milk powder scraped away from the roller and crumbled to the required powder size. The process is sometimes carried out under vacuum, which reduces the danger of oxidative rancidity developing (see §4.8). For *spray dried milk* powder, pasteurised milk is held under vacuum to partially remove the moisture. The milk is then sprayed into hot air drying chambers as fine droplets and any remaining moisture is removed. Roller drying is a cheaper process than spray drying.

Instant milks are prepared by further treatment of both spray and roller dried milk powders, involving a physical change. Sufficient moisture is added to cause the powder to form into porous clumps. This is effected by circulating the powdered milk through tunnels which contain steam and then hot air. Cooling and packing follows. Instant milk powder can only be prepared from low fat milk products. The bulk density is about half that of the conventional powders, being between 0·35–0·5 gr/ml. It has an improved solubility, a high rate of dispersion, flows more easily, has better wettability and, not surprisingly in view of the processing involved, costs more than the conventional powders.

The bulk density of roller and spray milks ranges between 0·55–0·8 gr/ml. Roller dried milk has a larger particle size—up to 250μ—than spray dried, where the particles range between 25μ and 75μ. It is possible to vary the particle size of spray dried milk by changing the diameter of the injection nozzles.

Reconstitution

The following recipe can be used to reconstitute milk powder for use in caramel manufacture

Ingredient	Parts by weight
Milk Powder	132
Cane or Beet Sugar	180
Water (1 gall weighs 10 lb)	100
Ammonium Carbonate	0·5
Yield	412

The simplest method for reconstitution is to mix the milk powder with an equal weight of sugar and to add as a thin stream to the required volume of water held at 50°–60° C. To improve the quality of the reconstituted milk, the mix should be passed through a homogenisation unit. Rapid cooling is necessary to prevent bacteriological growth. The prepared mix should not be stored in copper containers nor should more than one day's production be prepared at any one time. The ammonium carbonate in the recipe is to prevent curdling. If the reconstituted milk is prepared from the skimmed powder, and is to be used in place of sweetened full cream condensed milk then $6\frac{1}{2}$ lb of butter should be added to each 100 lb of the reconstituted milk.

Storage and deterioration

Three main types of deterioration can occur in dried milk: rancidity, insolubility, and caking.

High temperatures, light, and trace metals increase the likelihood that rancidity will develop, with the characteristic smell of butyric acid. Autoxidation gives rise to a tallow taste, while a fishy aroma is caused through chemical breakdown of the milk protein. A stale flavour and increasing insolubility arises through sugar/protein interaction (Browning reaction); moisture accelerates this. None of the milk types is truly soluble and mixing with water produces a suspension but not a solution of the milk proteins. The greater the heat treatment the greater the insolubility, due to protein denaturation. Roller dried powders are less soluble because of the higher heat treatment. Caking is caused when the milk sugar (lactose) dissolves in small traces of water condensing from damp atmospheres and then recrystallises.

Milk powder should be stored in sealed containers or bags; stocks should not be held for more than six months. In general, roller dried milk powder stores better than spray dried. The full cream variety has a shorter shelf life than the skimmed milk powder. Gas packaging can give milk powders a storage life of 5 years.

The protein content is mainly casein and albumen. Casein tends to produce a confectionery product which is hard and tough, while albumen alone gives a sweet which is soft and somewhat lacking in body. The use of the skimmed milk powder enables a manufacturer to use a higher proportion of the harder fats when exporting to tropical climates.

Full cream roller dried milk produces a good quality chocolate; the larger particle size is reduced during refining. The form of the lactose crystal affects the efficiency of refining in chocolate manufacture. Dried milk should be incorporated with the sugar and cocoa liquor at the melangeur stage. Roller dried milks are suitable for the manufacture of the cheaper grades of chocolate.

5.5   SODIUM CASEINATE

Sodium caseinate can be added to caramels to give them a firmer texture. It has excellent water absorbing properties and a good milk flavour. To use successfully it should be mixed with three times its own weight of sugar before being added to the remainder of the ingredients.

Commercial sodium caseinate has the following composition

	%
Sodium Caseinate	90·1
Milk Fat	1·6
Mineral Salts	4·1
Lactose	1·2
Moisture	3·0

5.6   LACTOSE

See under Sugars (§2.11).

5.7   BUTTER

See under Confectionery Fats (§4.7).

6

Gelling and Whipping Agents; Gums

6.1 CONFECTIONERY STARCHES

Starch has been used for many centuries in the manufacture of sweetmeats. Different cereal sources have been used to extract the starch and this has led to the regional development of sugar confections with very different textures. In sub-tropical regions the most readily accessible source for starch was rice while in the temperate zones, wheat and maize were used.

Starch is a white powdery substance whose main purpose in the plant is to provide a reserve food supply during the dormant and germination periods. In some plants, starch is found in the seed (for example maize and wheat); in others in the tubers or roots (potato and tapioca) or in the pith of the stem (sago).

Starch is used in sugar confectionery manufacture as a basic gelling ingredient, as a filler and as a moulding base.

Sources of Starch

Although many plants contain starch, only a few yield it in commercial quantities. The most important are wheat, tapioca, potato, sago, rice, arrowroot and maize. Microscopic examination reveals that starch is composed of tiny cells or 'granules' whose size and shape are characteristic of each source (Fig. 5, Corn Industries Research Foundation).

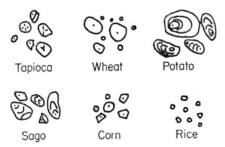

FIGURE 5. Microscopic appearance of six common starches.

73

Potato starch has relatively large oval granules with shell-like striations around an eccentrically placed centre. Rice starch is the smallest of the common starches. Maize starch (Corn starch) is likewise polygonal, due to compacting pressures while growing.

TABLE 31. Properties of Common Starches

	Maize	Wheat	Potato	Sago
Type of Gel				
(a) Clarity	Opaque	Opaque	Clear	Moderate
(b) Texture	Short	Short	Very Cohesive	Clear Soft
Stability to Retrogration	Poor	Poor	Fair	Fair
Freeze Thaw Stability	Poor	Poor	Poor	Poor
Resistance to Shear	Fair	Fair	Poor	Poor
Size of Granules in Microns	5–25	2–10	5–100	20–60
Amylose/Amylopectin Ratio	26/74	25/75	24/76	27/73
Gelatinization Temperature °C (Koffer hot stage method)	62–67–72	58–61–64	59–63–68	60–66–72

While the other cereal starches have been used by confectioners, none has been found so satisfactory as maize starch (Table 31). It is reliable, it imparts a better texture, and the wet-milling process for its manufacture yields a more refined product. A considerable range of speciality maize starch products has been developed (Table 32).

TABLE 32. Types of Starch used in Sugar Confectionery

Type	Use and Characteristics
Unmodified Maize Starch	Filler for cheap cream paste, toffee cigarettes, liquorice paste. Dusting powder. Can be mixed with fat for release agents; with icing sugar for Turkish Delight dusting.
Acid Modified Thin Boiling Starches: Fluidity Nos. 30, 40	Used in gums and jellies. Generally used for open pan cooking; can also be used for continuous processes where acid is present during cooking process.
Nos. 50, 60, 70, 85	Enable high solids production, good depositing capability, can be used in combination with other gelling agents. Produce gels of high rigidity, clarity and short texture and are capable of producing a wide range of textures (soft to hard); good shelf life.
Oxidised Modified Thin Boiling Starches	Similar range of fluidity available. Produce gels of increased clarity but lack the rigidity of acid modified starches. Produces soft eating products; can be used in combination with other starches and gelling agents.

TABLE 32—*continued*

Type	Use and Characteristics
Moulding Starches Oil Bound Moulding Starch (contains 0·12% – 0·2% mineral oil) Oil Bound 0·75%	Provides good moulding characteristics at low moisture percentages. Reduces explosion hazard by suppressing dust. Oil used is not susceptible to rancidity. Can be mixed with oil free starch in mogul plant to improve moulding. Increase total oil content to suitable range 0·2%.
Oil-Free Moulding Starches	Can be mixed with heavy moulding starch to rejuvenate after extended use. Excellent water absorption properties. (Moulding starches based on di-glycerides as binders are also available).
Amylopectin Thin Boiling (Range of fluidities)	Produces gels of excellent clarity with no set-back. Can be used at high concentration to produce hard texture; with other gelling agents, to provide a variety of textures. Also for continuous liquorice paste production.
Modified Waxy Maize Starches	Similar viscosity to gum arabic at same concentration. Excellent clarity, very soluble, low gelatinisation temperature.
Soluble Dextrin Starches (Range of fluidities; manu-factured from Maize or Tapioca starches.)	For adhesive coatings and glazes. Used in panning operation as a seal. In some cases can replace natural gums. Good sheen and clarity.
Pregelatinised Maize Starch	Cold water soluble; used as a tablet binder.
Physical Modified Oxidised Starch	Cold water soluble, easily dispersible, smooth texture, good film former, bland flavour. Used as tablet binder. Replaces gums and gelling agents in lozenge pastes, etc. Good seal for nuts, etc., in panning.
Modified Waxy Maize Starches Cross Bonded	For use in caramel and caramel coating, gives body with a soft eating texture, good clarity and flavour, acid stable and resistant to long storage. Also used as a gelling agent in deposited and extruded marshmallow. Acid, heat and shear stable.
Pregelatinised Cross bonded Acetylated Waxy Maize Starches	Used where moisture is a restriction, dissolves readily in cold water even in high concentra-tions to form a clear smooth short texture. Gel resistant to freezing and thawing.
High Amylose Starches	Very high gelatinisation temperature with strong set back used for quick setting starch jellies. (High Amylose can be blended with thin boiling maize starches to produce different amylopectin/amylose ratio.)

Chemistry and Structure

Chemically, starch is a carbohydrate synthesised from dextrose within the plant. Treated with certain acids or enzymes, starch breaks down into its constituent dextrose molecules. A similar reaction occurs when the plant calls upon its starch supply and when starch is consumed in food-stuffs by humans and animals.

Maize starch contains millions of individual granules each one of which possesses a highly complex chemical structure. The basic molecules of starch are arranged in an orderly pattern like a crystal; and for this reason the granules are referred to as *sphero-crystals*; that is round crystals. This crystalline formation can be readily seen when a granule is inspected under a high-powered microscope using a polarised light source.

Starch is a *polymer*; its molecules are complexes formed by the linking of simpler molecules of the same chemical formula, in this case dextrose. A plant may employ either or both of two different mechanisms to synthesise its starch polymers. It may form a long chain by the successive linking of several hundred dextrose molecules, or, from a short linear chain, it may form an attachment to a second similar chain in a branching configuration. Dextrose groups are then added to the branch points until new branch points are reached. The resulting structure is a large polymeric molecule comprising several thousand dextrose molecules.

Starch Fractions

Many starches contain both linear-chain (amylose) and branched-chain (amylopectin) types of starch polymers. These are called the *starch fractions*. The proportion of these fractions is characteristic and constant for any particular species of starch. For example, in tapioca starch the amylose fraction is about 17%; in potato starch about 22%; and in maize starch about 27%. In the so-called 'waxy' cereal grains, originating in China, and in some genetic varieties of maize, rice, and sorghum, the starch is entirely of the amylopectin type. Other starches are almost 100% amylose fraction; such as in wrinkled-seed green peas and in certain varieties of sweet corn.

Two recently-developed types of maize have very high amylose fractions one 55% and the other 70%. It is probable that one will eventually be developed which contains 100% amylose.

The amylose and amylopectin molecules are both very large in comparison with most molecular structures and for this reason exhibit characteristics quite different from those of simple molecules. For example, their starch-pastes (cooked and cooled solutions) possess unusual viscosity characteristics, and they are effective film-formers.

Another property peculiar to amylose polymers is their tendency to cling together and to line up parallelwise in bundles. This tendency is particularly pronounced with starch amylose polymers because of the great number of free hydroxyl groups along the chain. These exert a powerful attraction on similar groups in adjacent chains, and the result is to bind them together in tight, strong bundles.

The amylose fraction, moreover, forms insoluble compounds with the higher alcohols or fatty acids. For example, if a starch-paste is treated with amyl alcohol, the amylose fraction is precipitated as a micro-crystalline complex, leaving the amylopectin fraction in solution. This is the basis of a laboratory method for separating the two pure fractions.

The fractions exhibit other interesting differences in behaviour. Thus in combination with iodine the amylose fraction forms an intense blue complex, while the amylopectin fraction gives a red or plum colour. The familiar blue iodine colour of the common starches is due entirely to the amylose fraction, and starch from waxy maize is readily identified by its red-staining characteristic. The proportion of amylose polymers in a starch can therefore be measured by a simple titration with iodine or assessed from the intensity of blue colouring.

Granular Structure (*Corn Industries Research Foundation Inc., CIRF*)

The structure of starch granules can be described in terms of the attractive forces acting between adjacent molecules. In each of the concentric layers of the granule, the mixed linear and branded fractions are orientated radially. The linear fractions and the linear segments of the branded fractions tend to draw together into bundles or *micelles*. A single linear fraction may wander through several of these micelles; or the outer branches of a branched fraction may weave into several such micelles. This network holds the granule together and makes it insoluble in water. It also explains the dark-cross pattern of a sphero-crystal under a polarising microscope, since associated micelles simulate an essentially crystalline lattice. These attractive forces between molecules can be overcome if enough energy is applied.

Gelatinisation (*CIRF*)

Granular starch is insoluble in cold water. But if a starch-water mixture is heated beyond a critical temperature, the granules suddenly lose their polarisation crosses and begin to swell. This is termed the *gelatinisation* of the starch. Not all the granules in a given sample begin to swell at the same temperature but over a gelatinisation range, e.g. 64°–72° C (147°–162° F) for maize starch. As the cooking temperature is increased, the individual granules continue to swell until they begin to jostle one another. This produces the characteristic viscous consistency of cooked starch. The individual swollen granules are remarkably elastic. If the mixture is given a prolonged cooking or if it is vigorously stirred, some of the swollen granules break up, and so the viscosity decreases. Even so, enough granules survive to give 'body' or consistency to the mixture.

Heating a starch-water mixture opens up the looser regions between the

D

micellar bundles. Water therefore penetrates into the granular structure, causing these micellar regions to swell. This corresponds to the gelatinisation point, and the progressive swelling, in which persistent micelles continue to hold the granule together. Even prolonged cooking does not completely dissolve the structure. It can be dissolved, however, by application of high levels of energy; for example, by autoclaving (steam cooking under pressure).

Starches that have predominantly linear fraction (such as wrinkled pea) are gelatinised with great difficulty and do not dissolve even after prolonged autoclaving. On the other hand, the predominantly branched fraction in waxy maize causes the granules to swell rapidly and then break up with continued cooking. Between these extremes is the gelatinisation behaviour of maize starch, due largely to its content of linear fraction and the micellar structure within the granule.

Paste characteristics (CIRF)

The characteristics of a cooked starch-paste depend to a great extent on the botanical variety of the starch. Potato starch-pastes are relatively transparent and are stringy and cohesive in texture while maize starch-pastes are cloudy to opaque and tend to set to a jelly-like texture at room temperature. As a starch-water mixture heated beyond its gelatinisation point the viscosity increases. This change in viscosity can be conveniently followed with a recording viscometer. Maize starch, for example, thickens at first and then thins out slightly as cooking continues at 203° F. When the mixture is cooled, the viscosity increases quite sharply. Such curves are called *cooking and cooling curves*, or sometimes *pasting curves*.

In contrast to maize starch, potato starch starts to gelatinise at a lower temperature and reaches a higher peak viscosity for the same concentration. With continued cooking, the viscosity falls much more rapidly than that of maize starch, and the recovery of viscosity, or set-back, is less on cooling.

Wet Milling of Maize

Wet milling is a method for separating the maize kernel into its four main components—starch, gluten, fibre and germ (Fig. 6).

Maize from the silos is conveyed to steep-tanks where for 40–50 hours the kernels are soaked in water which contains sulphur dioxide. This softens the hard kernels which are transferred to Foos mills. These peg type mills tear open the kernels to free the germ but cause little other damage. Any underflow from the germ separators passes to centrifugal filters (Contessors) for the removal of the free starch and gluten. The main process stream then passes to the refining mills for complete grinding to release the remaining kernel components. Fibre is removed on reels—inclined cylindrical sieves —on which the fibre is retained, and by screen pumps.

Separation of the starch and gluten is effected by centrifuges of the

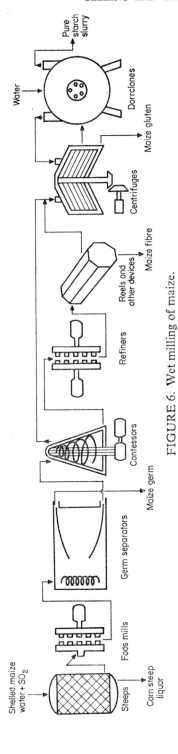

FIGURE 6. Wet milling of maize.

Alfa-Laval type. A very low protein content in the starch is obtained by treatment in highly efficient hydrocyclone installations in which the starch is washed upwards of nine times with warm water. The discharged product from the wet mill is a suspension of pure starch in water. Separated germ, fibre and gluten are normally used in the preparation of animal feed.

Starch suspension from the wet mill is first spun in preset, automatic operating, basket centrifuges to give a powder with an approximate moisture content of 33%. This starch is then injected into a stream of warm air being passed up a flash dryer (Fig. 7).

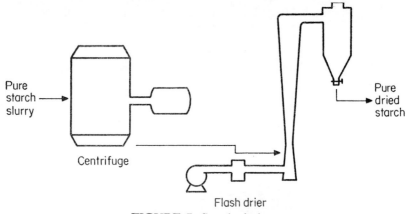

FIGURE 7. Starch drying.

6.2   MODIFIED STARCHES

Modified starches are produced by controlled chemical and physical processing of extracted starch, to produce oxidised and thin boiling starches and starch ethers. Oxidised and thin boiling starches can be used to prepare higher total solids content solutions than are obtained with the unmodified starches. A thin boiling starch gel is more firm than that obtained with maize starch. The gel of a starch ether is softer than an unmodified starch gel, with better film forming and film solubility properties.

A slurry of starch in water from the wet mill is treated (Fig. 8) under controlled conditions with either sulphuric acid (for thin boiling starch), caustic soda/hypochlorite mixture (for oxidised starch) or propylene oxide (for starch ethers). After the desired level of treatment, the reaction is stopped and the suspension thoroughly washed in a hydrocyclone, to remove any water soluble products which have formed. The speciality starches are then de-watered in a centrifuge, dried in hot air or flash dryers, sieved and packed.

Pregelatinised starches are prepared by passing a starch suspension over steam heated rollers which gelatinises and drys the starch in one operation (Fig. 9).

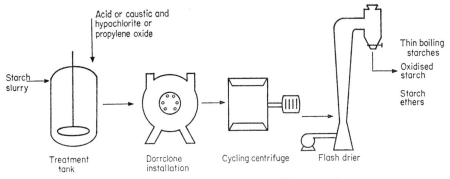

FIGURE 8. Manufacture of modified starches.

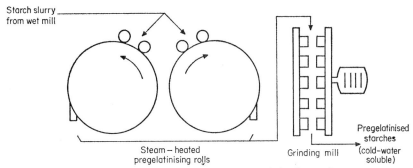

FIGURE 9. Manufacture of pre-gelatinised starches.

6.3 TYPES OF MAIZE STARCH

Regular or unmodified maize starch

Starch in dried form as prepared using the refining process is known commercially as regular, untreated, or unmodified starch. It is sometimes called pearl starch. When pulverised, it is known as powdered starch.

When regular starch is cooked in water, the solution is cloudy and non-cohesive and on cooling tends to paste, set, or gel, depending on the concentration. It is therefore also known as a thick-cooking starch. Massive quantities of regular starch are used, in either cooked or uncooked form, for such diverse purposes as sizing for papers and textiles, adhesives, salad dressings, puddings, canned foods, confections, refined brewers' grits, laundering, and medicines.

Waxy-maize starch

Waxy maize is a speciality maize originating in China and was long regarded as a curiosity. The term 'waxy' is misleading, since the maize has no relationship to wax. Its name derives from the waxy appearance of the cross-section of a kernel cut cleanly in two. To prevent cross-pollination with other types of maize, waxy maize must be grown in relatively isolated fields. Its starch, commercially termed amylopectin, as has been noted, comprises almost 100% branched chain molecules.

During growth, waxy maize has an appearance very like ordinary maize. The starch is extracted in the same manner and microscopically the granules look exactly the same. But the two types of starch have widely differing properties. Unlike normal maize starch, waxy-maize starch-paste is clear, fluid, and cohesive; and not only is it non-gelling, but it can stabilise other starches by reducing their tendency to gel.

Conversion of starches

By splitting, rearranging, or combining different molecules, refiners can produce custom-built starches for particular purposes. These processes are known by the general term *conversion of starches.*

A wide range of *pregelatinised* or *cold water swelling starches* have been introduced commercially. The starch is gelatinised and then dried on heated rollers. The dried material swells in water and forms a viscous paste, and has many applications, notably for 'instant' food products such as puddings. Virtually all types of starch product can be pregelatinised.

Thin-boiling or *fluidity starches* differ from regular starches in two respects. The cooked solutions have a lower viscosity, and they may be produced in a fairly wide range of viscosities. The principal starches of this type are given fluidity designations of 20, 40, 60, 75, and 85 representing progressively lower viscosities. Fluidity starches are usually converted in the form of 'milk'; i.e. a suspension of starch in water. A small quantity of acid is added to the starch-milk, which is then heated to a temperature below the gelatinisation point. When the desired degree of conversion has taken place, the acid is neutralised and the starch is filtered and dried. The action of the acid can be explained by reference to the earlier topic of molecular structure. By penetrating into the looser molecular areas between the molecular bundles, the acid hydrolytically breaks some of the molecular chains. Although the granule appears to be unchanged under the microscope, the links between the micelles have been weakened; and the granules literally disintegrate when cooked, giving pastes of greatly reduced viscosity.

Thin-boiling starches are used extensively in the manufacture of gums and jellies.

Oxidised starches are prepared in a similar way to thin boiling starches, but sodium hypochlorite is used instead of acid. This, by its oxidizing action, introduces random discontinuities into the linear molecules so that they are unable to associate into micelles, and thus stabilises the starch against gelling. Each of the oxidised starches has its own characteristic, but as a class their pastes are much more stable than those of thin-boiling starches, which are noted not for stability but for their gel strengths.

Speciality Starches

In addition to the general-purpose starches already discussed, many types with highly specialised properties are also available to the confectioner. Some of these are intended for a single, particular application while others are for more general use.

Starches with special gelatinisation properties

Speciality starches with important properties for some applications can be obtained by converting starch in such a way as to cause a cross-linking or bonding between some of the molecules. This treatment reduces the cohesive nature of the paste and stabilises the viscosity against breakdown on cooking or stirring. Further cross-linking and bonding causes the gelatinisation temperature to rise. The end-products, however, retain the desirable paste clarity and non-gelling property of the original starch.

The high gelatinisation peak of amylopectin is reduced by this kind of treatment, and the viscosity of the converted starch increases more gradually during cooking. With continued treatment, larger numbers of the molecules are cross-linked, and the cohesiveness of regular amylopectin is transformed into softer textured paste properties. These more highly polymerised starches are less prone to variations in viscosity during cooking, and smoother texture is retained on ageing. They also retain the excellent non-gelling characteristics of regular amylopectin.

It can be seen how control of cross-linking enables starches to be custom-built for virtually any cooking specification. A great number of new starches converted from amylopectin in this way are being extensively used especially in the food industries (see Table 33).

6.4   ZEIN

Zein, a prolamine, is obtained by settling and solvent extraction of the endosperm of maize. It is soluble in alcohol and can be used in association with shellac as a confectionery glaze.

6.5   PECTIN

Pectin is a natural carbohydrate found in most fruits, the most widely used source for manufacture being fruit residues.

The name pectin is derived from Greek and means to solidify or congeal; pectin is a strong colloid which will produce a tender gel given correct processing conditions.

In manufacture from citrus sources the peel is finely minced, washed to remove the bitter glycosides, mixed with water and heated to boiling point; the pH is adjusted to 2·0 using hydrochloric or sulphuric acid. The resulting solution is continuously filtered under pressure and vacuum. Pectin is

TABLE 33.   Properties of Modified Starches

Type of Modified Starch	Texture	Clarity	To Retrogradation	Terminal Viscosity	Shear Stability	Acid Stability	Heat Stability	Freeze Thaw Stability	Gelatinisation Temp. in Water
1. Roll Dried Maize	Short Granular	Average	High Set Back	Instant Cold Water Soluble; Thick	Good	Fair	Fair	Poor	Cold Water Soluble
2. Acid Modified Maize	Short Smooth	Average	High Set Back	Thick	Fair	Fair	Fair	Poor	63°–73° C in Water
3. Oxidised Maize	Short Smooth	Above Average	Soft Set Back	Thin	Poor	Fair	Fair	Poor	54°–64° C in Water
4. Moderately Cross Bonded Waxy Maize	Short Smooth	Average	No Set Back at Room Temp.; Some at Low Temp.	Thick	Good	Good	Good	Mod.	67°–77° C
5. Medium Cross Bonded Waxy Maize	Short Smooth	Average	No Set Back at Room Temp.; Some at Low Temp.	Thick	V. Good	V. Good	V. Good	Fair	69°–79° C
6. Highly Cross Bonded Waxy Maize	Short Smooth	Average	No Set Back at Room Temp.; Set Back at Low Temp.	Thick	Exc.	Exc.	Exc.	Poor	73°–83° C
7. Crossbonded Acetylated Waxy Maize	Short Smooth	Very Good	No Set Back	Thick	Exc.	Exc.	Exc.	Exc.	60°–72° C
8. Roll Dried Crossbonded Acetylated Waxy Maize	Short Smooth	Above Average	No Set Back	Instant Cold Water Soluble	Exc.	Exc.	Exc.	Exc.	Cold Water Soluble

then precipitated by adding an excess of organic solvent such as isopropanol. After further washing, the pectin is drained and then dried to within a final moisture range of 5–10%. Pectin made by this method is the quick setting variety. Modification is necessary to prepare slow-setting pectins.

Pectin is a partially esterified polygalacturonic acid. The degree of methoxylation (esterification) is a measure of the proportion of carboxyl groups (acidic groups) present in the pectin. A value known as the DM value is quoted for pectin which indicates the degree of esterification. Thus a DM value of 0·60 denotes a 60% esterification. A high methoxyl pectin has a DM value greater than 0·5; acid and sugar are needed to produce a gel with it and the high DM values gives increased rates of setting. With low methoxyl pectins (DM values less than 0·5) gels can be formed in the absence of sugar and acid, but to promote satisfactory gelation it is necessary to add a chemical promoter usually based on the calcium ion.

The grade strength of a particular pectin is defined as the number of grammes of sugar from which one gramme of pectin will produce a gel of standard firmness when tested under standard conditions of acidity and soluble solids content. Various methods are employed for quoting grade strength and, in purchasing, it is necessary to know which test method was used. The most commonly used is the American SAG using the Ridge-limeter Jelly Tester as detailed in method 5–54 of the IFT Committee on Pectin Standardisation [*Food Technology*, 1959, *13*, (9) 496–500]. This has been adopted by most of the leading suppliers in the UK. The standard grade strength of pectin for confectionery manufacture is 150.

An extensive range of apple and citrus pectins is available for specific purposes. Differences in the properties of corresponding grades of apple or citrus pectins are small and for most purposes the two types of pectins are interchangeable. The following details, together with the information given in §12.18, will assist in the selection of the most suitable type and grade.

Colour: Although the basic citrus or apple powders themselves differ little in colour, this is not true for the corresponding products made from them. Where the absence of any slight brown colouration is essential (e.g. in pale-coloured sugar confectionery, jellies and in certain preserves) the use of citrus rather than apple pectin is advisable.

Solution Clarity: Although solutions of apple pectin are normally clear, those made from citrus pectin are frequently hazy and opaque. This should not be taken as implying the presence of any undesirable impurity in the pectin and may, in general, be ignored, as it will not affect the clarity or brightness of the gel produced.

Composition: Unbuffered apple pectin will require slightly more acid than unbuffered citrus pectin to achieve the same pH fall. This is due to the slightly higher inorganic salt content of apple pectin.

Setting Temperature: Rapid set apple pectins (extra grade) will set under standard conditions, at a slightly higher temperature than the fastest rapid set citrus pectin.

Viscosity: Citrus pectins will produce more viscous solutions than the equivalent apple pectins. This property arises from the higher molecular weight.

6.6   GELATINE

Gelatine is derived from collagen, a constituent of bones and skin. The process of conversion is not clearly understood, and batches of a similar composition of raw material can produce gelatine with widely differing properties. Many of the commercial gelatines offered are blends of different extractions to maintain a consistent standard.

Gelatine is the term used to describe the commercial materials while *gelatin* is the 'pure' protein contained within that product. Two main types of gelatine are available—that from skin or hide and that produced from bone. Gelatines behave differently depending on whether they are produced by acid extraction in which there is some breakage of the long protein chain, or by lime treatment, where some of the amino groupings present are removed.

The bones are kibbled, treated with dilute acid and the mix neutralised. Skin and hide are washed and then chopped to small pieces using rotary cutters. Both types of raw materials, after pretreatment, are passed over magnets to remove any ferrous materials and then either soaked in a weak lime suspension or with dilute acid. After neutralisation, water at a controlled temperature is recirculated, with progressively warmer conditions to extract all the gelatine present. It is usual to bleach the early extracts of gelatine to produce a lighter product. The quality of gelatine produced is governed by the concentration of extract liquor, the extent of mechanical working and the temperature of extraction water. It is also related to the number of extractions though by no means linearly.

After concentration by heat and the addition of sulphur dioxide as preservative, the gelatine is dried. Traditionally this is carried out by passing deposited slabs through drying ovens but this has been largely replaced by continuous drum dryer or belt extrusion. The dried material is ground or kibbled and, after testing, blended to produce a gelatine with specified properties of gel strength, viscosity, colour, clarity, melting point and acidity.

The gel strength is quoted in a number of ways which refer to the method adopted for testing. Those in common use in the United Kingdom are Grams Bloom, Boucher units, FIRA degrees, jelly strength and units of gel strength determined on the BGGRA gelometer. Most of the available test instruments measure the weight or force needed to produce a depression or measured movement within a gelatine solution made up under standard conditions.

The strength of a jelly is affected by the pH of the solution, presence of other solids, type of gelatine in use, processing during manufacture, length of time the gelatine solution has been prepared, and the temperature of storage. At 5° C (41° F) storage, the jelly strength approaches the maximum level within an hour, while jellies held at 21° C (70° F) may take up to 8 hours to approach the same gel strength. Over longer times, small but significant rises in gel strength occur.

Varying the concentration does not greatly affect setting time. Acids adversely affect the ultimate jelly strength of the mix, according to their concentration and type. Citric and lactic acids have a markedly lesser effect on gel strength than does tartaric acid. Acid effects can be minimised by buffering the solution, by half the weight of the acid ingredient.

Heat received during processing has the most marked result on jelly strength. Once the temperature exceeds 80° C (176° F) gelatine degradation occurs. The lower the pH the greater is this breakdown. Holding a gelatine mix at 120° C (248° F) for a short period can result in a loss of over 25% in the gelling power of the solution. Hot syrups should always be cooled to 90° C (194° F) before being run in a thin stream into the prepared gelatine/water mix. The short processing times given in continuous cookers are usually insufficient to result in very large losses in strength.

According to L. H. LAMPITT and R. W. MONEY [*J. Soc. Chem. Ind.*, 55, 88 and 56, 290] the rigidity of jellies is approximately proportional to the square of the gelatine concentration. The relation of jelly strength and concentration is illustrated in Tables 34 and 35. Above 35° C (95° F) no gel will form with a gelatine solution. Quick setting gelatine solutions normally melt more quickly than those which are slow setting. Fast setting gelatines are available which will produce a jelly within 15 minutes.

Gelatine can never be a pure substance in the true meaning of the word,

TABLE 34. Relationship between Solutions of 100 Bloom Strength Gelatine and Equivalent Jelly Strength of other Bloom Grades

Solution Concentration 100 Bloom Strength Gelatine %	Bloom Strength of Gelatine							
	60	80	100	140	160	200	225	260
	Concentration of Gelatine needed to give a Similar Jelly Strength, %							
6·0	7·7	6·7	6·0	5·1	4·8	4·3	4·0	3·7
8·0	10·3	8·9	8·0	6·8	6·3	5·7	5·3	5·0
10·0	12·9	11·2	10·0	8·4	7·9	7·1	6·7	6·2
12·0	15·5	13·4	12·0	10·1	9·5	8·5	8·0	7·4
14·0	18·1	15·7	14·0	11·8	11·1	9·9	9·3	8·7

Note: pH and temperature can affect the performance of gelatines, the figures in Tables 34 and 35 are intended for guidance only.

TABLE 35. Relationship between Bloom Strength of various Gelatines held in Solution having Equivalent Jelly Strength.

Bloom Strength of Gelatine	% Gelatine needed to produce Equivalent Jelly Strength				
	60 Bloom	100 Bloom	160 Bloom	200 Bloom	260 Bloom
60	10·0	12·9	14·9	18·3	20·7
80	8·6	11·2	14·2	15·8	18·0
100	7·8	10·0	12·6	14·1	16·1
120	7·1	9·1	11·5	12·9	14·7
140	6·6	8·4	10·7	12·0	13·6
160	6·1	7·9	10·0	11·2	12·8
180	—	7·5	9·4	10·5	12·0
200	—	7·1	8·9	10·0	11·4
220	—	6·8	8·5	9·5	10·9
240	—	6·5	8·1	9·1	10·4
260	—	6·2	7·8	8·7	10·0

since it is produced from a mixture of different collagen molecules and therefore the commercial product contains a blend of different molecular weight materials. A gelatine which is free of impurities is colourless, clear, insoluble in alcohol, with an optical rotation of approximately +300 degrees. The appearance of the gelatine is dependent on the processing given during manufacture. It is available as a powder, kibbled and in sheet form. The kibbled or granular version is the most convenient for use being easier to handle, occupying less storage space and a shorter soak time.

To achieve maximum rigidity and rapid dissolving the gelatine should be soaked before use in cold water. Soak times for kibbled gelatine should be one hour while for sheet it is better to soak for five hours. The colder the water the better will be the swelling achieved. The mix should be stirred during the first one to five minutes of soaking but then left undisturbed for the remaining time. At least twice the weight of gelatine is required for soak water. The extent of swelling is dependent on the pH of the solution and the presence of any other components. Gelatine can absorb up to forty times its own weight of water under specified conditions. It is unwise to soak gelatine overnight, due to the danger from bacterial infection.

Bacterial growth can take place in the made up solution and in the powder or sheet. It is essential that all utensils used in conjunction with gelatine solutions should be kept scrupulously clean. Mould growth is likely to occur on gelatine powder if the moisture content exceeds 16%.

The composition of a typical gelatine is:

	%	
Moisture	14	
Total Solids		86
Protein	84	
Mineral Ash	2	

Gelatine picks up moisture in the air and bulk deliveries should be stored in cool dry conditions.

The colour and clarity of gelatine solutions vary according to the extraction run, whether the product has been bleached, the concentration, the presence of other salts and the pH of the solution. Gelatine becomes progressively deeper brown in shade with each successive extraction run. Clarity varies with the concentration of the jelly and the jelly may appear more cloudy as the solution is diluted. The iso-electric point of gelatine is that point at which the positive and negative charges in the gelatine cancel each other; at this point there is maximum turbidity and foaming. Lime-produced gelatines have iso-electric points which lie between pH 4·8 to 5·2 while acid extracted gelatines have a higher range of pH 5·5–6·0. It is essential when comparing gelatine samples to carry out any tests at the pH of use and at the concentration of gelatine to be present in the confection. The type of gelatine is indicated by the solution pH, lime-produced gelatines having pH of between 5·0 and 5·8 while acid gelatines are lower at 3·8–4·6. Cloudiness can also be caused by the presence of tartaric acid, which forms insoluble calcium tartrates with lime-produced gelatine. It is also caused by the incorporation of small bubbles in the mix.

The viscosity of gelatine solutions is of particular importance for assessing the whipping properties. A good quality gelatine for marshmallow production must have a high Bloom strength, (180–220), and a low viscosity. High viscosities affect the volume of foam produced, as does that from the concentration of sugar solids present. To hold the foam it is necessary to have at least 30% sugar in solution during whipping, but it becomes more difficult once this has risen to over 45%. The presence of citrate salts as buffers are helpful. Better foams are produced as the pH approaches 5·0. There is little change in viscosity of gelatine solutions above 40° C (104° F) but significant changes occur below 30° C (86° F).

Gelatine is difficult to disperse in hot syrups particularly if it is of a large grist (granule size). It is always advisable to remove more water from the cooked syrup fraction and to use additional water for the gelatine mix. A 7–8% level of gelatine, 220 Bloom, is suitable for table jelly manufacture while 10–12% of 100–120 Bloom gelatine should be used for fruit jelly lines. Marshmallow requires 2–3% of 220 Bloom low viscosity high grade gelatine.

6.7   AGAR AGAR

Agar agar, or Japanese Isinglass, is extracted from a wide range of seaweed varieties which grow in many areas of the world. The chief supplies of agar are from Japan, New Zealand, Denmark, Australia, South Africa and Spain. Each agar type has characteristic properties which influence its use in confectionery manufacture.

Agar agar is produced by hot water extraction followed by purification using successive freezing and thawing, or by concentrating under vacuum. It is usual for a bleach to be added during processing to lighten the colour of the agar [C. M. ADAMS, *BIOS Jap. Report*, PR 814, 1946]. Agar has a high gelling power at low concentrations; it is unique among the confectionery gelling agents in that gelling occurs at temperatures below the gel melting temperature. A 2% solution of agar will form a gel only upon cooling to around 30° C (86° F) but will not melt until the temperature has exceeded 85° C (185° F). The viscosity of agar solutions vary according to the source of the raw material. New deliveries should always be checked for gel strength.

Agar is commonly used in products such as Chinese figs and in certain types of fruit jellies and jams. It can also be added in heavy density marshmallow recipes. Agar is not absorbed in the body and can therefore be used in the manufacture of low calorie confections.

6.8   WHIPPING AGENTS

The term 'whipping agent' can be applied to a wide variety of materials to describe their role in confectionery manufacture as a means of holding air introduced into a product, to produce a uniform dispersion of air cells within the confection leading to a lower specific weight and considerable modification to the texture. This effect is an essential property of confections such as marshmallow, angel or negro kiss snowballs, chocolate bar line centres and various foam goods including frappés, sometimes called mazettas. Stable foams cannot be obtained by whipping high concentration sugar solutions without the presence of a 'surface-active' agent.

Many types of proteins have whipping properties and those used in the sweet industry are (*a*) egg albumen, crystal powdered and spray dried; (*b*) high Bloom gelatine and gelatine hydrolysates; (*c*) skimmed milk in spray dried form; (*d*) whey, or whey in a mixture with skimmed milk; (*e*) casein, the principal protein in milk, and (*f*) soya protein. Other egg albumen substitutes have been suggested including cellulose derivatives such as ethyl methyl cellulose, blood plasma, and fish protein but they have not been found to be satisfactory.

6.9   EGG ALBUMEN

Egg albumen is the most commonly used whipping agent, having excellent aeration properties together with a reasonable degree of stability, connected with its ability to coagulate. This coagulation can be considerably retarded or even prevented when used in high concentrations of sweetener solutions. Thus albumen dissolved in a sugar syrup of 40% concentration does not coagulate until a temperature of 65° C (150° F) is reached while albumen dissolved in a 60% syrup will require a temperature of 75° C (167° F).

Crystal dried egg albumen was traditionally produced in China, by drying liquid egg whites in shallow trays until they could be broken in pieces suitable for grinding. Pre-treatment consisted of storing the liquid egg whites in wooden vats for several days; usually fermentation would set in during this period. This resulted in the formation of a sour smelling and tasting product. However, during this procedure enzyme action also took place which improved the clarity and the odour. This effect was considered partly due to the process of de-sugaring in which reducing sugars were removed by yeasts or by other enzyme action thereby improving the keeping properties.

Several types of spray-dried albumens are now available which are free from odour and offensive taste, with excellent solubility whipping qualities and long keeping capability. New types of process and products have been recently introduced, such as the so-called 'fluff dried' albumen, produced by whipping the egg albumen solution into a foam and subjecting this to continuous rapid drying. Egg albumen dried in this manner has neutral taste and odour, good whipping and solubility properties.

6.10   GELATINE HYDROLYSATE

Gelatine hydrolysate, (US Patent 3206, 315) is produced by hydrolysing low-grade residue remaining after the removal of gelatine from collagenous material such as animal hides. It is then treated by the normal manufacturing methods of vacuum concentration, etc., used in conventional gelatine production. The hydrolysate so produced can then be blended together with normal high bloom gelatine, in proportions of up to 50/50. It is claimed that a considerable reduction in whipping time can be achieved by employing such an inexpensive mixture to produce the desired volume. This is particularly useful in batch production. Furthermore, a more tender type of marshmallow can be produced, free from stringing, with a short texture.

6.11   WHIPPING AGENTS BASED ON MILK PROTEIN

A well-established proprietary whipping agent based on milk protein is 'Hyfoama' (manufactured by Lenderink Co., Netherlands). This is prepared from casein, the principal protein in milk, by a process of hydrolysis and combination. Vegetable and solubilising agents are sometimes added. The treated milk protein is spray-dried to a low moisture content. Several types are available which have the following composition.

	Hyfoama Standard %	Hyfoama Double Strength %
Protein (nitrogen $\times 7 \cdot 20\%$)	41	80
Carbohydrate	46	—
Moisture	5	5
Ash	8	15

The grade normally used for confectionery manufacture is DS (double strength).

The general effect achieved with 'Hyfoama' is similar to that obtained with egg albumen, but it does not require pre-soaking, is not denatured by overbeating and is economical to use—0·3% is usually sufficient for optimum aeration while only 3 to 5 parts are needed as compared to every 10 parts of egg albumen. Full stability is developed in the presence of sugar; and 'Hyfoama' can be used in conjunction with other gelling agents where the concentration of soluble solids is low.

6.12   WHIPPING AGENTS BASED ON SOYA PROTEINS

Treated soya protein can be used as a whipping agent: one process has been patented under US Patent No. 2 844 486. This is based on the extraction of a highly concentrated protein from oil-free soya flakes. The protein is then modified by enzymic treatment and spray dried. It is claimed that soya proteins have similar properties to egg albumen when used for producing whipped confections; a similar level of it should be used. Soya protein is completely compatible with egg albumen and partial or full replacements can be made. Properties claimed for soya protein are:

(a) Good solubility with no pre-soaking: it should be dissolved by adding to 2–3 parts of water; stir to aid dispersion.

(b) Fast whipping together with a lower density, compared to a similar formulation based on egg albumen.

(c) Stability to heat: it is not impaired by very hot syrups, because this type is not denatured or desolubilised by high temperature, e.g. in continuous production methods of products such as nougat and for aerating high-boiled sugar goods. This also enables a degree of microbiological control over low soluble solid whips.

(d) Stability on over-whipping. Soya protein can be whipped well beyond maximum volume, without any signs of breakdown.

(e) Stability with fat. This is very useful in production of fudge, chocolate-based products, and nut-based pastes.

(f) Stand up properties. Soya protein foams do not suffer collapse with age. These types of vegetable proteins appear to give a more fluid body than do egg albumen-based products. A mixed batch of nuts, fat and cocoa for instance, after cooling, will be quite firm and will not be affected by cold flow.

The following recipes are based on Gunther Products Inc. using soya proteins, modified and manufactured according to the US Patent mentioned. The particular grade used for the manufacture of whipped confectionery products is G-400; the G-400V type is recommended for use in vertical or continuous beating machines, and G-400H for horizontal or slower types of machinery. These recipes are for the vertical mixer.

Typical Basic Frappés: (1) 50% Soya Protein; (2) 100% Soya Protein:

	Parts by weight	
	(1)	(2)
Soya Protein G-400V	1	2
Egg Albumen	1	—
Water	4	4
Glucose Syrup	60	60
Sugar	40	40

Method

1. Prepare a solution of G-400V and egg albumen in water.
2. Add this to 10 parts glucose syrup in a beating bowl.
3. Beat at high speed for 8 to 10 minutes until the desired increase in volume is obtained. (The foam should be light and fluffy.)
4. Boil the remaining glucose syrup with the cane or beet sugar and required amount of water, to a temperature of 116° C (240° F).
5. Add this boiled syrup to the foam batch and mix in, using a slow beater speed.
6. Beat at a high speed for several minutes.

6.13   Carrageenan

Carrageenan is obtained from a seaweed (*Chondrus crispus*) found on the shores of many European countries also the north east coasts of North America. The seaweed is well washed, before alkaline extraction with severe stirring, which breaks it up. The extract is then filtered, in some cases it is decolourised, and finally evaporated and roll dried, or, precipitated by alcohol; the resulting powder is then ground. A wide range of textures can be prepared by combining carrageenan with other gelling agents. It can be used in various types of jellies and generally as a thickening and gelling agent.

6.14   Chicle

Chicle is thickened latex of *Achras saporata*, a tree native to Mexico, South and Central America and British Honduras. Extraction is similar to that for rubber in which the tree is scored in a herring bone fashion and the extruded gum collected for purification. The blocks of raw gum contain also twenty to thirty percent of moisture and impurities such as sand, bark and twigs. Purification is by multiple washing with detergent solution followed by rinsing.

The gum is a transpolyisopene isomer of gutta percha which softens

TABLE 35A. Properties of Gelling Agents and Gums

Agent	pH	Solubility		Stability		Storage	Viscosity (aq. soln)	Gel-formation
		Cold	Hot	Heat	Acid			
Agar Agar	at 1%—:7	Insoluble (swells)	Soluble	Fairly stable	Fairly stable	Weakens	Viscous	Forms firm gel at 0·5% conc. Gels show syneresis. Swell less in acid media.
Alginate	Varies with type	Na salt soluble	Na salt soluble	Fairly stable	Stable	Stable	V. Viscous	Compatible with alkalis up to pH 11. Gels formed by divalent salts, the setting time controlled by phosphate.
Arabic Gum	at 10%—:4·6	Truly soluble up to 50%	Truly soluble	Degrades	Fairly stable	Weakens	Viscous at high concs.	Gelling power low. Electrolytes reduce consistency.
Carob Gum	at 1%—:5·3	Slightly soluble (swells)	Soluble	Fairly stable	Fairly stable	Stable	Viscous	Useful with agar. Gelling by addition of alkali.
Carrageenan	at 1%—:7·9	Fairly soluble (swells)	Soluble	Stable	Stable	Stable	Viscous	Forms firm gel with added K+ —hence regulation of gel strength by K+ salt. Gel thermally reversible.
Gelatin	Varies with type	Insoluble (swells)	Soluble	Degrades	Degrades	Stable	Viscous at low concs.	Gel thermally reversible its rigidity depending on pH, conc., temp, and additives.

Ghatti gum	at 1%-:4·5	Slightly soluble	Soluble	Fairly stable		Stable	Viscous	Mainly used as an emulsification agent concerning oil in water.
Guar gum	at 1%-:5·5 -6·1	Slightly soluble (swells)	Soluble	Stable	Stable	Stable	Viscous	Gel resistant to heat shock for long periods.
Karaya gum	at 1%-:4·6	Slightly soluble	Soluble	Not very stable	Stable	Stable	Viscous	Normally 3-4% conc. max. for uniform gel by cold water hydration.
Pectin	Varies with esterification	Slightly soluble	Soluble	Stable	Stable	Stable	V. Viscous	High degree of esterification or methoxylation gives rapid-set gels.
Starch: Unmodified	5·0-6·5	Slightly soluble	Soluble	Stable	Degrades	Stable	Viscous	Can be modified for many gels and textures.
Modified (see also Table 33)	Neutral or adjusted for acid conditions	Slightly soluble	Soluble	Stable	Stable	Stable	Viscosity controlled	Many starches when cooked have a low viscosity but form a rigid gel on cooling.
Tragacanth	at 1%:5·1 -5·9	Slightly soluble	Disperses	Highly stable	Stable	Stable	V. Viscous	2-4% of gum give thick gel when thoroughly dispersed.

considerably at temperatures above 60° C. It is associated with mixed resins and various waxes, sugars and mineral salts.

6.15   JELUTONG—PONTIANAK

This gum is the rubber sap of *Dyera costulata* of the family *apocyanesas*. It is found in the Far East and is extracted in the manner normal for gums.

6.16   GUAR GUM

This is extracted from the seeds of the guar plant, native to India and Pakistan. In the manufacture, the endosperm must be separated from the hull and germ, by roasting, mild acid treatment, grinding, and sifting. The endosperm is then ground to a fine powder.

Guar gum hydrates very well in cold water, the solutions giving a high viscosity. In aqueous solution a rate of usage of less than 1% is recommended. It is very stable to pH variation. Maximum viscosity is achieved at 25°–40° C (77°–104° F). One of the most interesting features of guar gum is its synergistic effect with other gums and starches.

6.17   LOCUST BEAN GUM (CAROB GUM)

The gum is extracted from the endosperm of the kernels of '*Ceratonia Siliana Linn*'. It is largely soluble in water giving a cloudy viscosity which exhibits its peak viscosity at 90° C (194° F). Locust bean gum has excellent stabilising and water binding properties. On adding to agar jelly recipes it enhances jelly strength and prevents weeping.

6.18   QUINCE SEED GUM

The quince is native to Central Asia and the apple growing areas of North America; the fruit and the method of growing are similar to those of the apple. Quince gum is extracted from the seed found inside the fruit, by seeping in an excess of water and filtering the extract through a filter cloth. The viscosity of solutions of quince seed gum is low and they are not very heat stable; the gum can be used as a stabiliser in chocolate milk. It is considered to have a shorter whipping time than gelatine and develops its maximum viscosity after processing has been completed.

6.19   PROPERTIES OF WHIPPING, GELLING AND THICKENING AGENTS

These are summarised in Table 35A.

7

Flavouring and Colouring Agents

7.1 FLAVOURINGS

Four types of flavourings are available to the manufacturers of sugar confections and chocolates: (1) essential oils; (2) essences; (3) fruit juices and pulps; (4) powdered flavours.

Liquid flavourings of all types should be held in sealed, full containers under cool, dark conditions. They are best held away from other ingredients to avoid the spoilage which can arise from flavour pick up. Essences and essential oils are often inflammable and should therefore be stored in metal-lined cabinets to reduce fire risk.

The headspace in containers, particularly those in a part-used state, can be a source of deterioration through oxidation of the flavouring. Opened containers of flavours should be used up as quickly as possible and never stored in hot processing areas unless required for that day's production. Unopened containers of flavourings should not be held on store for more than one year.

The containers used for storing flavouring materials can be in glass or metal. Glass bottles should be coloured, preferably deep amber, to reduce the catalytic effect of light which accelerates deterioration. It is possible to store some flavouring materials in plastics, but essences and essential oils tend to soften these materials and pick up off-flavours. Aluminium bottles are an acceptable packaging medium but are costly. PVC or polythene lined drums are satisfactory for some flavours. Lacquered tins are unaffected by powdered flavours and are the normally accepted packaging for these materials.

Glass or plastic measures are suitable for flavour dispensing. Plastic measures are slowly affected by essences and oils, though contact time is so short as not to rule out their use. Optic volumetric measures can be usefully adapted for delivering fixed amounts of flavourings. Flavour dispensing from a central point is preferable to individual operatives retaining their own flavour stock.

The level of flavouring needed for sugar confectionery varies considerably according to the product and the type of flavouring chosen. It is important to indicate to the flavour manufacturer the intended use for his product. Choice of solvent, binding agent, etc. can be varied to minimise flavour-loss and destruction for particular processing methods. Flavours must be chosen with care as some materials may adversely affect other confectionery ingredients, particularly gums. Experimentations carried out with a new flavouring should be at an initial level of 0·1%. The use of small amounts of salt enhances other flavourings. Ammoniated glycerhizin can also be used as a flavour intensifier in chocolate, chewing gum and butter confections.

Liquid flavours should be mixed with a small amount of dextrose to assist dispersion on adding to the batch. Flavouring oils and essences can also be diluted with ethanol, isopropanol, propylene glycol or carbitol.

7.2   ESSENTIAL OILS

Essential oils are produced in three ways: (1) distillation; (2) solvent extraction; (3) cold expression.

Distilled oils are improved by a short maturation period before use, while cold expressed oils are immediately available for use. In distillation, the chopped flowers, leaves, peel or pulped whole fruit are macerated with water. This mix is either boiled, or steam is bubbled through the mix. The steam and essential oil vapour is passed into a condenser and the condensed liquor collected. Filtration, separation and drying then takes place prior to packaging.

Essential oils are complex mixtures of alcohols, esters, aldehydes and lactones. The flavouring components of common fruits have been reviewed by H. E. NURSTEN and A. A. WILLIAMS [1967, *Chem. and Ind.*, (*12*), 486–497]. Some of the hydrocarbon components, particularly the terpenes, may produce cloudiness in confectionery jellies. Terpenes can be removed by dual solvent treatment or by vacuum distillation. The quality of oil is thus improved, but at a considerable increase in cost. Some essential oils contain small traces of antioxidants to reduce deterioration from oxidation; any such additive must be acceptable for the regulations in force in the country of sale.

Vanillin differs from most other natural flavourings in being available in crystalline form. It can be purchased either extracted from the plant or prepared synthetically. It should be added to caramels and fudge at 0·02% level to enhance butter flavour or at 0·05% to chocolate or coffee confections as a flavour intensifier. Vanillin should not be added to confectionery boils at temperatures greater than 90° C (194° F) if flavour loss is to be avoided.

7.3 ESSENCES

Essences are either diluted solutions of essential oils, or mixtures of synthetic chemicals blended to match the natural flavour of the fruit. They are cheaper to produce than essential oils and in the case of some of the synthetic blends, more accurately reproduce the flavour of the fresh fruit. Delicate flavours of soft fruits, such as strawberry, raspberry and blackcurrant, are particularly difficult to extract and it is only by the use of essences that these flavours of confections can be prepared. The simplest synthetic flavouring for butter is diacetyl. The safeguards previously listed for essential oils apply equally to essences.

7.4 FRUIT JUICES

Fruit juices are prepared by expelling the juice from the fruit after washing and scrubbing. The expelled juice is normally concentrated and a preservative such as sulphur dioxide added. Fruit juice will have a nutty flavour if too much seed is crushed during expellation. The acid content of the fruit juice is high, ranging from 0·5–2% expressed as citric acid. Lemon juice is exceptionally high in acid, between 4–7%. Aroma concentrates, stored under nitrogen, can be added to give a considerable increase in flavouring when using a fruit juice. Fruit juices are mainly used to enhance sales-appeal in products such as confectionery jellies. Their use lowers product quality rather than enhances it.

7.5 FRUIT PURÉES OR PULPS

The most commonly available purée and the cheapest is apple. This is best produced from ripe Champagne apples chosen for their thin, unblemished skins. Other purées available to the confectioner are apricot, blackcurrant, peach, pineapple and strawberry.

Apple purée should be sieved before use. It is high in water and in acid. Confections which contain a considerable amount of purée will develop high levels of invert sugar during boiling.

Most commercial purées contain considerable amounts of preservative, particularly sulphur dioxide, to prevent fermentation and possible mould growth. Much of the sulphur dioxide is boiled off during processing. Purées contribute insufficient flavour to confections and should be reinforced by the addition of essential oils and essences. Their main use is in the preparation of centre fillings for high boilings and fondants.

A typical analysis of apple purée is:

	%	
Moisture	90·0	
Total Solids		10·0
Total Sugars	6·8	
Acidity as Citric Acid	1·2	
Fruit Solids	2·0	

7.6   POWDERED FLAVOURS

Powdered flavours have poor aromas but produce a satisfactory flavour intensity. They are prepared by mixing the flavour with dry components such as dextrose; by spray drying, or by dropping the flavour on to a carrier such as gum arabic or tragacanth. The loss of flavour from powders is slow in comparison to the essential oils. Powdered flavours have a low solubility in water and may be affected by oxidation while on store. The choice of powdered flavourings should be based on flavour quality, free flow properties, uniform particle size and expected storage life.

7.7   ARTIFICIAL CHERRIES

The need for artificial cherries arises from the high prices commanded by the natural product. They can be produced by dropping small amounts of a cane or beet sugar/glucose syrup/water/sodium alginate mix into a weak solution of calcium chloride. The spherical droplets set under these conditions. This is due to the formation of an insoluble calcium alginate salt skin around the high viscosity sugar mix. Hardness of the artificial cherry is determined by the contact time between the alginate mix and the calcium chloride. The patent for this process is held by Alginates Industries Ltd., London who supply the necessary technical advice to potential users of their alginates.

Other forms of artificial cherry pieces can be produced by close chopping of a cherry-flavoured pectin jelly slab.

Artificial cherries have a low consumer acceptance when used in coated chocolate selections, but are of value for adding to other types of cheap confectionery lines.

7.8   DATES

Dates consist of 85% edible flesh and 15% stone, the flesh having the following composition:

	%	
Moisture	18	
Total Solids		82
Total Sugars	49	
Fat	0·3	

They are best stored at a low temperature, 5°–10° C (37°–50° F) and in conditions of medium humidity (60% RH). They can be used as a base material for centres in filled confections.

7.9 DATE SYRUP

The composition of date syrup is:

		%
Moisture	19	
Total Solids		81
Reducing Sugars as Invert	75	
Sucrose	1	

The high sugar content enables it to be used as a cheap replacement for glucose syrup in those countries having a ready supply of the raw ingredient.

7.10 FIGS

The fig consists of one-third peel and two-thirds edible flesh and seeds, which constitute one-fifth of the total weight. Fig flesh, without seeds, has the following composition:

		%
Water	89	
Total Solids		11
Sugar	9	
Mineral Ash	0·4	
Proteins	0·5	

Figs can be used as a base ingredient in recipes for centres used in filled confections.

7.11 GINGER

Ginger is obtained from the perennial plant *Zinziber officinale* which grows up to 2 ft in height. The edible stem, used in sweet manufacture, is an underground rootlike growth (rhizome) which contains both scaly leaves and buds. Raw ginger can be obtained from a number of areas, most commonly China, Formosa, Japan, Philippines and Thailand. The Chinese is the best type for processing as it lacks harsh flavour and is of a good texture. Successful cultivation requires frequent manuring, a sufficiently high rainfall and a high air temperature.

Ginger intended for preserving is lifted at an earlier stage than that grown for the manufacture of the spice. The rhizomes can be easily damaged by careless handling during lifting. They must be carefully peeled without damage to the flesh, and are then preserved in vinegar or in brine (at 14–18% salt content) and dispatched to the shippers. A preserving liquid is necessary to prevent mould developing on the cut pieces during transit [B. I. BROWN, A. C. LLOYD, *J. Fd. Tech.*, 1972, 7, (3), 309–31].

Good quality ginger should be free of tough fibrous strands, associated with the lower grade product, and should have a smooth taste, free of any back-flavour. Of the two types of ginger—'stem' and 'cargo'—'stem' has superior qualities and is accordingly more expensive. It is produced from the softer side shoots from the main stem. 'Cargo' is generally applied to the rest of the rhizome. Other factors governing price are source, size of pieces, flavour and texture.

7.12   LIQUORICE

Liquorice is used as a flavouring in sugar confectionery manufacture and for its consumer appeal as a medicant. It is always added as the block juice, which is a water extract prepared from the liquorice root. Cultivation is widespread; major sources are China, Greece. Italy, Spain, Syria, Russia and Turkey. Although all block juice that is sold is called liquorice it is extracted from a number of different varieties of the plant whose botanical name is *glycrrhiza*. The amount of glycrrhizin, as well as the flavour quality, varies according to the plant variety, the country of growth and the time when the root was dug out of the ground. Spanish liquorice, although having a lower glycrrhizin content, has a smoother, less harsh background flavour.

The plant develops by sending down a tap root which may reach a depth of 5 ft or more and issuing runners reaching over 20 ft. The roots are dug up at three to four yearly intervals leaving only the newer roots that have developed on the runners. All the roots are collected together, transported to a collection area, stacked and held to dry for up to three months. The stacks are periodically turned to assist in the release of moisture. After drying they are shipped to the extraction plants where aqueous extracts are prepared at high solids concentrations.

A typical analysis of a sample of block juice is:

	%
Glycrrhizin	14
Total Sugars	16
Starch and Gums	32
Ash	6
Moisture	20
Etc.	12

The glycrrhizin is present either as the calcium or as the potassium salt. It is extremely sweet and, depending on the conditions of test, it is reported as being up to fifty times sweeter than sucrose. Spanish root contains around 6% of glycrrhizin, Syrian 14% and Far Eastern produce around 20%.

Although glycrrhizin content can be used as a guide for the purchase of block juice it is by no means the only factor. Continuity of supplies to maintain a consistent taste and the lack of a harsh or bitter background

flavour are equally important. Oil of aniseed has similar flavouring characteristics to liquorice and can be used in moderation to boost the flavour
level of liquorice confections. Block juice should normally be added to
confectionery recipes at levels between $1\frac{1}{4}$–4% depending on the quality
of product being produced. It should be broken up before use and soaked
in three times its own weight of water prior to boiling to achieve solution.

Any adulteration of block juice is usually in the form of the addition of
sugar or starch and is difficult to detect. A good trustworthy supplier is
therefore essential.

7.13 NUTS

A wide range of nuts is available to the confectioner. In purchasing nuts,
great care must be taken to ensure that they are free of infestation and
foreign matter. Even with close specifications it is impossible to guarantee
complete freedom from impurities. Inspection procedures must therefore be
devised to avoid the unfortunate publicity which invariably surrounds
cases of infestation which come before the courts. Four methods can be
used depending on the usage of nuts in a particular factory, the cost of
labour and the types of nuts to be sorted. These methods are (1) hand
sorting, (2) vibratory sieving, (3) air flotation and (4) electronic sorting.
Deliveries of nuts should always be passed over a metal detector.

Batches of nuts offered for purchase which contain a high proportion of
broken or split seeds should be avoided, due to the enhanced danger of
rancidity. Nuts should be stored in cool conditions at 5°–10° C (41°–50° F)
with a medium air humidity (60%). Trace flavours may be due to insecticides sprayed on to the nuts prior to shipment. Mould growth is usually
indicative of a high moisture content and under no circumstances should
nuts so affected be purchased for use. Aflatoxins arising from mould growth
on groundnuts have been found to be responsible for many cases of
poisoning.

7.14 ALMONDS

Although almonds are grown in many areas, supplies for the confectionery industry originate from six main sources—California, France,
mainland Italy, Sicily, Spain and North Africa. The almonds from
European sources are generally sweeter than the softer shelled Californian
almonds.

The composition of sweet almonds is as follows:

	%
Moisture	6·5
Oil	59·0
Protein	23·0
Ash	3·1
Carbohydrate and Fibrous Matter	8·4
Including Sucrose	4·3

The ash is mainly potassium and magnesium salts with lesser amounts of sodium and calcium salts and some silica. The sucrose content of almonds varies according to the country of growth and to the season of harvesting. This can be of significance in calculating nut content based on chemical analysis.

Almonds are harvested when the hull splits to expose the hard inner shell containing the nut kernel. The almonds store well in the shell but require drying if they are to be sold as kernels. Once shelled the almonds should be sieved to remove any broken shell and blanched to remove the outer skin. Blanching can be carried out by plunging the nuts into water at 90° C (194° F) for 4 to 5 minutes and then passing them through a steaming chamber. The nuts should then be passed through fluted blanching rollers and washed with high pressure water jets to remove the skin. The excess moisture should then be removed to give the specified moisture content.

There are two basic groups of almonds, 'sweet' and 'bitter', according to the amount of prussic acid present. Analysis of almonds carried out by H. A. WILLIAMS [*Analyst*, 1943, *68*, p. 50–1] showed the following variations in prussic acid content.

	%
Prunus amygadulus amara (bitter)	0·22
Prunus amygadulus nana (bitter)	0·12
Prunus amygadulus praecos (sweet)	0·011
Prunus amygadulus dulcis (sweet)	0·005

Excessive incorporation of bitter almonds into sugar confectionery recipes would be likely to lead to illness though the use of a small proportion enhances almond flavour. Some countries limit the acceptable amount of prussic acid: in Canada the concentration limit was, in 1970, fixed at no more than 25 ppm. The outer layer of the cotyledons contain more than twice the amount of acid than the fleshy material in the centre of the kernels; the content varies from tree to tree, from country to country and, as previously shown, between varieties.

The count per lb of almonds supplied for use in the confectionery industry is within the range of 350–450 per lb for marzipan manufacture and 300–350 per lb for panning. The finest variety of almonds for sweet manufacture is Jordan, with Nonpareil as a good general nut. Neplus is a good variety for sugar panning.

Should the recipe require fried almonds, the nuts should be cooked in hot oil held at 145° C (293° F).

Almonds will store satisfactorily under cool dry conditions for 6 to 9 months. Cold storage at 5° C (41° F) extends the shelf life to at least 12 months. Ground almonds deteriorate more rapidly than whole almonds. The nuts will pick up odours from other components held in close proximity in the store.

The examination of a sample of nuts being offered should include:

Appearance   Freedom from moulds
Level of broken or deformed nuts   Freedom from infestation
Colour   Freedom from foreign matter
Flavour   Count per oz
Smell   Moisture content
                                    Quality of the oil

7.15   BRAZIL NUTS

Brazil nuts are cultivated primarily in South America. They are not true nuts but seeds contained in the fruit of a tree. They can be purchased in the shell, but during storage and transit there is a tendency for mould growth between the shell and the kernel. They are best purchased in sealed tins to minimise the pick-up of moisture, which in excess is responsible for the early development of rancidity. Edible flesh of the brazil nut has the following average composition:

	%	
Moisture	6	
Total Solids		94
Fat	69	
Total Sugars	9	
Fibrous Material	4	
Mineral Ash	1	

The high level of fat makes crushing difficult and therefore brazil nuts should only be crudely chopped prior to their addition to the rest of the batch. Once chopping has taken place a much greater surface area of nut is exposed to the atmosphere and rancidity is more likely to occur. Only sufficient nuts for 2 days' production should be prepared at any one time. Brazil nuts containing more than 7% moisture should not be purchased.

7.16   CASHEW NUTS

Cashew nuts are mainly supplied from Brazil, East Africa and India. The nut is found attached to the end of the fruit of the cashew nut tree. Although there are at least 8 known species of the tree only one produces an edible nut. Between the hard shell of the nut and the kernel is found a very alkaline liquor containing a high proportion of phenols. Because of the irritant nature of this liquor, cashew nuts are rarely imported in the shell.

The whole nuts are approximately two to three mm in length and average at a count of 300 per lb. As well as whole nuts, large and small pieces and butts (chipped kernels) are available to the confectioner. A typical composition for the nut is:

	%	
Moisture	6	
Total Solids		94
Fat	48	
Total Sugars	22	
Protein	21	

It is important to avoid buying nuts which contain more than 6% moisture. The preferable form of packaging is in sealed cans.

7.17   SWEET CHESTNUTS

Sweet chestnuts are not used to any great extent for the manufacture of sugar confectionery although they are widely grown in Europe, USA and Asia. There are many varieties, the best being the French Marron sweet chestnut used in the production of Marron Glacés. Bad nuts present in samples will float in water, and can thus be detected. The average composition of sweet chestnuts is:

	%	
Moisture	51	
Total Solids		49
Total Sugars	37	
Protein	2	
Fat	3	

The high level of moisture means that the stored product will readily go mouldy if left for any length of time.

7.18   COCONUT

Dried or dessicated coconut is probably the most widely used of all nuts in confectionery manufacture. The main supplier to the United Kingdom is Ceylon, with Philippines as the secondary source.

Coconuts are only harvested every other month; even so, tree yields are generally only 25 to 40 nuts per year. After harvesting, the nuts are cracked and immersed in water; they are then cut open, washed, dehusked and the outer dark skin removed by a spokeshave.

After shredding, the fragments are dried at 90° C (194° F) and graded on vibratory sieves. Delays between shredding and drying may be the cause of soapy flavours in batches of delivered coconut.

Various types of shredded coconut are available, the more useful being:

Fine Grade: The majority of coconut in use is of this type. It is in the form of $\frac{1}{8}$ in thick rope and is suitable for all types of sweets which have a guillotine action as part of the shaping process.

Medium Shred: Quarter-inch shavings which are highly suited for use in named coconut products, or coconut bars where the consumer would expect a more rough textured product.

Coarse Grade: A thicker variety than the medium shred where a distinct chewing action is desired in the sweet.

Long Thread: Long 2 in strips for use in the manufacture of specialist confections such as 'pipe tobacco'.

There have been many examples of *Salmonella* infection in dessicated coconut and purchase from a reputable supplier is advised. Methods attempted to destroy infection have included heating at 65° C (129° F) for 9 to 10 days; high temperature steam treatment; immersion in boiling water followed by drying; fumigation and roasting.

Roasting is frequently used to destroy bacteria though the margin of safety is small. The resultant product must be evenly brown and no white flesh visible.

If too high a proportion of dessicated coconut is used in sweet manu-facture, the product texture is dry and unappetising. Additions should be limited to no greater than 10% of the total weight of dry batch ingredients. Dried coconut always tastes better if it has been reconstituted before use. This can be done by adding the coconut to three times its own weight of invert sugar syrup, raising the temperature to 80° C (176° F) and then draining; about 40% of the syrup is taken up by the dessicated coconut. The weight of reducing sugar ingredients in the batch should be amended accordingly.

The drained reconstituted coconut should be added as late in the manu-facturing process as practicable. This avoids the excessive release of coconut oil into the main mass; it is more susceptible to rancidity than are the normal confectionery fats.

The average composition of dessicated coconut is:

	%
Moisture	3·1
Fat	39·4
Carbohydrate	53·0
Protein	3·8

The product is supplied in lined tea chests, tin-lined wooden cases and in moisture-proof paper sacks. If coconut is to be stored for any length of time it should be held in air tight, completely filled lacquered metal con-tainers at a lowered temperature.

7.19   HAZEL NUTS

Hazel nuts are mainly imported from Italy, Spain and Turkey; the best quality normally originate from Italy. Two main classes can be purchased:

a rounded nut which is easy to roast and has a white kernel, and a flatter almond-shaped nut which falls more erratically in the roasting units. As with all nuts, the moisture is of great importance to the keeping quality and nuts should not be purchased which contain more than 5% moisture. The composition of hazel nuts is:

	%
Moisture	3
Fat	69
Protein	15
Fibre	3
Mineral Ash	2
Total Sugars	4

7.20   MACADAMIA NUTS

These nuts are Australian and American in origin and have not yet found great use in other areas. There are two varieties—smooth shelled and rough shelled. The oil content varies according to variety (68% against 75%) as does the sugar content (7% against 4%). The water content of the nut is low at $1\frac{1}{2}\%$.

7.21   PECAN NUTS

The pecan nut is found in North America mainly in Southern USA. It is a plump brownish nut with a shell smoother and thinner than the walnut which it resembles. Pecan nuts have a good flavour and are useful for decorative purposes. Their average count size is 90 per lb though sorted nuts as large as 50 to the pound can be obtained.

The water content of the nut must be held below 4% to prevent browning, mould growth and rancidity from developing.

7.22   PEANUTS

The peanut, or groundnut, or monkeynut, as it is sometimes known, is not a nut at all but a bean. The major supplier is South Africa but large quantities are also grown in China, India, Israel, Libya, Mexico and West Africa. It is harvested from the seed pods which partially bury themselves in the ground at the end of the runners sent out by the main plant.

Two-thirds of the seed pod is edible nut flesh and one-third is shell. After the removal of the shell the nuts are dried at 60°–70° C (140°–158° F) to under 6% moisture. Shelled dried nuts keep satisfactorily for at least 4 months in dry cool conditions. Damp nuts will mould and become inedible. The higher the humidity the more rapid the development of rancidity.

Nuts for roasting and salting should have a count of 600–650 per lb while those for general confectionery manufacture can be much smaller, 800 per lb.

An average composition of the edible flesh of the peanut is:

		%
Moisture	6	
Total Solids		94
Oil	49	
Protein	31	
Total Sugars	10	

Not more than 2% of the peanuts should be deformed nor should more than 2% show signs of infestation.

The nuts are normally supplied in one-hundredweight sacks, usually out of the shell.

The cleaned nuts may if required be roasted at 110°–130° C (230°–266° F) for 45 to 15 minutes respectively. The shrinkage which occurs assists in blanching. If the nuts are not to be roasted then blanching can be carried out by the method described for almonds.

7.23   PISTACHIO NUTS

Pistachio nuts are imported from Arabia, India, Iran and Syria and are mainly used for decoration because of the green colour of the flesh. They have little other use in sweet and chocolate manufacture.

7.24   WALNUTS

Walnuts are grown widely the main suppliers being France, Italy, Poland and the USA. A special black variety is also harvested in California.

The walnut is very prone to infestation and it is advisable to heat all incoming deliveries to 60°–65° C (140°–149° F) to destroy any such contamination. Large stocks of walnuts should not be kept within the factory.

Moisture content is also critical and nuts should contain no more than 4% water. Above this value rancidity will occur at an enhanced rate. Walnuts should not be added to confectionery products which themselves contain high amounts of water. Staling is accelerated by storage in light and at high temperature. Walnuts which have been left on the ground too long before harvesting will be darker in colour than those harvested quickly.

If the walnuts are dried too quickly the nuts will split and spoil. High temperature drying also results in the development of an unwanted toasted flavour in the nuts.

The percentage composition of a typical sample of walnuts is as follows:

		%
Water	7	
Total Solids		93
Oil	60	
Protein	19	
Fibre	3	
Ash	3	
Total Sugars	3	

E

Walnuts are best purchased in sealed tins or in sealed 300 gauge polyethylene film bulk packs.

7.25   SULTANAS

Sultanas are produced from a particular variety of golden yellow grape which is grown in Australia, Turkey, Greece, South Africa and the USA. After harvesting, the bunches of grapes are dipped in an alkali–olive oil mixture or, increasingly in potassium linoleate solutions mixed with treated oils. The grapes are then washed, treated with preservative and dried.

7.26   CURRANTS

Currants are produced mainly in Greece and Australia from black grapes. The bunches of grapes are held on the frames or left on the vines to dry to the correct moisture level.

The main defects or contaminants found in deliveries of all these vine fruits are mould spores, sugar speckling on the surface of the fruit, stalks present in the dried fruit, and sand. Vine fruits should contain no maggots. They should always be thoroughly washed before being added to sugar confectionery batches.

7.27   RAISINS

The moisture content of raisins, which are dried Muscat grapes, averages 18%. Raisin paste, which is sometimes available, contains many fine crystals of dextrose which may be troublesome in manufacture. The solidifying of the paste can be slowed and, to a limited degree reversed by a short heat treatment at 50° C (122° F).

Dried raisins have the following composition:

	%
Water	14
Protein	1
Fat	0·2
Total Sugars	75

The raisins should be checked for foreign matter. Although they contain no natural fat, it is frequently reported to be present, because some suppliers prefer to oil the fruit with mineral or vegetable oil to prevent drying out and to improve the appearance. This may lead to difficulty, either because of local mineral oil regulations, or due to rancidity which may develop in the vegetable coating.

Raisins can be used for the manufacture of fruit centres for coated chocolate selections and to a lesser extent in sugar confectionery lines such as fruit bars.

7.28   VITAMINS

Vitamins may be added to sweets and chocolates to increase sales appeal by association with the properties of these materials. However, difficulties may arise when vitamins are added during the manufacture of the sweets. These include (a) contact with air resulting in vitamin breakdown (vitamins A B C E); (b) high temperatures involved in processing (most vitamins will, to a greater or lesser extent break down); (c) adverse effect of other ingredients, particularly acids; (d) presence of metallic impurities, particularly copper and manganese (vitamins B and C); (e) slow deterioration during storage of the sweets (most vitamins); (f) inherent strong flavour of the vitamins, which is difficult to mask; (g) effect of light on the stability of the vitamin (Table 36).

The present method of lettering the vitamins as a means of their identification is inconsistent with the present knowledge of their composition and relates to the order of their historical discovery.

TABLE 36.   Properties of the Common Vitamins

| Vitamin | Stability | | Solubility | | |
	Heat	Light	Water	Ethanol	Fat
A (carotene)	(st)	un	ins	st	sb
A (axerophthol)	(st)	un	ins	sb	sb
B_1	st	(st)	sb	sb	ins
B_2	st	un	st	(sb)	ins
B_5	st	st	sb	sb	(sb)
B_6	st	un	sb	sb	ins
C	(st)	st	sb	(sb)	ins
D_2	(st)	st	ins	(sb)	ins
D_3	(st)	st	ins	(sb)	ins
E	st	(st)	ins	sb	sb
F	st	(st)	ins	sb	sb
K	st	un	ins	sb	sb
P	st	un	sb	sb	ins

Key: st–stable; (st)–fairly stable; un–unstable; sb–soluble; (sb)–partially soluble; ins–insoluble.

The following vitamins are those of possible interest to the industry.

A   – When pure, vitamin A is a colourless to pale yellow material which regulates growth. It is normally added as 'pro-vitamin A', the prefix indicating that on breakdown in the body, it will form vitamin A.

B_1 – Thiamine is important in skin disorders; but prone to breakdown during the storage of prepared confections.

B_2 – Riboflavin, a growth-promoting vitamin which is stable in acid conditions.

B_6 – Pyridoxine.

C – Ascorbic acid, a white, water soluble crystalline material gives protection from
    scurvy and is claimed to give resistance to colds; rather less liable than the
    others to breakdown in stored confections.

D – A group of antirachitic vitamins which includes calciferol.

E – Mixed alpha and beta tocophenol which are found in wheat germ and in
    cottonseed and other oils.

K – A complex of vitamin components regulating the clotting of blood.

Vitamins should be stored in sealed containers (preferably glass,
aluminium or stainless steel) in dark and cool conditions; stocks should
be held for no longer than 3 months.

It is possible to add certain of the vitamins to sugar confections provided
precautions are taken during processing. Particularly suitable are carotene,
thiamine, riboflavin and L ascorbic acid. Debittered yeast, containing a
high level of vitamins, can also be used as an additive.

Vitamins may be used as follows:

Boiled Sweets: Fold in the vitamin with the flavour. The level of colouring
should be intensified to mask the induced colour of the vitamin. Water
insoluble vitamins will cause the boiling to appear cloudy. Pulling (see §9.1)
overcomes this problem but increases the breakdown of the vitamins.
Vitamins can also be incorporated with the jam in a filled boiled sweet.
Jam-centred blackcurrant-flavoured sweets are highly suitable for this type
of product.

Chocolate: Add the chosen vitamin to the chocolate mass a few minutes
before the completion of conching. Losses can be minimised by processing
in an atmosphere of carbon dioxide.

Other confections suitable for vitamin enrichment are caramels, tablets,
pastilles and cough sweets. Pastilles, which could contain dried fruit
powder and chopped nuts, with their higher moisture content will lose
greater amounts of vitamins through breakdown on store.

A 20% processing loss of the added vitamin weight should be assumed
in most types of confectionery. This is increased when higher temperature
and acid conditions are employed. Acid breakdown can be reduced by
using buffered lactic acid as the flavouring acid. Vitamin loss is considerably reduced by storage in the dark. Retailers and wholesalers should be
discouraged from overstocking lines containing added vitamins.

7.29 CONFECTIONERY ACIDS AND THEIR SALTS

Seven acids and their salts may be used in the manufacture of sugar
confections, four for their value as acidulents, one for its value both as
an acidulent and as a preservative and two as preservatives alone. The
acids are *citric, tartaric, lactic, malic, acetic, benzoic* and *sorbic.*

There is evidence to suggest that acid flavour is linked with pH but the tartness of a confectionery acid is also related to the type, ratio and amount of sugars that are present and the structure of the acid (see §1.7).

The pH values of 5% solutions of varying types of confectionery acids is shown below [DR. P. W. *Zucker und Süsswaren*, 1955, *8*, (25), 1246].

	%
Tartaric acid	1·7
Citric acid	1·8
Lactic acid	2·1
Acetic acid	2·4

7.30   CITRIC ACID

Citric acid has a mildly sour taste and the sweets produced using this acid are 'smoother' in flavour than those manufactured with tartaric acid. Pure citric acid is produced by the fermentation of sugar, using *aspergillus niger*. The acid is considered safe for use in food manufacture, being completely absorbed by the body.

It is normally sold in a solid hydrated form containing the equivalent of 8·6% moisture. On heating, it first softens at between 70°–75° C (158°–167° F); with increasing heat, water is driven off. Complete melting occurs at 153° C (307° F). Citric acid has a specific gravity of 1·54. It is quite soluble in water forming solutions varying from over 60% concentration at room temperature to over 80% at the boiling point of the solution. The acid should be stored under dry conditions as it will cake in atmospheres of high relative humidity. A 0·5% solution of citric acid has a pH of 2·4 while that of a 1% solution is 2·2.

7.31   SODIUM CITRATE

Sodium citrate is a valuable additive for confectionery manufacture because its buffering power enables small additions of acid to be made, either the pure component or present in another ingredient, without greatly affecting the acidic nature of the mix (see also §1.7). Buffering is particularly effective when an increase in acidity would affect the properties of the other materials that are present. Confections containing gelatine should always contain a buffer salt.

Two different types of sodium citrate are available, the differences being due to the number of molecules of water of crystallisation present. The pure material can be purchased either as crystals or as a white powder. Sodium citrate has a cooling effect on the tongue and a somewhat salty taste. This is not detectable at the level of use in sugar confectionery (0·3%) and at higher levels is masked by fruit flavours.

7.32   TARTARIC ACID

Tartaric acid is a by-product of wine production, making use of the sediment, press cake and crust. It is normally purchased as the colourless, translucent anhydrous form which has a moisture content of under 1%; being somewhat hygroscopic it should be stored under dry conditions. It melts at 170° C (338° F) and has a specific gravity of 1·76. The pH of a 1% solution of tartaric acid is 2·1 while that of a 0·5% solution is 2·2.

Tartaric acid is very soluble in water. At 20° C (68° F) solutions of over 65% concentration can be prepared while at a 100° C (212° F) the solubility rises to over 80%. The solubility in alcohol is lower than that in water, with a maximum of 20%. Sugar confections manufactured with tartaric acid have a sharper, more biting flavour than those produced with citric acid. Calcium tartrate is very insoluble and jellies using lime gelatines may appear cloudy when tartaric acid is used as the acidulant.

7.33   CREAM OF TARTAR

Cream of tartar (acid potassium tartrate, or potassium hydrogen tartrate) is produced by the action of tartaric acid on Rochelle salt (sodium potassium tartrate). It is relatively insoluble forming solutions of 6% in water at boiling point. The main use of cream of tartar in sugar confectionery manufacture is to bring about in-batch inversion during the manufacture of high-boiled sweets (see also §1.7).

7.34   LACTIC ACID

Lactic acid widely occurs in nature. It is usually sold as a mixture of two isomeric forms, as solutions of 50% or 80% concentration. The pure acid is very soluble and extremely hygroscopic and should be protected while on store (in steel or wooden drums) to prevent the further pick-up of moisture. It melts at 17° C (63° F) and decomposes above 250° C (482° F). A saturated solution has a pH of 1·7.

Lactic acid can be added to the batch of boiled sugar mass together with the colour and flavouring, to give a product with a pleasing acid taste which is not too bitter. It is preferable to use 2% quantities of partially buffered acid for the manufacture of sweets, as the buffered acid considerably reduces the amount of in-batch inversion that takes place. Partially buffered acids can be obtained in varying forms with pH values down to 3·0.

Sodium lactate is very soluble and unlike salts of fruit acids contributes an acid taste to the confection; used in excess, it may cause a saline taste. It is usually sold for use as a buffer as a 70% solution having a specific gravity of 1·38.

7.35   CALCIUM LACTATE

Calcium lactate is available in solution at a concentration of 50%. The salt is thought to act as plasticiser when used in conjunction with whipping agents and savings of up to 15% in gelatine, egg albumen and milk protein have been reported. It is also claimed that a 10% reduction in gelatine can be made in fruit jelly recipes when calcium lactate is incorporated.

7.36   ACETIC ACID (ETHANOIC ACID)

Acetic acid is prepared by the direct oxidation of the fractions of petroleum or by the oxidation of acetaldehyde. Commercial 'glacial acetic acid' has a concentration of 99·8%, a specific gravity at 20° C (68° F) of 1·051 and a boiling point of 117° C (243° F).

Acetic acid should be stored either in stoneware containers or in glass or PTFE coated steel tanks. Polyethylene containers or measures must not be used as they react with it.

7.37   MALIC ACID

Widely found in fresh fruit, the acid, when pure, is a white crystalline or granular powder which melts at 129° C (264° F) and will form solutions with concentrations up to 53% in water at 20° C (68° F). A 1% solution has a pH of 2·4. The acid taste produced in sugar confections is similar to that given by citric acid.

7.38   BENZOIC ACID

Produced by the air oxidation of toluene or by the chemical treatment of phthalic anhydride, this acid is a white powder with a purity of 99·5% which melts at 21° C (70° F) and sublimes at 100° C (212° F). It has a low solubility in water forming solutions of less than 0·3% at 20° C (68° F). The solubility in alcohol is high, it is 58% at 20° C (68° F). Where local regulations permit its use, benzoic acid can be added as a preservative.

7.39   SODIUM BENZOATE

Sodium benzoate can be used as an effective substitute for benzoic acid where a water-soluble preservative is required. It is available as a white powder with a purity of 99%. The solubility in water at 20° C (68° F) is 35%. The solutions are slightly alkaline and have a pH of 8·0. Sodium benzoate is an effective preservative when added at a 0·1% level and where the pH of the mix is below 4·5.

TABLE 37. Food Grade Dyes
Explanatory Notes on facing page

Name	UK Sub-Committee No	Type	Colour Index No 1924	Colour Index No 1957	Aqueous Solubility %	USA FD & C No Where Permitted	Stability in relation to				
							Sulphur Dioxide	Alkali	Confectionery Acids	Heat	Light
Ponceau 4R	2	Monoazo	185	16255	5	NP	F	G	G	S	8
Carmosine	3	Monoazo	179	14720	4	NP	F	F	VG	FS	8
Amaranth[1]	4	Monoazo	184	16185	7	Red No 2	F	F	VG	FS	8
Red 10B	5	Monoazo	30	17200		NP	G	G	VG	S	5
Erythrosine BS[2]	6	Xanthene	773	45430	2	Red No 3	G	F	P	FS	2
Red 2G	8	Monoazo	31	18050	6	NP	G	VG	G	G	10
Red 6B	9	Monoazo	87	18055		NP					
Red FB[3]	10	Monoazo	225	14780		NP	F	P	VG	VS	4
Orange G	28	Monoazo	27	16230	6	NP	F	F	VG	FS	10
Orange RN[4]	29	Monoazo	26	15970	4	NP	F	F	G	FS	8
Tartrazine	34	Pyrazolone	640	19140	6	Yellow No 5	VG	G	VG	VS	10
Yellow 2G	36	Monoazo	639	18965		NP	F	VG	VG	VG	10
Sunset Yellow FCF	39	Monoazo	—	15985	10	Yellow No 6	F	F	VG	S	10
Green S	50	Triarylmethane	737	44090		NP	G	P	G	VS	0
Indigo Carmine	58	Indigoid	1180	73015		Blue No 2	P	P	F	U	4
Chocolate Brown FB	73	Monoazo	—	—	15	NP	G	VG	VG	VS	4
Chocolate Brown HT	73a	Diazo	—	20285		NP	F	VG	VG	VS	8
Black PN	97	Diazo	—	28440		NP	F	F	G	S	6

7.40   Sorbic Acid

Sorbic acid is an unsaturated fatty acid which can be added to sugar confectionery products as an antimycotic agent. Under the mildly acid conditions used in sweet manufacture it is necessary to add up to 0·1% of sorbic acid based on recipe weights; higher levels may give rise to a detectable taste. Sorbic acid is effective in confections with pH up to 6·4. It inhibits both yeasts and the growth of moulds on high moisture confections. Due to the relative insolubility of sorbic acid in water, 0·2% at 20° C (68° F), it is preferable to use the potassium salt which has a solubility in water of 58% at 20° C (68° F).

Potassium sorbate will not decompose until the temperature is over 270° C (518° F). It has a specific gravity of 1·36.

7.41   Sodium Propionate

Additions of sodium propionate in 0·1–0·2% quantities may, subject to local legislation, be added to sugar confectionery as a mould inhibiter. For confections to be held under very adverse conditions, a light coating of the material in alcohol should be sprayed on to the surface of the confection.

7.42   Colour

Dyes contain chemical groupings which absorb light of a particular wavelength. Groupings within the dyes can be considered as falling within three main classes: *chromophores* (groups which have the potential to colour); *auxochromes* (groups enhancing the colour); and *solubility promoters*.

To qualify as a satisfactory colour for sugar confectionery manufacture, a dye must be resistant to sulphur dioxide, to the presence of reducing sugars and to confectionery acid; stable to heat and light; not likely to

---

Notes to Table 37

For details on UK permitted colours, see Reports, and their supplements on Colouring Matters, of the Food Standards Committee of the Min. of Agriculture Fisheries and Food, published by HMSO.

References in Col. 1: (1) Goes off-brown with traces of copper. (2) Precipitated by acids. (3) Recommended for removal from UK permitted list. (4) Goes yellow with SO_2.

Solubilities: By weight; so far as published. All are water-soluble. Oil soluble colours omitted as of little interest to the industry.

Light stability: Graded from 0 (poor) to 10 (excellent).

Abbreviations: NP Not permitted. F, FG, G, VG: fair, fairly good, good, very good. P poor. U unstable. FS fairly stable. S stable. VS very stable.

separate into basic colours; and unaffected by the presence of minor components.

It must also comply with current legislation. The number of dyes meeting this last criterion is limited, and unfortunately varies from country to country. These permitted dyes do not satisfy all the requirements stated above. Amaranth will turn brown in acid conditions and greenish when in a confection which has a high proportion of invert sugar. Confections coloured with indigo carmine are prone to fading when held in sunlight such as occurs in retail displays. The properties of the common dyes are given in Table 37.

In manufacturing coloured confections, it is possible to avoid the likely adverse effect arising from the use of a particular dye by referring to this table and assessing whether to make the following recipe changes: (*a*) vary pH of the batch; (*b*) use an alternative dye or blend; (*c*) improve packaging to avoid adverse storage conditions; (*d*) vary the temperature for the addition of the dye; (*e*) do not add the dye at the same time as the acid; (*f*) lower the amount of preservative present.

Intermediate colourings can be made by blending basic colours. Three useful blends are as follows:

Pea Green	*Purple*	*Chocolate Brown*
10 parts tartrazine	1 part erythrosine	6 parts tartrazine
2 parts indigo carmine	1 part indigo carmine	4 parts amaranth
		2 parts indigo carmine

Black confections can be prepared using food grade carbon black. Titanium dioxide may be used as a whitener; it is particularly useful in pan goods.

Colour mixes can be prepared by mixing the dye with a 50:50 solution of glycerine and high DE glucose syrup. Should the colour be dissolved in water it must not be kept longer than one day. An acceptable alternative is the use of measured quantity colour sticks in which gelatine is used as the setting agent.

A number of mineral and natural products are available to replace synthetic colours and these are widely permitted under European and US food regulations. These include carbon black, titanium dioxide (limited to 1% in the USA), annatto, caramel, cochineal and saffron.

The European Brewing Convention has published (*Analytica*, 2nd edn) a method of assessing colour values by EBC numbers, using slides or discs (see also §2.12).

8

Cocoa, Chocolate and Related Products

8.1 SEQUENCE OF PROCESSES

The manufacturing processes for cocoa and chocolate are similar up to the stage of the production of cocoa nib (cocoa beans which have been deshelled, degermed and split into segments). Fig. 10 illustrates the early stages in cocoa and chocolate manufacture while flow sheets for the later stages of processing cocoa and chocolate are given in Figs. 11 and 12.

8.2 CLEANING

It is necessary to clean cocoa beans after delivery to remove any earth, fragments of sacking, broken beans and other foreign matter that may be present. The process is one of screening, brushing and conveying over powerful magnets. Storage and cleaning should be carried out away from the main factory premises. Insect infestation control can be better maintained in a restricted area. Beans, from the storage hoppers, should be conveyed over a counter-current air flow to remove the lighter material. They should then be passed to high energy vibratory screens of different mesh size which incorporate mechanical brushing; these will remove bean fragments and dust.

Magnetic separators will take out some of the metallic fragments and metal detector heads will isolate any remaining metallic fragments. Hot air of predetermined velocity should then be blown through meshed conveyor bands to cause the beans to float, leaving behind any heavier contaminants. By the choice of careful temperature conditions, the beans can be cracked through differential heat strains without any adverse effect on the contained cocoa butter.

8.3 ROASTING

Five changes occur during the roasting of cocoa beans. These are
(a) development of flavouring components which enhance both cocoa taste

119

and aroma; (*b*) textural changes in the shell thereby permitting its removal in subsequent processing; (*c*) development of colour; (*d*) removal of moisture; and (*e*) chemical changes in bean constituents.

Roasting was originally carried out by soaking the cocoa beans in water, draining and, lastly, rapidly heating to break the husk. The breakthrough in roaster design came with the large batch open flame heating methods now developed into continuous procedures using gas, electrical, hot air and infra-red heating.

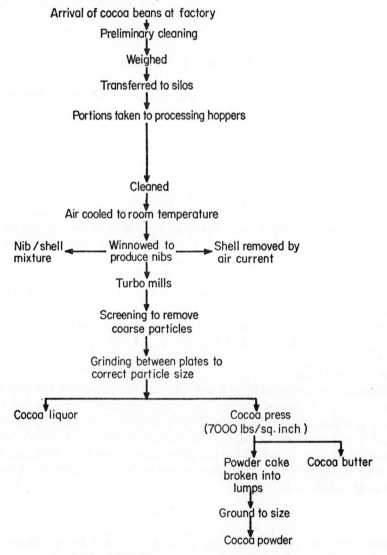

FIGURE 10. Treatment of cocoa beans.

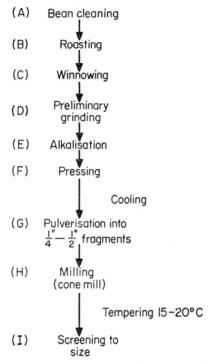

(A) Bean cleaning

(B) Roasting

(C) Winnowing

(D) Preliminary grinding

(E) Alkalisation

(F) Pressing

Cooling

(G) Pulverisation into
$\frac{1"}{4} - \frac{1"}{2}$ fragments

(H) Milling
(cone mill)

Tempering 15–20°C

(I) Screening to size

FIGURE 11. Manufacture of cocoa powder.

In the Lehmann roaster the beans fall through stepped beds which automatically close on filling. Air, which has been used as a coolant, is drawn over heating elements and used for roasting. The Buhler roaster depends on heated air passing upwards through the beans which are tumbling downwards in a diagonal motion on to the trays. Barth's Sirocco roaster depends solely on heated air, while the Nalder and Nalder plant employs steam heating over a cascaded flow. According to G. WOLF [*Nährung*, *3*, 11/12, 1075–8] the quality of cocoa beans roasted by infra-red heating was disappointing. However other workers have claimed that infra-red heating gives a more even roast with less flavour-loss. A mixture of light and dark radiators has been proposed for this system. Fluid air bed systems have been successfully used for roasting cocoa beans [H. J. MILLEVILLE, *Food Proc.*, *23*, (11), 67–9; *Candy Industry*, 31 Dec. 1963]. In this method powerful jets of heated air are forced downwards on the beans, which float and roll, giving even roasting in under five minutes. Flavour and fat loss are said to be reduced.

Whichever procedure is used, a sampling technique should be used to check the progress of the roast. Withdrawn samples of the beans should be broken and the ingress of roasting examined. The aroma is indicative, as is the amount and colour of blue smoke that is emitted. Continuous temperature recorders fitted on the roasters are a useful guide to the processing that a particular group of beans have received.

It is difficult to specify conditions for roasting; these are dependent on the variety of the bean, the harvesting season, the district of growth, subsequent treatment received after harvesting, and the type of flavour required in the chocolate. Ultimate roasting quality is still very much dependent on the skill and judgement of the machine operator. A particular difficulty is that the temperature produced at the surface of the bean can differ greatly from that in the centre. The amount of roasting affects the colour, flavour and aroma of the final chocolate. Adjustments must be made to take account of changing moisture content and the size and shape of the beans. Flat beans are particularly difficult to roast as they do not tumble easily, while split or fragmented beans tend to become rapidly over-roasted.

Suitable roasting temperatures are 115°–140° C (239°–284° F). The time given for roasting is dependent on the peak temperature reached. Roasting should be so arranged that the beans are brought quickly up to temperature, held at this for the full roast period, and rapidly cooled after discharge. A short roast for 20 minutes at 200° C (392° F) may give a better product than longer but lower temperature conditions.

The fine beans of the Criollo type should be given a lower temperature, 110°–115° C (230°–239° F), to prevent loss of the more delicate flavouring components. Colour development in these beans will therefore be slight.

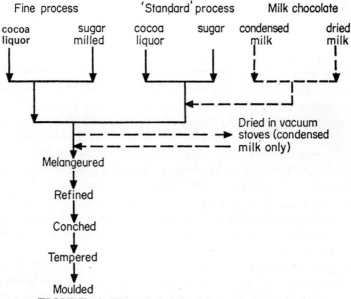

FIGURE 12. Flow sheet for chocolate manufacture.

Roasting temperatures used on beans for cocoa powder production should be high to develop full colour and a slightly caramelised flavour.

A low temperature roast can take up to 60 minutes to complete, a medium roast up to 40 minutes and the full high temperature from 15 to 25 minutes. American roasting conditions tend to be lower than the British and Continental practice.

The discharged beans must be rapidly cooled to prevent over-roasting with attendant discolouration and spoilage of flavour. This is detectable as a sharp disagreeable background flavour imparted to the prepared chocolate. Without rapid cooling only a slow liberation of the internal heat occurs. In these circumstances the husks appear charred and they quickly crumble. Too short a roasting period will also result in a low quality product.

Roasting as a single process is insufficient to develop a full chocolate flavour. Beans which have not been fermented will not develop a chocolate flavour on roasting.

There is very little loss of volatile acids from the beans during roasting. Up to 10% of acetic and propionic acids are however released from the shell [W. DIEMER, L. ACKER, H. LANGE, 1959, *Süsswaren*, *3*, (8) 372–5]. The removal of these volatile acids is greatly assisted by the steam generated from the moisture losses from the bean. Diemer et al [W. DIEMER, L. ACKER, H. LANGE, 1959, *Süsswaren*, *3*, (9) 488–90] has shown that losses of carbohydrate and amino acids also occur during roasting. Bailey [S. D. BAILEY, et al, 1962, *J. Fd. Sci.*, *27*, 165–170] found that the content of higher aldehydes fell during roasting but there was a rise in the lower aldehydes. A reaction of Maillard type probably occurs during this process which involves the sugars and the amino acids.

Some fat is also lost during roasting. Mohr, Heiss and Gorling [W. MOHR, R. HEISS, P. GORLING, 1957, *Gordian*, *57*, (1383), 349] found this to be 0·2% of the dry nib weight while Kleinert [J. KLEINERT, 1957, *International Chocolate Review*, *12*, (12), 512–520] in measurements made on a different bean variety found a loss of 0·5%. It is suggested by Kleinert (loc cit) that some fat transfers to the shell and the rest migrates from the broken nibs onto the dried pulp residues. The higher the roast temperature the greater will be the loss of fat. This can be reduced by rapid cooling of the beans on leaving the roasters.

Properly dried beans have moisture contents of 4–6%. During storage there is a gradual pick-up of water from the atmosphere and the moisture content can rise to 10–20%; this is largely driven off during roasting. Well-stored beans can show weight losses during roasting of 4–7%, the greatest part is accountable to the removal of moisture, but some arises from the abrasion dust taken away by the circulated air. The loss in weight is accompanied by shrinkage which together with loss of moisture assists in the later removal of the shell. Cocoa beans tend to reabsorb moisture after roasting, and the winnowing process should not therefore be greatly delayed. W. Mohr [*Fette Seifen AnstrM.*, 1970, *72*, (8), 695–703] has suggested that control of bean moisture before roasting is important for flavour development. It is proposed that beans are dried at 100° C (212° F) before roasting is commenced.

8.4   CHOCOLATE RECIPES

The development of a recipe for chocolate should be based on three criteria: (i) the intended market or use; (ii) the limitation being placed on material and production costs; and (iii) the desired quality.

The amount of fat present in the chocolate will affect the flow properties, and fat content must therefore be varied according to the intended use. The ranges for different types of chocolate are:

Moulding chocolate	30–34%
Covering chocolate	35–40%
Ice-cream-covering chocolate	50–55%

Increases in sugar content should be matched by increases in fat content for a similar viscosity to be maintained. Milk chocolate requires a lower fat content than dark chocolate used for similar purposes. Commercial lecithin or its synthetic alternatives in a chocolate recipe can save up to 5% of added cocoa butter.

Dark chocolate is expected to have a stronger cocoa aroma than milk chocolate; the quality of cocoa beans used in a recipe for dark chocolate will therefore be higher than for the product containing milk solids. Milk flavour tends to mask the more delicate chocolate flavouring components and the use of small proportions of aroma beans will not greatly contribute to the overall effect. The type of cocoa beans used in a recipe should be balanced to produce a desired taste quality compatible with the limitations on cost. Table 38 lists common types of cocoa beans and their suggested value in recipe compilation.

TABLE 38.   Characteristics of Cocoa Beans from Various Sources

Base or Bulk Beans	Flavour Beans	Aroma Beans
Accra	Ceylon	Arriba
Bahia	Java	Caracas
Cameroon	New Hebrides	Grenada
Nigeria	Samoa	Machala
San Thomé		

Cheap couvertures (covering chocolate) can be developed from a blend of 90% base beans (Accra or Nigeria) and 10% flavour beans (Samoa). A standard chocolate should contain 75% base beans and 25% mixed aroma and flavour beans. Good covering chocolate for box assortments should contain 50% base beans and 50% mixed aroma and flavour beans. High quality cocoa powder can be manufactured from a mix containing 50% blended Accra and Nigerian beans, 30% Samoan and 20% Arriba (or Trinidad). Although it is common practice first to blend the beans and then to roast, a higher quality product can be produced by roasting each type of bean individually and then blending. A more detailed consideration of the variation between bean varieties has been prepared by L. RUSSELL COOK [*1963 PMCA Conference Report and Conf. Prod.*, 1964, (2), 115–142].

Recipes for a range of chocolate products are given in Table 39. Some guide to the quality of a sample of chocolate can be given by comparing the product on the six point scale detailed in Table 40.

TABLE 39.   Recipes for Chocolate Products (parts by weight)

Ingredient	Coating	Easter Egg or Liqueur	Moulding	Piping
Dark Chocolate				
Nib	38	30	43	50
Sugar	47·6	47·6	48	47·6
Cocoa Butter	14	22	8·6	2
Lecithin	0·4	0·4	0·4	0·4
Dried Milk	—	—	—	—
Milk Crumb	—	—	—	—

Ingredient	Coating		Easter Egg or Liqueur	Moulding
	Milk Crumb	Dried Milk		
Milk Chocolate				
Nib	12	14	9	12
Sugar	—	46	44	45
Cocoa Butter	18	16	23	20
Lecithin	—	0·4	0·4	0·4
Dried Milk	—	23·6	23·6	23·6
Milk Crumb	70	—	—	—

TABLE 40.   Check List for Rapid Evaluation of Chocolate Samples

Property	Desired Quality
Colour	Even, rich
Surface Appearance	Smooth, lack of bloom spots
Texture	Smooth, no detectable grittiness
Break	Good snap
Flavour	Pleasant, good chocolate taste, no back flavours
Aroma	Strong cocoa aroma

8.5 MILK CRUMB

Milk crumb is a homogeneous blend of cocoa solids, milk solids and sugar. It has found wide acceptance in the manufacture of chocolate as its use avoids the necessity of adding dried milk powder. Although milk crumb is more expensive, when considered on a comparable solids content basis, the milk chocolate produced is of better quality and improved cocoa flavour; it has a tendency to be harder than that manufactured using equivalent amounts of cocoa bean, dried milk and sugar. The method of manufacture is depicted in Fig. 13.

Milk crumb can be purchased either kibbled (usually more convenient) or as a powder produced by milling the blocks after drying. Incoming deliveries should be checked and purchased on the declared specification for: (a) sugar to milk solids ratio; (b) milk solids not fat content; (c) cocoa butter content; (d) total fat content; (e) cocoa mass content; (f) cocoa shell content; (g) moisture.

Results obtained by J. SAUNDERS [J. Sci. Fd. Agric., 1956, 349] indicated that no reaction takes place during manufacture if only milk solids, not fat and chocolate liquor, are present, or when sucrose is processed with chocolate liquor. However, when all three components are mixed a chemical reaction was found to take place. Later work by this author [Chem. & Ind., 1957, 52–53] suggests that a complex reaction occurred involving reducing groups present in the ingredients. Saunders found that a significant change occurs in the proteinous material during the manufacture of milk crumb.

Milk crumb can be used in a number of different ways, namely (a) extra cocoa butter is added to the milk crumb and, after warming and refining, is processed as for chocolate; (b) refining is followed by an addition of extra cocoa butter and commercial lecithin; (c) milk crumb is blended with additional cocoa mass, sugar and cocoa butter and processed in the standard manner for chocolate.

It is more usual to purchase milk crumb from the available range of a producer rather than to order crumbs manufactured to a specified composition. A typical composition for a commercial milk crumb is as follows:

	%
Moisture	1
Full cream milk solids	37
Sucrose	54
Cocoa mass solids	8

This crumb is intended to be used with additional cocoa butter, cocoa mass and sugar. The advantage is that the additional cocoa beans incorporated produce a distinctive chocolate flavour which is specific to one

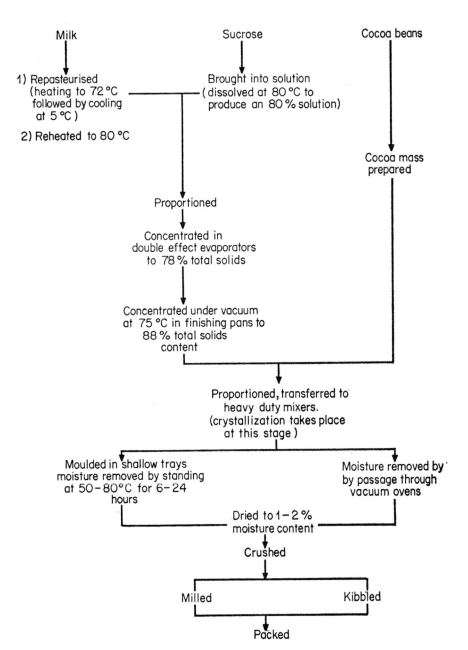

FIGURE 13. Manufacture of milk crumb.

product. Milk crumbs are available which do not require the addition of extra cocoa mass or sugar, the proportion of cocoa solids being increased at the expense of the full cream milk solids. A milk crumb intended for the manufacture of chocolate which needs only the addition of cocoa butter, commercial lecithin and flavourings should contain at least 13% non-fat cocoa solids.

Conching (see §8.10) should commence at 35° C (95° F). Due to the sugary composition of the milk crumb and to the presence of milk solids, conching should not be taken to higher than 50° C (122° F). If higher temperatures are used the chocolate will develop a caramelised flavour which affects the ultimate flavour quality of the chocolate. Conche times can be substantially reduced when chocolate is manufactured from milk crumb. The length of the conching period is dependent on the desired characteristics of the product being produced but values of between 10 to 20 hours are normally sufficient to achieve the required flavour development.

CHOCOLATE USING MILK CRUMB

| | Parts by weight | |
	Wholly Crumb	Part Crumb
Milk Crumb	77	50
Cocoa Butter	$22\frac{3}{4}$	$23\frac{3}{4}$
Lecithin	$\frac{1}{4}$	$\frac{1}{4}$
Cocoa Beans		8
Cane or Beet Sugar		18

Deterioration can occur in milk crumb through the pick up of moisture. The work of Saunders (loc cit) has indicated the equilibrium relative humidity of milk crumb to be approximately 60%. At high air relative humidity levels, milk crumb will pick up moisture and the water content level rises to an equilibrium value of 3%, after which deterioration rapidly occurs. It is, therefore, essential to package and store it so as to reduce the danger of ingress of moisture; e.g. in plastic-lined paper or waterproofed jute sacks. Bulk storage is more difficult because of the blocking of the powder due to the weight of the head of raw material. Silos must, therefore, be designed to minimise the pressure effect. Purchases of milk crumb should be controlled to keep within a factory life of 6 to 8 months.

8.6 WINNOWING

The purpose of winnowing is to separate the shell and germ and to split the cocoa bean into its natural segments (cocoa nibs). Roasted cocoa beans can contain between 10% and 15% shell, depending on source, and 1% germ. The presence of significant amounts of shell in chocolate will affect both colour and flavour and, in addition, reduces the effectiveness of refining. Chocolate manufactured from cocoa beans which still retain the germ is more bitter than that produced from de-germed beans.

The separation of shell and germ can be carried out separately or together, depending on the choice of commercial plant. Cocoa beans are first cracked by passing through rollers or rotating cones. An air current is then used to blow away the lighter shell. The velocity of this air stream is critical: it should be sufficient to remove the undesirable shell but not too high to blow off the costly cocoa nib, and must be varied to suit the changing size of cocoa bean from differing sources. Dust can be collected separately and should be periodically examined to determine the level of efficiency being achieved in separation. Discharged cocoa shell may contain as much as 20–25% of cocoa fat. Provided the plant throughput is sufficiently high, the solvent recovery of this fat may be a viable proposition.

The nib and remaining shell fragments should be passed to the germ separator. Here vibratory, perforated screen cylinders or sieves can be used to separate the germ from the nib. It may be necessary to consider a second winnowing to remove the smaller sized nibs. Yields of between 80–86% are normally achieved by winnowing. The 'pure' nib still contains some shell; a limit of 1·75% shell is in force in the USA.

The action of the Nalder and Nalder winnower depends on the difference in weight and density of the nib and shell. They can be separated by dual action of air flow and sieving. The beans are emptied into the elevator hopper and carried upwards by steel cups to the breaker box where toothed breaking rolls crush the roasted cocoa bean into fairly large pieces of nib and shell, with a minimum amount of dust. A permanent magnet removes any ferrous metals which might damage the rollers. These are spring-loaded, self-cleansing and adjustable from a hand wheel.

The broken beans now enter a horizontal rotary cylinder with a feeding and forwarding worm and a number of grades of woven wire to give the required number of separations. As the separated nib passes through the wire mesh and down chutes—it is subjected to aspiration, which draws off the husk. To determine precisely the separation of husk from nib, the machine is fitted with a series of baffles which can be finely adjusted. A rotating airlock is arranged on the shell discharge side.

The husk or shell and the various graded separations of nib are delivered through separate series of sacking spouts, but, when required, nib and shell collecting worms may be incorporated instead. The overfull is returned to the elevator by a worm conveyor sited beneath the machine. A germ separator is sometimes fitted to winnowers so that the germ and fine nib can be discharged separately.

The capacities of such winnowing equipment depend upon the number of separations, but for between 4 to 7 separations, the capacity would be 600 lb (275 kg) per hour to 4000 lb (1800 kg) per hour.

After winnowing the cocoa beans, a typical breakdown would be:

	%
Clean nib	86·0
Nib with little shell	1·0
Clean shell	8·0
Shell with little nib	4·0
Nib shell mixtures	1·0

8.7   Cocoa Powder

Cocoa powder is produced from the grindings of the press cake after the partial removal of cocoa butter. A flow diagram for the method is given in Fig. 11. It is usual to roast the cocoa beans to a higher temperature for cocoa powder than that given during chocolate manufacture. This is to develop a more pronounced flavour in the powder with a better colour. Winnowing is carried out as described for chocolate manufacture.

A typical analysis of cocoa powder is:

	%
Moisture	3·9
Fat	24·0
Nitrogenous Matter	18·0
Fibre	5·5
Ash	5·2
Starch	10·5

A pressure of 5–6000 lb/ft² leaves 20–28% cocoa butter in the powder against 10% left in cocoa butter production. In blending beans for cocoa powder it is preferable to use mainly the cheaper bulk type such as Accra or Nigerian and, if considered desirable, to incorporate 10–25% of the more expensive aroma beans to improve flavour; these are best added as liquor after alkalisation. Small traces (0·01%) of vanillin and cinnamon improve the overall flavour.

Various additives proposed include sucrose esters and tripolysodium phosphate [Y. NAKANISHI, *International Chocolate Review*, 1965, *20*, (4) 142–156], diosodium sulphosuccinate NS [*Canad. Fd. Ind.*, 1969, *40*, (10), 345] and alginate salts. It is claimed that these improve the dispersability and increase the wettability of the cocoa powder.

Cocoa powders are produced in 'Natural' or in 'Dutch' form (so named from the origin of the process). The latter involves the alkalisation of the cocoa powder prior to final grinding, to improve dispersability. It only slightly increases the solubility which ranges between 19–25% dependent on the conditions of production. Untreated cocoa powder has a pH of around 5·6 while that of the alkalised powder is nearer 7·1. Some medical claims have been made for the alkalised powder based on its less acid nature.

Roasting (see also §8.3)   Low roast treatment at about 85° C (184° F) gives a mild flavoured cocoa powder; high roasts should be carried out at 125° C (259° F). Small changes in roasting temperatures can give significant alterations both in flavour and colour.

Alkalisation   One to two per cent of various alkali salts should be added to the beans at a chosen stage (see Fig. 11): either to the raw bean (at Stage A); or to the unroasted nib (at Stage C with B omitted), or to the chocolate liquor (at Stage E).

The alkaline chemicals used are ammonia; potassium, sodium and ammonium carbonate; ammonium and sodium bicarbonate; or, on occasions, magnesium oxide. Potassium or sodium carbonate gives the best all round result.

Alkalisation prior to the removal of the shell will require a considerably higher quantity of alkali than when added at stage E, because some becomes absorbed by the shell. In general the principle is to add sufficient alkali to nearly neutralise the acid content.

The commonest method is to take the chocolate liquor produced after the initial grinding and to heat it up to 70°–80° C (158°–176° F). Sufficient 40% potassium carbonate solution is gradually added to produce an approximately 2% alkali/chocolate mix, which will then gradually thicken. This temperature is held for one to two hours, then raised to 110°–115° C (230°–239° F) to drive off the excess moisture.

A continuous system for roasting, winnowing, alkalising and roasting nibs has been developed by Dunford and Elliot Ltd. In this equipment a rotary louvre mixing system is used to alter air flow and temperatures, and roast temperatures.

Nib alkalisation produces a darker cocoa powder than that given by liquor alkalisation. The nib should be soaked in the alkaline solution, which is held in suitable non-corrosive vats, and then dried. Continuous plant has been devised which will alkalise, dry, and roast in automatic sequence.

Expeller cake can be alkalised to produce a low grade cocoa powder, identifiable by its larger particle size.

Grinding   Grinding may be carried out using granite rolls, roll refiners, or rotating and fixed steel disc pulverisers and micropulverisers. The most useful equipment is the disc pulveriser in which multiple revolving plates are used to produce low particle size.

The cocoa powder should be cooled to 20°–23° C (68°–74° F) immediately on discharge from the grinding unit. It is necessary to sieve the cocoa powder as there is a tendency to aggregate. Oversize granules should be returned to the grinding unit, the final powder all passing a 100 mesh sieve.

Quality   The quality of cocoa should be judged on a six point examination of (*a*) pH; (*b*) fat content; (*c*) moisture content; (*d*) particle size; (*e*) colour; and (*f*) flavour of the made up drink. The product should also be examined to determine bacteriological purity and freedom from moulds and yeasts.

Cocoa powder has a density of 1·39 and a specific heat of 0·38.

Storage   Cocoa powder can be stored in a paper, or similar inner lining, in tins or in sealed plastic bags, suitably at 18°–22° C and a relative humidity of 50–60%. It will take in only sufficient moisture to the equivalence of its own relative vapour pressure in relation to the air humidity. Mould will develop if it contains more than 4% moisture.

Cocoa powder which has been exposed to excessive heat is lighter in colour and has a speckled appearance.

8.8   MIXING/MELANGEUR PROCESS

The sugar, cocoa butter and cocoa liquor are brought together in a melangeur or similar equipment designed to produce a homogeneous chocolate mix. A melangeur (French; mixer) of traditional design consists of two vertically positioned rotating heavy rollers standing on a hardened, horizontal, heated bed. During loading, the melangeur should be heated to 40° C (104° F); the mixing operation is carried out at 50°–60° C (122°–140° F). The rollers are usually of granite or similar hard stone but frictional wear necessitates from time to time their dressing (refurbishing). The melangeur bed is normally constructed from planed cast iron and this too wears with use. Melangeurs should be fitted with effective covers to prevent excessive loss of flavouring components and to reduce any deterioration of the fat. The equipment must however be vented to permit the release of volatiles such as acetic acid from the chocolate mix. Mixing should not take longer than 20 to 25 minutes.

During the mixing process, there is little effect on the size of the cocoa particles but some breakdown of sugar crystals will occur. A better quality chocolate will be produced if the added sugar has previously been milled. This can be done on equipment such as the pin or stud disc mill in which the crystal sugar is passed between rotating high speed studded steel discs (e.g. KEK Mill, Alpine Killopex Mill). The full crushing effect of the rollers in a melangeur should not be applied at the commencement, but a gradual reduction made in the gap between the rollers and the bed throughout the mixing period.

Several alternative systems are available to melangeuring. In the Buhler mixer the input of raw materials and mixing process are automatically controlled and the roller action of a melangeur is replaced by a kneading action on the paste. The Contimixer is automatically controlled, using punch card inserts. Mixing times are short, 3 to 5 minutes, and a bank of mixers can be arranged to give a continuous flow of paste to the refiners. Bauermeister disc milling depends on the mixing effect achieved by passing a steady stream of sugar and cocoa nibs between a fixed and a rotating cone disc.

Vacuum kneading is sometimes suggested in place of the conventional melangeur process. Due to the loss of some of the minor flavouring components, this process is best restricted to the manufacture of milk chocolate. The heated paste is worked hot under vacuum conditions, moisture thus being drawn off, and the paste quickly becomes less viscous. A reduction in cocoa butter content can therefore be made and, because a higher proportion of undesirable volatiles are removed, conching time is reduced.

8.9   REFINING

Refining involves the crushing, abrasion, attrition and shearing of cocoa and sugar fragments to produce a product which has the desired particle size. Over-refining can be costly, the final size reduction taking considerable amounts of power. Power economy may be improved by feeding in paste which contains materials that have already been partly reduced in size. The variable factors in any refining process are the feed rate and the degree of reduction that is desired.

C. L. Hinton [12th Pennsylvanian Manufacturing Confectioners Association Conference, 1958] has claimed that the limit for the detection of particles by the tongue is 25 microns. Chocolate is usually composed of a mixture of particle sizes which can range from 3 to 100 microns; less than 10% of particles in well refined chocolate lie below 5 microns. Even a small proportion of large particles can produce a gritty effect on the palate. It is the distribution of particle sizes in a sample of chocolate which is more important for comparative purposes than an average size of the particles. During refining the particle size falls and the total surface area of the particles rises. Hinton (loc cit) has found that a reduction in size of the larger sugar crystals of the order of 20% produces an increase in surface area of around 40%. Table 41, taken from Hinton's paper, illustrates this effect.

TABLE 41.   Increase in Surface Area with Fall in Particle Size in Chocolate

Specific Surface Area cm²/gm	Particles above 12·5 microns %
8 700	44
12 000	35

Increases in surface area in chocolate particles require the addition of more cocoa butter to maintain the same flow properties. Comparisons between chocolate samples with similar compositions show that the smaller the particle size, the greater the viscosity. It follows that an increase in the amount of refining will inevitably change the behaviour of the chocolate for later stages in processing.

It is only during refining that any significant reduction in particle size occurs. A small reduction in the size of the sugar crystals takes place during melangeuring but very little, if any, change occurs during conching. The effect of varying the conditions for grinding has been examined by GROB [*Fette Seifen Anstr.*, 1961, *63*, (8), 729–36].

Chocolate for the United Kingdom or USA markets should be refined to an average particle size of between 20 to 30 microns. Continental tastes demand a lower size range of 15 to 22 microns. A chocolate containing particles of 35 to 40 microns or over in size will find little acceptance among consumers; conversely low particle size chocolates, under 15 microns, are clinging and generally unpleasant to the palate. Irregularities in the particle size of refined chocolate can usually be traced to variations in the setting along the length of the rolls of refiners, vibration occurring on the rolls, and worn or pitted rollers that have not received attention.

The simplest form of refining is by stone mills in which the nib is gravity-fed from hoppers on to horizontally positioned stone grinding wheels, often grooved to improve performance. During this crude grinding, the cocoa butter melts and the mix liquefies. A resting period for the liquor of 12 to 24 hours before refining will then greatly improve quality, as some of the astringent flavours will be lost, and this will reduce the time needed for conching. It is not necessary to grind milk crumb in a stone mill before refining.

The most widely used refining equipment is the 3 or 5 roller mill. Each roller operates at different speeds, arranged to cause the chocolate to flow from the lowest roll vertically upwards to the top roll. The lowest or feed roll is operated at the slowest speed. Each roll is adjustable for spacing, the evenness of compression being typically achieved using compressed air and floating the rolls on an oil bed. The spacing between the rolls does not directly relate to the size of particle produced particularly when comparing different refinery equipment. By the time the chocolate is discharged from the top roll it is travelling eight to ten times faster than it did on the feed roll. Greatest throughput is achieved with the lowest pressure setting, but particle size reduction is poor. The faster the speed setting, the more accurate should be compression ratios. The throughput of a modern refiner is around a half ton per hour. A low fat chocolate is faster to refine than a high fat chocolate. Processing speeds may therefore be increased by a partial pressing of the mix followed, after refining, by making up with additional cocoa butter.

The most efficient size-reduction occurs when the rolls are slightly concave, because inward flexing occurs and there is a natural tendency for the chocolate to flow towards the middle of the roll. Uneven wear occurs from this effect, hence it is necessary periodically to dress the rollers.

A considerable amount of frictional heat is generated—progressively with smaller particle sizes—during refining and an efficient internal water cooling system should operate within the grinding rollers. Uneven cooling can result in distortion of the rolls. Feed rate and temperature should be kept constant; the latter may be fixed within the range 20°–40° C (68°–104° F). Losses in chocolate flavour will occur if the refining temperatures are allowed to become excessively high.

An effective refiner should be fitted with overload cut out devices, temperature control and indicator equipment, independent and controlled speed settings and even-spread feeds. The hydraulically operated rolls should be capable of being finely adjusted for gap settings.

Refined chocolate should be removed from the top roll by accurately positioned scraper blades and discharged into containers or on to conveyor belts as fine, dry flakes. The powdery nature of the mix is due to the large increase in surface area that has taken place in comparison to the surface volume that is occupied by the fat. Increasing the extent of refining will give a chocolate with a lighter colour. Rises in refining costs do not however have a straight line relationship with the extent of particle size reduction: they become progressively steeper as smaller sizes are achieved.

Water-cooled ball mills may be used as an alternative to roll refiners: the particle size reduction is achieved by the grinding effect of entrapping chocolate between a mass of agitating chromium or ceramic balls. This principle operates in the 'Altriter' equipment in which the chocolate is placed into a grinding tank where a bar agitator revolving at 100–400 revolutions per minute stirs the chocolate. The pot contains, in addition to the stirrer, the balls used for grinding. Ball mill equipment can be used for batch processing or for continuous manufacture. In the continuous method, a stream of chocolate is pumped through a jacketed cylinder which contains the grinding balls, which are removed at the end of their travel by screening.

The size of the balls is important for the efficiency of grinding. Up to 80% of the mix volume should be composed of balls; these should be within a size range of $\frac{1}{8}$–$\frac{1}{4}$ in (0·3–0·6 cm). The grinding effect is achieved by the interplay between the balls, and not between the ball and the vessel wall. It is claimed that this form of grinding produces a superior size reduction, power economy in usage and reduced conching period (see §8.10).

The Drais-Schoko-Perl Mill consists of a vertical stainless steel cylinder in which grinding is effected by the agitation of a mixed size range of ceramic balls. Throughput is claimed as one ton/hour.

In the Wiener automatic process the sugar, cocoa liquor, milk powder and lecithin are mixed in an homogeniser unit and fed to a batch style agitator. Following screening, the chocolate is transferred to a further homogenising tank and passed through rollers operating in an atmosphere of hot humidified air. It is claimed that the product is smoother and finer, and occupies a smaller space than with roll refiners. Processing takes some 18 hours, during which the product is cycled eight to ten times.

A micrometer can be used to measure the particle size but the results only represent the size of the more irregularly shaped particles. Sedimentation and Coulter counter techniques give more precise information on the number and range of particle sizes present.

8.10   CONCHING

The process of conching is primarily one of flavour development, by removing the undesirable volatile acidic components remaining after fermentation and by the chemical changes that take place in the flavouring components in the chocolate mix.

Other secondary effects; are (a) the removal of moisture from the mix; (b) a smoothing of the sharp edges of the sugar crystals; (c) colour changes arising from fat emulsification and from a lowering of the fat globule size; (d) changes in viscosity of the mix; and (e) thorough mixing which, in particular, breaks up the aggregates of sugar and cocoa particles.

The different conches developed for use in chocolate manufacture are designed basically to produce an effective mixing action with maximum exposure to air, and are capable of operating over a lengthy period. One of the older and commonly used types is the longitudinal conche, with two, four or more pots to hold the chocolate; a granite, steel or iron bed; and roller unit for each pot. The paired rollers operate in a forward and backward action between the ends of the pot. Chocolate is forced forwards in front of the roller and eventually falls back over the top of the roller to return to the main central mass. This circulatory action is caused by the small clearance between the roller and end wall. Steam or hot water jackets initially heat up the equipment and the mix. The frictional heat generated during the process is usually sufficient to maintain the required temperature. During the operation of the conche the slapping sound, caused by the movement of the chocolate and the incorporation of air, changes character and this is indicative of the progress of conching. Over and under loading of the conche, or wrong mixing speeds, can result in poor processing.

The heat transfer and mixing characteristics of the longitudinal conche are not very efficient by modern standards, and there has been a gradual acceptance of dry conching, in which the internal friction, caused by working the mixture dry, results in temperature rises up to 55° C (131° F). The designs are such that the powerful mixing arms can cope with large batch sizes and still give maximum surface exposure to air. Effective ventilation systems remove the volatile acidic components and excess moisture. Most commercial equipment is designed for a three stage mixing—dry, semi-liquid and liquid. The product from refining is transferred to the conche and a small amount of cocoa butter added. Cooling should be given to remove excess frictional heat and the mixture conched till balling occurs. Selective additions of more cocoa butter should then be made until the whole of the recipe weight of fat has been added. As a crude rule, dry conching should be carried out for 12 hours followed by a 12 hour 'wet' conche period. At no time should the conche temperature used for milk chocolate rise above 60° C (140° F). Many types of conches produce a higher quality product if the cocoa butter is progressively added throughout the process.

The McIntyre unit (Low and Duff Equipment Ltd.) is a useful means of achieving low cost conching/refining for the cheaper chocolate mixes, particularly those containing substitute fats. Cocoa powder, icing sugar and the required fats are placed in the feed hopper of the unit. Heating and blending takes place and air is drawn through. The mix is circulated through a cylinder unit in which rotating cylinders press against spring loaded grinding bars to achieve the required particle size reduction. Processing is discontinued when the desired flavour and particle size range has been achieved. A McIntyre unit can be considered as reproducing the partial action of a rotary conche.

Rotary conching involves a whisking action of the mixer blades which permits effective exposure of the chocolate surface to the air. Higher temperatures can be used in this form of conching as the blades are designed to scrape the mix from equipment walls, thereby avoiding local over-heating and increasing the amount of air incorporated into the mix. In some versions the mixing blades are designed to achieve a partial throwing action akin to that obtained in the longitudinal conche. However it is the basic whipping motion that is instrumental in lowering processing times.

Variations on the more usual conching procedures include circulating bed systems in which chocolate is continuously pushed through heated piping by passage through turbines, and ultrasonic conching in which ultrasonic vibrators are used to develop an erratic motion in the chocolate so exposing new surfaces to the air. Two major developments in conching have recently occurred. The Cadbury system, being commercially exploited by Baker Perkins Limited, is a five stage process by continuous agitated flow through tubing. Cocoa butter and lecithin are added during the fourth flow stage. A process developed at the British Food Manufacturing Industries Research Association achieves complete roasting and conching within 30 minutes. The temperature during processing is maintained at 140°–160° C (284°–320° F) to achieve maximum flavour development.

During conching new surfaces are continuously exposed to air. Oxidation of the chemical components and caramelisation occur, and further development of the characteristic chocolate flavour. Gas chromatographic examination of chocolate concentrates before and following conching has shown that such changes occur [W. MOHR, 1958, *Fette, Seifen, Anstrl., 60*, 661–9]. In addition there is a further loss of the undesirable volatile acids developed at the fermentation stage. The figures in Table 42 are those obtained by Aasted [K. AASTED, 1941, *Studier over Concheringsprocessen,* 148 pp, Copenhagen].

TABLE 42.   Changes in Acid Content during Conching

Hours in Conche	Volatile Acid %	Total Acids %
0	0·089	0·67
24	0·079	0·61
48	0·071	0·51
72	0·058	0·42

(percentage figures are relative to cocoa mass)

As conching proceeds the mix thins due to the loss of moisture. This point is illustrated in Table 43 by the work of Spagnoli [G. SPAGNOLI, F. ROSI, 1958, *Scienza Alimentazione, 4*, (3–4), 123–8] on a chocolate coating which contained 1% of lecithin and was produced in a Lehmann Conche.

TABLE 43.   Changes in Chocolate during Conching

Hours	Temperature °C	Viscosity 40°C	Moisture Content %
23	64	284	0·55
49	64	280	0·40
74	64	256	0·37
75	67	154	0·30

The viscosity can be controlled by varying the stage at which cocoa butter is added, and the amount used. As a general rule one quarter of the lecithin should be added at the start of conching and the remainder towards the end of the conching period. Small amounts of sugar syrup can be added to control the viscosity of the chocolate mix during conching. Work carried out by Heiss [R. HEISS, 1957, *Süsswaren, 1*, (15), 640–4] has shown that the yield value and plastic viscosity diminishes during the first five hours of conching (see §1.9). When the value for moisture falls below 0·7%, Heiss could find no correlation with viscosity. In a later paper [R. HEISS, 1962, Pennsylvania Manufacturing Confectioners Association Conference] the same worker found that the apparent viscosity was lowest after five to six hours regardless of the type of conche. Viscosity effects are minimised with high fat chocolate. Milk chocolate thickens during conching due to chemical changes occurring in the milk protein. The fat content should be raised, to maintain the same viscosity, when the sugar content of the mix is increased. Lecithin in the chocolate during conching reduces the amount of cocoa butter required, probably by the added lecithin coating the sugar crystals, thereby reducing frictional drag. Both natural and added lecithin undergo some breakdown during conching.

The time needed to complete conching has been the subject of considerable debate. Below a 20 hour conventional conche period the process is considered uneconomic. Some manufacturers conche for 5 to 7 days to produce a high quality product. In milk chocolate comparatively little flavour development occurs through conching, but considerable improvement occurs with so called 'plain' or 'dark' chocolate. It is doubtful whether any further improvement will occur in milk chocolate after a 24 hour conche period. A 48 hour conche is necessary for plain chocolate; beyond that the palate of the average consumer is unlikely to detect additional improvement. It is therefore preferable to allocate the savings achieved by reducing the conche period to purchasing higher quality beans.

The temperature chosen for conching depends on the choice of bean and the process unit used. Milk chocolate contains a lower proportion of nib and should have a delicate flavour. It should therefore be conched at a lower temperature of between 45°–60° C (113°–140° F). Plain chocolate should be conched at between 55°–85° C (131°–185° F) for British taste and up to 100° C (212° F) for Continental tastes. Chocolate intended for a high temperature conche should be given a low temperature roast. Well roasted beans release less moisture during conching and this minimises the initial viscosity change. Mixes containing spray dried milk should be conched up to 5° C (9° F) higher than those containing roller dried milk.

8.11 THE TEMPERING OF CHOCOLATE

Tempering is a method of inducing cocoa butter to crystallise in a stable form in the fluid chocolate mass. This process is necessary to ensure a long shelf-life; incorrectly tempered chocolate has a short shelf-life, poor gloss and inadequate stability. A fault known as bloom can develop. This appears in two forms (a) the most common, which is the development of crystals of unstable fat on the surface of the chocolate and (b) which arises from sugar crystallisation on the surface of the product (this is not due to poor tempering). Fat bloom formation occurs more readily with plain chocolate than in milk chocolate. This is because of the presence of milk fat and milk phosphatides in the latter.

The handling of chocolate during tempering, enrobing and dipping is governed by a number of factors: (a) composition of the chocolate, (b) viscosity of the chocolate, (c) condition, type and composition of the centre being coated, (d) temperature of use and (e) state of temper. The composition of the chocolate has a significant effect on the handling properties of the material. In particular, the type and amount of fat has a major effect on the behaviour of the melted mass. The higher the content of cocoa butter, the thinner will be the chocolate, but the greater will be the risk of bloom formation. This thinning action can be achieved by the addition of lesser quantities of certain other materials of which lecithin is one. Cocoa butter is not the only fat suitable for use in chocolate and certain other substitute fats enhance stability. In certain countries chocolate, unless otherwise labelled, may only contain cocoa butter.

Chocolate normally contains approximately one per cent moisture; more results in the thickening of the melted mass and indirectly the greater use of the material during enrobing. A given viscosity, as already mentioned, implies a given sugar-to-fat ratio. The viscosity is important in that it can effect the amount of coating during enrobing and dipping as well as varying the depositing rate of the material. Finally, the particular size of both the sugar and cocoa mass affects the flow properties of the melted chocolate.

The condition, type and composition of the centres can have significant effects on the keeping quality of the enrobed confections. The centres should not be hotter than the enrobing temperature, and preferably somewhat cooler. Centres which are too hot cause loss of temper, while refrigerated centres give rise to bad enrobing. Certain centres can accelerate bloom formation. Nut centres can cause seepage of the nut oil into the enrobed casing causing bloom formation; wherever possible they should be sealed to reduce oil transfer.

The shape of centres can affect the amount of chocolate coverage, a factor often explaining variable usage rates for enrobing.

The 'state of temper' is the description of the amount of stable fat crystals in the melted chocolate. Vaeck [S. VAECK, 1955, *Zucker und Süsswaren*, 718, *Manuf. Conf.*, 1960, 35–74] has suggested that there are four different forms of crystallisation for cocoa butter in chocolate. Each form has a different melting point and these are, it is suggested, as follows:

Type of Crystal	°C	°F
α	23·5	74·5
β11	28·0	82·5
β1	33·0	91·5
β	34·5	94·0

Only the β form is stable and does not give rise to fat bloom formation. Duck [W. DUCK, 1964, Pennsylvanian Manufacturing Confectioners' Association Conference] found that in the commercial samples of chocolate he examined, the best result showed only a 50% content of stable β crystals. Tempering is therefore a method of achieving the crystallisation of cocoa butter in the stable β form. All the indications are that fat bloom is composed of other crystalline forms of cocoa butter held near or on the surface of the chocolate. During tempering there is a slow crystallisation of cocoa butter in the β form. This is achieved by tempering the chocolate at a temperature in which only stable cocoa butter can exist. Feuge [R. O. Feuge, U.S. Dept. of Agriculture] has found that the forced mechanical working of chocolate can result in the correct type of crystallisation of the cocoa butter. This is carried out by forcing the chocolate through narrow orifices at high pressures. The stages in the normal method for tempering chocolate are (1) complete melting; (2) crystallisation of cocoa butter; (3) removal of unstable seed.

Chocolate should first be heated to 48·8° C (120° F) (not more) in the holding kettle. At this temperature all the cocoa butter will become liquid; no further treatment should be undertaken until all the chocolate has melted. The melted chocolate should now be cooled to 26·6° C (80° F), when both stable and unstable forms of fat are crystallised. On reheating to 31°–32° C (88°–90° F), all the unstable crystals will remelt leaving the stable cocoa butter crystals to act as a seed. Subsequent crystallisation will occur predominantly in the stable β form. The final warming process must be carried out slowly to avoid local overheating. The melting kettle must be continuously and efficiently stirred, and the tempered chocolate is fed into the enrober. In many cases, using this batch method, the chocolate becomes too thick to use. A more satisfactory method is a process known as drip feeding.

Drip Feeding entails cooling untempered chocolate to about 36° C (96° F), and drip feeding into the enrober tank, where it becomes mixed with the tempered chocolate. The rate of feeding in should be synchronised to the rate of usage. This process, however, can cause a variation in the degree of temper, due to such factors as different rates of throughput of centres, plant breakdowns and stoppages.

AUTOMATIC CHOCOLATE TEMPERING

Automatic methods of tempering have largely replaced the batch and drip feed process. These fall into two main systems: (1) where the tempering device is built into the chocolate enrober, and (2) a separate tempering unit. Fig. 14 shows the former; this particular version is called a single stream continuous system.

The chocolate is circulated by pump A from tank B to flow pan C, the surplus returning to B. De-tempered chocolate is circulated from storage kettle J and metered by pump E through tempering tube D to the tank B. The quantity of chocolate in B is controlled by adjustable overflow F, the overflow chocolate being pumped by pump G back to storage. The chocolate in B is held in a tempered condition and acts as a 'seed bed'. The fresh chocolate from J is gently cooled by tempering tube D and is mixed with the tempered chocolate in B. The quantity in the holding tank B is varied according to the type of chocolate being used, and by continuously replac-

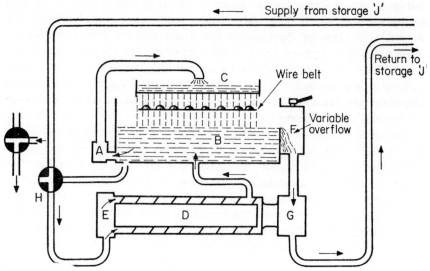

FIGURE 14. Single-stream continuous tempering and enrobing, of chocolate.

ing it with fresh chocolate at a constant temperature, independent of the rate it is being taken away by the product being coated.

An automatic by-pass H stops the flow from J during the initial tempering period, when the machine is first started-up and chocolate is drawn by pump E from B and returned to it via the tempering tube D. As the chocolate in B is tempered, H automatically returns to its normal running position.

For such a process, hot de-seeded chocolate is taken from a bulk storage ring main at 50° C (122° F) and is continuously pumped, metered at a pre-determined quantity, through a heat exchanger, where it is reduced in temperature to 28°–30° C (82°–86° F) by cooling water at approximately 13°–16° C (55°–61° F). This introduces a fast growing nuclei of tiny crystals in which are contained stable Beta prime, and a small amount of unstable alpha, crystals. The continuous agitated stream of freshly seeded chocolate enters the enrober reservoir with a constant and very fine crystal growth, due to precise metering and temperature control. This pattern of crystals is growing at relatively low temperature, so, to ensure adequate seeding times giving only the most stable Beta crystal form, the whole mass is raised in temperature in the reservoir up to 31°–32° C (88°–90° F), over a controlled time period. Beaters provide mixing action and any unstable Alpha crystals are melted out as the mass reaches 31°–32° C (88°–90° F), thus only the stable Beta crystals can form and are kept small in size by high speed mixing action. Since only heating is applied to the coater reservoir and coating control, no unstable crystals form, due to low temperature water (i.e. no riser pipe control cooling). The rate and amount of crystal growth in the coater reservoir is controlled by time, and the coating temperature automatically. The time period is determined by the type of chocolate being tempered and the coating temperature desired.

The 'time period' is accurately maintained by the overflow circulation principle, which ensures that by pumping a continuous stream of freshly tempered chocolate into the reservoir tank in a quantity in excess of that required for maximum product requirements, a continuous overflow of tempered chocolate is maintained at the overflow device built into the coater reservoir. The excess flow of chocolate from the reservoir is tempered chocolate and is returned to bulk storage for de-seeding. The 'time period' or changeover time fresh to well-tempered chocolate, therefore, remains constant, a 'state of equilibrium' is reached and maintained because the overflow is continuous (i.e. chocolate level in reservoir is accurately maintained).

The state of equilibrium is the balance of temper to viscosity and is related to the setting of accurate flow rates, temperature, time and agitation.

An overflow device controls the 'time period' of chocolate in the coater reservoir; varying levels can be selected (i.e. seeding or graining times) to suit any kind of chocolate since different couvertures require varying periods to induce the correct amount of the right size of stable crystals in the reservoir.

Coating temperature is determined by the amount of temper (seed or grain), since the coating temperature is proportional to the amount of crystal growth in the coating. It will be remembered that different couvertures require different seeding times. Therefore, coating temperatures will also vary slightly: 31°–31·5° C (87°–88° F) for milk chocolate, and 32°–33° C (90°–92° F) for plain chocolate, as general examples. Coatings at these temperatures give good clean coverage and good all round quality control. Tempering and coating temperatures are very precisely controlled by electronic resistance type indicator controllers.

The tempered chocolate is circulated from the coater reservoir by a pump independent of the tempering system. This gives maximum flexibility to the flow systems.

Due to the flexibility of the system for time, temperature and agitation, any type of chocolate may be tempered, continuously and accurately to any desired degree of temper (seed or grain). The accuracy over viscosity control can give from $1\frac{1}{2}$–2% saving in total chocolate usage.

Tempering tests show constant and repeatable cooling curves during runs of up to 144 hours duration (6 days) before re-heating is necessary. The large capacity enables high flow rates to be maintained enough to full coat at 70 ft/min.

Separate Tempering Unit

A typical unit is manufactured by Sollich; in this process a twin-steam circulation system is employed (Fig. 15). The enrober is fed with a considerably larger amount of freshly tempered chocolate than the actual requirement over the same period. The resulting excess is continuously returned to the circulation tempering unit, where half of the chocolate is heated up to approximately 40° C (104° F), so that it is freed again from any solidifying crystals. The remaining half of the chocolate is again immediately fed into the tempering unit, where it seeds the untempered chocolate with stable Beta crystals. When passing through the tempering unit, the complete chocolate mass, while being stirred constantly, is again cooled down to the required temperature and subsequently fed to the machine where it is to be used. This system is able to keep the chocolate mass in freshly tempered condition over an unlimited period, and also a constant viscosity is obtained. Twin-steam circulation tempering units can be used for feeding hollow goods, depositing plants and spraying plants.

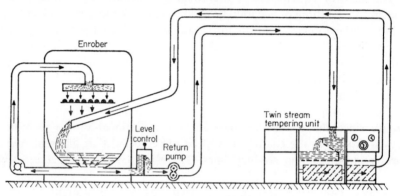

FIGURE 15. Sollich tempering unit feeding enrober.

The thickness of the chocolate coating on enrobed goods is dependent on a number of factors: (a) coating temperature; (b) flow properties of the chocolate; (c) degree of temper; (d) size of the centre; (e) amount of blow off air used; (f) band speed.

Too low a coating temperature may give rise to air bubbles within the coating. Ripples on the surfaces of the coated centres are produced if the blow off air blast is too strong.

The most accurate methods for measuring the flow properties of the chocolate are, naturally, those carried out under controlled conditions within a laboratory. There are four commonly available instruments for operation in the factory, which can be used to rapidly determine or indicate (with greater or lesser degrees of accuracy) the viscosity of chocolate. These are the *torsion wire viscometer*, the Redwood Cup, the *Koch viscometer* and the *Ferranti viscometer*. The torsion wire viscometer depends on measuring the angle of swing of a metal cylinder suspended in the chocolate while the Redwood Cup is based on the time taken for a fixed volume to flow through a standard orifice. The Koch viscometer is dependent on the time of fall of metal balls through the molten chocolate. The results so obtained can be converted into actual viscosity readings. The Ferranti instrument is the most expensive of the three types and is primarily intended for laboratory use. Measurement of the drag on a metal cylinder inserted in the chocolate is carried out electrically.

The other major item of scientific control instrumentation that has been introduced is the *temper meter*. A large amount of heat is evolved before cocoa butter changes from the liquid state to the crystal form. This evolution of heat can be followed by measuring the temperature change during cooling. Easton et al. [N. R. EASTON, D. J. KELLY, and L. R. BARTON, 1951, *Food Tech.*, 5, 521–3] investigated the cooling curves of both pure cocoa butter and chocolate. The method used was to remove sample tubes of material and measure the heat change against time over a 14° C temperature range. The plotted results indicated three phases: (*a*) an initial rapid temperature fall; (*b*) a slow fall, and even, under certain circumstances, a temperature rise; (*c*) a rapid drop.

The extent to which stage (*b*) occurs is related to the degree of temper. The Greer temper meter, described by Gardiner [J. GARDINER, 1960, *Manufacturing Confectioner*, 40, (5), 21–2], adapts this changing cooling rate at the second stage as a means of control. The equipment consists of a temperature-sensitive element, a recorder, an amplification unit and an ice bath. Chocolate is sampled into a tube which is then held in a cold bath. The cooling curve of the material is automatically recorded, which, on examination, indicates the degree of temper. A further system has been described by Duck [W. DUCK, 1963, 1964, Pennsylvanian Manufacturing Confectioners' Association Conference]. This method is dependent on the recording of viscosity changes shown by a Brookfield RVT viscometer. It is, at present, more suitable for laboratory use as opposed to the Greer temper meter, which can be used in both factory and laboratory.

Fat bloom can develop from the incorrect storage of the enrobed confections in heated conditions. Other causes of fat bloom are the use of centres which are too hot, the addition of fresh untempered cocoa butter, the use of incorrect enrobing temperatures and the use of the wrong type of substitute fats. The main cause of sugar bloom is the condensation of water on the surface of the chocolate. This can occur when the chocolates are too cold leaving the cooling tunnel, or by storage in humid conditions. Properly tempered chocolate takes longer to cool than badly tempered chocolate.

The cause of common faults arising during chocolate enrobing and means of overcoming them are listed in Table 44.

Use of Lecithin in Tempering (see also §4.10 and 4.11)

Commercial lecithin or its synthetic substitutes can be added to chocolate to improve its enrobing properties. The use of oilseed lecithins has three

TABLE 44.   Faults and their Prevention in Coverture Enrobing

Fault	Cause	Action to Prevent Recurrence
Fat bloom (grey or white patches).	Adding cocoa butter to the kettle.	Never add cocoa butter to the tempered chocolate.
	Incorrect enrobing temperature.	Enrobe at 90° F for plain and 88° F for milk.
	Not tempering the chocolate.	Melt the chocolate at 120° F, cool slowly to 80° F, raise to above limits.
	Failing to melt all the chocolate.	Ensure all the chocolate has melted before cooling to 80° F.
	Kettle stirrers not satisfactory.	There must be only a minimum space left between the stirrer and kettle side.
	Cooling the kettle too quickly.	Cool the chocolate slowly and steadily.
	Hot and cold spots in the kettle.	Take up with the kettle manufacturer.
	Being in the kettle too long without retempering.	Retemper after 3 hr, or if the temperature exceeds 92° F.
	Use of oily centres.	Avoid if possible particularly peanut and Brazil nut centres.
	Using a substitute fat.	Only use fats specially developed for chocolate work.
	Too rapid a cooling run.	Slow down the band speed.
	Severe chilling in the cooling tunnel.	Never allow the tunnel temperature to fall below 45° F.
	Poor storage conditions.	Store between 63°–68° F and a relative humidity between 40–50%, and away from walls and floors.
Sugar bloom (irregular crystals, reddish brown hue).	Handling with sweaty hands.	Wear gloves or finger stalls.
	Pack has been stored near heat.	Check on storage conditions in the warehouse and shops.
	Fluctuations in packing room condition.	Check if the packing room temperature is varying.
	Presence of air bubbles.	(1) Enrobing too cold.
		(2) The stirrers of the kettle are too slow.
	Chocolates have been over-chilled.	Never allow the tunnel temperature to fall below 45° F.

Fault	Cause	Remedy
Bursting, weeping.	Incomplete coating.	(1) Increase coating thickness. (2) Use a pre-bottomer.
	Cold centre expanding. Fermentation setting in. Not allowing the marzipan centre to mature before covering.	The centre should be at 75° F prior to coating. See under fermentation. Stand for 6 to 8 hr before coating.
Lack of smoothness, poor flavour.	Cocoa and sugar particles too large. Milk chocolate has been overheated.	Take up with the supplier or with the production department. Never allow the temperature to rise above 120° F.
Greasiness.	Badly tempered.	Temper by the method given under 'Bloom'.
Variable results.	Lack of a uniform tempering method. Poor rotation of stock.	Check on the method being used. Take up with the storekeeper.
Thickening of the chocolate	Being in the kettle too long. Excessive use of lecithin.	Retemper after 3 hr or use the drip feed method. 0·3% lecithin should be added during the manufacture of the chocolate.
Variations in the coating thickness.	Cocoa butter content varying. Band speed varying.	Take up with the supplier or the appropriate production department. Check on the speed of the band.
Ripples, wavy lines.	Using too fierce an air blast.	Alter the air speed.
Finger marking.	Do not allow the chocolates to be handled with the bare hands. Packing room temperature too high.	Use gloves or finger stalls both in the enrobing department and in the packing room. The packing room should [bet]ween 60°–65° F.

TABLE 44—contd.

Fault	Cause	Action to Prevent Recurrence
Marking.	Dropping off the enrober band on to trays.	Take off the band just before the chocolates reach the end.
Strong foreign odour or flavour.	The chocolate has picked up the odour or flavour from its surroundings.	Avoid storing the chocolates near anything with a strong odour.
Air bubbles.	Enrobing too cold.	Enrobe at 90° F. for plain chocolate and 88° F. for milk chocolate.
	The stirrers of the kettle are too slow.	Speed up the stirrers.
Poor gloss.	Worked at too low a temperature.	Enrobe at 90° F for plain chocolate and 88° F for milk chocolate.
	Using a poor quality paper wrapping.	Use foil wrapping.
	Overchilled chocolate.	Do not allow the tunnel temperature to go below 45° F.
Mould.	Humid storage conditions.	Store at 63°–68°F and a relative humidity of 40–50%.
	Imperfectly covered centre.	(1) Increase the coating thickness. (2) Use a pre-bottomer.
	Overchilled chocolate.	To avoid water condensation do not allow the tunnel temperature to fall below 45° F.

advantages: (a) it reduces viscosity, thereby enabling a lower level of cocoa butter to be used; (b) it lessens the danger of fat bloom developing; (c) it increases the range of temperatures that can be used in processing; (d) it improves the texture of the chocolate; (e) it reduces any increase in viscosity arising from moisture; and (f) it improves the snap of the chocolate.

It should be used at levels up to 0·5% and achieves savings of up to 4% cocoa butter. Nakanishi [Y. NAKANISHI, 1965, *Rev. Int. Choc.*, **20**, (4), 142–156; 1962, *New Food Industry (Japan)*, **4**, (4)] has suggested that sucrose esters have good viscosity reducing properties. More widely known are the sorbitan esters of the Span and Tween types (Span and Tween are registered trade marks of Honeywell-Atlas Ltd.). These have been investigated by Easton et al. [N. R. EASTON, D. J. KELLY, L. R. BARTON, S. T. CROSS, W. C. GRIFFIN, 1952, *Food Technology*, **6**, (1), 21–5] and have been found to have good bloom resistant properties and gloss retention. The suggested rate of addition of mixed polyoxyethylene (20) sorbitan monostearate (Tween 60) and sorbitan monostearate (Span 60) is one per cent. Other research on the use of additives in enrobing has been carried out by Alikonis and Farrell [J. J. ALIKONIS, T. FARRELL, 1951, *Food Technology*, **5**, (7), 288–90] and Du Ross and Knightly [J. W. DU ROSS, W. H. KNIGHTLY, 1966, *Confectionery Manufacture and Marketing*, 1966, 190–191, 226–237].

8.12   THE APPLICATION OF SPAN 60 AND TWEEN 60 IN SWEET DARK CHOCOLATE (see also §4.13)

Maximum gloss retention and bloom prevention in dark sweet chocolate can be achieved with a blend of Span 60® and Tween 60® emulsifiers, by closely following the steps described below.

Chocolate Production

Span 60/Tween 60 must be added to the chocolate at the batching stage in a 60/40 ratio to the extent of 1% based on total weight; and the chocolate containing the emulsifier blend must be properly tempered.

In view of the melting point of Span 60 (51° C or 124° F), the surfactant blend is most effectively added at the batching stage. The blend can be melted and added to a small portion of liquid cocoa butter, or it can be added directly to the batch, where sufficient heat is normally present to insure adequate dispersion of the Span 60.

The emulsified chocolate then goes through mixing, the refiners, and the conche. After spending the required time in the conche, viscosity should be checked and adjusted for that particular type of chocolate, with lecithin, cocoa butter, or a blend of the two. The emulsifier blend reduces interfacial tension of the cocoa particles in a similar manner to lecithin. It follows that the amount of lecithin also being added to the batch should be carefully controlled.

Span 60/Tween 60 are not, however, a replacement for lecithin, because their functions are different when added to chocolate, they form a mono-layer on the surface of the fat crystal that reduces the rate of crystallisation. This effect must be overcome in order for the fat to crystallise and develop temper. One of two methods may be followed, depending on plant practices and equipment; both are adaptable to tempering units producing bulk items as well as those used to enrobe the finest centres.

(i) *Batch Method.* The most effective way to temper batch chocolate is to add 1–3% (based on total weight) of finely ground seed that contains Span 60 and Tween 60 in the 60/40 blend. In this case the seed provides the nuclei for fat crystallisation. Stable fat crystals will develop in chocolate, in the same proportion they existed in the seed. That is, the more stable the seed, the more stable the chocolate. Hence the seed must be from chocolate containing 1% Span 60/Tween 60 blend, and finely ground to 90% through a 10 mesh screen.

The amount of seed added to the batch also affects in direct proportion the rate of fat crystallisation.

To temper chocolate in a line enrober, settings should be as follows:

Tempering State	*Maximum*	*Minimum*	*Preferred*
Enrober Feed	34° C (93° F)	33° C (91° F)	33° C (91° F)
Ist Cooling	31° C (88° F)	30° C (86° F)	30° C (86° F)
Seeding (1·3 % seed)	31° C (88° F)	30° C (86° F)	30° C (86° F)
(10–15 min crystallisation and viscosity increase, cut off determined visually or with Brookfield)			
Heating	34° C (93·5° F)	32° C (90° F)	33° C (91° F)
Unit Stabilisation Temperature	34° C (93·5° F)	32° C (90° F)	33° C (91° F)

To add seed, cool the chocolate in the kettle to 86° F and add 1–3% seed. Allow viscosity to build until a 'heavy mush', or 'heavy string' forms. Raise the temperature of the chocolate to 33° C (91° F). The chocolate can then be deposited in moulds, or used to enrobe centres, and run through a cooling tunnel. Tunnel temperature should be set 2°–5° cooler than normally used for dark chocolate.

(ii) *Continuous Tempering.* With a continuous tempering unit chocolate containing 1% Span 60/Tween 60 may be tempered without the use of seed, because the high heat transfer (high energy input) in the continuous unit induces fat nucleation. The unit should be set as follows:

Zone	Maximum	Minimum	Preferred
Unit Feed	37·7° C (100° F)	33·5° C (92° F)	35° C (95° F)
1	30° C (86° F)	28·5° C (83° F)	29·4° C (85° F)
2	28·5° C (83° F)	28° C (82° F)	28·5° C (83° F)
3	32° C (89° F)	31° C (88° F)	32° C (89° F)

After leaving the unit, the chocolate may be moulded and run through a cooling tunnel set at 1°–2° C (3°–5° F) cooler than temperatures normally used for a dark sweet chocolate. Where possible, the depositing temperatures should be 33°–33·5° C (91°–92° F).

8.13 MOULDING

The production of chocolate shells for subsequent filling can be achieved by spinning, or by inverting chocolate filled moulds. In the first method the shell is produced by a centrifugal effect on chocolate in a totally enclosed mould, while in the inversion method the excess chocolate is drained away under gravity. The production of chocolate shells by spinning is described under chocolate liqueurs (§8.18).

Filled bar production by inversion involves: (1) preheating of the moulds; (2) tempering of the chocolate; (3) depositing into the mould; (4) inversion; (5) removal of the excess chocolate by heated wipers; (6) filling; (7) bottoming (coating the remaining exposed face with chocolate); (8) ejection.

Stepped cooling is used between stages 4 and 7 to promote solidification. The time taken to produce the filled confections ranges between 15 and 45 minutes according to the type of plant and the shape being produced.

The working of the Bindler Grbr shell plant illustrates the operation of this type of equipment. Radiant heaters are used to raise the temperature of the mould before receiving its charge of chocolate. The chocolate is tempered in a Rasch unit and is deposited in the individual moulds by transfer through piston blocks and directional nozzles. As with all shell plant, the temperature of the chocolate and of the moulds is critical at this stage and should be controlled within ±1° C (2° F). The moulds are then passed over vibrators to remove any entrapped air, and rotated to produce the thin shell of chocolate. Wall thickness of $\frac{1}{16}$–$\frac{1}{8}$ in can be produced by this process. The moulds are then passed through stepped chilling units which produce slow cooling thereby preventing the cracking of the shells. Excess chocolate is removed by heated scraper blades. Following filling, resuction is used to give a consistent level of centre which may vary with changes in wall thickness.

Other shell plant is based on the inversion of the chocolate filled mould and the removal of the excess chocolate by draining. A controlled warming unit is used to improve the intermingling of the bottom coating with the chocolate shape. The most effective coverage is achieved by double enrobing using a low viscosity first coating, followed by a second coating with a more viscous enrobing chocolate. The first coating can be applied by spraying on chocolate using compressed air. Filled blocks can then be handled through conventional bottoming units. Effective demoulding of the filled shapes is linked to the careful control of temperature and humidity whilst the snap of the bars is closely related to effective tempering and the composition of the chocolate. Snap is poor if the moulds are used too cold.

The effect of tapping or vibrating the moulds has been investigated by D. W. BARTUSCH [*Int. Choc. Rev.*, 1962, *17*, 438], who found that shaking affected the flow properties of the chocolate and significantly reduced yield value. The viscosity that was achieved after shaking depended on the frequency and operating amplitude of the vibrating unit.

The moulds used for chocolate shell or block manufacture can be constructed in plastic (polycarbonate), stainless steel, or nickel deposited on copper. Plastic moulds are cheaper and less liable to deteriorate on store but take longer to cool due to their lower thermal expansion. Moulds represent a large capital investment and should not be overstocked. Only small changes in weight can be accommodated using conventional mould designs, and extensive variation in pack sizes should be avoided if mould stocks are to be kept low.

Small scale production of shell goods of the type such as Easter Eggs can be easily achieved provided sufficient moulds are held. The moulds should be warmed to 22° C (72° F), filled with a charge of tempered chocolate, rapidly tapped to remove any entrapped air, and inverted to produce a smooth coating of chocolate. They should be stood on racks to allow the chocolate to drain. A short cooling at 10° C (50° F) for 30 to 45 minutes is necessary to permit the chocolate to become sufficiently firm to allow its removal from the mould. One surface edge of the half shell should be melted on a warming plate to join the two halves together.

Choice of Filling

Three points must be observed when deriving a filling for a chocolate shell: (1) moisture content must be carefully controlled, so that there will be no loss following filling; (2) the viscosity of the filling must be low as it will be deposited at a low temperature; (3) solidification must take place quickly if effective handling is to be achieved.

Most types of sugar confections can be adapted for use as a centre filling. The only exceptions are those with high viscosities and with setting temperatures such as high boilings. Depositing temperatures can be lowered by reducing the moisture content though difficulties may arise from fermentation or from graining. The use of fructose or high dextrose equivalent glucose syrup is helpful in this context. High melting point fats can be used to increase the setting rate of the centres following depositing. The deliberate inducement of grain by the addition of prepared fondant will have a similar effect. Emulsifier addition using GMS (see §4.12) or lecithin YN (see §4.11) will greatly improve the handling properties of fat-containing fillings.

If the centre temperature is too hot, then the chocolate shell will melt. As a general guide, creams should be deposited at 50° C (122° F) while caramels will need a higher temperature of 60° C (140° F). During depositing the holding moulds must be kept sufficiently cool to preclude melting.

8.14   FAT MIGRATION

During the storage of chocolate coated items, the milk fat content of the covering will fall due to the migration of the fat into the centre. M. BARNET and E. C. WOOD [*J. Assoc. Public Analysts* 1969, *7*, 99–103] have shown that this can significantly affect the analytical constants reported for coating chocolate. Vegetable fats present in biscuit centres also migrate during storage but in the opposite direction thereby changing the fat composition of the chocolate couverature. The fat migration effect with chocolate coatings has previously been noted by E. KRACKHARDT [*Mitt.-B.G.D. Ch Fachgr. Lebensmitt Chem.* 1956, *10*, 148]. M. WOOLTON, D. WEEDON, and N. MUNK [*J. Sci. Fd. Agric.*, 1971, *22*, 184] believe that fat binding is due to a starch–fat interaction which is not specific to fat type.

8.15   STORAGE OF CHOCOLATE

Chocolate does not develop its full flavour immediately on manufacture; this may take up to 1 month for milk chocolate and 2 months for dark. Production geared to sales demand should be adjusted accordingly.

Chocolate should not be stacked directly on floors or against walls. The storage area should give adequate air circulation, conditions being held at 60% relative humidity and within the range 16°–18° C (61°–64° F). Properly tempered chocolate will then remain in good condition for at least 6 months. Lower storage temperature ranges of 8°–10° C (46°–50° F) have been proposed [J. KLEINERT, *Gordian*, 1968, *1619*, 393 6–9] as a means of extending shelf life but this necessitates more careful control of air humidity. The storage areas should be constructed with flat roofs carefully sealed against water penetration; during the summer, flooding the roofs with water will cool the store by evaporation.

Reduced Temperature Storage of Coated Confections

Production difficulties, caused through seasonal variations in demand, can be minimised by storing chocolate and confectionery products at low temperatures. Quick freezing techniques do not improve or change the properties of the stored chocolates or sweets but keep them in a good saleable condition prior to distribution.

Most of the research into cold storage of confections has been carried out in the USA. This has shown that not all products can be held under cold storage. Suitable confections however can have their shelf life extended from 2 to 3 months to upwards of 2 years.

Adverse factors in adopting cold storage are that costs are increased and that more floor space has to be found in the stock room. Certain confections show adverse effects when held under low temperatures. Chocolate coated hard centres crack when held in cold conditions. Confections which can successfully be held under cold store include starch jellies, turkish delight, caramels, fudges, nut bars, cream and french pastes and soft pan work. Each product must be adequately tested under proposed storage conditions before freeze techniques are adopted.

The confectionery packs should be wrapped in heat sealed moisture proof cellophane and then outer wrapped in sealed polythene liners. The cold store should be held at −10° to −12° C (10°–14° F). Suitably wrapped the packs can be brought directly into air at atmospheric temperature rather than being held for a period at an intermediate temperature. The packs should preferentially be of the single variety type. Cartons should not contain staples or any other metal fixings. These cartons should be stacked on pallets and it is essential that gaps should be left between the stacks and the walls and ceiling. The refrigerated room used must have an effective means of air circulation.

8.16 NUTRITIONAL VALUE OF CHOCOLATE

The nutritional value of chocolate has been investigated by R. A. McCANCE and E. M. WIDDOWSON [1967, *Composition of Foods*, HMSO, Special Report 297]. Their research has indicated the average calorific value of 100 g of plain and milk chocolate to be 544 and 588 respectively. The same workers list the nutritionally valuable elements as follows

	Plain	Milk
	mg/100 g	
Potassium	257	349
Sodium	143	275
Phosphorus	138	218
Magnesium	131	59
Calcium	63	246
Chlorine	5	170
Iron	3	2
Copper	0·8	0·5

Published research on the nutritional value of cocoa powder and chocolate has been reviewed by P. H. WIGGALL [1969, *Cocoa Growers Bulletin*, (*13*), 4–7].

8.17   BULK DELIVERIES OF CHOCOLATE

This can be advantageous in three ways because less storage space is required, handling costs are reduced, and chocolate is normally cheaper when delivered in bulk. Against these factors must be set the economic through-put level, the amount of money that will be tied up in raw material stocks, heating costs, and the initial costs for installation of the storage tanks.

The temperature for holding the liquid chocolate should be above the crystallisation point of the constituent fats. For most purposes, a suitable range will be 38°–43° C (100°–109° F). The tanks should be capable of being agitated to prevent the separation of the fat. Chocolate can be transported by passing through positive displacement pumps feeding into heated, jacketed pipes. Cleaning may conveniently be carried out by blowing a rubber plug through the piping system.

8.18   LIQUEUR CHOCOLATES

Two different types of liqueur chocolates may be produced depending on the choice of production method: *Crusted Liqueurs*, in which the liqueur syrup centre is held in a sugar shell that is then coated with chocolate; and *Crustless Liqueurs*, in which the liqueur syrup is held in a pre-formed chocolate shell. A crusted liqueur does not have the same eating quality as a crustless liqueur but has a longer storage life. The methods for preparation vary for the two types of liqueurs.

Crusted Liqueurs
(1) Prepare a high sugar-content syrup by dissolving two parts, by weight, of refined cane or beet sugar to one of water. Add 0·2% sodium citrate buffer.
(2) Concentrate the syrup to 74% solids by boiling to 108° C (226° F).
(3) Allow to cool and when below 70° C (158° F), add 10–20% liqueur or flavouring spirit, 0·25% gum arabic (dissolved in an equal weight of water) and a small amount of flavouring essence. Mix gently.
(4) Cover with anti-evaporation balls (see later).
(5) Remove portions of the prepared mix and deposit into preformed impressions made in moulding starch that is held at 32° C (90° F).
(6) Sprinkle a fine layer of starch over the filled impressions.
(7) Allow three hours to elapse and then gently invert the liqueur shape.

(8) Allow to stand for two days and then remove the liqueur shapes from the starch. Blow free of starch using a gentle stream of air.

(9) Double enrobe the formed shapes using a dark covering chocolate.

Crustless Liqueurs

The method for the preparation of crustless liqueurs is dependent on the choice of manufacturing plant. The procedure for the preparation of a syrup is similar to that described for crusted liqueurs except that the preferred composition is 40 parts cane or beet sugar, 20 parts high DE glucose syrup, 39·75 parts water, and 0·25 parts gum arabic (in an equal weight of water) boiled to 105° C (221° F) to which is added 10 parts liqueur and a trace of flavouring essence.

Commercial units for this process depend on injecting a predetermined weight of chocolate into moulded impressions. In the simplest type, the moulds are inverted on several occasions to produce adequate coverage of the walls by the chocolate, while in others the shells are spun in high speed rotary equipment to produce even chocolate coating. In the processes in which the chocolate shells are produced in two halves, they should be sealed by warming the connecting surfaces. Once liqueur syrup has been run into the chocolate shell, the moulds should be tapped to release any incorporated air. In the automatic methods, the chocolate shell, which has been released from its plastic mould, is filled by syrup injected through holes drilled in the surface. This hole is then filled with chocolate. Plant for the automatic production of chocolate liqueurs is available from equipment manufacturers Collmann Spezialmaschinenbau, Lübeck, Germany and Gunther and Waller, Pfaffikon ZH, Switzerland.

In the traditional procedure for the manufacture of crusted liqueurs described earlier, the liqueur shapes in starch can be produced on Mogul equipment (see §12.6) or in simple impressions pressed into filled starch trays. Depositing can be from hand held funnels, depositing troughs on movable trolleys, or mogul heads. Great care must be taken to avoid excessive vibration, which may cause the shock crystallisation of the syrup.

Syrup Preparation

This is the first stage in the manufacture of chocolate liqueurs. Sugar solids should be lower in a crustless liqueur syrup than for liqueur crusted confections. The prepared syrup should be held at 60°–70° C (140°–158° F) for crusted liqueurs and 16°–18° C (61°–64° F) for crustless liqueurs. During the mixing and holding period a significant evaporation of alcohol can take place, which can be considerably reduced by up to 90% by covering the mix with a carpet of non-absorbent plastic balls $\frac{3}{4}$–1 in diameter. This technique may be adapted in many confectionery processes to reduce both evaporation and heat losses; it was developed from one devised for fire suppression. A suitable type of covering ball is 'Allplas' (Capricorn Industrial Services, London).

The cooling of the liqueur syrup for crustless liqueurs can be carried out with an Asbach cooler in which it flows over a tubular cooling unit into a depositing trough. Providing the chilling process takes place quickly, crystallisation will not occur, due to the rapid rise in viscosity of the syrup.

The factors which affect sugar crystallisation in liqueurs are the same as those described elsewhere for fondants and creams. Significant factors for the prepared syrup are (i) degree of supersaturation; (ii) holding temperature; (iii) viscosity; (iv) composition; (v) mechanical treatment.

Moulding starch tends to act as an instant seed for crusted liqueur syrup, which commences to crystallise immediately on casting. A light covering of starch should always be sprinkled over the syrup deposit to induce crystallisation on the upper surface.

Liqueurs should be manufactured from pure white cane or beet sugar which has an ash content of less than 0·015% [A. BAUCKER, *International Chocolate Review*, 1954, *9*, (5), 134–6]. The solubility of sucrose is depressed by the presence of alcohol and this is shown by the figures reproduced in Table 45 which are based on the work of L. A. REBER [*J. Amer. Pharm. Ass.*, 1953, *XLII*, (4), 192–3].

TABLE 45.   Solubility of Sucrose in Solutions of Alcohol in Water

Alcohol % by weight	Solubility of Sucrose % by weight
0·0	67·1
8·6	65·2
15·8	62·2
24·9	58·1
33·5	52·9

According to Reber (loc cit) there is no demonstrable effect on the optical rotation of sucrose in solutions containing up to 50% w/w alcohol.

A simple type of liqueur can be prepared by dissolving flavouring materials in alcohol and adding a high sugar content syrup (66%) containing a small proportion of glycerine as a thickener and conditioner. Factory prepared liqueurs can also be produced by standing suitable base materials, fruit, etc. in alcohol prior to boosting the solids content by adding additional sugar. Legal opinion in the United Kingdom however is that it is reasonable to expect that genuine liqueur should be included in named liqueur chocolate varieties.

The usual means of expressing the alcoholic strength of liqueur is by its declared proof. Proof spirit weighs 12/13ths of the weight of an equal measure of distilled water at 10·6° C (51° F). A proof solution is one containing 57·1% v/v or 49·3% w/w alcohol. The difference in the degrees proof is the amount of distilled water needed to reduce to, or bring up to, proof strength (see Table 46). US practice is different from that adopted in Europe.

The flavouring agents present in liqueurs vary considerably from type to type. They are mainly fruits, herbs, spices, seeds and roots. Some chemical constants for common liqueurs are given in Table 47.

TABLE 46. Relation between Degrees Proof and Alcohol Content

Proof Degrees (UK)	Alcohol % by weight	Specific Gravity at 15·6°C
5	2·2	0·996
10	4·6	0·992
15	6·9	0·988
20	9·2	0·985
25	11·6	0·982

TABLE 47. Composition of Liqueurs and Spirits

Type	Specific Gravity	Alcohol % by vol.	Total Solids %	Sugar %	Acidity %
Benedictine	1·070	52·2	35·7	32·4	3·3
Chartreuse	1·080	43·2	36·4	34·7	1·7
Cherry Brandy	1·079	17·2	32·7	31·9	0·8
Curacao	1·032	54·4	29·1	29·0	0·1
Kummel	1·083	33·9	32·0	31·2	0·8
Port	1·045	21·4	6·0	4·4	1·6
Rum	0·940	49·1	0·4	0·2	0·2
Sherry	0·999	21·5	4·0	2·1	1·9

The pH of liqueurs lie mainly within the range 3·2 to 4·2 .

Liqueur Chocolate Characteristics

Chocolate Liqueurs are heavy by comparison to other confections. Reasonably sized individual chocolate liqueurs should weigh 8 to 15 g. Crustless liqueurs should consist of around 75% centre and 25% chocolate shell; the liquid contents comprising 50%–60% sugar and the equivalent of 10%–25% liqueur, of 5%–7% proof strength.

Crusted liqueurs may contain higher levels of alcohol, as the sugar shell has a better resistance to alcohol penetration. Eating characteristics are quite different for the two types. The crustless product is generally more enjoyed, but has a shorter shelf life and requires more expensive plant for its manufacture. The thickness of the sugar crystal wall varies considerably between individual crusted liqueurs and the evenness in crystal build up is dependent on operator skill in turning the formative shell. A typical crusted liqueur contains 25% sugar shell, 40% liqueur syrup and 35% chocolate coating. The alcohol content of the syrup varies between 10–14% proof spirit depending on the type of base material used.

Both crusted and crustless liqueur syrups increase in invert sugar content while on store. This arises from the acidic nature of the liqueur base. J. WURZIGER [*Gordian*, 1954, *13*, (1275), 9–10] found a rise in reducing sugar content from 6% after manufacture to 27% after storage. These changes result in a thinning of the syrup and additional sucrose from the sugar crust going into solution or being leeched from the chocolate.

Syrup seepage can occur with badly manufactured chocolate liqueurs. Small starlike clusters of sugar crystals develop on the surface. These clusters grow and eventually lead to the collapse of the confection. The use of gum arabic or cmc in liqueur syrup recipes is helpful in preventing the development of incrustation.

Collapsing may also arise through the transfer of sugar from the walls of crusted liqueurs to the base. Chocolate liqueurs contain in addition to the syrup centre, an air bubble. The movement of this air bubble during transport produces a mixing action which causes a more rapid take up of sugar into solution. Investigations by M. FLUGE and H. MEYER [*International Chocolate Review*, 1963, *18*, 150] have indicated that microorganisms are not responsible for collapsing.

Chocolate liqueurs should be packed into preformed plastic shells, and preferably individually foiled. While handling, the operatives should wear thin cotton gloves. Breakages during packing are most frequently caused by the sugar shell walls being too thin or uneven. They should be stored at 50–60% relative humidity and at 16°–18° C (61°–64° F), when they have a shelf life of three to four months. An absorbent liner inserted into the pack will improve storage performance. Crusted liqueurs have a longer shelf life than crustless liqueurs.

8.19 THE TROPICAL WAREHOUSE MOTH

This is the most troublesome pest which affects both chocolate and sugar confectionery products, the signs being webbing, excreta and larvae on the surface of the sweet. The life span of the larva is one month at 25° C (77° F) and 3 months at 20° C (68° F). Larvae are killed by prolonged holding at 40° C (104° F) and the processing times and temperatures used in sweet manufacture are sufficiently high to ensure that few, if any, larvae survive. Thus infestation nearly always occurs after manufacture, in the packaging or stock departments or at the wholesalers or retailers. Products containing nuts are particularly susceptible.

The moths emerge from their pupa casing in May to July and within a few days lay their eggs; one to two days later, the larvae leave the eggs and commence feeding. At the end of ten weeks a cocoon is spun and the larvae go into hibernation for the winter. (See also §3.11.)

9

Boiled Sweets

9.1 CHARACTERISTICS

The art in producing high-boiled sweets with satisfactory shelf life is manufacturing boilings which contain the minimum amount of residual moisture and a satisfactory balance between cane or beet sugar, and glucose syrup or invert sugar syrup.

The main physical change during the storage of high-boiled sweets is the formation of small crystals in the confection, usually referred to as graining, due to recrystallisation of sucrose. These spoil the appearance and cause an unpleasant roughness on the tongue.

For high-boiled sweets it is impossible, using the normal proportions of cane or beet sugar (sucrose) and glucose syrup, to obtain a product of 97% solids content, which is not supersaturated with respect to sucrose. In practice, however, one-and-a-half parts of sugar (sucrose) to one part of forty-two DE glucose syrup will produce a high-boiled sweet stable against graining.

High-boiled sweets are an example of a product in the 'glassy' state. In appearance they are solid, but they are supercooled, non-crystalline liquids, which are so far below their melting or softening point that they have assumed solid properties without crystallising. They can be considered as liquids with very high viscosities, a property which interferes very considerably with the process of crystal formation. For this, there must be a 'nucleus', that is a completely sub-microscopic crystal to act as a 'seed'. These nuclei are formed spontaneously if the supersaturation is sufficiently high, but the higher the viscosity the slower the rate at which they form. Molecules of the substance crystallising have to hit and stick to the nucleus, being brought to it by their continuous, very rapid movement; which however is very severely limited in a solid or in a liquid of extremely high viscosity. The transition point of boiled sweets has been investigated by W. DUCK [*Manuf. Conf.*, 1957, *37*, (8), 17–22].

However, if the supersaturation is sufficiently high, graining *can* take place, and this will occur if the level of 'doctoring' is too low (see §2.11, Table 8). When the boiling has been poured onto the slab and whilst it is being manipulated at a raised temperature, it is still extremely viscous. During the cooling period on the slab and the later manipulation an insufficiently doctored boiling will grain.

The solubility of carbohydrates increases as the temperature rises. The moisture remaining after boiling at atmospheric pressure means that the supersaturation with respect to sucrose is less than at the lower temperatures experienced during a vacuum boiling process. A higher proportion of 'doctor' must therefore be used with the latter.

Pulled high-boiled sweets, however, are an example of graining being induced to produce a particular texture. The mechanical action of pulling is used to beat in air and to produce very fine sucrose crystals, though in a much smaller number than in fondant. The amount of doctor is much higher than for fondant, and the viscosity is higher owing to the increased solids content: both factors combining to reduce the number of sucrose crystals formed.

The choice of the most suitable type of doctor, for example, glucose syrup or invert sugar, depends on several factors, the most important of these being the hygroscopic properties.

The equilibrium relative humidity of a high-boiled sweet is around 30% [J. W. GROVER, *J. Soc. Chem. Ind.*, 1947, *66*, 207] and as the normal humidity is nearly always well above this value, there is always a constant tendency for the sweets to absorb moisture.

The relative vapour pressure of a high-boiled sweet can be calculated using the Money-Born equation [*J. Sci. Food Agric.*, 1951, *2*, 180]. The storage behaviour of boiled sweets has been investigated by W. DUCK (loc cit) and by R. HEISS [*Food Tech.*, 1959, *13*, 433–439].

Where invert sugar is used as a doctor, the relative vapour pressure is lower than with 42 DE glucose syrup. Thus high-boiled sweets doctored with 42 DE glucose syrup will be less liable to moisture pick-up from the atmosphere than when invert is used—an important point in the relatively moist atmospheric conditions which apply in Europe and other areas of the world.

A high-boiled sweet containing 34% of invert sugar would be unacceptably hygroscopic: the difference between 34% invert sugar (unacceptable) and 34% DE glucose syrup solids (perfectly satisfactory) is too great to be explained solely by the difference between 23% and 28% relative vapour pressure. This difference is probably due to the ability of 42 DE glucose syrup to 'skin' when it is exposed to the air. In a high-boiled sweet the 42 DE glucose syrup component has probably imparted a 'skin' to the outer surface of the sweet, which greatly hinders the penetration of moisture into the sweet. The lower the moisture content of the sweet the greater this 'protective skin' action.

Another important factor is the viscosity of the glucose syrup to be used as 'doctor'. The viscosity of glucose syrup (at constant solids content) depends upon its chemical composition, and particularly upon the percentage of high carbohydrates present. At the high solids content of high-boiled sweets, the effect of the higher carbohydrates is very significant. Further, the viscosity of the boiling mass in the pan (and during its subsequent manipulation) can be significantly affected by quite small variations in the amount of higher carbohydrates present in the glucose syrup. In addition, this variation can significantly affect the 'break' of the sweet in the mouth, i.e. its brittleness and toughness.

The high viscosity of glucose syrups at very high solids contents greatly aids the crystal retarding action. Thus, solids concentrations of the order of 70–80% invert sugar and glucose syrups will have the same effect on the solubility of sucrose in very high viscosity and high solids content sugar confections (which are in reality supersaturated with respect to sucrose). The anti-graining action of glucose syrup is however much higher than that of invert sugar.

When a high-boiled sweet absorbs moisture it is initially only the surface which becomes moist. A very thin film of a solution with a solids content apreciably lower than that of the sweet itself is formed, the viscosity of which is very much lower than that of the sweet. In this film the inhibiting effect of high viscosities is much lower than in the body of the sweet, and this, in many cases, permits the crystallisation of sucrose to take place. A close examination will, frequently show that in stored, grained, high-boiled sweets the crystallisation of sucrose has started on the surface and has spread into the body of the sweet.

Additionally a much higher proportion of glucose syrup can be incorporated in a high-boiled sweet, as compared with the safe quantity of invert sugar. This results in any surface film being more highly 'doctored', and thus more resistant to 'graining'.

All these effects, particularly the resistance to moisture absorption imparted by it, make glucose syrup a more acceptable 'doctor' for use in high-boiled sweets.

Cane or beet sugar is the major constituent of high-boiled sweets and their manufacture calls for a grade of the highest quality in terms of freedom from colour, colour forming impurities and mineral salts (see §2.1). Glucose syrup is the second major constituent of high-boiled sweets. It is a clear syrup of non-crystallising character, composed of a mixture of carbohydrates. These are dextrose (glucose) and its higher homologues (extending normally to about dextrose polymer 15 max.).

Several types of glucose syrup are available for the manufacture of high boilings, varying in the extent to which they have been hydrolysised (see §2.3). The degree of hydrolysis is characterised by the 'dextrose equivalent' (DE). Low DE syrups (under 35 DE) contain a high proportion of high molecular weight constituents. In consequence a syrup of this type is viscous, with a low sweetness and moisture absorption. Conversely the high DE syrups (over 50 DE) which are available are low in viscosity, are sweet and, due to the simple sugars they contain, are fairly hygroscopic.

The type of glucose syrup normally offered for hard-boiled sweets is a 'regular conversion' at about 40 DE. Under certain circumstances (e.g. rock manufacture) a product at about 36 DE is sometimes used with advantage. Many new types of glucose syrup, produced by enzymic conversion are available with improvements over the traditional acid hydrolysed types. Of these enzymic converted products, the most suitable for high-boiled confections are the high maltose syrups. A comparison of the composition of two grades of glucose syrup is given in Table 48.

TABLE 48. Composition of Acid and Enzymic Converted Glucose Syrup

Type of Conversion	Acid (Traditional) %	Acid-enzyme (High Maltose) %
Dextrose Equivalent	42	43
Dextrose	18·5	5·9
Maltose	14·5	44·4
Maltotriose	12·0	12·7
Maltotetrose	10·0	3·3
Maltopentose	8·5	1·3
Maltohexose	6·5	1·5
Maltoheptose and higher	30·0	30·4

The acid/enzyme 'High Maltose' glucose syrup is characterised by a low dextrose content, a high maltose content and a low 'heptasaccharides and higher sugar content. 'High Maltose' glucose syrup is now being used for boiled sweet manufacture in many different countries, and the experience so far gained has indicated the following advantages as compared to the conventional acid converted glucose syrups used in the manufacture of high-boiled sweets:

(1) Owing to its lower 'high carbohydrate' content, the actual mass being boiled is 'freer' and less viscous than when traditional glucose syrup is used.

(2) For the same reason, the mass on the slab is also 'freer' and is easier to work. It does not form hard outside crusts so easily.

(3) The amount of air entrapped is less and any air that does become entrapped escapes more easily. This results in sweets which are of appreciably greater clarity.

(4) The sweets are more plastic during forming with better surface flow and have a much higher gloss and improved finished appearance.

(5) The sweets during storage do not become so sticky on the surface and in multi-coloured sweets there is less tendency for the colours to 'bleed'.
(6) There is less discoloration during the boiling process.

An interesting point concerning 'High Maltose' glucose syrup is that its boiling point elevation is somewhat lower than that of the traditional type. For this reason and to ensure sweets of the same solids content, the final temperature to which the boiling is taken should be reduced by about 1° C or 1·8° F.

It is essential that the glucose syrups used for hard boilings should not discolour too much during processing. This can be achieved by the addition of up to 450 ppm of sulphur dioxide (permitted under the UK Preservatives in Food Regulations 1962). Glucose syrup should not foam excessively during boiling and should preserve the glassy state of the confection during a shelf life of around six months.

Glucose syrups are quite viscous but can be conveniently delivered and stored in bulk if held at higher than ambient temperatures—45° C (113° F). They may also be purchased in a mixture with sugar and will thus be directly available for boiling without the necessity for premixing.

Flavouring can be provided by ingredients such as malt, butter, treacle, honey or fruit juices; but the flavours most commonly encountered are oils, either natural or synthetic, the amount needed varying considerably. Popular flavours are mint, lemon, orange; increasing use is also being made of peach, apricot and high strength flavours such as menthol, eucalyptus and thymol. Amounts required range from 1–12 oz/100 lb batch (60–750 g/100 kg). Flavours for use in high-boiled sweets must not be sensitive to heat degradation or to loss by volatilisation, and must have good stability during storage (see also §7.1–7.3).

Colours must be only those legally permitted; constant revision is required to fulfil the requirements of the home trade and export markets. Colour should be metered precisely in the sugar mass to obtain consistent results. Colour sticks or cubes are quite useful, provided that they are quick dissolving. Pastes prepared by mixing colours in solution with sorbitol, propylene glycol or glycerine can also find application (see also §7.42).

Acid flavours of four main types are used in high-boiled sweets: tartaric, citric, lactic and malic. Acids may also affect sweetness by causing inversion of the sucrose into invert sugar.

Citric acid is a tribasic acid with good solubility and is quite mild in taste. Tartaric acid has a sharper bite and should be used for acid drops. The use of lactic acid, nearly always in buffered form, is advisable in the production of deposited high-boiled sweets, because it can be held in a more highly concentrated solution. Greater clarity is usually possible with this acid and there is more control over inversion. Increasing use is being made of malic acid, which has a rounded flavour and can be used in smaller amounts than citric acid; it has a lower melting point and a more rapid dissolving rate. It is also said to help fix flavourings (see also §7·29–7.37).

Although cane or beet sugar and glucose syrup form over 97% of a high-boiled sweet, trace elements can have a significant effect on taste, properties and appearance. Sugar contains minute amounts of ash (less than 0·02–0·04%). Ash and any protein matter present can cause foaming and additionally the protein can react with reducing sugar to form coloured impurities. Water may also have a considerable effect on the quality of boiled sweets. Acidic water can cause inversion while alkaline water can lead to degradation of the sugar (sucrose) and thereby cause discoloration.

9.2 THE PRODUCTION OF HIGH-BOILED SWEETS

There are three main production methods for high-boiled sweets namely open pan, vacuum cookers and continuous cookers. Each of these requires a different ratio of sugar to glucose syrup, to give the best results. The ratios set out below are percentages. For example, a 70/30 mixture means 70 parts by weight of standard granulated sugar (always given first) mixed with 30 parts by weight of glucose syrup. The water requirement is 20 lb (2 gal) per 100 lb of total sugars (20 litres per 100 kg).

The following ratios indicate the varying usage of 'doctor':

Open pan	70/30 to 66·5/33·5
Vacuum Cookers	65/35 to 50/50
Continuous Cookers	60/40 to 45/55

The reason for the increasing glucose content is twofold. First, as the methods become more advanced, the amount of agitation to which the syrup is subjected is greatly increased, and, second, the amount of time for which the syrup is subjected to high temperatures is considerably reduced, lessening the danger of inversion (see §1.7).

The effects of different degrees of vacuum on the boiling point of cooked solutions, compared to the residual moisture content, is given in Table 49.

TABLE 49. Effect of Changing Operating Conditions on the Moisture Content of Boiled Sweets

Average Residual Moisture Content %	Inches of Vacuum		0	5	10	15	20	25
3·0	Boiling pt.	°C	149	142	135	125	112	92
		°F	(300)	(285)	(274)	(257)	(234)	(198)
2·0	Boiling pt.	°C	160	153	145	135	121	101
		°F	(320)	(307)	(293)	(275)	(250)	(213)

Using open pan cooking, there is a limit to the temperature to which the syrup can be boiled without a considerable discoloration taking place: approximately 156° C (315° F). For cooking using steam pans it is lower, at 149° C (300° F). The process of vacuum cooking is used to get over this difficulty, for, as the amount of vacuum increases, so the temperature at which the same total solid content is obtained is lowered. If the syrup is boiled to the same temperature, but under vacuum, there is an apparent rise in boiling temperature. If a standard sugar syrup is boiled under the same conditions to the same temperature, then the resulting boiling will have the same total solid content.

Open pan methods produce boilings with a total solids content of 95–96%, while using vacuum methods, the total solids are around 98%, and occasionally as high as 99%. The less moisture left in the sweets, i.e. the higher the total solids content, the greater the shelf life of the products.

With a vacuum cooker, it is important that the stirring of the boiled syrup should be discontinued as soon as the correct temperature has been reached, otherwise graining may be caused. In continuous cookers, to get constant results, there must be a standard syrup, a fixed pump stroke and a constant steam pressure. It is also most important that the pre-cook temperature (usually between 110°–115° C (230°–239° F), should be fixed and rigidly adhered to if a consistent product is to be obtained. In this low temperature range, a difference of only 1° F can mean a loss of 1% moisture, while in the higher temperature ranges, 1° F only means a loss of an additional 0·1% moisture. It is for this reason that a syrup takes so long to boil from 104°–115° C (220°–240° F), and yet rises quickly from 127°–138° C (260°–280° F). Differences in the syrup moisture entering the cooker will mean differences in the syrup viscosity, and this will affect the pump stroke on a continuous cooker.

9.3   CHEMICAL CHANGES DURING BOILING

There are two main types of reactions which occur and the first takes place in three stages.

(1) Sucrose (cane or beet sugar), is changed into Dextrose and Fructosan; (2) The Dextrose is then changed into Dextrosan and water; (3) The Dextrosan and Fructosan then recombine to form Isosaccharosan.

This reaction is complicated by the formation of side products, such as dileavodextrosan and dihetrofractosan.

The second type of reaction is the formation, at high temperatures, of breakdown products such as formaldehyde and hydroxymethylfurfural which cause discoloration of the syrup.

As stated earlier the product of a sugar boiling is a glass, which is a super-cooled liquid. The molecules in the glass are rigidly bound with the same forces as would be found in a crystal, but they are in a more disordered state. When the glass is in an atmosphere of high relative humidity, the surface changes to a liquid.

9.4   INVERT SUGAR IN HIGH-BOILED SWEETS

Sweets containing no glucose syrup can be manufactured either by using a sugar/invert sugar syrup mix, or, more traditionally, by relying on the inversion taking place during boiling. In either case, the boilings will go sticky unless the humidity conditions are very favourable, good protective packing is used, or there is only a very short delay between production and retail sale. Inversion during boiling can be induced by adding an acid salt, such as cream of tartar to the recipe. There is very little control over the quantity of invert sugar produced by this method, external factors influencing the rate of inversion. Variations in boiling times can be caused through irregular steam pressure, gas supply, coke quality, external atmospheric conditions, batch loading, etc. A batch may be produced which is completely satisfactory while the next one may be 'greasy' or 'too fat' (over-inverted).

9.5   BATCH COOKING

Batch cooking of high-boiled sugar mass can be undertaken using the cooker shown in Fig. 16(a), manufactured by Otto-Hansel. The cooking pan 2 is steam jacketed and fitted with stirrers driven by a fully enclosed

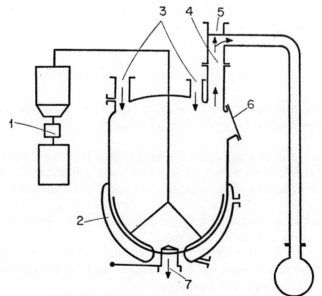

FIGURE 16(a). Otto Hansel sugar cooker.

motor 1. Raw material enters at openings 3 in the upper part of the kettle. Vapour generated during cooking escapes by pipe 4 and is controlled by a flap 5. Vacuum can also be applied via these valves. The manhole 6 provides visual inspection during cooking. The cooked mass is emptied through bottom valve 7. The capacity is 300 kg (660 lb) per hour and batch sizes are 100 kg (220 lb).

9.6 BATCH TYPE EARLY VACUUM PROCESS

Fig. 16(b) shows an early type of system. The unit consists of two steam jacketed boiling pans, in between which is the vacuum holding chamber. The procedure is as follows:

(1) Sugar and water are dissolved in the boiling pan.
(2) When the temperature reaches 110° C (230° F), the glucose syrup is added.
(3) Boiling is continued until the temperature attains 129° C (265° F).
(4) The cooked solution is then sucked into the vacuum chamber.
(5) Cooking is then continued under vacuum until a temperature of about 149° C (300° F) is reached.
(6) The finished cooked mass can then be drawn off at the bottom valve.
(7) In the meantime, a batch in the second boiling pan should have reached the required temperature and be ready for vacuum treatment.

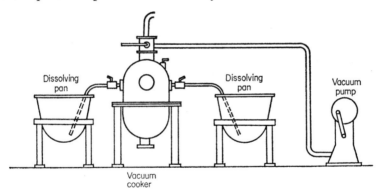

FIGURE 16(b). Early vacuum cooker design.

9.7 RECIPES FOR HIGH-BOILED CONFECTIONS

ATMOSPHERIC PRODUCED HIGH-BOILED SWEET
(using open pan—or forced gas fire)

	Parts by weight
Sugar	12
Water	4
36 DE glucose syrup	5

Method

1. Dissolve sugar in water and bring to boil.
2. Add glucose syrup.
3. Boil as rapidly as possible to 154° C (310° F).
4. Pour on to an oiled slab fitted with retaining bars.
5. Add acid (fruit flavour), colour and flavour.
6. Turn in until uniform in temperature and of the required plastic consistency.
7. Shape as required—for example through drop roller or batch roller and dies.

BUTTERSCOTCH

	Parts by weight
Sugar	50·0
36 DE Glucose Syrup	12·5
Water	15·0
Butter	2·0
Salt	0·12
Oil of lemon	0·12

Method

1. Dissolve sugar in water bring to boil.
2. Add glucose syrup.
3. Boil to 295° F (146° C).
4. Add the butter in small pieces.
5. Add oil of lemon and salt.
6. Pour onto an oiled cooling slab.
7. Whilst still plastic apply a frame cutter.
8. Wrap as soon as possible preferably in waxed paper or waxed foil.

HIGH-BOILED BUTTER BATCH

	Parts by weight
Brown Sugar	100·0
42 DE Glucose Syrup	60·0
Water	30·0
Butter Fat	10·0
Salt	1·0
Lecithin	0·12

Method

1. Dissolve sugar in water, add glucose syrup.
2. Add butter, salt and lecithin, pre-cook to 110° C (230° F).
3. Transfer to vacuum cooker reservoir fitted with a stirrer.
4. Cook in vacuum cooker at a temperature of 127° C (260° F) using a vacuum of 25 in, or equivalent ratios of temperature and vacuum.
5. Pour onto the cooling slab and process as required.

CINDER TOFFEE

	Parts by weight
Sugar	20
Water	6
36 DE Glucose Syrup	8
Bicarbonate of Soda	0·25

Method
1. Dissolve sugar in water, bring to boil.
2. Add glucose syrup.
3. Boil rapidly to 145° C (293° F).
4. Sieve bicarbonate of soda in to cooked batch and stir in quickly.
5. The volume of the mass will increase rapidly.
6. Pour onto a well dusted slab and level to equal thickness.
7. Cut with frame cutter whilst batch is still soft.
8. Wrap or enrobe with chocolate immediately.

EDINBURGH ROCK

Although most types of boiled sweets are produced ungrained, sugar crystallisation is deliberately induced in Edinburgh Rock. A recipe for this confection is given below.

	Parts by weight
Sugar	50·0
42 DE Glucose Syrup	12·5
Water	15·0
Citric Acid	0·5
Colour and Flavour to Taste	

Method
1. Dissolve sugar in water boil to 100° C (212° F).
2. Add glucose syrup.
3. Boil to a temperature of 135° C (275° F).
4. Pour onto a cooling slab.
5. Add acid colour and flavour.
6. Turn in the batch until uniform in temperature.
7. Place on a pulling machine until light and spongy.
8. Using a batch roller pull out to the required diameter. Allow for some shrinkage.
9. Cut to required lengths.
10. Place the sticks on dusted trays in a stove maintained at 33° C (100° F) for 48 hours until the typical grained creamy texture is obtained.
11. Wrap preferably in waxed paper.

Note: To speed up the development of graining, finely powdered icing sugar 0·5 lb/kg may be added at stage (5).

9.8   LETTERED OR 'SEASIDE' ROCK

The production of lettered rock still involves the art of the sugar confectioner, being a process which can only be completed using hand methods (Figures 17–20). Apart from inscriptions, many designs are possible, including flowers and figures.

A sugar/glucose syrup (36–38 DE) mix in the ratio of two to one with a boiling temperature of 146° C (295° F) should be prepared. A batch of 56–112 lb (or 25–50 kg) is convenient for manipulation on the slab. After boiling to the required temperature, the batch is poured on to a slab and flavoured (usually with peppermint). About two-thirds of the batch is removed and pulled. Of the remainder, sufficient is coloured deep red, to form the letters, and the remaining portion coloured pink to form the outer skin; the suitable dimensions are shown in the diagram.

Pulling can be achieved by hand which involves doubling, pulling and stretching over a hook mounted on a wall bracket, about 5 ft from the floor; machines are available. This has the effect of incorporating air, which considerably increases the bulk and modifies the texture. Pulling is completed when the mass is still plastic enough for formation.

Formation of the Letters (Figures 17–20)

A is formed with two equal strips of deep red (1 and 2) and a narrower strip (3). A piece of pulled white is shaped as a V and put on top of strip No. 3. Another piece of white is shaped to form the white section under the V and put under No. 3. Taper to point and place pieces 1 and 2 on each side.

For B there is one broad strip of deep red to form the upright of the letter and two narrow strips to form the two loops. Lay round pieces of white on Nos 2 and 3 and shape them as if the B was resting on a vertical base. Place on top of No. 1.

Only one oblong piece of deep red is required for the letter C. Roll a piece of pulled white and place in the middle of the red. (Make sure that the edges do not meet.)

D is a simple letter. There is one piece of deep red for the upright leg, another for the round back, and one roll of pulled white for the inside filling of the letter.

E requires one piece of deep red for its upright leg and three other pieces of less depth for the three branches. The branches are filled in with two rolls of white and the whole is shaped into a neat oblong.

F is almost the same as E, but is minus the bottom branch of deep red. Again form as neat oblong.

G is much like the letter C but has a little tail added.

H requires two large pieces of deep red for the two upright legs and one

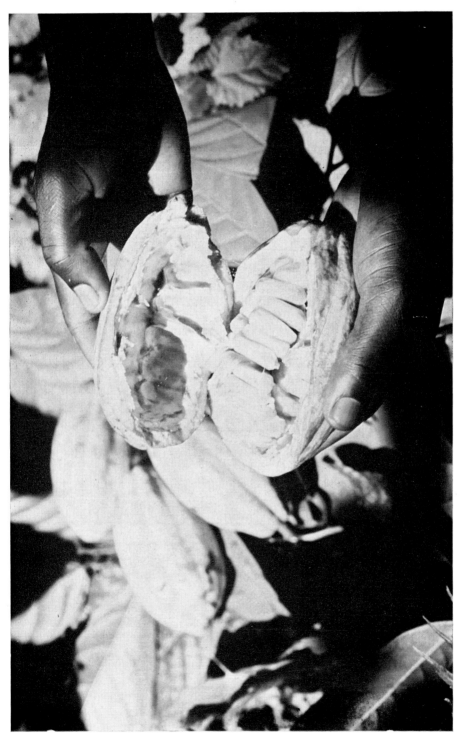

Plate 1   Split cocoa pod showing beans

Plate 2   Ter Braak Coolmix

Plate 3   Baker Perkins continuous microfilm cooker

Plate 4   Baker Perkins multi high-boiled sweet depositor

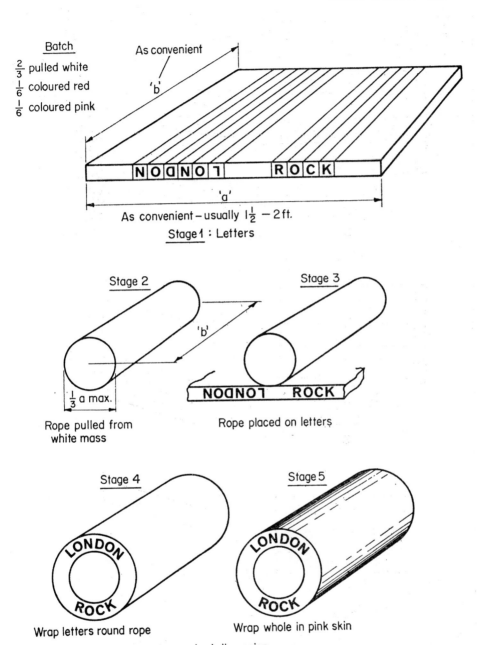

Batch
$\frac{2}{3}$ pulled white
$\frac{1}{6}$ coloured red
$\frac{1}{6}$ coloured pink

As convenient

'b'

NOᗡNOⰀ   ROCK

'a'

As convenient – usually $1\frac{1}{2}$ – 2 ft.

Stage 1 : Letters

Stage 2

'b'

$\frac{1}{3}$ a max.

Rope pulled from
white mass

Stage 3

NOᗡNOⰀ   ROCK

Rope placed on letters

Stage 4

LONDON
ROCK

Wrap letters round rope

Stage 5

LONDON
ROCK

Wrap whole in pink skin

Roll out to required dimension

FIGURE 17. Formation of lettered 'rock'.

G

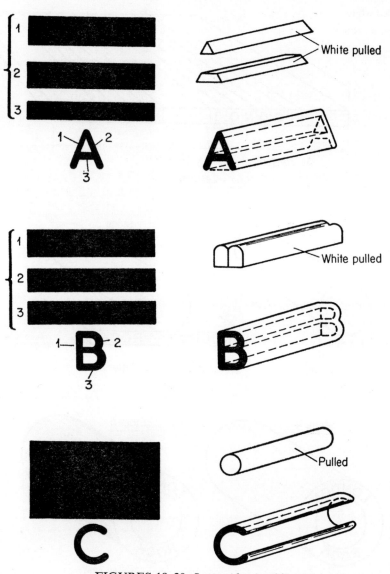

FIGURES 18–20. Letters for 'rock'.

piece for the centre cross piece. The centre piece is topped and bottomed with white and the two uprights put on either side.

I only requires one piece of dark red to stand upright. It is preferable if the dark red is supported on each side with a layer of white.

J is almost a twin of I. It has to be made longer to allow for the half loop. Shape a piece of pulled white and loop red round the base.

K requires one large piece of deep red for the upright leg and two other pieces for the sloping branches. Form two V-shaped pieces of white, add the branches, and fill in with pulled white in centre.

L has one upright leg and a smaller piece to branch off at the base. Fill in with a neat oblong of white. Another method is to make the full letter with one piece shaped and bent over a steel bar.

M has two upright legs and two pieces to form a V shape to be placed between the upright. Fill in with white and form into a square.

N needs three deep red pieces and two pieces of V shaped white. The sloping piece connects the upright at opposite ends.

O In one piece of deep red place one round roll of white. Allow the letter to flatten a little and thus form itself into an oval.

P has an upright and a loop which is filled with white. This letter requires neat sloping.

Q follows the letter O, with the addition of a tail on its base. Make sure the tail juts out on one side.

R again the outline is self-explanatory; there is an upright, a sloped half-leg, and a top loop, all filled in with white.

S one large piece of deep red. Roll two pieces of white of equal size and place one on each side of the red. By being placed on the reversed side and not allowing the edges of red to meet the letter will be formed.

T is an upright leg and a top crosspiece, filled in with white.

U requires only one piece of deep red. Fill in with one round of white and flatten slightly on either side.

V has two pieces of deep red. Shape letter V piece of white and lay on the two pieces of red. Taper to a fine point and fill in with white.

W requires four deep red pieces. Form two V shaped parts. Join them with V shape pulled part going up to centre of the two Vs.

X can be formed by making the letter V big enough to divide. Place top and bottom with white pulled to fill in each side.

Y: form V with two pieces of deep red. Place on a half upright and fill in with white on each side.

Z: of the three pieces of dark red required, the sloped piece is a little longer than the other two. Fill in with white.

After formation of the letters to form a name, they are laid side by side. (If to be read centrally, they will need to be laid out upside down.) They are divided by a strip of pulled sugar between each, and the whole line is then wrapped around the pulled sugar mass to form a cylinder and the outside covered with the pink colour sugar skin. The whole mass can be pulled out by hand or placed in a batch roller and spun out to a continuous rope and cut to required stick lengths.

9.9   CONTINUOUS DISSOLVING METHODS

Fig. 21 shows a sequence diagram of a Theegarten 01 continuous dissolver, which will produce a hot pre-mix suitable for feeding to a cooker. Crystalline sugar is fed by metering worm (1) into the dissolving chamber (2). Water is introduced into the dissolving chamber by a metering pump (3). The solutions flow over the heating surface plates (4) and (5), after which glucose syrup is metered in by pump (6). The mixed solution is then subjected to further surface heating and holding in heated vessels (7) and (8), flowing over into a holding tank (9), ready for pumping to the cooker. The ingredient flow through the machine is in a turbulent stream producing

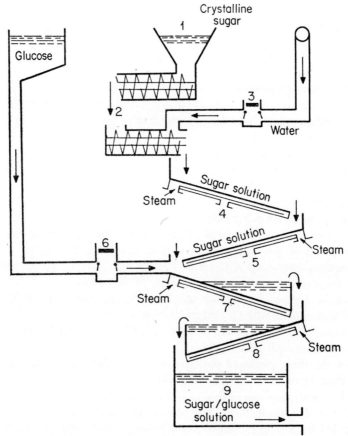

FIGURE 21. Theegarten 01 continuous dissolver.

internal blending. The output of such a machine is about 10 000 kg or 22 000 lb of pre-cooked syrup per eight hour day.

A recent development in continuous dissolving is the Autobatch, (Confectionery Developments Ltd). Using a fixed 50 kg (110 lb) batch, a particular blend may be chosen from a range by throwing a selector switch. The required amount of water, sugar and glucose syrup and any other additives is then metered into the top chamber by weight. The solution is transferred to the dissolver, where it is circulated until the required temperature is reached. Circulation is continued until the holding tank reaches the predetermined capacity, whereupon the pre-cooked solution is transferred by integral pump. During the dissolving cycle a further batch is under preparation, thereby providing a continuous supply of pre-cooked solution.

The Ter-Braak Coolmix (Photo 2) is a method of producing a slurry at ambient temperature. This machine will handle up to two dry and six liquid raw materials, which will be accurately weighed automatically into batches of 135–180 kg (300–400 lb). These batches are mixed for a predetermined variable period and discharged automatically to a holding container, which can be used to feed a ring main for supply to more than two take-off points. A low level probe in the holding container is used to send a signal to the control panel to start the weighing cycle.

Providing the circulating pump is kept in operation, there is no necessity to empty the system over the week-end or even over a longer period. This machine is capable of supplying pre-mixes for other types of confectionery as well as high boilings. Using dissolving units, it is possible to have 'on tap' a constant supply of mixed raw materials held at ambient temperature, with little risk of discoloration or inversion.

It is also possible to have a machine operating in the same manner with heating units in the holding tank thereby enabling a pre-cooked solution to be obtained.

9.10 Continuous Cooking Methods

The *Microfilm cooker* (Fig. 22) was designed some thirty-five years ago by Baker Perkins Ltd. It is a continuous cooker which both cooks and discharges continuously, an essential point in any automated production process. The cooker is essentially a scraped film evaporator and consists of a vertical jacketed cylinder into which is fitted a high speed rotor. Down the centre of the cooker is a shaft, supported in bearings at the top and bottom and on this shaft are fitted five flanges. A series of rods, about 5 mm in diameter, pass through holes at the outer edge of these flanges, and extend from the top flange to the bottom flange, supported at each end, thus forming a cylindrical cage. On each rod and between each pair of flanges is a hinged blade with a series of notches along the blade tip.

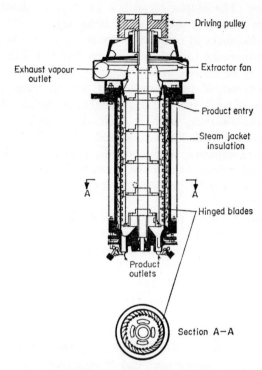

FIGURE 22. Microfilm cooker.

When the cage rotates (the shaft being driven by vee belts on the pulley shown at the top of the cooker), the tips of the hinged blades are thrown outwards by centrifugal force and make contact with the inner wall of the cylinder.

Sugar/glucose syrup solution is introduced continuously at the top of the cooker, just above the topmost blades and is immediately spread in a film around the inner surface of the jacketed cylinder. The force of the blade tips is just sufficient to penetrate the film and to reach the inside of the tube.

As a result of gravity and the special form of the blade tips, the sugar is cooked in a turbulent film about 1 mm thick.

This heat exchanger has an overall heat transfer coefficient of 195 cal/cm^2/hr/$^\circ$ C (400 Btu/ft^2/hr/$^\circ$ F). The other important feature is that the syrup takes only about 8 sec to pass through, hence it remains clear and white, not discoloured by prolonged heat.

A fan, at the top of the cooker between the vee rope pulley and the cooking cylinder, extracts the water vapour from the centre of the cylinder. Holes in the rotating flanges support the blades through which the vapour can pass.

Fig. 23 shows the moisture content compared to temperature when using the microfilm cooker for sugar-glucose syrup solutions.

The *Candy Maker* plant is well-known in the continuous production of high-boiled sweets. A continuous microfilm cooker is employed, and continuous mixing in of granular acid, colour and flavour is achieved by a rotating cone at the bottom of which is a short cylindrical section, the whole being not unlike an enlarged funnel.

The cooked solution is dropped on to the rim of the rotating cone and spreads as a film on to the sloping inner surface. Powdered acid or any other granular material falls on to the surface of the sugar, together with the liquid flavouring, and as the film of sugar with the acid and flavouring on its surface falls through the bottom cylindrical section, it assumes the shape of a tube with the acid and flavouring imprisoned on the inside. The tube stretches as it falls with increasing velocity and collapses as it hits the spreading-chute underneath. It is claimed that this method of flavour

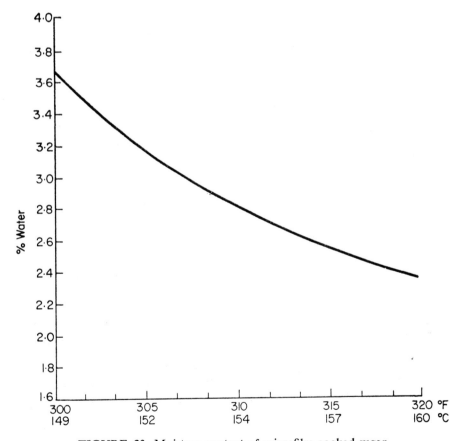

FIGURE 23. Moisture content of microfilm cooked sugar.

incorporation can save as much as one-third of the weight of flavour used, with such volatile flavours as peppermint.

After the sugar mass leaves the mixing unit, it has to be cooled to prevent over-inversion, particularly with an acidulated product. The rate of cooling depends upon the final moisture content of the sugar, and its thickness, and it is achieved by conduction. The sugar falls on to a steel band about 1 mm thick, and the heat is removed by water spraying on to the underside.

It is not possible to cool sugar uniformly through its depth, and it is first essential to remove heat through the bottom surface which results in a skin forming. This must be hard enough to allow the sheet of sugar to be lifted off the band without sticking, but not too hard, otherwise the sugar will fracture.

The sheet varies in temperature and, therefore, plasticity, throughout its thickness, but it must pass to the plastic forming equipment in a uniform state throughout; non-uniformity in plasticity causes most breakdowns on forming plants. This is achieved by rolling the sheet of sugar into a rope, like the coil of a watch spring, bringing the colder under surface of sugar into contact with the hotter and more liquid upper surface and thus equalising the temperature of the mass.

The steel band is divided into two cooling zones, the first zone for controlling the initial cooling in sheet form up to the plough which rolls the sheet into a rope, the second controlling the final condition, before the forming machine.

The lower the final residual moisture content, the more rapidly the sugar cools to the required plastic state. This effect is primarily due to the fact that lower residual moisture, produces a substantial increase in the viscosity of the cooked sugar mass. Given the same degree of inversion, low-boiled sugar requires more cooling to reach a similar plastic state.

By controlling the thickness of the sugar and the cooling water temperature, the sugar can be tempered to the ideal plasticity.

There is an ideal thickness for cooling sugar on a steel band. Below this thickness the sugar becomes more difficult to remove from the band and above it the varying temperature through the depth of the sugar becomes a problem, in that, at the desired final mean temperature, the sugar in contact with the band will be hard and brittle, whilst the surface remains liquid.

Air bubbles in the cooled sugar, which appear as lines in the final formed sweet, have not been eliminated on the candy maker. However, by altering the diameter of the tube of sugar falling from the mixing cone in relationship to the output, and other small adjustments, the air bubbles can be kept to a minimum and are certainly less than those incorporated during the batch kneading process, where the sugar is in a more plastic stage.

Candy makers are built in pairs so that both plants can be looked after by one operator. They can also be obtained with various take-off positions for the rope of sugar: Fig. 24 shows a typical layout feeding three forming plants.

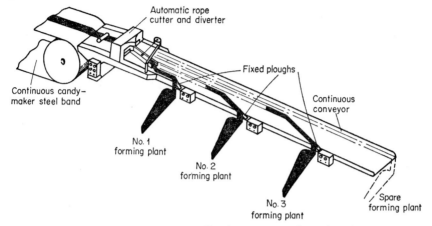

FIGURE 24. Take-off points on a candy maker.

9.11 CONTINUOUS VACUUM COOKING

By cooking under continuous vacuum conditions, the cooked sugar can be discharged at a lower temperature—for example at a vacuum of 10 in (25 cm) of mercury, the boiling temperature is reduced by 20° F (11° C). A first stage cooker can also be added to increase the capacity. The moisture evaporated from the syrup is removed from the cooker through a pipe connected to the condenser of the vacuum pump. At the base of the cooking chamber, an outlet is fitted with sight glasses, through which the stream of sugar can be observed. At this point, buffered lactic and citric acid, colours and certain flavours can be added continuously. A discharge pump extracts the cooked sugar continuously via a connecting pipe. The sugar is discharged continuously into the hopper of the depositor or into a rotary mixing unit (as used on Baker Perkins 'Continuous Candy Maker' plants). Fig. 25 shows this principle in diagram form, see also Photo 3.

The vacuumised microfilm cooker has the following advantages: (1) continuous discharge; (2) cooks rapidly in a film; (3) low process inversion giving a very clear syrup; (4) a very wide range of recipes can be dealt with; (5) maximum glucose syrup can be incorporated. It may be necessary to increase the amount of glucose syrup in the recipe when using this type of cooker.

Operation of a Typical Continuously Working Vacuum Cooker

In the Otto Hansel vacuum cooker, called the Sucromat (Fig. 26), the sugar and glucose syrup are pre-cooked to 110° C (230° F). The feeding pump 1 forces the pre-cooked solution through the cooking coil 2 into the steam zone B1, where it is cooked to 120°–144° C (248°–291° F). The solution then leaves the cooking coil 3 and the steam is flashed off in zone B2, the vapour passing out at 14. The separated cooked solution flows into vacuum chamber B3 by way of a regulated needle valve 5. The solution is sprayed into the vacuum chamber B3, in such a manner to secure maximum surface area, hence efficient separation of water from the sugar mass. After cooking a predetermined amount, the foot pedal 10 is actuated and valve 5 closed, and vacuum valve 7 opened, permitting a rise to atmospheric pressure in the vacuum chamber B3. Thereby, kettle 11 is released from the seating, and by the weight of cooked sugar inside, swings through 180°, to allow empty kettle 12 to seal itself automatically to surface 9. After completion of this movement, vacuum valve 7 is closed, and valve 5 opened, by actuating the foot pedal 10. Once a batch size has been determined, it will remain constant, irrespective of whether the cooker operates at maximum or minimum capacity. It is only necessary to actuate the foot pedal for all operations to follow automatically. The capacity of this cooker is 400–1200 kg (880–2640 lb) cooked sugar mass per hour, the batch sizes are adjustable between 20 and 40 kg (44 and 88 lb).

After cooking, the boiling is discharged, not onto a rotary cooling table, but uncooled into a depositor or on to water-cooled steel bands. This is to achieve a uniform plastic state at the delivery point into batch rollers, etc. Using this equipment it is possible to produce a finished sheet of flavoured, coloured and acidulated sugar for continuous frame cutting.

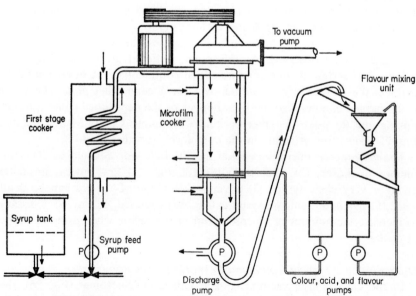

FIGURE 25. Baker Perkins continuous candy maker unit.

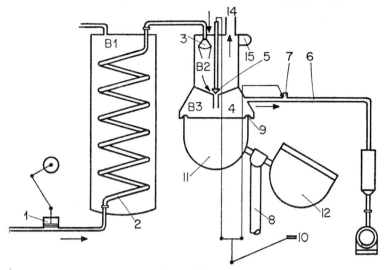

FIGURE 26. Otto Hansel Sucromat vacuum cooker.

BOILED SWEETS:

PRE-MIXED SOLUTION FOR VACUUM PROCESS

	Parts by weight
Sugar	240
Water	80
42 DE Glucose Syrup	160

Method

1. Dissolve sugar in water.
2. Add glucose syrup.
3. Pre-heat to 82° C (180° F).
4. Transfer to cooker and pre-heat to 110° C (230° F) before cooking.

PRE-MIXED SOLUTION FOR CONTINUOUS PROCESS

	Parts by weight
Sugar	200
Water	70
42 DE Glucose Syrup	160

Method

As described for vacuum process.

These solutions can be prepared by automatic dissolvers using the sugar-glucose syrup ratios shown above, (up to 15% of recovered scrap syrup can be added to this recipe).

9.12 DEPOSITED HIGH-BOILED SWEETS

Deposited sweets have several advantages over traditional produced high-boiled sweets. The deposited process (Fig. 27) can save up to 60% in

labour costs, compared to the traditional batch method. The sweets produced by the deposited method have a very much higher degree of clarity
and are more uniform in size and shape. This factor of uniformity is of
great importance, particularly with regard to high speed wrapping machines.
Sweets produced by the deposited method normally contain a slightly higher
residual moisture content. The residual moisture content is usually about
the 3% level, which means the sweets should be wrapped as soon as
possible after depositing. Because the metal moulds are usually lubricated
with edible oil, some stickiness is prevented and the absorption of moisture
is reduced.

Buffered lactic acid is used because it contributes less additional moisture
after cooking. It contains the equivalent of 80% lactic acid. The highest
concentration of other acids in solution would be approximately 58% by
weight. For example, if 1·6% acid is required in the finished sweet (2% of
80% lactic acid), then the lactic acid introduces less moisture than the same
equivalent amount of other acid solutions. A claim is also made for
enhanced clarity when using buffered lactic acid, due to the high solubility
of calcium lactate compared to that of calcium citrate or tartrate. This is
because water used for manufacturing purposes usually contains small
amounts of calcium salts.

TYPICAL RECIPE FOR A DEPOSITED HIGH-BOILED SWEET

	Parts by weight
Sugar	120
High Maltose Glucose Syrup (42 DE grade)	90
Water	30

Method
1. Prepare the solution by batch or continuous methods.
2. Pre-cook the prepared syrup to 110° C (230° F).
3. Pass through a continuous cooker (the setting suitable for a continuous
   vacuum microfilm cooker would be 140° C (285° F) and a vacuum of
   10 in Hg (234) mm).
4. Add buffered lactic acid at a rate of 32 fl oz per 100 lb (2000 cm³ per
   100 kg).
5. Flavour, depending upon type of confection, at the approximate rate
   of 3 fl oz per 100 lb (190 cm³ per 100 kg).
6. Colour at the approximate rate of 3 gm per 100 lb.
7. Deposit into metal moulds using a suitable machine, such as the CD
   Multi Depositor (Photo 4).

The range of high-boiled sweets can be extended by the use of different
colours and flavours and also by means of design, such as stripping and
pulling. The size and shape also add to other possible variations. By far
the most influence on variety is the introduction of a centre. The most

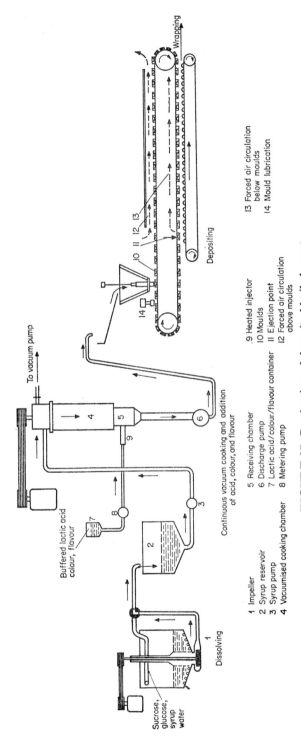

FIGURE 27. Production of deposited boiled sweets.

1 Impeller
2 Syrup reservoir
3 Syrup pump
4 Vacuumised cooking chamber

5 Receiving chamber
6 Discharge pump
7 Lactic acid/colour/flavour container
8 Metering pump

9 Heated injector
10 Moulds
11 Ejection point
12 Forced air circulation
   above moulds

13 Forced air circulation
   below moulds
14 Mould lubrication

common method was box filling, but this requires a degree of skill by experienced staff, who are not always available. To overcome these difficulties, the pump filling centre machine was introduced. These machines are capable of pumping quite viscous fillings with proper control.

9.13   PUMP FILLING

The injection of various centres into a high-boiled syrup casing calls for close control over the range of possible viscosities. Centres which can be pumped range from low viscosity materials, such as jelly solutions and jam to caramel and coconut pastes which have high viscosities. The following factors should be considered as essential when operating centre fillers.

(a) Preparation of the Centre

The centre should be manufactured using a constant temperature control in relationship to the temperature of the boiled syrup casings. The temperature of the centre should be maintained between 60° C (140° F) minimum, and 82° C (180° F) maximum at the time of injection. If the centre is hotter than 82° C (180° F) it may cause the filler tube to stick to the inside of the boiled syrup casing. A cold centre will prevent the sealing of the boiled syrup mass at the ends. The centre filler hopper and pipes should always be pre-heated to 82° C (180° F) before operation commences. All centres should be of smooth texture and when using jam type material, they should be sieved to remove seeds or pips. Lecithin can be added to centres containing fat to help prevent separation.

JAM CENTRE

	Parts by weight
Sugar	50
Glucose Syrup, (42 DE grade)	45
Apple Pulp	50
Colour, Flavour	To taste

Method
1. Boil the apple pulp in an open pan for ten minutes.
2. Add sugar and glucose syrup, boil to 113° C (235° F) for pump filling, 123° C (254° F) for hand filling.
3. Mix in colour and flavour, pour into suitable holding containers.

CARAMEL CENTRE

	Parts by weight
Brown Sugar	100
Glucose Syrup (42 DE grade)	70
Condensed Milk	70
Hardened Palm Kernel Oil	23
Invert Syrup	47
Lecithin	0·2

Method
1. Load a pan, which is steam heated and fitted with stirrers, with all the ingredients and pre-mix for twenty minutes.
2. Boil to a temperature of 110° C (230° F) for pump filling and 125° C (257° F) for hand filling.

TREACLE PASTE CENTRE

	Parts by weight
Brown Sugar	120
Glucose Syrup (42 DE grade)	100
Hardened Palm Kernel Oil	30
Condensed Milk	45
Treacle	20
Salt	1
Lecithin	0·25

Method
1. Load all ingredients into a steam heated boiling pan fitted with stirrers, with the exception of the treacle.
2. Boil to a temperature of 110° C (230° F).
3. Add treacle and raise temperature again to 110° C (230° F).
4. Transfer to cooling slabs.

LIQUORICE PASTE CENTRE

	Parts by weight
Glucose Syrup (42 DE grade)	100
Brown Sugar	66
Salt	0·20
Block Liquorice Juice	8
Aniseed Oil	0·20

Method
1. Load into a steam heated pan, fitted with stirrers, glucose syrup, brown sugar and sufficient water to dissolve.
2. Boil to 124° C (255° F).
3. Add block liquorice juice dissolved in 8 lb/kg water and mix in.
4. Add salt and aniseed oil and mix in.
5. Transfer to cooling slab.

9.14 POWDER FILLING

In addition to fluid centres, it is possible to produce high-boiled sweets which contain a powdered centre. This can be achieved by traditional hand methods using a box filler or by using specially designed powder filling machines. These machines contain a continuous screw feed held inside a tube, with a hopper at one end and the other open end feeding into the hollow sugar mass.

SHERBET CENTRE

	Parts by weight
Icing Sugar	50
Bicarbonate of Soda	4
Tartaric Acid	5
Lemon Oil	0·1

Method
1. Sieve together and mix.
2. Pre-heat before use to 60° C (140° F).

SHERBET CENTRE
(containing Dextrose Monohydrate)

	Parts by weight
Dextrose Monohydrate	100
Bicarbonate of Soda	3·5
Tartaric Acid	4·5
Lemon Oil	0·2

Method
1. Sieve together and mix.
2. Do not pre-heat before use. Keep temperature below 60° C (140° F).

TABLE 50.   High-boiled Sweets – Faults and their Prevention

Fault	Cause	Action to Prevent Recurrence
Graining.	Sugar balance incorrect.	Use at following relative weights (sugar to glucose syrup): Open pan 70 to 30; Vacuum cookers 65 to 35; Continuous cookers 60 to 40
	Vacuum kettle not clean.	Clean before use.
	Adding scrap which has already a slight grain through standing in damp cooker section.	Either reprocess or boil up for cheap clearing lines.
	Inadequate dissolving of the sugar.	All the sugar must be dissolved before going under vacuum.
	The sweets are damp before wrapping.	Wrap at 32° C (90° F) if possible.
	The steam from the cookers is causing a slight stickiness which subsequently causes graining.	Shield the cooker section from the rest of the production machinery.
	Standing too long before packing.	Pack as quickly as possible.
	Addition of powdered flavours (seeds the grain).	With flavours like menthol, dissolve in alcohol, propylene, glycol, etc.
	Leaving the stirrers on after the boiling has been completed.	Switch off the stirrers as soon as the boil has been completed.

TABLE 50—*contd.*

Fault	Cause	Action to Prevent Recurrence
Dull finish, poor gloss.	Too slow cooking.	Use less water for making sugar syrup.
	Batch warmer too hot.	Cool before using.
	Table too hot.	Allow the table to cool down.
	Excessive pulling of the batch.	In subsequent batches do not pull to the same extent.
	Pulling a batch which is too hot.	Allow the batch to cool down more next time.
	Rollers and forming equipment too hot.	Allow to cool before continuing to use.
	Poor syrup colour.	Check glucose syrup colour. Add small amount of blue to the clear batches as a 'whitener'.
	Poor packing.	Pack in sealed tins or jars at 32° C (90° F).
	Folding the batch too much.	Only fold as much as required.
Stickiness.	Using natural flavours high in acid.	Use synthetic flavours.
	Batch cooking too slowly.	Try to shorten boiling times.
	Too much water added at the syrup stage.	Use 2·5 parts of water to every 10 parts of total sugars.
	Using a weak sugar.	Use only standard grade sugar.
	Using cream of tartar and having varying boiling times.	Use if possible a glucose syrup sugar boil at the following rates (wt. sugar to wt. glucose syrup): Open pan 70 to 30 Vacuum cooker 65 to 35 Continuous cooker 60 to 40 Ensure constant steam pressure and batch size.
	Adding the acid while the boil is hot.	Never add the acid to the pan.
	Cooking acid scrap.	Reprocess the scrap neutralising the acid with bicarbonate of soda. Then add this syrup at rates up to 10% per batch.
	Atmospheric conditions at the factory.	Pack the sweets while hot into tins to await wrapping. Wrap at 32° C (90° F). Pack as soon as possible.
	Conditions in retail shops and stores.	Have the traveller explain the ideal storage conditions for sweets.
	The cooking temperature or vacuum is too low.	Increase the cooking temperature and vacuum.
Varying acid content.	Batch weights varying.	Check the weight the operator is taking from the cooker.

TABLE 50—contd.

Fault	Cause	Action to Prevent Recurrence
	Acid not properly mixed in.	Check the mixing technique.
	The acid weight is incorrect.	Check the scales on which the acid is weighed.
Lack of flavour.	Batch weights varying.	Check the weight the operator is taking from the cooker.
	The flavour has been added while the boil is very hot and has evaporated.	Add at a time which ensures that the machine can still handle the batch but when the first heat has dissipated.
	The wrong type of flavour is being used.	Check with the suppliers that the flavour is suitable for use in high boilings.
Speckling.	Speckling caused by cube colours containing insoluble matter.	Check by dissolving a cube in hot water and filtering. If this is the cause, inform the supplier.
	Adding the powdered colours directly to the batch.	Always dissolve in a minimum amount of water.
Air pockets in pulled work.	Excessive pulling.	Do not pull to the same extent next time.
Cracked sweets.	Dies too cold.	Warm the dies slightly.
	Boiling higher than machines will handle.	Reduce boiling temperature.
Dark sweet.	Holding batch too long.	Use as quickly as possible.
	Varying steam pressure.	Ensure a constant steam pressure.
	Heating the batch too high.	The upper limit is 156° C (315° F), (149° C (300° F) steam cooking).
	Leaving the syrup in pan after cooking.	Get the batch out of the pan as quickly as possible.
The batch is lumpy.	Leaving batch too long.	Do not allow the work to pile up.
	Folded incorrectly.	Always fold the cold side inwards.
Batch sticking in machines.	Dirty rollers.	Keep the rollers clean.
	Rollers too warm.	Do not overheat. Lightly lubricate with cocoa butter if necessary.
	Dirty dies.	Keep the dies clean. Lubricate lightly with cocoa butter if necessary.
	Poor mixing of the acid.	The acid must be adequately mixed in.

10

Caramels, Toffees and Fudge

Caramels and toffees are produced by blending glucose syrup, refined and/ or brown sugar, milk solids (usually in the form of full cream condensed milk), fats and salt. The mix is then concentrated to a high total solids content. Differences between caramels and toffees lie normally in the amount of residual moisture left in the confection and in the amount of fat incorporated. Both products can be prepared by the traditional batch procedure or in the newer continuous production equipment.

CARAMEL: GOOD QUALITY

	Parts by weight
Glucose Syrup (42 DE grade)	170
Full Cream Condensed Milk	140
Brown Sugar	115
Hardened Palm Kernel Oil	45
Butterfat	30
Salt	3
Flavouring	0·9

(Variations on this recipe are given later in the Chapter)

Batch Production Method
1. Load the open boiling pan with the glucose syrup, full cream condensed milk, refined or brown sugar.
2. Turn on the stirrers and then the heating and warm the mix to 35° C (95° F).
3. Add the hardened palm kernel oil and butter.
4. Mix for 10 minutes.
5. Turn on the heating and bring the batch to the boil.
6. Boil until the temperature reaches 124° C (255° F).
7. Release the heat from the pan.
8. Add the flavouring and mix for a short period. (The temperature of the batch should not rise to over 125° C (257° F) at this stage.)

TABLE 51.   Recipes for Caramels and Related Products
(parts by weight)

Ingredient	Chewing Mint	Butterscotch	Caramel Strips	Mint Chews	Toffee Whirls	
					Caramel Casing	White Centre
Glucose syrup (medium DE)	100	100	100	100	200	100
Refined cane or beet sugar	100	100	60	70	68	60
Brown sugar		20		14	60	
Hardened palm kernel oil	12		15	18	80	10
Egg frappé	12			2		8
Butter		30		5		
Condensed milk: Full cream sweetened					180	
Condensed Milk, skimmed			12			
Condensed whey			3			
Gelatine solution 140 Bloom (50:50)			5			1
Salt		2	1	2	3	1·5
Peppermint oil	0·2		0·25	0·25		
Spearmint oil	0·12					
Vanillin crystals			0·02		0·02	0·01
Colouring			0·5	0·5		
Lecithin						
Boiling Temperature	126° C (259° F)	140° C (284° F)	129° C (265° F)	135° C (275° F)	125° C (257° F)	122° C (252° F)

Notes

(1) Method of preparation is as described for caramels with following exception: Egg frappé and gelatine (dissolved in its own weight of water), where indicated, should be added after boiling has been completed and the batch then lightly pulled. (2) Butterscotch develops its flavour if about 14 lb (7 kg) portions from the premix are taken and cooked on forced gas fired pans. The butterscotch should be deposited at 136° C (275° F) on to moulds in PTFE coated trays, previously lightly greased with mineral oil. (3) Caramel strips should be coloured red, yellow and green and cut into 12in × 3 in ×3/16in lengths. (4) Toffee whirls are prepared by laying the white centre on the caramel casing and rolling up to produce a circular strip in the centre of the caramel. Liquorice or fruit whirls can be made by omitting the full cream sweetened condensed milk and adding an additional 110 parts by weight of refined cane or beet sugar together with suitable colouring and flavouring.

9. Turn out the batch on to oiled slabs.

Note: Stages 1 to 4 can be carried out in bulk provided no more than 24 hours of mix is prepared on any one day.

Continuous Production
1. Prepare the premix as described above.
2. Heat to the boiling point of the mix and pump to the caramelisation unit.

Note: Processing conditions are described in §10.4 and 10.5.

10.2 Modifications to the Basic Recipe

Clotted Cream Caramels. Increase the butter content to 10%, reducing the vegetable oils accordingly, and add 1–2% of clotted cream.

Summer Caramels. Coat the caramel shapes with fondant mass at 40° C (104° F) in an enrober type equipment. At this temperature the fondant will flow and still contain sufficient crystals of sucrose to set up on cooling. The caramels should be placed on the enrober band at 20° C and quickly returned to this temperature after coating has taken place.

Oriental Fruit Toffees. These should be prepared using the following recipe:

	Parts by weight
Mango Pulp	50
Cane or Beet Sugar	25
Skimmed Dried Milk	7
Hardened Palm Kernel Oil	6
Glucose Syrup, (42 DE grade)	4

Method
1. Load the pulp into the cooking pan and cook to 33% total solids.
2. Add the remainder of the ingredients and cook to 127° C (261° F).
3. Deposit and cut to shape.
4. Stand for 24 hours and wrap.

[See D. N. KERAWALA, G. S. SIDDAPPA, *Food Sci.* Central Fd. Tech. Res. Inst., 1963, *12*, (8), 221.]

10.3 Dulce de Leche

This milk-based chewing-sweet is popular in South America and the Middle East.

	Parts by weight
Fluid Milk	200
Cane or Beet Sugar	50
Glucose Syrup	15
Sodium Bicarbonate	0·5
Lactose	10

Method
1. Boil the milk and cane or beet sugar to 60% solids content (check on a refractometer).
2. Add the glucose syrup and the sodium bicarbonate.
3. When the frothing has stopped continue cooking to 70% total solids content.
4. Allow to cool to 90° C (194° F) and mix in the lactose seed.
5. Discharge and pack.

10.4   CARAMEL RECIPE COMPILATION

A number of inter-relating factors must be considered when balancing the proportions of the various ingredients in a caramel recipe. The more important of these factors are (*a*) texture of the confection; (*b*) flavour characteristics of the product; (*c*) grain (crystallisation) prevention; (*d*) protection from moisture absorption; (*e*) chew; (*f*) colour; (*g*) flow characteristics of the sweet; (*h*) behaviour on the forming and cutting units.

A caramel is a complex blend of fat globules in varying size groupings surrounded by a high concentration sugar solution in which the milk solids not fat are dispersed or dissolved.

The greatest single factor affecting texture and chew is the amount of moisture left in the caramel. Open pan production methods usually employ boiling temperatures of 125°–130° C (257°–266° F). At this boiling range, 6–8% moisture is left in the caramel mix. Provided sufficient fat is present, the caramels so produced will have pleasant chewing characteristics. Higher boiling temperatures of up to 145° C (293° F) must be used with caramels for hot climates. The moisture left in the product is substantially less, around 3%, and chew characteristics are poor. Higher boiling temperatures produce caramels which are less likely to grain (crystallise) on store.

The ratio of cane or beet sugar and lactose to the totalled glucose syrup solids and invert sugar solids is of prime significance in keeping quality. In deriving this ratio the amount of reducing sugars present in the brown sugar and in any treacle present must be added to the glucose syrup solids. Sucrose in the condensed milk should be added to the weight of cane or beet sugar being used. A stable caramel should contain 1·2 to 1·4 parts of sucrose (cane or beet sugar) to every part of reducing sugars. A high level of reducing sugars invariably leads to a poor keeping quality caramel.

Increasing the level of sucrose will increase the toughness of the caramel and the likelihood of graining while on store. Grained caramels find acceptance with some consumers but in general sucrose crystallisation is an undesirable development which must be prevented by the careful balancing of ingredients during recipe compilation. Grained caramels frequently develop unacceptable stale flavours. Fudge is a form of grained caramel but the crystallisation that occurs is deliberately induced and of controlled grain texture. In this instance it is normal to add a fondant seed which acts as a crystallisation promoter. Grain in caramels is sometimes described as sugar crystallisation and sometimes as fudging.

Grain can often be detected at the ends of the caramel where the loose wrapper twist had allowed the entry of air which had a high humidity. The condensed moisture leaches out some of the sugar to form a syrup which, with changes in temperature, undergoes evaporation and then crystallises. Once graining has commenced it cannot be reversed and it will travel throughout the whole of the caramel. Low temperature storage of well protected products prevents the early development of graining. Conversely, high temperatures for storage accelerate the development of graining. The presence of milk solids in caramels is helpful in that it raises viscosity which lessens the likelihood of crystallisation taking place.

Graining is particularly sensitive to moisture content. The lower the moisture, the less the tendency to grain. Consumer acceptance is closely linked to texture and therefore a balance must be maintained between an acceptable texture and a reduced tendency to grain. For most caramel recipes, a moisture content of 6–7% is satisfactory. Caramels exhibit an increased proneness to grain when they are left for extended periods on warm slabs. Once boiling has been completed, the batch should be given the minimum of mechanical agitation. Added scrap, which has not been freshly used up, invariably increases the likelihood that graining will occur.

The glucose syrup chosen for caramel manufacture should be of the 'regular grade' i.e. 42 DE. Varying the type of glucose syrup used for caramel manufacture will affect viscosity, colour development and firmness of the batch. Caramels exhibit great stretch properties as the glucose syrup solids level are increased but keeping properties are lowered. According to H. H. VOLKER [*Zucker und Süsswaren*, 1969, 22, (3), 114–6] the level of glucose syrup used does not significantly affect the speed at which caramels are dissolved in the mouth.

The higher the dextrose level in the glucose syrup, the greater will be the tendency of the caramel to flow. Raising the dextrin level produces a caramel which is both harder and less chewable. Maltose syrup gives caramels which are considerably lighter and therefore more creamy in appearance.

The presence of milk solids is the essential feature of a caramel recipe and it is these which cause the product to be different in its properties to other types of confectionery. Milk solids are normally added as full cream or skimmed sweetened condensed milk though dried milk and condensed whey are sometimes used. Condensed milks are employed because a considerable amount of the water has been removed from the original milk. Liquid milk, from the cow, can be used but boiling times are considerably lengthened. With these extended cooking periods, increased sucrose inversion occurs with consequent falling off of storage quality. Liquid milk from the cow contains 87% moisture as against only 28% in sweetened condensed milk.

The presence of milk solids has a pronounced effect on texture, flavour and colour. The higher the level of milk solids present in the caramel, the harder will be the caramel. Casein—a milk protein—is a major component of the milk solids and it is this compound which contributes hardness. Additional casein may be added to caramels being exported to hot climates to increase their resistance to graining.

During manufacture the milk protein and some of the sugars undergo a chemical reaction to form complex components. This is known as the Maillard reaction and the compounds that are formed enhance both colour and flavour. The reaction is slow at low temperatures of around 40° C (104° F) but rapidly increases once the temperature exceeds 95° C (203° F). The higher the temperature, the greater the flavour development and the darker the colour. However as the temperature is raised so the caramelisation of the sugar occurs and therefore the flavour development is not solely due to the Maillard reaction. According to A. W. HOLMES [Third International Congress Food Science and Technology, 1970] only the dextrose and glucose syrup solids take part with the milk protein in the formation of colour and flavour.

The lactose present in the condensed milk can cause difficulty during the storage of the prepared caramels. Lactose is not a very soluble sugar and if present in too high an amount will cause graining. The combined solubility of sucrose and lactose is considerably lower than the combined solubility of sucrose and invert sugar.

The fat content found when samples of a wide range of price quality of commercially produced caramels were analysed, ranged from 4–20%. Fat has a significant contribution to the texture, chewing characteristics, colour and flavour of caramels. Low fat levels tend to produce caramels which are sticky and difficult to chew while a high fat usage without the addition of an emulsifier leads to oiling on the surface of the confection.

The most important fat in a caramel recipe is the milk fat derived from the condensed milk and this should be boosted by the addition of extra butterfat.

These two sources of fats give caramels which have the best flavour but which are more likely to become rancid on store. Where permitted, small proportions of antioxidant should be added at the end of the cooking period to maintain the fresh taste of the product. This use of antioxidants in particular BHA and PG has been shown to be effective in extending the storage life of caramels [L. F. MARTIN, Progress in Candy Research, Report No. 20, 1950]. During the investigations it was found that a peroxide value of at least 20 was needed before rancid taste could be detected.

The main bulk fats in caramel are vegetable oils, in particular hydrogenated or hardened palm kernel oil. The choice of fat is dependent on the ultimate market for the caramels. Controlled hydrogenation can give a range of differing melting point fats. The fat most suited for temperate climates should melt at 32°–35° C (90°–95° F). Higher melting fats melting at 35°–45° C (95°–113° F) should be used when producing caramels for export to areas with hotter climatic conditions. Other fats have been used for caramel manufacture notably hardened coconut and hardened fish oil. In both instances there may be some difficulty from flavour carryover. Commercially blended fats for caramel manufacture are on offer to the sweet manufacturer. In general caramels produced from vegetable oils alone and non-fat milk solids, do not need the addition of an emulsifier.

During the storage of caramels there is a slow but gradual migration of fat from the body of the confection to the surface. This increases the susceptibility of the milk fat to rancidify through the increase in exposure of fat surfaces to the atmosphere. Rancidity arising from this cause can be minimised by purchasing wrapping paper which contains or has been slightly coated with antioxidant.

Good caramels are only produced when there has been effective emulsification of the fat and sugar liquor. Emulsification improves the dispersion of the fat thereby lightening the colour of the sweet and giving a more creamy taste. It can be carried out by giving the caramel ingredients an initial premix prior to boiling and by stabilising the blend by including an emulsifier in the recipe. A convenient and inexpensive emulsifier is lecithin extracted from oilseed. Some lecithin is present in the milk but this is less heat tolerant than that which is extracted from oilseed. Soyabean lecithin is the most effective oilseed emulsifier having greater stability and wider availability. The breakdown of the oilseed lecithins during heating is not usually sufficient to produce detectable fishy flavours in the confection.

Other useful emulsifiers are glyceryl monostearate (GMS) and glyceryl mono-oleate (GMO). Better cutting characteristics during cut and wrap operations are claimed for caramels containing these emulsifiers. In all cases the emulsifier should be added after the fat addition has been made.

In addition to the vanillin flavouring, or one of the alternative commercial caramel flavourings, salt enhances consumer acceptability; without it, caramels and toffees are bland and undistinguished in flavour. A suitable usage for salt is 0·4–0·65% of the final cooked batch weight.

There are a number of other raw materials which can be included in confectionery recipes according to the type of product being produced. These include:

Pregelatinised maize starch	To give body to the cheaper grades of caramels and toffees containing lowered amounts of milk solids. Use at 5–10% level. Some loss in quality occurs.
Ammonium carbonate	To neutralise any acidity present in the added milk thereby improving milk flavour. Use at 0·1% level.

Waxy maize starch	To improve the water binding power. Use at 5–10% level. Some loss in quality occurs.
Milk protein (whipping grade) or Egg albumen foam	To lighten the batch. Use at a 2% level.
Soya protein	For cheaper caramels to improve texture and reduce the tendencies to flow and become sticky. Use at a 1% level.
Sodium propionate or potassium sorbate	In caramels for export to hot climates to reduce the danger of mould spoilage. Use at 0·1% level.
Vitamin C	As a sales inducement. Add at the end of boiling at a rate of 500 mg/lb declaring 20 mg/oz on the label of the confectionery pack. Care must be taken as heat stability is poor.
Whey solids	As a complete replacement of condensed milk solids for cheaper confections.

The traditional method of manufacture described earlier can be used with open pan cooking employing forced gas or coke, electrical or steam heating methods. Care must be taken to avoid burning on the side of the container. Cooking must be temperature controlled and the batch transferred to oiled slabs as soon as the specified boiling point has been reached.

In the continuous system, the basic caramel mix is rapidly cooked by passage through scraped film evaporators. A separate caramelisation stage must be given to achieve the required level of flavour and colour development. Moisture loss can take place under vacuum and this accentuates the lack of flavour production. The mix should be prepared to have a moisture level of 17–22%. This blend, after adequate emulsification should be fed into the scraped film evaporators at 70° C (158° F).

10.5   CONTINUOUS MANUFACTURE OF CARAMELS

Caramel manufacture can be considered as taking place in five stages: (i) preparation of premix; (ii) evaporation and caramelisation; (iii) further ingredient addition; (iv) cooling; and (v) shaping, cutting to size and wrapping.

Plant for continuous manufacture usually caters for stages (ii) to (iv). Baker Perkins equipment follows closely the method used in batch processing, excepting that surplus water is evaporated before, instead of during, caramelisation and that these parts of the process are undertaken as separate stages. The advantage of this is that it is possible to produce most types of caramel with more flexibility than with the batch process. Caramelisation is determined by two factors—time and temperature while the amount of moisture retained in the caramel, which contributes to its hardness, depends upon the temperature to which it is boiled. By separating the process into two distinct stages, the caramelising time is not dependent upon the temperature to which the caramel is taken to reduce the moisture to the required amount. It is therefore, possible to produce a hard, lightly caramelised product or a softer, highly caramelised product or any required combination.

A flow diagram for the Baker Perkins Continuous Caramel Plant is given as Fig. 28 and the plant shown in Photo 5.

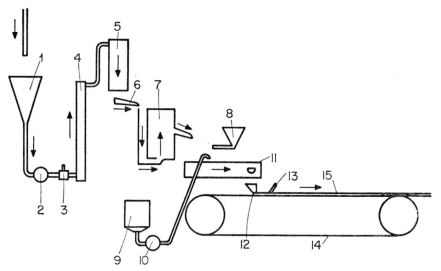

FIGURE 28. Baker Perkins continuous caramel plant.

The cold premixed and emulsified ingredients are pumped into the conical receiving hopper (1) which is fitted with level controls and is hot water jacketed. From here, it is drawn into a metering pump (2) and pumped through a vertical preheater and dissolver (4). This is a steam jacketed tube and contains a worm stirring device. In this tube, the premix is preheated and subjected to pressure so that the small fragments of crystals remaining in the cold premix are dissolved in the available water before passing to the evaporating stage.

The premix continues on to a microfilm cooker (5) where the surplus water is evaporated and the cooked mixture is now discharged and falls by gravity to the caramelising unit.

The caramelising unit (7) consists of two vertical cylindrical chambers connected together at the bottom by ducting. The whole unit is surrounded by a steam jacket and the walls of the chambers are continuously scraped. The cooked premix enters the top of the smaller vertical cylinder, in which is fitted a mixing worm to assist the material on its passage down to the interconnecting ducting and through to the main caramelising unit.

In the C and B continuous caramel plant (Tourell (Sales) Ltd., Cornwall) the premix is held in a heated hopper before being screw fed through vertical sugar dissolver into the steam jacketed (120 lb/in²) cooker unit. Moisture evaporation and caramelisation take place during the passage through the cooker unit. The extent to which these occur is governed by adjustments to the rate of flow and by varying the contact time in the cooker using weir type outlet points positioned along its length. Following cooking, the caramel boil is discharged into a blender unit, similar in design to the cooker unit, which acts both as a constant temperature holding vessel and as a means of incorporating flavouring, emulsifiers or any other ingredient liable to be affected by exposure to high temperatures. Throughput is approximately 1000 lb per hour.

Premixing is best carried out in bulk mixing pots and the required charge drawn off as necessary. Adequate emulsification is usually achieved after mixing for 10 minutes at 40° C (104° F). Not more than one day's production should be premixed and held on store at any time. Effective premixing can also be achieved by passing the crudely mixed blend in a stream past an ultrasonic whistle.

Depositing should be from heated hoppers on to a moving release coated conveyor band. The lower the depositing temperature, the less the tendency to stick but the poorer the flow properties and the slower the production rate. The deposited caramel can be allowed to flatten on the stainless steel or PTFE coated band or be dropped into individual coated moulds. Light mineral oil or commercial blends of fat release agent are suitable for this type of sugar confectionery product. Polytetrafluoroethylene or, to a lesser extent, silicone coated implements give improved release for this type of confection.

When depositing is not used, the batch should be kept on hot slabs until transfer to the cut and wrap units. Long standing periods on these heated slabs will lead to a lowered effective storage life through surface graining. Alternatively cutting to size may be carried out by allowing the batch to flow warm to take up the space enclosed by pre-greased iron bars. The batch, when cooled, is then scored to the required shape by passing over circular blade cutters/markers.

Continuous cooling of caramel-based confectionery bars can be achieved by passing the extruded ribbon over brine cooled rollers. Thin thermocouples, which contain a sensitive registering tip should be positioned to brush the surface of the bar and signals from these used to control the temperature gradient of the confection during cooling.

Thickness control may be carried out by passing the strip over a PTFE slide which responds to changes in size. Any change in movement of the slide can be amplified and the resulting signal used to control the setting of the sizing rollers.

10.6 PROPERTIES OF CARAMELS

In general, the larger the batch, the darker will be the colour of the final confection. Dark patches on the surface of the caramel are indicative of the blending of two batches of caramel or burning through imperfect mixing action in the pan or an insufficiently large charge of caramel mix for the size of pan.

The browning of the batch through the Maillard reaction occurs following an induction period [L. C. MAILLARD, *Compt. Rend.*, 1912, *154*, 66]. It takes place initially between the amino acids and the aldehyde groupings of sugars of the dextrose type. The reaction is very heat sensitive, the higher the temperature the greater the browning. Moisture accelerates the reaction that occurs with milk protein [C. H. LEA, *Chem. and Ind.*, 1950, 155]. Accompanying the browning are flavour development, lessened solubility of the protein and an increased tendency to froth. Stale flavours have been found [S. ADACHI, T. NAKANISHI; *Nippon Nogei Kagahiu Kaishi*, 1957, *31*, 189–93] to develop during browning when the mix is subject to aeration. Debruin (21st Pennsylvanian Manufacturing Confectioners' Association Conference) found browning to increase with higher levels of glucose syrup and fat and with the use of whey powder.

The hardness of caramels increases linearly with rising boiling temperature [J. W. GROVER in G. W. SCOTT BLAIR; *Foodstuffs their Plasticity, Fluidity and Consistency*, 1953, North Holland Publ. Co.]. It is not relatable to the effectiveness of the fat emulsification but does vary according to the type of fat present. E. J. DEBRUIN and P. G. KEENEY [*Manufacturing Confectioner*, 1969, *49*, (6), 31–5] using a compression testing and shearing apparatus to test samples of caramels, have found that high compression values are given when low DE glucose syrups were used and that there was little tendency to flow. High DE glucose syrup gave softer caramels but cold flow occurred. Increasing the milk fat and whey solids raised the recorded compression values while vegetable fats only slightly changed these values when used as a substitute for milk fat. According to W. DUCK [*Manufacturing Confectioner*, 1960, *40*, (6), 99–105] caramels have similar properties to those predictable from the Maxwell theoretical model; he found a relationship between the elasticity of caramels and stress. GROVER (loc cit) developed a hardness index for relating hardness to changes made in recipe compilation:

$$\text{Hardness Index} = 2 - \log P$$

where P is the rate of penetration found on test.

The hardness index was found to vary with water content, proportion of glucose syrup solids and milk solids. J. C. DAKIN [*Chem. and Ind.*, 9 Dec. 1968] has used the Instron Universal Test Rig to measure the stickiness of toffee. In this instrument a stainless steel rod is inserted into the caramel sample and the force required to remove the rod is measured.

The viscosity of a cooked caramel batch is relatable to (a) residual moisture content; (b) milk protein; (c) higher carbohydrates and starch. Caramels are non-Newtonian in flow character. During the cooking process, the viscosity of the caramel first falls in a non-smooth manner up to about 80° C (176° F). Changes in the milk protein then commence and the viscosity rises as heating is continued. High viscosities considerably reduce the danger of graining. It follows that caramels of the same moisture content which are low in milk solids will be more liable to grain than those which are high in milk solids. Increasing the milk protein but lowering the moisture content increases the viscosity but lowers the elasticity [W. DUCK, 1959, Pennsylvanian Manufacturing Confectioners' Association (PMCA) Conference]. According to DUCK an increase of 0·8% in milk protein doubled the viscosity and increased elasticity by 10%. The same author has in earlier work [*Manufacturing Confectioner*, 1957, 1, (6), 24] found that chewiness is increased with viscosity changes but not with changes in elasticity. Increasing the water content by 1% reduced the viscosity of a caramel sample by a half. Sticking during manufacture can be greatly reduced by using PTFE stainless steel surface coatings on equipment. Production speeds are increased, processing temperatures can be raised and wear significantly reduced. The coating can be applied to mixing vessels, gears, valves, cutting knives and holding bars.

Research by P. G. KEENEY and E. J. DE BRUIN [26th PMCA Conference, 1972] using a scanning electron microscope and compression testing studies, has shown that the sugar phase is the supporting medium in caramels. Below a critical moisture, structural strength is dependent on protein content. The number and size of fat globules are also important for mechanical properties. Fat dispersion seemed to depend upon degree of agitation and sequence of mixing. Numerous inclusions were detected on the caramel surface which were found to be entrapped water or air; the size being influenced by milk protein. The butter fat globule size was from 10 to 100μ with many interconnected. Some nucleation was found to develop at the fat globule–sugar syrup interface.

The equilibrium relative humidity value of caramels varies according to composition but is normally 30–45%. Storage conditions are therefore important because they tend to attract moisture from the air; their high viscosity is helpful in that it minimises these effects. Some variation in e r h can be achieved by lowering or increasing the glucose syrup and invert sugar levels. The lower DE glucose syrups gives caramels that are less hygroscopic than those made with the high DE glucose syrups, but this affects texture. The higher the level of cane and beet sugar, the less the tendency to go sticky; but the greater the possibility of graining. To counteract this, the higher sucrose content caramels should be produced with a lowered moisture content. Irrespective of recipe, higher humidity will cause increased graining and stickiness.

10.7   PACKAGING AND STORAGE

Caramels are normally wrapped as moulded pieces or transferred for continuous chopping and wrapping of a rope of caramel on cut and wrap units. This latter method is more economical but causes greater strains to be set up in the cooked mass. A recipe which has been used for moulded caramels should be modified for use on cut and wrap machines by raising the glucose syrup level. Caramels should at all times be worked at as low a temperature as practicable during wrapping.

During storage, caramels which are less viscous tend to flow and take up the internal shape of the wrapper. High milk protein levels can cause the reverse action in that the caramels contract after wrapping. This can result in the wrapping paper becoming detached from the sweet. Caramels and toffees should be rapidly cooled immediately following wrapping. At the point of wrapping the confections are at around 60° C (140° F) and they must be rapidly cooled to 20° C (68° F). Wrapping the caramels hot and at high speeds can result in the bursting of the wrappers. In this instance the fault arises by the reformation of those components in the recipe which contribute to elasticity. Caramels soften at around 25°–30° C (77°–86° F). Caramels held above 25° C (77° F) will become misshapen during storage. Suitable cooling conveyor belt speeds are from 50–60 ft per hour.

The space occupied by wrapped caramels depends on the size of the sweet. This can vary from 25 lb/ft³ (88 ft³/ton) for the larger size of caramels to 60 lb/ft³ (37 ft³/ton) for the smaller wrapped caramels. Both twist wrapped and foil wrapped caramels have 5–6% of their weight attributable to the wrapping while for regenerated cellulose acetate film the figure is lower at 4–5%.

Quality control and comparisons of competitive caramels and toffees should be carried out according to the schedule described in Table 52 and the cause of faults determined by reference to Fig. 29.

10.8   EXPORT CARAMELS

Caramels produced in, or for export to, tropical climates should be harder and have a higher softening point than those for sale in temperate areas. This can be achieved by (1) lowering the moisture content by raising the boiling temperature; (2) using a higher melting point; (3) increasing the casein content by raising the non-fat milk solids; (4) using a lower DE glucose syrup; (5) adding a binding material such as waxy maize starch and cornflour; (6) lowering the content of butterfat.

TABLE 52.   Scheme for Assessing Quality of Caramels

Flavour	Texture	Analytical Quality
(i) Assessed by panel testing.	To be assessed by a panel test in which the most appropriate of the following terms are underlined	Depth of graining
(ii) Quality control by triangular testing[1] (in which two similar and one dissimilar sample are presented).		Fat—total butterfat Milk solids, not fat

(iii) Competitor comparison, by assessment on a ten point scale in which 1 represents unacceptable flavour and 10 of excellent flavour	Brittle Powdery
	Creamy Sandy
	Crunchy Short
	Fudgy Soft
	Greasy Sticky
	Gritty Tacky
	Hard Tender
	Lumpy Waxy
		Moisture content
		Sugars—reducing sugar content
		         sucrose content
		         glucose syrup solids
		         proportion of non-reducing
		         sugars to reducing sugars
		Starch (presence of)
		Salt

[1] Lees, R., *Handbook of Methods of Food Analysis*, 1971, Leonard Hill Books.

Plate 5   Baker Perkins continuous caramel plant

Plate 6   Ter Braak pressure whip

Plate 7   Steinberg twin spray unit in pan room

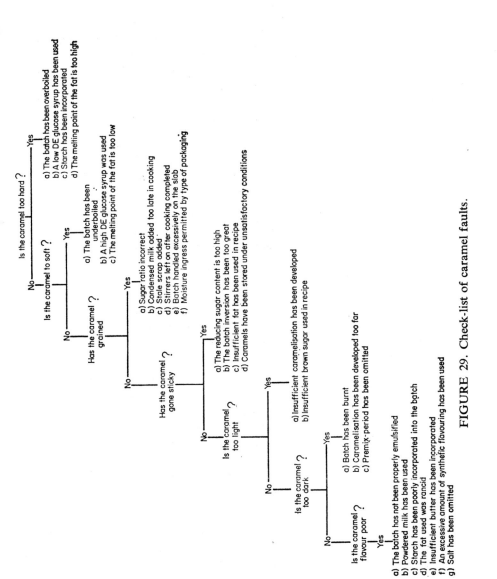

Is the caramel too hard?

Yes
a) The batch has been overboiled
b) A low DE glucose syrup has been used
c) Starch has been incorporated
d) The melting point of the fat is too high

No

Is the caramel to soft?

Yes
a) The batch has been underboiled
b) A high DE glucose syrup was used
c) The melting point of the fat is too low

No

Has the caramel grained?

Yes
a) Sugar ratio incorrect
b) Condensed milk added too late in cooking
c) Stale scrap added
d) Stirrers left on after cooking completed
e) Batch handled excessively on the slab
f) Moisture ingress permitted by type of packaging

No

Has the caramel gone sticky?

Yes
a) The reducing sugar content is too high
b) The batch inversion has been too great
c) Insufficient fat has been used in recipe
d) Caramels have been stored under unsatisfactory conditions

No

Is the caramel too light?

Yes
a) Insufficient caramelisation has been developed
b) Insufficient brown sugar used in recipe

No

Is the caramel too dark?

Yes
a) Batch has been burnt
b) Caramelisation has been developed too far
c) Premix-period has been omitted

No

Is the caramel flavour poor?

Yes
a) The batch has not been properly emulsified
b) Powdered milk has been used
c) Starch has been poorly incorporated into the batch
d) The fat used was rancid
e) Insufficient butter has been incorporated
f) An excessive amount of synthetic flavouring has been used
g) Salt has been omitted

FIGURE 29. Check-list of caramel faults.

H

10.9   FUDGE

Fudge is a cross between a caramel and a fondant. It is a grained medium boiled confection which contains both milk solids and a high fat content. The confection can be prepared by seeding with fondant or by mechanically inducing a grain in the cooked batch.

SEEDED FUDGE

	Parts by weight
Glucose Syrup (42 DE)	100
Brown Sugar	180
Prepared Fondant	100
Egg Frappé	30
Full Cream Condensed Milk	100
Hardened Palm Kernel Oil	20
Glyceryl Monostearate	1
Glycerine or Sorbitol	15
Salt	2
Vanillin	0·025
Ammonium Bicarbonate	0·25

Method
  1. Load the pan with the glucose syrup, full cream condensed milk, brown sugar and hardened palm kernel oil.
  2. Switch on the beaters and the steam.
  3. When the mix has reached 60° C (140° F) add the glyceryl monostearate and premix at this temperature for 10 minutes.
  4. Turn on the full steam pressure and cook to 114° C (237° F).
  5. Turn off the steam and add the fondant, frappé and the vanillin crystals as soon as the temperature has dropped to 90° C (194° F). Mix in.
  6. Pour at 80° C (176° F) on to warm greased or waxed paper lined slabs and score to size while still molten.
  7. Hold till set and cut to size.

Note: (*a*) space can be used more economically by pouring the cooked fudge on to wooden or metal released coated trays which are then stacked; (*b*) Glazes should not be applied to the deposited fudge until it has cooled to room temperature.

10.10   VARIATIONS ON BASIC VANILLIN FUDGE

A. *Chocolate Fudge*
  Add 4% unsweetened chocolate (the use of cocoa powder will give a dryer, tougher product) to the basic fudge recipe.

B. *Layered Fudge*

Use 250 parts of caster sugar in place of the weight of full cream condensed milk and brown sugar specified in the basic recipe. After boiling has been completed split the batch into two and colour either yellow or red. Lemon and raspberry flavouring should be used to flavour the two parts in place of the vanillin.

C. *Maple Fudge*

Flavour the basic fudge recipe with maple flavouring (0·1%) in place of vanillin.

D. *Eastern Fudge*

Add 5% of a mixture of equal parts of chopped hazelnuts and raisins to the basic vanillin flavoured fudge recipe.

E. *Winter Cough Candy*

	Parts by weight
Brown Sugar	100
Fondant	50
Glucose Syrup	10
Water	30
Cough Mixture Essence	0·5
Brown Colour	to desired shade

Method

1. Load the sugar, glucose and water into the cooking pan, mix and boil to 118° C (244° F).
2. Cool to 85° C (185° F) and add the fondant. Mix.
3. Add the cough mixture flavouring. Mix.
4. Pour on to oiled paper held on a warmed table.
5. Spread and equalise.
6. Score and cut to a count of 60 pieces per lb.
7. When set break into pieces.

F. *Fudge Icing*

(for dipping or coating purposes)

	Parts by weight
Cane or Beet Sugar	25
HPKO	18
Water	15

Cook to 102° C (215° F) stop heating. Transfer to powder mixer which contains:

	Parts by weight
Fine Brown Sugar	15
Icing Sugar	60
Milk Powder	5
Mix and add glycerine.	1

10.11   COMPOSITION OF FUDGE

Fudge contains both a solid and a liquid phase. The solid phase is mainly composed of sucrose crystals and to a lesser degree milk solids and fat crystals. Similar factors to those which influence the crystal size of fondant will also affect fudge. Increasing the doctor solids level in a fudge recipe will give a product which is slower to crystallisation. This is due to the changes that are brought about in the proportion of solid and liquid phases in the manufactured product.

Fudge can be manufactured in which the crystal nuclei are produced by beating. Growth takes place on these crystal nuclei. Rapid cooling and stirring produce a large number of crystal nuclei which then develop into fine crystal matrix. Using a fondant seed reduces the time required for the development of nuclei and produces a satisfactory level of growth points in the mix. Natural graining produces a fudge which contains coarser sugar crystals than are found in the seeded product.

A holding period is essential before the fudge is cut and packed. This holding or maturing period is to enable the product to develop a sufficiently high level of crystal phase that will prevent spoilage while handling. During the maturation period the confection becomes softer in bite and smoother in texture. Crystallisation continues for a number of weeks after the fudge has been cut and packed and an unbalanced recipe may lead to such a high degree of crystal phase as to make the product unpalatable. Work carried out by J. DU ROSS and W. H. KNIGHTLY [*Manufacturing Confectioner*, 1963, *43*, (7), 26–31] indicates that the finer the crystal matrix that is present in fudge the slower will be the migration of contained water and fat to the surface of the confection. Increases in the fat content of the surface layer will accelerate the rate at which fudge stales due to oxidation.

The proportion of cane or beet sugar to doctor solids (glucose syrup solids, invert sugar, sorbitol and glycerine) should approximate to 4 parts to 1 part for an acceptable fudge. Regular grade glucose syrup (42 DE) should be used in preference to other grades. High maltose glucose syrups produce fudge which is chewy while high DE syrups give rise to confections which although initially more tender, harden excessively while on store. Sorbitol can be added to extend shelf life though it is best used in combination with glucose syrup. One-fifth of the glucose syrup solids weight should be replaced by sorbitol solids where an extended shelf life is required.

The use of full cream condensed milk is necessary to produce a full flavoured fudge. Milk solids will slow the hardening of the confection while on store. An addition of 0·1% of ammonium bicarbonate is helpful in preventing hardening due to milk protein. Straight replacement of milk solids from full cream condensed milk by whey solids will significantly affect the properties of the fudge. This is due to the differences in the type and content of milk protein. Should it be necessary to cheapen the confection an equal mixture of condensed milk and whey should be used. When no milk solids are added a small amount of gelatine solution (0·25% of a 50:50 solution, 140 Bloom) should be included in the recipe. Fat is a necessary component of fudge to give the desired texture and to produce a smooth bite. The presence of a crystal phase in fudge causes fat oxidation to occur more quickly than in a one phase confection. Butter should not be used in fudge recipes and only stable fats such as hardened palm kernel oil incorporated. Egg frappé should be included firstly to lighten the fudge, secondly to increase the volume and lastly to produce a paler colour to the confection. M. F. STAINSBURG and P. R. DAWSON [*Manufacturing Confectioner*, 1961, *41*, (3), 25–7] have found that the addition of 2% calcium carbonate can be used as an alternative seeding material to prepared fondant.

The gloss on fudge is unaffected by the type of fat used in the recipe. It can be developed by working the surface. This may be carried out by drawing a spatula over the surface of the deposited fudge. It is thought by W. DUCK [*Confectionery Manufacture*, 1962, *8*, 32–4, 6, 49] that working increases the amount of syrup fraction on the surface by reorientating the sucrose crystals that are present. Too much working at too early a stage after pouring can however impair the gloss. The amount of syrup fraction present influences the degree of gloss exhibited by the fudge. Increasing the glucose syrup/sorbitol/invert sugar fraction increases gloss but weakens the structure of the fudge. According to DUCK (loc cit) the weakest structure of fudge is obtained when the ratio of sucrose to doctor solids is 1·75–1·0. This researcher found that any other ratio of sugars gave a stronger structured fudge.

If the fondant is added to the boiled fraction of the recipe at too high a temperature then the fudge will have both a mottled appearance and be coarse in texture. Fondant should be added when the temperature of the cooked mass has dropped to within the range 65°–90° C (149°–194° F). The addition of fondant will make little difference to the amount of crystal phase that is ultimately developed when compared to a fudge made by beating which has a similar sugar ratio. Mottling may also be developed when the fudge batch is poured onto slabs which have not been preheated.

The storage of fudge at low relative humidities or at high temperatures can result in a lowering of gloss. Fudge should be preferentially stored at between 50–55% relative humidity and at 5°–20° C (59°–68° F). Sweating may occur when fudge is packed in sealed moistureproof containers and this can give rise to mould growth. Depending on composition of the syrup phase the equilibrium relative humidity of fudge will be between

65–75%. Fudge should be turned on the slabs after 12 hours of maturing to permit even drying.

The eating qualities of fudge should be judged according to the following gradings:

Light	Chalky	Sandy
Short	Chewy	Tough
Soft	Greasy	
Smooth	Gritty	
Tender	Rough	

Fudge can be produced on a continuous basis by feeding fondant at 32° C (90° F) into a caramel mix held at 75° C (167° F) in a Tourell Unit (see §10.5).

11

Fondants, Creams and Crystallised Confectionery

11.1 FONDANTS, CREAMS AND CRYSTALLISED CONFECTIONERY

Fondants and creams are sugar confectionery products which contain mixed sugars held in two phases. The sugar crystals which constitute the solid phase, are dispersed in a high sugar solids syrup. Fondants and creams are similar in composition though creams contain slightly higher residual water and a greater proportion of doctor solids. Five recipes for these products are given in Table 53 overleaf.

Method
Basic Fondant
1. Dissolve the cane or beet sugar, glucose syrup and/or invert sugar in the specified weight of water.
2. Cook to 120° C (248° F) by open pan cooking or in a heat exchanger or concentrate to 88% total solids using vacuum cooking.
3. Cool to within the range 38°–45° C (100°–113° F).
4. Beat and discharge into holding containers.
5. Mature for 1 day before use.

Cream
1. Dissolve the refined sugar and glucose syrup in the stated weight of water.
2. Cook to the specified temperature by open pan or heat exchanger procedures or vacuum cook to 88% solids (86% in the case of cream centres).
3. Cool to within the range 60°–70° C (140°–158° F).
4. Add the specified weight of basic fondant previously melted at 60° C.
5. Add acid (dissolved in twice its own weight of water), colouring, flavouring and, after mixing in the other ingredients, invertase.
6. Mix and transfer to the depositing hopper.

TABLE 53.   Recipes for Fondant Products

Ingredient	Basic Fondant A	B	Fruit Cream Centre	Mint Creams	Fondant Cake Decorations
			parts by weight		
Refined cane or beet sugar	100	100	50	100	100
Glucose syrup (42 DE)	25		14	50	50
Invert sugar syrup (70%)		25	—	—	—
Water	50	50	12	50	50
Basic fondant			100	75	70
Citric acid			0·3		
Invertase			0·25		
Flavour			0·75	0·25	0·25
Colour	trace	trace	0·01	trace	trace
Suggested colours	blue	blue	yellow, orange, red, green	blue	yellow, orange, red, green, purple
Suggested flavours	—	—	lemon, orange, strawberry, lime	peppermint	lemon, orange, strawberry, lime, blackcurrant
Boiling temperature	120° C (248° F)	120° C (248° F)	115° C (239° F)	119° C (246° F)	120° C (248° F)

11.2   PRODUCTION OF FONDANT

The traditional method for the manufacture of fondant is to pour the boiled syrup on a cooling table, splash water on the surface to prevent skinning and when the temperature has fallen to 40° C (104° F), to beat with a spatula.

The continuous procedures that have been developed are based on drum or cylinder cooling. In the drum method. a thin film of cooked syrup is dropped on a rotating, cooled drum to achieve a temperature fall to between 38°–43° C (100°–110° F). The cooled syrup is removed by a scraper blade and transferred into a beating chamber where a revolving bladed shaft produces the agitation necessary to rapidly crystallise the fondant syrup. The procedure described is that employed on the Baker Perkins plant which has an output of over 1000 lb of basic fondant per hour. In the Hansel fondant unit, the syrup is cooled in a chilled cylinder prior to passing to a second cylinder beater unit.

The discharged fondant can be held in wax paper lined cardboard boxes, lacquered tins and plastic containers until required. Tins or plastic materials are unsuitable for the long storage of fondant. The atmosphere of the headspace above the fondant held in sealed tins varies in humidity with changes in external temperature. When the headspace humidity exceeds the e r h value of the fondant, water will be deposited on the surface. The deposited water will leach out the sugar, the resulting weak syrup acting as an ideal media for mould growth. Fondant can be similarly affected when stored in plastic bags. In this instance it is the entrapped air pockets which give rise to localised deposition of water.

Fondant should be matured for at least one day before being used in the manufacture of creams. Although the majority of sugar crystallisation takes place during the beating process, a further small amount of crystallisation takes place during storage. During the maturation process a redistribution of crystal sizes and changes in the concentration of the syrup phase takes place. The total solids content of the syrup phase falls and the syrup water content is evenly distributed throughout the mass. Fondant becomes detectably softer during maturation. During the beating process there is a sudden liberation of heat as the sugar crystallises. This rise is of the order of $10°$ C ($18°$ F) and is due to the release of the latent heat of crystallisation. Some heat is also released during maturation but this is normally too small to be detectable.

11.3 CREAMS

Creams can be prepared in four ways: (1) diluting melted fondant with a thinning syrup; (2) increasing the doctor sugars in the fondant recipe and then producing creams using a continuous fondant unit; (3) blending a prepared fondant powder with water and using without further processing; (4) preparing a syrup and adding a fixed amount of prepared fondant.

Method 4 is the one adopted in the recipe section given at the beginning of this chapter. This procedure is generally known as the 'bob batch' method. Creams produced using this technique are of good quality and the method is less subject to operative error. The temperature at which the basic fondant is added to the bob syrup is critical to the whole process. Basic fondant should not be added to the bob syrup when the temperature is higher than $70°$ C ($158°$ F) if a fine crystallised product is to be obtained. Even at this temperature there is some change in the ratio of the crystal phase to syrup phase in the fondant which ultimately results in the raising of the number of coarse crystals that are present. This is due to the ease by which the smallest crystals redissolve leaving the larger crystals to act as seed. If the crystals in the cream are too large, the sweet will develop white spots due to the drainage of syrup at various points in the crystal network. Coarser crystals are produced when powdered sugar is substituted for basic fondant.

The prepared cream mix should be deposited at 60°–70° C (140°–158° F). It can be deposited from a mogul unit into impressions cast in moulding starch (described in §12.6) or in to shapes formed in flexible rubber or plastic mats. Casting into starch will produce confections that have a crust containing less than half the moisture level present in the remaining mass of cream. Cream centres intended for chocolate covering are best cast in starch as the presence of the crust is helpful in the subsequent handling on to the enrober band. A redistribution of syrup takes place after the cream has been coated with chocolate and the crust will normally disappear by the time the product is placed on sale. Creams that are intended for sale without being covered with chocolate are preferentially deposited into flexible rubber or plastic mats. They can be expelled from the mats by a simple bending action. Silicone mats have particularly good release properties and resist moisture though greater care must be taken during cleaning: they must not be sprayed with live steam.

New rubber moulds should be held in a 1% solution of sodium hydroxide for 15 minutes and then washed in running water before use (this solution is caustic and when handling operatives should wear rubber gloves and goggles). Highly viscous confections are poorly released from rubber or plastic mats which find their greatest use for the manufacture of fondants or creams.

Creams and fondants can be produced by depositing the prepared mix into impressions made in trays of moulding starch. The impressions are formed by pressing plaster of Paris moulds into the starch. These moulds are relatively fragile and can be easily disfigured by chipping. Surface treatment with a silicone release fluid will improve moulding but should only be carried out when the moulds have been newly purchased or prepared. New shapes can be produced in modelling clay or similar materials or in wood. A casting may then be taken using a 4% agar agar solution and the final moulding obtained by using a 1:2 plaster of Paris to water mix. The prepared moulds should be dried in warm air stoves operating at around 60° C (140° F).

The moulding and removal of creams from starch mats is particularly costly in process time. A continuous manufacturing procedure has been developed by the Cadbury Research and Development Department, in association with Baker Perkins Ltd., which reduces the manufacturing time to 30–45 minutes. Creams are cast into metal moulds at a rate of up to 1440 impressions each minute. These moulds are sprayed with a fine mist of acetylated monoglycerides to improve release. Air pressure, exerted through small holes positioned in the moulds is used to expel the creams. To obtain rapid production on this plant all crystallisation should take place immediately following depositing. Cream recipes to be used with this plant have to be varied to produce a product which has satisfactory crystal to syrup phase immediately after casting.

Another significant development is the increasing availability of powdered fondant. This material is composed of mixed fine cane or beet sugar and invert sugar solids, 100 parts by weight of powdered fondant can be reconstituted by blending with 11 parts by weight of water. The resulting product does not contain the same fine crystal range as a well made factory produced fondant.

11.4   Composition of Creams and Fondants

Sugar crystals in fondants and creams are evenly dispersed throughout the syrup phase. More crystal phase is present (50–60%) than syrup phase (50–40%). The syrup phase is saturated with respect to the crystallised sugars that are present. During storage the saturation level of the syrup phase changes with varying temperature. These changes may cause quality defect arising after the confections have left the factory.

One of the main quality criteria of a sample of fondant or cream is the size of the sugar crystals present in the solid phase. Above 35μ the crystals will appear coarse to the palate while a very low crystal sized fondant will appear tacky to the tongue. A good quality fondant or cream should contain the majority of crystals within the $12–17\mu$ size range with a spread of other crystals from $5–30\mu$. During storage it is the smallest crystals which tend to dissolve and later cause growth on larger sized crystals. An incorrect balance of crystal to syrup phase may result in selective drainage of syrup from certain parts of the confection. This causes the appearance of white spots on the surface of fondant. The syrup phase is only loosely held in a fondant or cream and this can be demonstrated by squeezing the confection. Beads of syrup will be noted on the surface of the squeezed material.

Water content is of great importance in the manufacture of fondants and creams. Creams should contain rather more water than basic fondant —13% against 11–12%. A change of only 1% in water content can produce a 3–4% change in the amount of syrup phase that is present. Cooling is of significance in governing the quality of fondant. Slow cooling or beating at too high a temperature produces fondants or creams with large sugar crystals. Rapid cooling gives small crystals which if present in excess result in a fondant with adverse storage properties. Overcooling produces a confection which has a translucent appearance.

The manufacturing variables which influence crystallisation are (i) type of raw materials used; (ii) proportion of raw materials to each other; (iii) residual water content; (iv) beating temperature; (v) extent of beating; (vi) speed of cooling.

A fuller review of the crystallisation in sugar confectionery products has been given by one author elsewhere [R. Lees: *Factors affecting Crystal-*

lisation in Boiled Sweets, Fondants and other Confectionery, 1965, British Food Manufacturing Industries Research Association].

Both fondants and creams contain incorporated air. The amount of air does not normally exceed 2% of the finished batch volume and is dispersed throughout the mix. Badly creamed confections may contain large air cavities which give an unsightly appearance to the product and accelerates localised syrup drainage.

The composition of a fondant and cream varies in the ratio of sucrose to doctor solids. Basic fondant should contain 85 parts sucrose to every 15 parts doctor solids while that for coating fondants is 87.13. Creams should contain 70 parts sucrose to every 30 parts doctor solids. The presence of doctor solids is necessary to prevent hardening on store such as occurs with all sucrose creams. Doctor solids may be developed during manufacture by the addition of 1·5% cream of tartar. It is better however to add predetermined weights of glucose syrup than to depend on in-batch inversion. Medium DE glucose syrup (42) is suitable for the manufacture of these confections but high DE syrups (63) give an enhanced tenderness to the confection.

A number of additives have been proposed for use in cream or fondant manufacture. These are mostly aimed at raising the viscosity of the syrup phase which affects both the crystallisation rate and character of the crystals formed. The use of 0·25% carboxymethylcellulose added at the end of the boiling period has been patented in the Netherlands as a means of reducing overall crystal size of fondant. Small proportions of agar agar and gelatine have been suggested as producing similar lowering in crystal size. Egg frappé can be added to increase the amount of air incorporated thereby whitening the fondant. It is also thought that egg frappé prevents the aggregation of existing air bubbles and prevents hardening. A small trace of blue colour increases the 'whiteness' of a fondant or cream. The use of modified high amylose starch has been suggested [Anon., *Food Proc. Dev.*; 1970, *4*, (5), 84] as a replacement for basic fondant. The addition of 2–3% fat, such as HPKO, will improve bite and assist release from the moulds. Rancidity may develop in fondant held on long store when fats are incorporated and any whipping effect is lost.

The equilibrium relative humidity of fondant is 75–80% and for creams is 80–85%. E r h values can be lowered by the introduction of between 2–4% glycerine or sorbitol to the recipe. Conditions such as these will reduce the e r h values by 5–10%. High e r h values mean that the confections will sweat while on store. Coating fondant used on cakes will tend to absorb moisture from the cake (e r h values 82–90%).

For cake decoration the stock fondant should be warmed to 40°–50° C (104°–122° F) and then diluted with sufficient warm water to achieve the desired coating consistency. If too high a warming temperature is used the coating will be hard and lack gloss. Cakes with a high fat content should be firstly coated with fondant which has been heated to 80° C (176° F) and then with fondant melted at the normal temperature. The hard shell of glazed fondant mix reduces the extent of fat transfer from the cake.

Coating fondant can be applied continuously using an enrober. If sugar confectionery centres are covered with fondant they are known as fourres. The fondant should be diluted with water and the coating operation carried out at 43° C (109° F). Cracking of the coating is due to the expansion of centres under differing temperature gradients. Centres should therefore be warmed to 32° C (90° F) before being placed onto the wire coating bands. Drying is necessary to achieve a fondant coat of sufficient strength to be handled during packaging. Coated confections should be passed through drying tunnels in which overhead heating is provided by infra-red elements and lower heating by aluminium warming plates under the conveyor band. A low air humidity should be maintained in the drying tunnels.

Creams prepared for chocolate enrobing should be firm enough to permit handling prior to covering but soften quickly while on store. To develop this softening some of the crystallised sugars should be brought back into the syrup phase. This can best be achieved by converting sucrose into the more soluble invert sugar. One way of carrying out inversion is to add a high level of fruit acid but inversion achieved in this way is uncontrolled and a variable quality product results. The most effective method is to add invertase to the other ingredients. Invertase should only be added to the cream after the temperature has fallen to below 70° C (158° F), within a desirable pH range 4·5–5·5 and at a rate of 0·12% of the final batch weight. A 4–5% rise in syrup phase will take place with the conversion of sucrose to invert sugar.

Fermentation in fondant or creams arises mainly because the syrup phase contains too little solids or because too great an amount of thinning water has been added. Spotting on the surface of creams is caused by the use of unclean mats, overheating and, more occasionally by the use of high quantities of incompatible flavouring materials. Poorly coloured creams or fondant can be frequently traced to scorching at some stage in processing but the presence of trace metals, particularly iron, can give rise to discoloration. Cupping, the most frequent fault exhibited by creams, is manifested by the sinking in at the centre of the base of the cream. Too dry moulding starch, depositing at too high a temperature or excessive water left in the cream after boiling are the usual causes. The rate of drying out of creams while on store can be lowered by increasing the viscosity of the syrup phase. Creams produced from less viscous syrup phase materials, such as invert sugar, are more likely to dry out in adverse storage conditions.

Creams containing dextrose as the crystal phase can be prepared in a similar manner to that described for mixed sugar creams. A mix containing 50 parts dextrose, 20 parts high dextrose equivalent glucose syrup (63),

20 parts invert sugar syrup (70%) and 10 parts water should be prepared at 80° C (176° F) and passed through a swept heat exchanger to produce a cream with a total solids content of 84%. The cream should be passed through a cooling chamber to chill to 40° C (104° F), beaten and discharged at 20° C (68° F). The development of equilibrium between crystal to syrup phase is slower than with sucrose crystal phase creams and may take up to 24 hours. Crystallisation can be accelerated by adding a 2% dextrose crystal seed.

11.5   WET CRYSTALLISATION

Creams and similar confections which are sold uncovered and which dry out should be protected from moisture loss by wet crystallisation. In this process a tight shell of sucrose crystals is developed around the confection to act as a moisture barrier. Gloss is also improved by wet crystallisation. A poor crystal shell is inevitably due to bad operating practice.

A 74% cane or beet sugar syrup should be prepared at 40° C (104° F). This syrup should also contain 0·2% sodium citrate buffer. The syrup should be passed through sieves and transferred to the crystallising tank.

The confections to be treated should be loaded into 9 in×12 in×3 in wire baskets constructed from stainless steel and placed on holding rails. The syrup temperature should be allowed to fall to 25°–27° C (77°–81° F) and the baskets carefully lowered into the syrup. Great care must be taken to avoid sudden movement or excessive vibration as this can cause shock crystallisation of the syrup. Any syrup crust must be removed before the baskets are lowered into the liquor. Raising the syrup concentration will give a thicker but coarser shell. The confections should be held in the syrup until a sufficiently thick crystal shell has been developed.

Once the shell has developed, the baskets should be raised out of the syrup and agitated slightly to allow even drying. After draining, the confections should be transferred to wire trays and held for one day to permit drying. Any baskets not in use should be washed to remove the deposits of crystal which can act as seed.

Careful checks should be made in the crystallising syrups to determine the reducing sugar content. This must not be allowed to increase above 4%. Syrups containing higher proportions of invert sugar should be used as a base syrup for the manufacture of confections such as gelatine jellies. The wash water used in cleaning the tanks or baskets can be employed as dissolving liquor in the manufacture of other confections.

Each time wet crystallisation takes place, the syrup loses around 3% of its sugar content. This must be brought back to the operating level of 74–75% by the addition of more refined cane or beet sugar.

Confections which are ineffectively drained of crystallising syrup will have a glazed appearance. A dull crystal shell is invariably due to the syrup containing excessive invert sugar. Sweets will stick together if too great an amount is loaded into the crystallising baskets. Each contact point can be an entry area for the ingress or loss of moisture while on store. If the creams are found to collapse while being crystallised it can be due to insufficient solid phase, the use of excessive glucose syrup or the use of too hot crystallising syrup.

11.6 CANDIED FRUIT AND PEEL

Candied (crystallised) fruit and peel are sugar confections in which water in the raw material has been exchanged for a high sugar content syrup. Candying can be carried out using traditional batch processing or in continuous concentration candying equipment.

Traditional Method
1. Prepare a sugar syrup containing cane or beet sugar, a high dextrose glucose syrup and dextrose in the proportion of 70:25:5. Boil to 55% solids (103° C or 217° F).
2. Load the fruit or peel into wire baskets and lower into the hot syrup.
3. Stand for 48 hours, remove baskets and drain.
4. Reheat the syrup and at the same time raise the solids content by a further 10% using additional cane or beet sugar.
5. Stand for 1 day. Remove baskets and drain.
6. Repeat for four further periods slowly raising to a syrup concentration of 70% (107·7° C or 226° F).
7. Following the sixth draining, run in new syrup at 75% concentration, raise to boiling (110° C or 230° F) and hold for 5 minutes. Allow to cool to room temperature and hold for 3 days.
8. Remove the baskets from the tank and allow to drain.
9. Remove the candied fruits and spread on wire trays to dry, turning periodically.

Semi Continuous (Carle and Montanari Plant)
1. Transfer the inspected washed fruit into wire baskets and load into the holding retort.
2. Fill with water and blanch for 10 minutes.
3. Drain and refill with a weak sugar syrup (for composition see traditional procedure) at 30% concentration.
4. Commence candying by slowly increasing the vacuum and allow the temperature to rise from 50° C (122° F) at the start of the process to reach 80° C (176° F) at the finish.
5. Concentration should be gradual and spread out over 12 hours for small fruit and peel to 36 hours for large items such as half cap oranges. At the final concentration level the syrup solids should be between 73% and 75%.

6. Drain off the syrup and lower the temperature in the holding chamber by circulating cooling water.
7. Remove and allow the candied materials to dry.

The first stage in any method for candying is to blanch the fruit or peel. This is necessary to break down the fruit tissues and so improve the speed of ingress of the syrup with lowered shrinkage. During blanching, the enzyme is destroyed and the fruit becomes less likely to discolour. Blanching is achieved by subjecting the fruit to hot damp conditions. It may be carried out using steam, boiling in water or boiling in a weak 10% sugar syrup. Times allowed for blanching should vary from 2–15 minutes according to the softness of the fruit.

Most varieties of fruit are suitable for candying though delicate soft fruits loose both colour and flavour. Fruit chosen for candying should be firm and unblemished. Overripe fruit will collapse during the candying process. Prior to treatment with candying syrup, fresh fruit should be pricked with stainless steel or silver forks to increase the rate of penetration of syrup. During candying the sugar solids content rises from between 10% and 20% to between 70% and 80%. The extent to which candying takes place is related to the size of the fruit. Fruit should be graded before use.

To maintain continuity of production, fruit may be stored in brine or a high sulphite level solution until required. The fruit should be held in wooden barrels made in oak or in a similar hard wood, which has been inner coated with wax. Tanks used for fruit storage should be epoxy or polytetrafluroethylene (PTFE) coated. Any barrel which has been left empty for any period will shrink and to prevent seepage when used, they should be well soaked in water. Additional preserving liquor should be added to ensure coverage of the fruit during storage. Crushing occurs if too much fruit is loaded into the barrels. The concentration of salt (sodium chloride) most suited to preserving fruit is 16%. Hard fruits can be softened by initially brining in 8% strength liquor and increasing over a 6 week period to a concentration of 16%. The fruit should be washed free of salt prior to candying. Some loss of colour may occur during brining or sulphiting which is mainly restored during candying. Fruit colour may be boosted by the addition of small traces of synthetic colour to the candying syrup.

Special precautions should be taken with certain fruits prior to candying. In particular:

Angelica The stalk should be trimmed from the roots and leaves and then soaked in 1% brine solution for 10 minutes. Following rinsing, the stalk should be boiled in water for 10 minutes and then candied according to the standard procedure.

Cherries   Cherries should be held for at least one week after harvesting before being candied. Stones should be removed by punching out of the flesh. Some colour loss occurs on candying and this should be compensated by adding a small amount of edible colour to the syrup. 'Morello' and 'Flemish Red' are good candying varieties but 'Lightharts' should be avoided. The presence of high amounts of tannins in cherries may cause darkening after candying [P. BUTLAND, *Food Tech.*, 1952, 208–209].

Pears, Peaches   The fruit should be peeled, halved, destoned if required and
and similar fruit soaked in 1 % brine solution for 10 minutes before being candied.

Peel   Peel should be stored in brine until required. Prior to candying it should be thoroughly rinsed to remove any residual salt and then scrubbed. A light steaming should then be given.

The transfer of moisture from the fruit and its replacement by a high sugar concentration syrup takes place by diffusion. The rate of transfer and final concentration of incorporated sugar is influenced by (i) ripeness of the fruit; (ii) size of the fruit; (iii) sugar concentration of the syrup; (iv) temperature at which candying takes place.

The amount of sugar transferred into the fruit is of particular significance in connection with the product's keeping qualities. Candied fruit should contain at least 75% sugar and candied peel around 65%. Confections containing less sugar than the minimum figures quoted above are liable to ferment while in store. Immature fruit absorbs significantly less sugar than ripe fruit. Although it is possible to vary transfer rates this should only be undertaken after a careful consideration of the effect on keeping quality. The influence of varying the conditions for candying has been investigated by F. E. ATKINSON *et al.* [*Food Tech.*, 1952, 431–6] and by D. R. MACGREGOR *et al.* [*Food Tech.*, 1964, (1219), 109].

According to A. L. GROSSO [*Confectionery Production*, 1965, *31*, (5), 295] the speed of candying can be predicted using the formulae developed by M. Catenacci in consultation with Grosso. That is

$$\text{Speed of Candying } (V) = \frac{ST(C-c)}{vD} \times k$$

where S = surface area of fruit; T = absolute temperature; C = sugar concentration of syrup; c = sugar concentration of fruit; v = viscosity of syrup; D = thickness of the pieces; k = constant depending on fruit and type of syrup.

The amount of sugar syrup prepared for candying should occupy approximately double the volume of the fruit. The composition of the syrup should be 70 parts of cane or beet sugar: 25 parts high dextrose equivalent glucose syrup: 5 parts dextrose. Some dextrose is advantageous in that it produces a softer texture and increases the rate of candying. Invert sugar syrup (70%) can be substituted for glucose syrup but the prepared fruits are more likely to go sticky on store. A syrup which incorporates invert sugar is 70 parts cane or beet sugar: 20 parts invert sugar syrup: 10 parts dextrose. A small quantity of salt, 0·2%, added to the final candying syrup will improve flavour.

GROSSO [*Confectionery Production*, 1965, *31*, (4), 293] has suggested the use of 2 ppm of either calcium phylate or EDTA as a metal inhibitor to prevent discoloration arising from the presence of trace metals. The same author suggests the use of nacconyl (sodium alkyl aryl sulphenate) to inhibit damage through softening.

Toughness in candied confections can normally be traced to the immaturity of the fruit that was used or to a fast rate of candying. The latter processing fault also causes a shrivelled appearance to the fruit. Inadequate blanching also produces toughness though this is frequently associated with poor colour.

There are a number of causes for poor or off colour. The presence of trace metals, high sulphur dioxide content or low pH values may result in loss of colour quality. Tannins, associated with the fresh fruit and extracted from the storage barrels may cause browning during processing. Enzymes not destroyed by the blanching process also produce discoloration.

A gritty taste in the candied fruit is due to large crystals of grained sugar present in the confection. This can be overcome by increasing the amount of glucose syrup incorporated in the candying syrup. Over doctored syrups produce sticky candied fruits. The equilibrium relative humidity values of candied fruit are high and there is a constant tendency for the confection to lose water while on store. Candied products should not be packed in airtight containers.

Disfigured products will arise if too much material is packed into the crystallising baskets or if overripe fruit are processed or if the candied sweets are packed too hot.

11.7   CRYSTALLISED AND PRESERVED GINGER

Crystallised ginger is produced by soaking cut rhizomes of ginger in progressively increasing strength sugar solutions and finally wet crystallising or tossing in crystal sugar. Preserved ginger is prepared in a similar manner with the omission of the final wet crystallisation and the inclusion of storage in high sugar content syrup. The qualities required of the ginger to be used in manufacture have been fully discussed in Chapter 7 (§7.11). In general ginger originated in China produces a higher quality sweetmeat. High batch weights should be used in processing as the procedure is time consuming and uneconomic with low ginger weights. The method to be adopted for processing is given below.

Batch Method
1. Drain off all the preserving liquor.
2. Soak the ginger rhizomes in water to remove all traces of the salt.
3. Chop or slice the pieces so as to achieve a count per lb of 60 to 80 or a count per kg of 130 to 170.
4. Transfer the chopped pieces into open mesh wire baskets and lower these baskets into the crystallising tank.
5. Prepare a crystallising syrup, which contains 30% sucrose and 10% glucose syrup (63 DE) solids, using the weights given in Table 54. Check the concentration using a pocket refractometer.
6. Fill the tank with this syrup and hold at 120° F for 24 hours.
7. Remove the baskets, allow the syrup to drain returning this liquor to the main mass of syrup.
8. Add additional sugar to the crystallising syrup to bring the total soluble solids content up to 55% (Table 54). Raising the syrup temperature to 180° F and cooling to 150° F will help to achieve solution.
9. Check the total soluble solids content with a pocket refractometer.
10. Return the baskets of ginger into the tank and hold for 24 hours at 120° F.
11. Repeat the cycle 7 to 10 raising the syrup concentration to 70%.
12. Repeat cycle 7 to 10 raising the syrup concentration to 75%.
13. Add a 1% seed of caster sugar to syrup and stand for 3 hours.
14. Remove the ginger and dry in a stove held at 110° F for 12 hours.
15. Wet crystallise as described earlier in this Chapter.
16. For preserved ginger, omit 13 to 15 and pack in 36 Baumé sugar syrup.

Continuous Method
The equipment is the same as that used for crystallised fruit and described earlier in this Chapter. Stages 1, 2, 3 and 13 to 16 are required in the continuous method.

Notes on Manufacture
It is essential to remove all trace of salt, an easily detectable taste, before the commencement of manufacture. The presence of a small proportion of high conversion glucose syrup in the processing syrup is advisable to promote the transfer of sugar into the ginger and to produce a more tender product.

Preserved ginger takes longer to mature than does crystallised ginger. It can take as long as two months before the product develops its finest quality. Once bottled it should last for at least 18 months. Crystallised ginger has a much shorter keeping life and after 4–5 months becomes heavily crusted and generally unattractive. Ginger for subsequent use as a

TABLE 54. Syrup Composition for the Treatment of Ginger

| Syrup Stage | Method Stage | Approx. Soluble Solids % | Weight of Ingredients | | | | | |
| | | | Avoirdupois | | | Metric | | |
			Cane or Beet Sugar lb	Glucose Syrup lb	Water Gal	Cane or Beet Sugar kg	Glucose Syrup kg	Water Litres
1st	5	40	180	75	34·5	85	35	160
2nd	8	55	200			95		
3rd	11	70	400			190		
4th	12	75	240			110		
			Batch Yield			Batch Yield		
			1440 lb			675 kg		

chocolate centre should be processed as described up to stage 12 and then receive a light wet crystallisation coat.

The waste syrup can be used for the manufacture of ginger creams, or in strongly flavoured sweets such as cough toffees, or be recovered as a scrap syrup. Syrup used in the treatment of ginger is unsuitable for re-use when the reducing sugar content (excluding that contributed by the glucose syrup) rises to over 4%.

12

Gums, Jellies and Pastilles

12.1 PRODUCTION

Gums, jellies and pastilles constitute a large class of confectionery products which can be manufactured with many interesting variations. They are comparatively low boiled and contain about 20% moisture. The texture of these products, which can be firm or solid, is obtained by the use of various types of water binding gelling agents principally gum arabic, starch, gelatine, agar and pectin. After a boiled mixture of mixed sugars has been prepared it is mixed with the gelling agent and then processed into the range of shapes by depositing into starch moulds. Other methods may be used principally depositing into rubber moulds or pouring onto a slab. After forming into shapes, the confections are dried to their final moisture content and texture by stoving.

Hard gums are normally prepared from gum arabic alone which is the major ingredient constituting some 50% of all total solid matter that is present. The texture produced is hard and short, but malleable. If the level of gum arabic is reduced to produce a softer eating product then another gelling agent such as gelatine will be required. These products are usually called pastilles.

Gelatine jellies have a soft texture which is inclined to be rather rubbery. It is normal to use an additional gelling agent, such as thin boiling starch, to improve the texture and to give a shorter bite. The traditional 'wine gum' confections contain a large percentage of lower bloom gelatine, and it is this ingredient which produces the characteristic texture.

Starch gums and jellies are becoming increasingly popular in Europe, compared to the United States of America where they have been manufactured in large amounts for many years. The gelling agent employed is thin boiling starch although many types of modified starches are now available and a wide variety of texture can be obtained. The texture of a traditional thin boiling starch based jelly is short and tender with a reasonable degree

226

of resilience. Starches can be combined with any of the mentioned gelling agents.

Agar jellies are low boiled and soft, with a very short eating texture. It is usual to mix either jam or pastes such as minced figs together with the jelly to develop an acceptable texture.

Pectin jellies also have a short soft texture, but provide an excellent base for fruit-flavoured products; normally the pH will be on the acid side, to enable the necessary gelling to take place. New types of pectin, such as the low methoxyl grades can be used in the manufacture of Turkish Delight. This type of pectin gives stable gels over a wide range of pH and blends well with thin boiling starch. Table 55 lists the general characteristics of these gelling agents and the method of use in the manufacture of confectionery.

12.2   Processes for Gums and Jellies

Using different gelling agents, these follow the same general flow line, namely (1) cooking or concentrating; (2) depositing or moulding; (3) drying or stoving; (4) removal from starch moulds, cleaning; (5) sugar sanding or crystallising or glazing.

Cooking and Concentrating

The preparation of gums and jellies has for many years been carried out in steam heated open boiling pans. This method is, however, rather time-consuming and is inefficient in steam usage. New methods of cooking by continuous means are now available which match the advances in depositing and moulding. Of these, three will be considered in this chapter namely the Unimix method, the Votator equipment and the continuous jet cooker. The use of this equipment will be illustrated by reference to starch, but the basic principles apply to all confectionery products.

Unimix Cooker

This batch-type plant (Fig. 30) made by Daniels of Stroud, is for use under either vacuum or pressure and will speedily produce good-quality confectionery jellies; mixing can be programmed to demand minimum operator skill while ensuring constant quality control. The 500 litre mixing chamber is surrounded by an external insulated jacket for heating or cooling. Liquid and semi-liquid products can be discharged under pressure through an optional bottom vacuum-tight valve; solids and semi-solids by tilting the machine bowl through 120° whilst the mixing head and scraper attachment are rotating. The lid is opened hydraulically through 100° and incorporates a light, sight-glass, various connections for dosing, and vacuum or pressure systems. All shaft seals are vacuum-tight and are above the working area of the product.

TABLE 55. General Characteristics of Gelling Agents used in Gums and Jellies

		Gum Arabic	Starch	Gelatine	Agar	Pectin
Usage levels for gelling agents in confectionery products		35%-45%	9%-12%	5%-12½%	1%-1½%	1%-1½%
Percentage of gelling agent to water to effect solution water/agent		50/50	10/1	2/1	50/1	40/1
Temperature of solution required to bring about solution	°C	25°	71°- 82°	60°- 65°	87°- 93°	93°-100°
	°F	77°	160°-180°	140°-150°	190°-200°	200°-212°
Sweetener Ratio Sucrose/Glucose Syrup		66/33-50/50	66/33-50/50	66/33-50/50	66/33-60/40	50/50-60/40
Temperature of Acid Addition	°C	82°	93°	71°- 82°	76°	93°
	°F	180°	200°	160°-180°	170°	200°
Depositing Temperature	°C	71°- 82°	82°- 93°	71°- 82°	65°- 76°	82°- 93°
	°F	160°-180°	180°-200°	160°-180°	150°-170°	180°-200°
Setting Temperature	°C	20°- 37°	20°- 37°	20°- 37°	35°- 37°	71°- 82°
	°F	68°-100°	68°-100°	68°-100°	95°-100°	160°-180°
Setting Time		24 hours +	12 hours +	4 hours +	3 hours +	1 hour +
Time in Starch Moulds		36-72 hr	12-36 hr	12-24 hr	12-24 hr	6-12 hr
Starch Moisture %		5%-8%	5%-8%	5%-8%	5%-8%	5%-10%
Starch Temperature	°C	26°- 37°	37°- 49°	26°- 37°	26°- 43°	37°- 49°
	°F	80°-100°	100°-120°	80°-100°	80°-110°	100°-120°
Total Solids Depositing		68%-70%	72%-78%	72%-78%	76%-80%	76%-78%
Final		85% +	78% +	78% +	80% +	78% +

Texture	Smooth Malleable Hard Bite	Short	Tough—Long	Short—soft Some insolubility	Short—Ridged Clean bite
Complementary Gelling Agents	Starch Gelatine	Gum Arabic Agar Pectin	Agar-Starch	Starch Gelatine	Starch
Temperature at final solid atmospheric pressure °C / °F	124° / 256°	108° / 228°	115° / 240°	107° / 226°	108° / 228°
Effect of cooking or holding time on gel strength	Decrease in strength due to extended time and low pH	Prolonged cooking at low pH decreases gel strength	Prolonged time in liquid state and low pH causes loss of gel strength	Lengthy cooking causes weak gel with discolouration	Prolonged boiling causes some degradation
pH During Cooking Recommended	pH 5·0–6·0	pH 5·0–6·0	pH 5·0–6·0	pH 5·0–6·0	pH 4·0–5·0
Percentage of Acid for Flavouring	0·3%–0·45%	0·2%–0·4%	0·2%–0·3%	0·2%–0·3%	0·4%–0·7%
Buffer Salt Recommended	Only required for low pH products	Not normally required	0·1% if acid is added	0·1% to prevent degradation of agar at high temperatures and low pH	0·1%–0·2% to retard setting
Final pH of Product	pH 4·2–5·0	pH 4·2–5·0	pH 4·5–5·0	pH 4·8–5·6	pH 3·2–3·5
Shelf Life—Approximate	6 months +	5 months +	4 months +	3 months +	5 months +
Flavour Carrying Performance	Good	Good	Poor	Fair	Very Good
Ease of Manufacture	Good	Excellent particularly continuous production	Good	Fair	Fair
Preparation of reclaimed waste material for re-use	Good	Fair	Good	Fair	Difficult

Votator Heat Transfer Equipment

A Votator heat exchanger (Fig. 31) is essentially a shaft rotating within a cylinder: the product is pumped through the annular space between the shaft and a concentric tube, outside which is the cylindrical jacket through which flows the heat-transfer medium (Dowtherm, steam, water, ammonia, etc., as appropriate). Two rows of scraper blades, fitted diametrically opposite on the shaft, scrape the internal surface of the tube, removing any film of material which might hamper heat transmission. A back-pressure valve on the outlet enables the annular space to be kept full of material. For the production of starch-based articles, two such units are

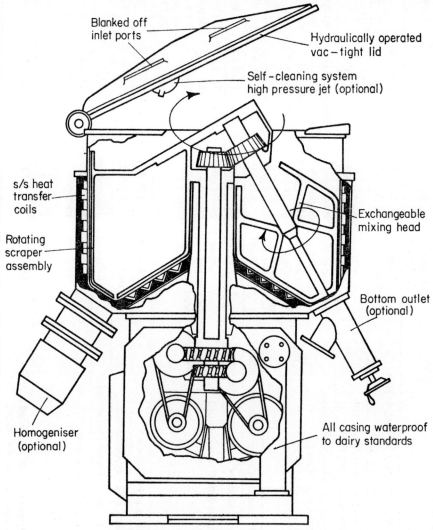

FIGURE 30. Daniels unimix cooker.

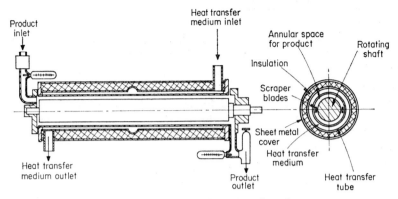

FIGURE 31. Votator heat transfer plant.

connected in series, one with a steam heated and one with a water-cooled cylinder.

Heat transfer coefficients, with starch-sugar mixtures, are obtained of 350 Btu/ft²/deg F/hr as against 80 by traditional open-pan methods.

The basic recipe is broken down to discover the total moisture content and re-assembled containing only that amount of free moisture in the mix that will be required for transfer to the Mogul hopper. This is usually between 20% and 22% moisture. As the cooking and cooling processes are conducted in a closed system under pressure there is little loss of moisture. When the product is cooled to between 80°–95° C (176°–203° F) an allowance of 2% moisture loss is made. The recipe for the pre-mix should be pumpable and this will control the composition to some degree. The pre-mix should be prepared in an open steam heated pan fitted with stirrers, and circulated with a recycle pump to reduce the time necessary to produce an homogeneous pre-mix.

Preparation of the pre-mix

The glucose, followed by the water, is warmed to about 38° C (100° F) and part of the granulated sugar added. It is necessary to dissolve the sugar as soon as possible, as its abrasive nature can cause difficulties should it enter the processing unit. The starch can then be added after dry mixing with the remainder of the sugar; this will prevent it balling. Alternatively the starch can be made into a slurry with the cold water and added to the warm glucose/sugar mixture. The pre-mix should be heated to above 60° C (140° F), and stirring stopped to de-aerate the mixture.

The pre-mix is then pumped to the cooking unit, where the temperature of the material is raised to 127°–143° C (260°–290° F) in about 24 sec, under a pressure of about 100 lb/in². Under these conditions the individual starch granules will be completely gelatinised.

Continuous Starch Jet Cooker

Fig. 32 shows the layout of a typical continuous starch jet cooker, developed for the production of starch gums and jellies, or other types based on agar-gelatine gum arabic and pectin by modifying the processing method. These gelling agents can be manufactured in conjunction with each other, or combined with suitable modified food starches.

The cooking temperature used for starch jelly processing in continuous jet cookers should be about 140° C (285° F) and within the range 135°–145° C (275°–290° F). The actual conditions used will depend on the product total solids and recipe.

The steam pressure valve should be adjusted to about 80 lb/in². To obtain the correct operating temperature, the back pressure valve range should be kept within 40–60 lb/in². At maximum pump speed the steam pressure should make about 80 lb/in², by adjusting the valve on the steam reducers; when operating, the inlet supply of steam to cooker should be 100–120 lb/in².

When depositing, the total solids should be as high as possible to reduce drying time in starch trays. This necessitates good depositing practice with no tails and an accurate measure of the size of piece.

12.3   MODIFICATION OF RECIPES FOR CONTINUOUS PRODUCTION

The original open pan recipe cannot be translated directly to continuous cooking methods. If the original recipe is reproduced for Votator work, the product turns out to be tougher than normal. This can usually be rectified by either reducing the quantity of starch in the recipe or changing to starch of a high fluidity. Another way would be to increase the moisture content of the recipe up to say 30% but then some of the real benefits of the system would be lost. Although satisfactory results from recipes with as low as 17% moisture have been achieved, generally a minimum of 20% is necessary to get a tender product.

Another problem that can occur is that of tailing during depositing. Tailing due to the cooling off of material towards the end of a batch can be eliminated. The outlet temperature of the material can be very closely controlled as we have already seen and the amount of material held in the Mogul hopper can be maintained only high enough to ensure good deposits.

12.4   STARCH DRYING AND CONDITIONING

Moulding starch will pick up moisture from the deposited sweets and must be dried and conditioned before it can be re-used, so as to have the correct moisture content and correct temperature at the time of depositing.

There are two main types of dryers generally in use: steam heated tubular dryers, such as manufactured, e.g. by R. SIMON, England, and flash

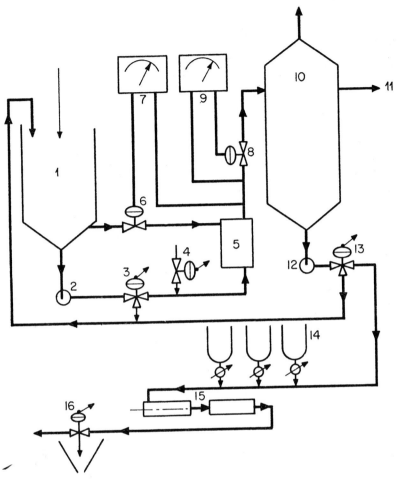

1. Premix slurry tank
2. Feed pump
3. Three way valve
4. Control valve
5. Cooking chamber
6. Steam control valve
7. Temperature recorder
8. Back pressure control valve

9. Back pressure recorder
10. Vacuum chamber
11. Vacuum pump
12. Cooked slurry pump
13. Three way valve
14. Dosage system for acid colour and flavour
15. Mixing units
16. Feed to Mogul hopper via two way valve

FIGURE 32. Ter Braak jet cooking system.

dryers, manufactured by e.g. NID, Australia and Winkler-Dunnebier, Western Germany.

Tubular Drying is exemplified by the Simon drying plant; the amount of moisture evaporated is regulated by adjusting the steam pressure to the dryer. The temperature of the starch leaving the dryer is approximately 77°–82° C (170°–180° F). This is fed back through a Russell screen into the mogul and mixed with cold starch to produce a moulding temperature of 40° C (104° F). Typical moisture contents are 10% entering dryer, reduced to 6% at outlet.

An important feature and advantage of this type of dryer over the flash dryer is the elimination of the explosion risk when drying to a very low moisture content. It may be necessary to pass the dried starch through a cooling unit, if large quantities have been removed for treatment. Where desired, one large drying machine can deal with the starch from a number of Mogul moulding units.

Flash Drying Plant such as the Winkler-Dunnebier unit is for continuous drying, which has three major advantages; the dried starch has a consistent moisture content; there is a reduction in the quantity of starch in use at any time, and there is no longer a need for lengthy re-conditioning of starch in trays stacked in a hot room. A pre-selected but adjustable proportion of the starch is fed by worm conveyors towards the tray-filling station and is continuously withdrawn by passing through an air-tight rotary valve into a drying tube beneath. Here the starch is caught up in a stream of heated air and is conveyed into a large cyclone separator. Clean air is drawn by a fan from outside and heated either by steam or by electricity. The great bulk of the starch is separated by the action of the cyclone; the extremely fine particles are carried on with the air into a cloth filter for the final separation. This filter delivers completely dust-free air and is fitted with intermittent working automatic tapping equipment. The dried starch coming out of the cyclone is continuously fed back into the Mogul by a worm conveyor and enters immediately before the tray filling station. Before being transferred to trays it is intimately mixed with the remainder of the starch that was not removed for drying.

12.5   GLAZING OF GUMS

It is possible to produce an attractive glaze on hard gum type products without the use of oils or fats. This can be achieved using continuous glazing machines of the type manufactured by the NID Company. The purpose of this unit is to wet medium-hard or hard gums or jujubes using steam and then dry off the moisture. This results in an attractive shiny surface and clear transparency of the finished product without the use of oils or greases for polishing.

The cast gums or jujubes are received directly from the starch mould-

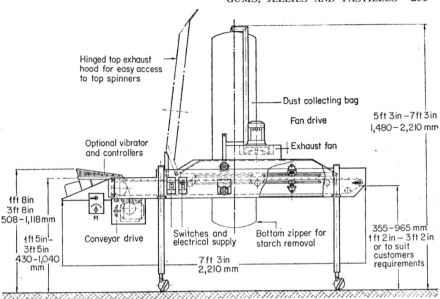

Hinged top exhaust
hood for easy access
to top spinners

Dust collecting bag

Fan drive

5ft 3in – 7ft 3in
1,480 – 2,210 mm

Optional vibrator
and controllers

Exhaust fan

1ft 8in
3ft 8in
508 – 1,118 mm

1ft 5in
3ft 5in
430 – 1,040
mm

M

Conveyor drive

Switches and
electrical supply

Bottom zipper for
starch removal

355 – 965 mm
1ft 2in – 3ft 2in
or to suit
customers
requirements

7ft 3in
2,210 mm

FIGURE 33. NID brushless candy cleaner.

ing machine sometimes via a secondary cleaner (Fig. 33) where they are
brushed again. They are then collected in a hopper at the infeed end of
a 24 in wide wire-mesh conveyor. From there the goods proceed to a
motor-driven circular nylon brush which spreads them evenly over the
full width of the conveyor belt. The capacity of a continuous Glazing
Machine is determined by the total length of the machine supplied and
can cope with the production of a starch moulding machine operating at
speeds up to 20 trays per minute. In the NID unit an inspection area of
3 ft belt length is left before the goods enter the steaming section where
steam of approx. 40 lb/in^2 pressure is evenly played out of nozzles over
the whole surface of the goods while the condensate is removed by drains
below. The surplus steam encounters a stream of heated air of considerable velocity so that condensate is minimised, while the excess steam is
removed by exhaust ducts. From the steaming section the goods proceed
through the heating and drying tunnel with the tunnel operating on a
closed system of air circulation. Surplus moisture is continuously discharged through air outlets, while adjustable air inlets are provided where
the circulating air enters the steam radiator heater under the suction of a
blower which generates an air flow of a suitable velocity.

Depending on the existing room temperature the air is heated to approximately 40°–60° C (104°–140° F). Temperature controls at this stage in
processing should be automatic but require a manual override. The system
circulates the air for maximum steam economy and to keep the heated
air inside the unit and, therefore, isolated from the rest of the plant. The

rate of production is controlled by the setting of the speed of the conveyor band. Speeds of 20–40 ft per minute can be used to achieve satisfactory drying. Where immediate packaging of the finished glazed gums or jujubes is required a second cooling conveyor with air circulation operates with the glazing unit. This may be arranged to pass the glazed sweets through an air conditioned area on the way to the packaging stations, and if provided with refrigeration, can act as a cooling tunnel.

Sugar Sanding of Jellies

The sugar sanding of jellies is illustrated in Fig 34 by the NID unit. Moulded jellies are damped by treatment with steam, dropped into fine sugar crystals, and then dried at raised temperatures. Poor sugar sanding invariably occurs from the inefficient removal of the moulding starch from the surface of the jelly.

12.6   STARCH MOULDING MACHINES OF THE MOGUL TYPE

A number of starch moulding units of the Mogul type are available from Winkler and Dunnebier, NID and Meket. The operation of these machines is similar, differences being in the engineering concepts adopted to achieve the depositing and filling sequences. Typical of these machines is the Helios 262 manufactured by Winkler and Dunnebier, Fig. 35. Stacks of trays can be brought to the machine by any of the customary methods— dolly trucks, lifting trucks, etc, and are simply placed on to the roller conveyor close to the feed entry point of the machine. Trays stacked on pallets or wheeled platforms can also be used.

A stack of trays is always in the 'ready' position and the tray lifters take away trays one at a time, working from the top of the stack downwards. The next stack in line is automatically drawn into position when the preceding one has been disposed of.

The same tray grippers which picked the tray off the stack turn the tray through a full circle when they have reached the top of the machine. The contents of the tray—starch and finished sweets—fall out on to a coarse mesh sieve for preliminary separation. A system of brushes then loosens up any starch still adhering whilst the sweets are resting on the wire band conveyor which subsequently transfers them to the starch blowing station. Four pairs of air jets, mounted alternatively above and below the wire band, clean the sweets. The starch dust which results is continuously withdrawn from the chamber and is separated from the air stream in a cloth filter. In the meantime, the empty trays, now upright, are lowered to the normal working level and are transferred to the main tray conveyor. This is a chain conveyor provided with lugs which control the precise positioning of each tray.

The starch which passed through the first sieve is further sieved and

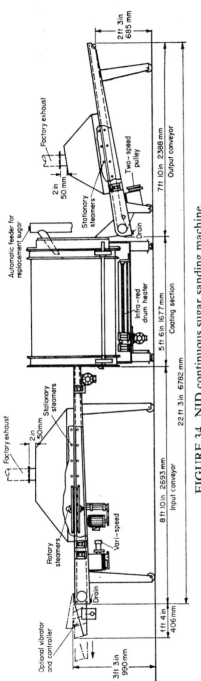

FIGURE 34. NID continuous sugar sanding machine.

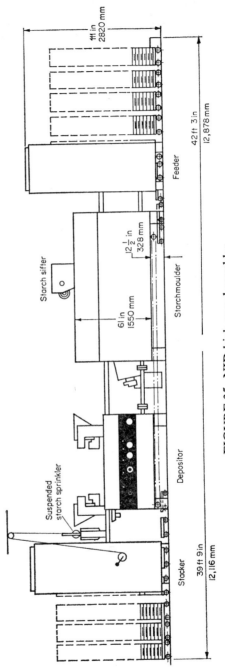

FIGURE 35. NID high-speed moulder.

cleaned falling directly into the empty trays passing beneath. Any excess starch is conveyed back by worm conveyors to the starch charging position. The filled trays are smoothed off on the top surface and also cleaned on all sides. All operations are performed on the moving tray and there are no intermittent motions in this section of the machine.

The starch printing machine has an elliptic motion. It grips and steadies each tray during the return half of its cycle, thus ensuring rigidity during the starch printing operation itself. An accelerated return movement and a slow action forward movement permits a clean printing action with little risk of collapse of bridges between the impressions.

The standard depositor used on this machine has a swinging head action which follows the movement of the tray. For liqueur work, however, an intermittent chain motion is introduced, permitting deposit into a stationary tray. The weight of the deposit and the precise travel of the swinging head can be varied, allowing work with a very wide variety of consistencies of filling. The depositor is normally set to deposit from two to six rows of sweets at each stroke. A single depositor can be arranged one after the other.

When the trays have been finally filled, they are picked up by the tray lifters of the automatic tray stacking unit to be built into stacks of pre-selected height. As soon as the correct height of stacking has been reached, the completed stack is ejected from the machine and building of a fresh one is started without interruption.

12.7   OTHER POINTS IN PRODUCTION

Starch gums and jellies manufactured using open steam pan cooking methods require a high degree of practical knowledge, in order to achieve satisfactory products. Thin boiling starches and other types of modified starches may be used as a total replacement for agar, gelatine or gum arabic, however they are more often used in combination with other colloids.

When cooking starches at atmospheric pressure in open steam heated pans, a steady simmering is desirable, rather than by rapid boiling: it should be maintained just above the gelatinising point of the particular starch being used. During simmering the starch mix begins to thin and then becomes viscous—this effect is sometimes referred to as 'cutting' the starch. Once this effect has been achieved, rapid boiling can be commenced. The end point of final cooking can be judged when the consistency is such that the cooked mixture falls into strings, which spring back on dipping a suitable spatula into the mixture.

The use of various additives to improve the process of starch gelification has been examined by W. J. KNIGHTLY [*Manuf. Conf.*, 1961, (2), 32–33].

12.8 STARCH GUM JELLIES AND PASTILLES BY ATMOSPHERIC COOKING METHODS

	Parts by weight			
Ingredient	A B Gums	Hard	Soft Fruit Pastilles	Medium Hard Pastilles
Sugar	40·0	34·0	30·0	40·0
Glucose Syrup	40·0	54·0	48·0	48·0
Thin Boiling Starch	12·5	12·0	12·0	11·0
Water	100·0	120·0	110·0	100·0
Jam			10·0	

Colour, Flavour, Acid   As required

General Method
1. Boil the sugar and glucose syrup with two-thirds of the water in a steam-jacketed pan.
2. Prepare a starch slurry using the remaining water.
3. Slowly add the starch slurry to the boiling sugar mixture, the speed of addition being such as not to cause the mixture to cease boiling. Vigorous stirring at this stage will help.
4. Continue cooking until the necessary consistency is reached.
5. Add the colour, flavour and acid solution.
6. Deposit into starch impressions and stove in a hot room for 24 hours.

Note: The jam can be prepared by boiling 50% sugar with 50% fruit pulp. The types of thin boiling starches which are recommended are acid or oxidised, with a fluidity of 20, 30, 40 and 50.

12.9 STARCH JELLIES FOR CONTINUOUS PRODUCTION

BASIC STARCH JELLY

	Parts by weight
Sugar	25
Glucose Syrup 42 DE	25
Water	19
75 Fluidity Thin Boiling Starch	10
Colour, Flavour and Acid	As required

Method
1. Add water to pre-mixing pan ⎤
2. Add sugar and mix   ⎬ Cold
3. Add starch and mix   ⎦
4. Add glucose syrup and mix.
5. Raise the temperature to 80°–90° C (176°–194° F).
6. Check total solids of pre-mix at 20° C (68° F) on refractometer. The jelly should be within the range 76–82%.

7. Pump to cooker.
8. Check total solids content after cooking; this should not vary by more than 2% water.

ORANGE SLICES (Starch Base)

	Parts by weight
Glucose Syrup	200·0
Dextrose	104·0
Sugar	200·0
Starch (85 fluidity)	60·0
Water	100·0

Total Solids 76%–80%. Cooking Temperature 278°–283° F. Texture: Short/Tender.

JUJUBES

	Parts by weight
Glucose Syrup	200·0
Sugar	160·0
Starch (75 fluidity)	64·0
Dextrose	80·0
Water	80·0

Total Solids 78%. Cooking Temperature 275°–285° F. Texture: Short/Harder; more Chewy.

JELLY BEAN CENTRE

	Parts by weight
Water	132·0
Starch (70 fluidity)	60·0
Glucose Syrup	330·0
Sugar	130·0

Total Solids 68%–70%. Cooking Temperature 285°–295° F. Texture: Firm/Chewy.

12.10 GELATINE JELLIES

Gelatine is available in sheet, granular or powdered form. Granular and sheet gelatine require pre-soaking before use while powdered gelatine is immediately ready for incorporation.

The gel strength of gelatine can be determined in various ways but that commonly used in the confectionery industry is the Bloom Gelometer. The higher the Bloom number, the stronger will be the gel formed by the gelatine. Bloom strengths normally used in the confectionery industry are between 100–220 Bloom, 180 Bloom gelatine being used for gelatine jellies. The amount of gelatine required to produce a satisfactory gel varies between 5–12% depending upon the final texture of the sweet required and the Bloom strength. Gelatine is not soluble in cold water, but it softens when soaked and absorbs up to ten times its own weight of water. Over soaking, however, can tend to reduce the gel strength of the gelatine, like-

TABLE 55A.   Starch Based Gum and Jellies Produced
by Continuous Jet Cookers

Type	Hard	Parts by Weight Medium	Soft
Sugar	33	40	50
Glucose Syrup	66	60	50
Thin Boiling Starch 70 Fluidity	12–13	11·5–12·0	11·0–11·5
Water	26	22	22
Total Soluble Solids pre-mix	74%	78%	78%
Temperature of pre-mix	82° C (180° F)	82° C (180° F)	82° C (180° F)
Cooking Temperature	140° C (285° F)	137° C (280° F)	137° C (280° F)
Depositing Temperature	93° C (200° F)	93° C (200° F)	93° C (200° F)
Depositing Soluble Solids	73%–74%	76%–78%	76%–78%
Stoving Time (Days)	3	1	1
Final Soluble Solids	85%	82%	82%
Finished Surface	Oiled	Sugar sanded	Sugar sanded

wise high temperature or extended heating has the same effect. In general
it is normal practice to add sugar/glucose syrup solution to the gelatine
solution at a temperature below 82° C (180° F). Any acid addition should
be added at the end of the process.

12.11   Production of Gelatine Jellies

	Parts by weight
Powdered Gelatine 180 Bloom	25
Hot Water	50
Sugar	80
Glucose Syrup	80
Water	40

Method
1. Prepare the gelatine solution in advance, by slowly adding the specified weight of powdered gelatine to warm water. Mix to obtain a
   solution and allow to clear.

TABLE 56. Gelatine Jellies—Faults and their Prevention

Fault	Cause	Prevention
Syneresis (weeping)	Excessive inversion	Use glucose syrup in place of acid inversion. A ratio of 50% sugar to 50% glucose syrup is recommended.
	High reducing sugars	Reduce glucose syrup percentage. Reduce boiling time.
Graining	Low reducing sugars	Increase the amount of glucose syrup or use a high DE type of glucose syrup.
	Low gelatine percentage	Increase the gelatine to inhibit crystallisation.
	Low total soluble solids	Total solids should be within range 78–82%.
	Age of product	Avoid long storage.
Lack of Body	Gelatine hydrolysis due to adding acid at high temperature	Acid should always be added at last stage compatible with adequate mixing.
	Low strength gelatine	Determine percentage of gelatine in relating to its bloom strength.
	Undissolved gelatine	Ensure adequate solution: if powdered, add slowly to water at 90° C (194° F) with slow stirring. Cool syrup before adding to gelatine solution.
	High syrup temperature	Check amount of acid being added. pH range should be 4·5 to 5·0. Use buffer salt (0·2%) if a lower pH required.
	High pH	
Cupping	Low solids depositing	Range 72%–78% is recommended.
Poor Surface	Damp starch at depositing	Moisture content of moulding starch should be 5–8% and temperature 26°–37° C (80°–100° F).
	Cold moulding starch depositing at a low total solids content	
Texture Variations	Variations in drying	Control time and temperature of stoves. Ensure circulation of hot air.
Off Flavours	Low Bloom gelatine or poor quality	Check storage and use a high Bloom strength.
Poor Colour	Low Bloom gelatine	Use a higher Bloom strength gelatine.

2. Dissolve the sugar in water and add glucose syrup. Boil to a temperature of 116° C (241° F).

3. It is advantageous at this stage to cool this solution to approximately 70° C (158° F), before adding to the gelatine solution.

4. Add the boiled solution to the gelatine solution and mix in.

5. Add the dissolved colour and acid solution and mix. Add the required flavour and mix in.

If sheet or granular gelatine is used, it should be pre-soaked for a minimum of three hours in its own weight of water. In most factories it is usual to soak overnight.

12.12   FRUIT PASTILLES

A : STARCH-BASED PASTILLES

	Parts by weight
Sugar	90·0
36 DE Glucose Syrup	90·0
Water	35·0
Thin boiling Starch (60 fluidity)	20·0
Gelatine (medium Bloom)	12·0
Fruit Pulp	16·0
Tartaric Acid	3·5
Colour and Flavour to taste	

Method

1. Add sugar to water bring to the boil.
2. Add glucose syrup bring to the boil.
3. Slowly add starch slurried in 50 parts cold water boil 10 mins.
4. Add fruit pulp boil to 110° C (230° F).
5. Cool to 93° C (200° F).
6. Add gelatine dissolved in 24 parts hot water.
7. Add colour, flavour and acid dissolved in 5·0 parts water.
8. Deposit in warm dry starch.
9. Place in a stove at 54° C (130° F) for 48 hours.
10. Clean off starch and coat with crystal sugar or wet crystallise.

B : GUM-BASED PASTILLES

	Parts by weight
Sugar	100
Glucose Syrup	75
Water	30
Prepared Gum Arabic Solution	100
Gelatine	10
Water	20
Colour, Flavour and Acid to taste	

Method

1. Dissolve sugar in water, add glucose syrup, boil 127° C (260° F).
2. Stir the prepared gum arabic solution.
3. Dissolve gelatine in double its own weight of hot water.
4. Add to batch at 82° C (180° F).
5. Add colour, flavour and acid dissolved in an equal weight of water.
6. Deposit in warm dry starch.
7. Stove at 54° C (130° F) to required texture.

12.13 TABLET JELLIES

Tablet or table jellies are products made from sucrose, glucose and/or invert sugar syrup, gelatine, fruit acid(s), buffer, flavouring, colour and water which on dilution with additional hot water and cooled, set to form a loose jelly structure that can be served as a dessert. It follows that the amount of gelatine, acid, flavouring and colour must all be greater than normally present in conventional gelatine jellies.

Two main methods are used, batch and continuous. The dessert product made using either method should, when considered comparatively differ very little in its properties. A schematic summary of the processes used in manufacture are shown in Fig. 36 and amplified below.

TABLET JELLIES: BATCH PRODUCTION

	Parts by weight
Cane or Beet Sugar	280
Invert Sugar Syrup (70%)	245
Water	70
Batch yield	595

Method

1. Run the required quantity of hot water into a large heated pan.
2. Raise the temperature to 90° C (194° F).
3. Add the specified weight of cane or beet sugar and dissolve.
4. Add the specified weight of invert sugar syrup, mix.
5. Run through a filter press.
6. Hold at 60° C (140° F) until required.

Boiling

7. Draw off 590 parts of syrup.
8. Rapidly boil until the temperature reaches 123° C (252° F). Alternatively pass through a heat exchanger to concentrate the syrup to 90% total soluble solids.

Cooling

9. Turn on the cooling units and bring the syrup temperature down to 100° C (212° F).

Preparation of Other Ingredients
  Gelatine
  10. Slowly add 80 parts of gelatine to 145 parts of hot water at 90° C (194° F) in a mixer tank.
  11. Operate the mixing blades at low speed until the syrup is discharged into the tank.

Acid
12. Dissolve 12 parts of citric acid in 12 parts water.

Buffer
13. Dissolve 2·5 parts sodium citrate in 2·5 parts of water.

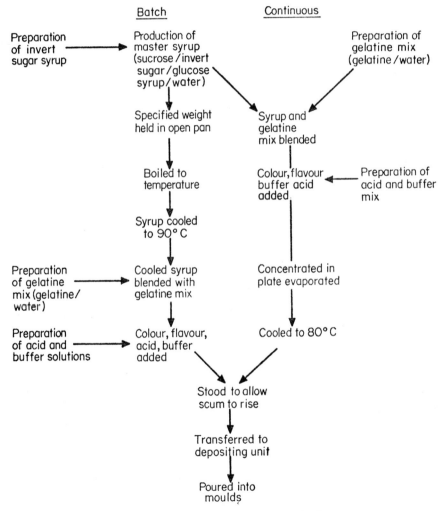

FIGURE 36. Production of table jellies.

Flavouring and Colouring (as desired)

14. Measure 0·45 parts flavouring and add to the batch.
15. Dissolve 0·025 parts of colouring in 0·25 parts water and add.

Mixing

16. Gravity feed or pump the syrup after the completion of stage 8 into gelatine mix at stage 11.
17. Allow to mix for 3–5 minutes.
18. Up to 5% scrap jelly can be incorporated at this stage.
19. Add the buffer solution, flavouring, colouring and finally the acid.
20. When the mixing is complete stop the paddles and transfer to the pouring hopper passing the jelly liquor through a wide mesh sieve.

Depositing

21. Allow the scum to rise.
22. Ensure that the holding slabs or moulds are well covered with release agent.
23. Deposit at a sufficiently slow rate to avoid the incorporation of air bubbles.

Notes

(*a*) Suitable slab release agents are the acetylated monoglycerides or a food grade mineral oil which contains some of the higher paraffins; the agent can be removed by hot water washing and drying.
(*b*) Greasing can be carried out by hand wiping or by spraying from fixed or movable atomisers.
(*c*) To prevent the incorporation of air care should be taken to avoid too great a temperature drop prior to pumping.
(*d*) Some loss of moisture occurs on storage and this requires compensation in the deposit weights used. Up to an additional 3% tablet weight should be allowed for this loss.
(*e*) Jellies can be wrapped in wax paper, glassine or any other close wrapping moisture proof 300 gauge film.
(*f*) The incorporation of scrap normally lowers the quality of the tablet jelly. One solution is to prepare mixed flavour 50% scrap jellies for institutional use.

Continuous Production (stages 1 to 6 as for batch production)

7*a*. Mix the prepared syrup with all the other ingredients.
8*a*. Pump the jelly mix through a thin film evaporator/plate evaporator to concentrate the total solids to 72%.
9*a*. Transfer to the depositors.

Note: If the flavour and colour loss is high or excessive inversion occurs, meter the acid, colour and flavour into collected quantities of evaporated mix or inject these ingredients into the stream of jelly leaving the evaporators.

In both procedures the jelly is deposited after the scum has been allowed to rise. Depositing can be as large slabs which, after setting, can be cut to tablet size or into individual tablet moulds, suitable large size moulds can be constructed from cast iron, nickel or PTFE coated moulds. The latter has good release properties but heat transfer characteristics are lowered. Individual mould depositing can be conveniently carried out by the continuous transport of moulds under the depositing heads. These filled moulds can either be stacked to allow setting or slowly run through a cooling tunnel at 5°–10° C (41°–50° F). Cooling times will be shortened with increase in surface area of the cast jelly. This can be achieved by producing thin jelly tablets with indented surfaces. Such jellies have better sparkle from the reflected light and dissolve more rapidly when diluted with hot water.

The quality assessment of table jellies should be carried out according to the scheme given in Table 57 and faults can be overcome by adopting the procedure suggested in Figs. 37 and 38. Samples of the jellies should be regularly checked to ensure that they have the necessary setting quality. The jelly should be made up according to the packet instructions and 80 ml amounts held in 100 ml squat form beakers for 18 hours at 10° C. On turning out at least 5 of the 6 jellies should retain the shape of the beaker. Generaly $4\frac{3}{4}$ oz (135 gr) or 5 oz (143 gr) of jelly are required to be diluted to 1 pint (568 ml). The jellies should melt and dissolve in 70–100 seconds after hot water has been added.

The choice and amount of gelatine plays a significant part in determining the quality of the table jelly. Various quality criteria and the methods used in the manufacture of gelatine are discussed in Chapter 6. Gel strength determinations carried out on the use of gelatine intended for table jelly production must be carried out at the expected pH of the diluted jelly. Tests on commercial products show this varies between pH 3·3–4·4. It is useful to standardise on testing at pH 3·97 which can be conveniently obtained using a standard buffer solution. The degree of cloudiness exhibited by a gelatine solution is also pH dependent and erroneous impressions will be obtained unless comparisons are made at the pH of the made up jelly. The variation in clarity is caused when the pH approaches the isoelectric point of the gelatine. At the isoelectric point the positive and negative charges within the gelatine molecule are cancelled and turbidity and foaming are at a maximum. For lime gelatines this point is reached at a pH of around 4·8. Viscosity will also vary with changing pH and this may be the cause of difficulties experienced when pumping the

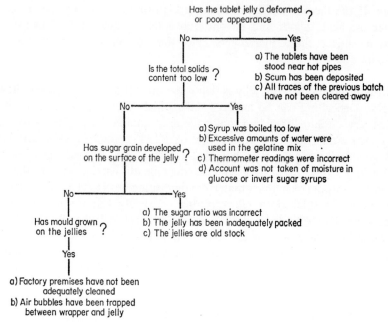

FIGURE 37. Check-list of table jelly faults: A (manufactured).

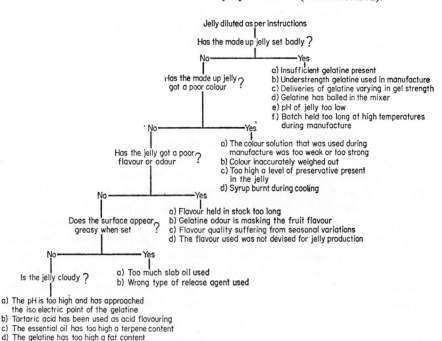

FIGURE 38. Check-list of table jelly faults: B (made up).

jelly if the supplier of gelatine has been changed though the product is apparently of the same Bloom strength. A low viscosity gelatine is easier to disperse than a high viscosity gelatine, the latter variety requires more mixing water.

It is common for raw material suppliers to blend different grades of gelatine during the production to achieve products with a particular gel strength. Some separation of the blends may occur during jelly manufacture which, together with the finer grist material, will clump during mixing. These small balls of gelatine are held back during sieving together with the scum. If the balling of the gelatine is excessive, the overall setting power of the diluted jelly is impaired.

It is advisable to use 230–250 Bloom grade gelatine for the production of tablet jellies. The amount of gelatine used in manufacture is dependent on the Bloom strength. A satisfactory level for 250 Bloom gelatine is between 7·0–7·5%. Low Bloom gelatines require to be used at a considerably higher level and the jelly is more rubbery in texture.

The jellying power of gelatine is severely affected when subjected to high temperatures. Very hot sugar syrups should not be run directly on to gelatine solutions and gelatine mixes should never be added to a hot syrup. Savings of between 10–20% can be achieved by cooling the syrup. Boiled sugar syrups are best cooled to 100° C (212° F) before adding to the gelatine mix. Holding temperatures for the mixed sugar and gelatine should be between 75°–80° C (167°–176° F) to achieve maximum economy in the use of this raw material. Gel strength can also be severely affected by very acid conditions. Buffer salts should be incorporated in table jelly recipes to minimise the acidic nature of the other ingredients. Suitable buffers are sodium citrate and sodium tricitrate added at a rate of 0·2–0·25% at the flavour mixing stage. In preparing the gelatine mix each part of gelatine will require 1½ parts of soak water.

In addition to the cloudiness caused by the effect of pH it may also arise by the choice of flavouring acids. Traces of calcium salts are left in gelatine during the lime treatment received in manufacture. Calcium tartrate is relativity insoluble and produces a cloudy haze in the prepared jelly. It is therefore advisable to use either citric or lactic acids for flavouring purposes. A satisfactory level of usage is between 1·0–1·25%. The buffered versions of these acids, though more expensive, give a product with improved properties. Cloudiness can also be caused from traces of fatty material left in the gelatine during processing.

As a general rule, the best type of flavouring for tablet jellies is the most expensive. Essential oils high in terpenes will cause cloudiness when the jelly is diluted to the 'dessert' strength. This can be overcome using the terpeneless oils that are available. Essences produced specifically for jelly manufacture and not as general flavourings, will give a satisfactory quality. These should (1) be only minimally affected by addition at 80° C (176° F);

TABLE 57.   Quality Assessment of Table Jellies

External Characteristics			
Tablet	Made Up Jelly	Ease in Use	Chemical Tests
Clarity	Clarity	Comparative viscosity of diluted jelly	Acidity content
Colour	Colour		Colouring used
Light reflection	Firmness of set	Ease in cutting or breaking into segments	Gelatine content
Moulded shape	Odour	Time taken to melt down	Greasing agent used and content
Nett and gross weights	Taste	Time taken to set	Sugar content, individual and total
Oil on surface			Ratio of sugar types
Sugar grain			Total solids content
Wrapping quality (Tightness of wrap, ease in opening, quality of materials, protection given)			Water content

(2) be of good odour strength which will be held on storage; (3) have a good natural flavour which blends and is not overcome when the jelly is served in conjunction with other foodstuffs.

Care should be taken to reduce the amount of acid used in the jelly recipe when fruit juices are used.

The ratio of sucrose to doctor solids is important but not to the same extent as in other confections. This is because the total water content is high in comparison to other types of sweets. It is noticeable when drying out has taken place. Invert sugar syrup is better suited for jelly manufacture than glucose syrup. The latter increases viscosity, lowers sweetness, gives a flatter taste and a tougher product. High DE glucose syrup has a noticably less adverse effect than the regular grade syrups. Invert sugar solids will slightly raise the sweetness of the product. An acceptable ratio of sucrose to invert sugar solids is 2:1.

The high sugar content should prevent the growth of moulds on table jellies. This however is not the case and a number of different mould spores have been detected on the surface of table jellies which have included such unlikely types as 'Xeromyces bisporus'. The effect of a steamy atmosphere in the manufacturing area together with the presence of sugar dust produces conditions acceptable to mould growth. Spores may be found in many parts of a jelly department in particular on piping, girders and supporting stands of the cooling slabs. Good factory hygiene must be maintained and efforts made to keep doors and windows closed. The inclusion of small traces of sorbic acid in the slab release agent is helpful in controlling mould growth. Acetic acid should be added to the jelly recipe at a 0·1% level to increase the resistance to mould growth. Pockets of air trapped between the moistureproof wrapper and the jelly give conditions which may cause the development of mould.

12.14   JELLY DROPS

A recent development in jelly manufacture has been the production of sugar coated jelly droplets. The traditional jelly mix is deposited on a conveyor band completely covered with powdered sugar. More sugar is sprinkled on the surface and the drops are packed in the normal 4¾ oz pack. Some readjustment in the total sugar content is required to account for the additional sucrose on the coating. With this method of manufacture the need for the consumer to tear apart the jelly is removed and the greater surface area of the product shortens dissolving time. (British Patents 856,078 and 905,850.)

12.15   GUM ARABIC GUMS

Fruit gums are normally of a hard texture and are produced using various grades of gum arabic or gum acacia. In many recipes the amount of gum

TABLE 58. Gum Arabic Gums—Faults and their Prevention

Fault	Cause	Action to Prevent Recurrence
Insufficient body	Total solids content too low	After drying, should be over 85%.
	Reducing sugar content too high	Should not be above 40%.
	Low percentage of gum arabic	Should be over 35%.
	Acid added to gum arabic solution	Should be added after sweetener addition at final stage before depositing.
Stickiness	Reducing sugar content too high	Over inversion during cooking. Reduce pH and cooking time.
	Too much glucose syrup	Maximum glucose syrup 50% of total sweeteners; normal for hard gum, 20%.
	Low total solids	Increase drying time—total soluble solids should be over 85%.
	Surface stickiness associated with gums	Add glyceryl monostearate (0·2%).
Cloudiness	High oil content in gum arabic	Use centrifugal filtration when preparing gum arabic solution.
	Poor quality gum arabic	Check solution clarity before purchase.

arabic exceeds the quantity of other ingredients and is therefore a major factor in determining the texture of the final product.

Gum arabic varies greatly in colour from a very pale yellow colour to a deep reddish amber. Pale grades are normally selected for the manufacture of best quality confectionery gums. Before processing, it should be broken into small pieces to achieve easier solution, by means of a kibbling machine.

The kibbled gum arabic should be dissolved in cold water in the proportion of 80 parts of gum arabic to a 100 parts of water. The gum should then be slowly steam heated at low pressure to bring about solution; on no account should the mixture be allowed to boil. After the gum has completely dissolved, it should be sieved and cleaned, by passing through a series of sieves or filter cloths, or by centrifugal methods; all grades are liable to contain matter such as fibre bark or sand.

To aid filtration, the sugar solution may be added to the gum prior to cleaning. Gum arabic has a high solubility; solutions of 40% concentration can be prepared at 25° C (78° F) in water. It has found many applications in sugar confectionery manufacture which include its use as a gelling agent in gums, binding agent in pastes and lozenges, a sealant for coating the outside of nuts prior to sugar coating and as a glaze on liquorice and chocolate panned products.

GUM ARABIC GUMS

	Parts by weight
PART A	
Gum Arabic	100
Cold Water	120
PART B	
Sugar	90
Glucose Syrup	14
Water	15
Colour, Flavour and Acid to desired shade and taste	

Method

1. Slowly dissolve the gum arabic pieces in water.
2. Carefully sieve the solution through a fine sieve or cloth, to remove impurities and extraneous material.
3. Dissolve the sugar in the water, add the glucose syrup and boil to 124° C (256° F).
4. Add the boiled solution to the gum arabic solution and mix well.
5. Mix and allow to stand for at least one hour. (During this standing time, the mixture will begin to clear and foam will rise to the surface. This crust should be removed before continuing.)
6. Add the colour, flavour and acid solution.
7. Mix.
8. Deposit into starch moulds.

9. Transfer the moulded impressions to a drying stove and hold until the desired hardness is achieved.
10. Thoroughly clean the gum jellies and glaze.

12.16 TURKISH DELIGHT

Turkish delight has been produced for many hundreds of years from honey, cereals (probably ground corn or maize) and flavoured with rose water. It originates from the Eastern Mediterranean.

Traditional turkish delight is made from a boiled mixture of sugars and a starch based gelling agent which is poured onto a slab, cut when set and dusted with icing sugar.

Many other modifications are possible using starch and pectin, the latter being referred to under pectin jellies. Agar and gelatine can be combined with starch to produce the characteristic texture. Turkish delight produced in this way is usually deposited into starch moulds and later covered with chocolate. The best-known brands of turkish delight are manufactured using starch as the only gelling agent.

Of starches which can be used in turkish delight manufacture, the most suitable is modified maize starch; others are unmodified maize, wheat, tapioca and arrowroot. These starches give a less firmer bodied delight than does modified maize starch and in certain cases have a greater tendency to foam and give 'off' flavours. Nearly all the major faults in turkish delight arise with the incorrect treatment of the starch. With most starch products, for example pastilles, there is often another gelling agent, but for a tender turkish delight only starch should be used.

The main essential during the manufacture is that the starch should be completely broken down—gelatinised. If this is carried out correctly then the residual water left after boiling is tightly held. Failure to obtain complete gelatinisation will result in a 'cheesy' or 'spongy' texture. The sweet has a natural tendency to extrude water which is absorbed by the protective icing sugar. Poor gelatinisation greatly increases this tendency. Complete gelatinisation gives the maximum body to the product. When the starch slurry is run into hot water the starch granules slowly swell and at the completion have lost their characteristic shape. Gelatinisation of starch is more effective when the mix pH is between 5·0–6·0.

The sugar used in turkish delight should be standard granulated white sugar with either invert sugar formed using cream of tartar or from added invert sugar syrup or with glucose syrup as doctor. As with all confectionery recipes which use cream of tartar, the result of inversion is very variable being dependent on external conditions—length of boiling time, when added, buffering effect of the water etc. The most suitable addition therefore is glucose syrup or invert sugar syrup (75%) at a rate of 35 lb (kg) of syrup to every 65 lb (kg) of sugar. Some recipes advocate honey in place of the glucose syrup as a source of reducing sugars. The use of honey increases the dangers of sweating and the flavour it imparts is by no means universally acceptable. Powdered dextrose can be added at a rate of up to 10% to give a more tender product and to help bind the water. Excess usage will increase the danger of the turkish delight going sugary. Recent studies by E. K. HEATON and J. G. WOODROOF [*Food Engrg.*, 1952, *24*, (10), 95] have shown that the use of sorbitol in starch jellies has a detrimental effect on storage. Other research work applicable to turkish delight manufacture is that of W. J. HAMER [*J. Natl. Res. Bur. Standards*, 1947, *39*, (1), 29] and of L. F. MARTIN, H. H. ROBINSON and F. J. FAHS [U.S. Dept. Agr. Report, *Progress in Candy Research*, 1953, (27), p. 3]. These workers showed that the tenderness can be increased for long periods by the addition of small traces of a surface active agent. Suitable agents used have been stearic acid, polyoxyethylene stearate and glyceryl monostearate. The disadvantage of these agents is that the product is so tender it is difficult to handle.

The generally accepted flavourings for turkish delight are rose for the red and lemon or geranium for the white batch. Other flavours used by some manufacturers produce fruit starch delights rather than turkish delight.

In manufacturing turkish delight, a cold well-mixed slurry of starch should be slowly added to the boiling sugar solution. If the slurry is prepared well before it is needed then the starch will absorb some of the slurrying water making ultimately a quicker and easier achievement of gelatinisation. An alternative method is to add the starch slurry to the boiling water in the pan and then after a few minutes add the glucose syrup or invert sugar syrup followed by the sugar. Starch should be slurried in at least five times its own weight of water. When the slurry/sugar mix is being boiled, the starch swells and finally bursts giving its maximum viscosity which then falls on continued boiling; this additional boiling is often necessary, to obtain a satisfactory body.

It would be an advantage if in making the turkish delight the batch could be boiled to a specific temperature; but because a starch skin forms over the thermometer bulb, preventing a rapid passage of heat, thermometers give false readings. A different method must be used to establish the end of the boil. A spatula is dipped in the boil, and withdrawn, allowing the sugar/starch mix to drip off. With the thickening of the mix, the portion removed on the spatula drips in a long rod-like stream. As the boiling continues this changes to a triangular-shaped drip which sets up, this is known as the 'duck's web'. A further check can be made with a pocket refractometer to check the total solids content of the boil. A sample of turkish delight should have a solids content of between 78–80%. A low solids content increases the danger of sweating, while a high solids content gives a rubbery texture.

When the batch has been completed it should be poured into wooden trays which have been well dusted with a sieved 50:50 icing sugar and starch mixture. After a standing period the turkish delight should be picked up, cut, dusted again with icing sugar and then left to stand for three days. During this period a crust is formed which prevents drying out.

The moisture content is quite important due to the effect it has on the relative vapour pressure. When the relative vapour pressure is above the surrounding humidity the sweet will dry out and when it is below it will attract moisture from the air. Turkish delight with a solids content of 76% has an e r h of 78%; when its solids are 80% its e r h is only 73½%. The higher the solids, compatable with eating texture, the less the tendency is to dry out.

In packaging the turkish delight the box should be constructed so that the confection is on one layer only. A box designed with a large depth may only be used with turkish delight of a high solids content in the region of 82%, at which the sweet is hard and leathery. When packing the delight it should be carefully positioned so that on ageing the pieces do not stick to one another. It is the usual practice to add icing sugar to the pack to absorb the traces of water which occur during the shelf life. The use of small traces of anticaking agents in icing sugar will improve the appearance.

STARCH BASED TURKISH DELIGHT

	Parts by weight
Sugar	90
Glucose Syrup, high DE grade	50
Dextrose Monohydrate	10
Thin Boiling Starch	20
Water	92
Colour and Flavour	

Method
1. Dissolve the sugar, glucose syrup and dextrose in 46 parts by weight of water in an open steam heated pan.
2. Prepare a slurry of the thin boiling starch with 46 parts by weight of cold water.
3. Commence heating, bringing the solution of sugar, glucose syrup and dextrose to boiling point.
4. Add the starch slurry but do not allow the mixture to cease boiling.
5. Boil the final solids concentration, indicated by 'Duck's Web' formation.
6. Check the total solids content using refractometer, this should be over 78%.
7. When the final solids are reached turn off the steam and add colour and flavour.
8. Pour the mixture into wooden or plastic trays, which have been dusted

with an equal mixture of starch and icing sugar and leave until firm
enough for cutting.

9. Lift from the trays and cut into the required sizes, redusting with the
   icing sugar/starch powder. Leave to harden a little before final packing.

Note: A suitable usage rate for dusting powder is 7 gr ($\frac{1}{4}$ oz) per 113 gr
(4 oz) pack. To prevent this icing sugar from becoming lumpy, about 1%
of either calcium phosphate or magnesium carbonate can be added; these
additives improve the free running characteristics of dusting powders.

12.17   AGAR JELLIES

Agar is relatively insoluble when added to a boiled sugar glucose syrup.
It should be added to the dissolving water and brought into solution by
heating. Solution only occurs near the boiling point of water. Agar requires
a higher dissolving temperature to gelatine, the latter going into solution
at about 54°–60° C (130°–140° F), as against that for agar of around
85° C (185° F). The actual temperature will depend on the source of the
agar, but it is invariably over 85° C (185° F) and usually over 93° C
(200° F).

An exceptionally large amount of water is required to prepare a satisfactory solution of agar. A ratio of 50 parts water to 1 part agar is
recommended. Unlike gelatine, agar is not greatly affected by heat provided
it is held in a neutral solution. However, in acid solutions it is very rapidly
hydrolysed, a process which is used to good effect in the production of
piping jelly. Acids affect hot agar solutions to a much greater extent than
gelatine solutions. A temperature over 66° C (150° F) causes the agar to
become hydrolysed. However, by adding a buffer salt, such as sodium
citrate, the temperature at which hydrolysis takes place will be raised to
76° C (170° F). The buffer salt is added to minimise the change in pH due
to the acid. The normal rate to add is about 20% by weight of the total
acid, by dissolving in an equal weight of water.

The pH range for agar products should be within pH 4·5–5·5, at the
final stage. If the product falls outside this range, the acid or buffer salt
content should be adjusted.

Unlike gelatine, agar does not exhibit an iso-electric point and is
negatively charged. This means that solutions of agar do not exhibit
maximum cloudiness and foaming at a specific pH. Agar jellies will set at
approximately 37° C (100° F) but considerably higher temperatures are
needed to bring about melting. In comparison to gelatine jellies, agar jellies
have a short texture but not so short as that produced using pectin. Agar
jellies take considerably longer to set in moulding starch impressions than
pectin jellies. Agar can be used in conjunction with all types of gelling

TABLE 59.   Agar Jellies—Faults and their Prevention

Fault	Cause	Action to Prevent Recurrence
Insufficient body	Undissolved agar	Soak agar prior to use.
	Not enough water used for solution	Recommended ratio 50/1.
	Acid added at too high a temperature	Maximum temperature for acid addition 76° C (170° F).
	Total soluble solids content too low	Ensure that after depositing the minimum solids content is 78%.
	Insufficient agar	Percentage agar used should be 1–1½%.
	Not enough glucose syrup	Increase the glucose syrup content to 50% of total sweeteners.
Too much body—solid texture	Too high soluble solids	Maximum solids content after cooking should be reduced to 80%.
	Percentage agar too high	Reduce to recommended percentage, as above.
Weeping	Excessive inversion	Do not add acid after cooling—measure the amount of any added fruit pulp.
	Low pH during solution stage	Use a recommended buffer salt (0·1%).
	Packing problems	Change the type of packaging. Jellies of this type are subject to e r h change and packing material must allow some passage of air.
Starch crust	Low solids at depositing	Ensure that the solids content after cooking is more than 76%.
	Damp starch	Maintain starch moisture in the range 5–10% and temperature 37°–49° C (100°–120° F).
	Depositing into starch too hot	Deposit at between 65°–76° C (150°–170° F).

Fault	Cause	Action to Prevent Recurrence
Graining	Low reducing sugars	Increase the glucose syrup content to 50% of total sweeteners.
	Excessive invert sugar content	Under certain circumstances it is possible to get crystallisation of dextrose, and, for this reason, reducing sugar should be kept below 30%.
	Added dextrose	For the same reason dextrose monohydrate should not be used in agar jellies as a conditioner.
Cloudiness	Poor quality agar	Check clarity of agar solution sample before buying.
Sugar crystal not adhering to product	Starch surface on jellies	Consider producing this type of jelly by starchless moulding using rubber moulds, particularly suitable if the jellies are to be chocolate covered.
Deformation	Low total solids Packing too hot	Increase drying to yield total solids over 85%. Products should be cooled after glazing, before packing.
Graining	Reducing sugar low Undissolved sugar	Increase the usage of glucose syrup and/or invert syrup. Ensure complete solution of sugar by cooking to 124°C (256°F).
Cupping	Very low total solids content at the depositing stage	Depositing solids should be over 60%. Normal practice is over 68%. Close control is necessary to obtain desired shape and smooth rolled edge. Stoving temperature should be 49°–66°C (120°–150°F).
Dull surface	Starch crust	Depositing at low solids or depositing in damp starch. Starch temperature should be 26°–37°C (80°–100°F) and moisture content 5–8%.

agents, but only combination with pectin or starch produces a satisfactory confectionery jelly.

AGAR JELLIES

Part A

	Parts by weight
Agar	2·0
Water	70·0
Sodium Citrate	0·7

1. The agar, depending on source, should be pre-soaked in cold water for 3–12 hours.
2. Slowly heat the mixture in an open steam pan to bring about solution.
3. Add the sodium citrate.
4. Strain through a fine sieve.

Part B

	Parts by weight
Sugar	60
Glucose Syrup	40
Colour, Flavour and Acid	to taste

5. Add sugar and glucose syrup to the agar solution and boil until a temperature of 107° C (225° F) is reached.
6. Cool to a temperature not exceeding 76° C (170° F), and add any acid solution.
7. Add the colour and flavour.
8. Deposit in warm dry starch moulds.
9. Hold the jellies in starch moulds for 12–24 hours.
10. Check that the total soluble solids content of the finished jellies is in excess of 76% before removing from starch.

Note: The moulding starch should be in the range 5–8% moisture and be held at 26°–43° C (79°–110° F).

12.18   THE USE OF POWDERED PECTINS IN CONFECTIONERY MANUFACTURE

Pectins used for confectionery manufacture are (1) slow set buffered; (2) slow set unbuffered and (3) low methoxyl grades. The range of products they are capable of producing are grouped under the general title of pectin jellies; the texture of these is quite different from that of gums or pastilles. Typical pectin confections are jelly fruits, jellied chocolate centres, fruit

slices, and, in combination with starch, turkish delight. For these products
the use of a slow set pectin is essential to give the necessary flexibility in
manufacturing methods.

Soluble Solids Content

The normal depositing solids for pectin jellies should be in the region
of 76–78%, as measured by a sugar refractometer. In some cases (e.g.
orange–lemon fruit slices a high total solids content of 83% is sometimes
used. Under these conditions it is advisable to use a higher pH mix. By
increasing the soluble solids to 83% the rate for setting will be increased.
Raising the pH will lengthen the time available for depositing or pouring
to take place. Higher temperatures and longer boiling times used to raise
the soluble solids, result in the formation of increased invert sugar unless
the recipe is modified to give a higher pH.

Sugar-Glucose Syrup Ratio

Glucose syrup should be used as an ingredient in pectin jelly recipes,
to prevent sugar crystallisation developing on store, at a rate of 30–40%.
This rate is based on the total soluble solids concentration; higher amounts
of regular grade glucose syrup (43 DE) will cause toughness in the jellies.
This can be overcome by using the higher conversion glucose syrups (63
DE), which will enable the amount used to be increased to 50% or more
of total soluble solids content, and bring about increased sweetness, reduced
viscosity and improved humectant properties.

pH

The pH of a pectin jelly can be measured on a 50% by weight solution
of jelly dispersed in water. Jellies manufactured with slow set pectins should
be within the pH range 3·3–3·6 and for those with high total solids content,
within the pH range 3·6–3·8. The pH can be controlled by the amount of
buffer salt (such as potassium or sodium citrate) used and the type of acid
present. The pH will remain constant if these two ingredients are held in
the same ratio. pH can be lowered by increasing the proportion of acid and

TABLE 60.   Relationship between pH and Acid Taste

Type of Acid	Relative Amounts to Produce an Equal pH drop (by weight)	Relative Amounts to Produce an Equal Acidic Taste (by weight)	Relative Acidic Taste for Equal pH Drop
Citric Acid	1·00	1·00	1·00
Malic Acid	1·00	0·80	1·25
Lactic Acid	1·00	1·25	0·80
Tartaric Acid	0·56	1·00	0·56
Phosphoric Acid	0·23	0·90	0·25

raised by increasing the amount of buffer salt. Buffered pectins usually contain all the buffer salt and part of the acid required for confectionery manufacture.

Citric acid is commonly used for pH control. However, other acids, such as tartaric, lactic, malic and phosphoric may be substituted, if these are permitted by local food additive regulations.

The type of acid used not only governs the pH but also the acidic taste (Table 60).

Depositing Time

The depositing time is dependent upon three factors: (a) type of pectin; (b) pH and soluble solids; (c) temperature. It is advisable to aim to deposit at a temperature not lower than 82° C (180° F) and within twenty minutes of adding the final amount of acid. This is to ensure that any sugar inversion is kept within safe limits—excess inversion leading to sweating and possible crystallisation. Below 82° C (180° F) there is a considerable risk of setting before depositing is completed. Raising the pH will slow the rate of setting. It is therefore advisable when manufacturing large sized batches to work at the upper end of the pH range.

Material which has set prematurely can be added to subsequent batches at a rate not exceeding 5% of the batch. The scrap should be added after the pectin has been dissolved in the water and completely dissolved before any further sugars are added.

Addition of Buffer and Acid

The acidic taste of the final product depends more on the concentration of the acid than the pH. The acid taste can be increased without alteration of the pH by increasing the acid and buffer salt in proportion, up to a total of about 0·6 parts potassium citrate and 1·1 parts citric acid per 100 parts of the jelly. The acid should be added in two portions, first about one-third of the total, the remainder at the end of boiling. This procedure is to control the rate of sugar inversion during boiling and thereby extend shelf-life. It is not usual for pectin jellies to dry out. If drying does occur, a higher percentage of acid should be added at the start of boiling to increase the amount of inversion. Where the product sweats or becomes damp the amount of acid added at the beginning of cooking should be reduced.

Firmness of Jelly

This can be altered by increasing or decreasing the amount of pectin, the quantities of the remaining ingredients remaining the same; this will not affect the total setting time. The texture can also be altered by the addition of fruit pulp, juice or sieved fruit.

Size of Batch

The size of the batch depends on the process and equipment available for production. Provided the boiling time is not less than 15 minutes and the depositing time 20 minutes or less, there is no limit to the size of batch that can be produced. Where suitable equipment is available, to use a continuous processing will also produce optimum results.

Methods of Manufacturing (Batch Production)

1. Dissolve the potassium citrate (unbuffered pectins only) and one-third of the citric acid in the water and heat to 70° C (158° F).
2. Mix the pectin in the dry state with three times its own weight of sugar and pour into the water, stirring continuously.
3. Bring the mixture to the boil, and keep boiling for one minute to ensure that all pectin is dissolved.
4. Add the glucose syrup and the remainder of the sugar and boil to 76% soluble solids, i.e. 108° C (227° F) (see Table 2).
5. Dissolve the remainder of the citric acid in an equal weight of water, stir well into the mixture.
6. Add colour and flavour.

A batch size of approximately 100 lb or 50 kg should be deposited within twenty minutes into starch or release treated rubber moulds.

PECTIN JELLIES

(A)   *Buffered Slow Set Pectins*

	Parts by weight
Pectin	1·25
Citric Acid Monohydrate	0·4
Sugar	51
Glucose Syrup 42 DE	29
Water	40
Colour and Flavour	As required
Yield	100

(B)   *Buffered Slow Set Pectins (using 63 DE Glucose Syrup)*

	Parts by weight
Pectin	1·25
Citric Acid Monohydrate	0·4
Sugar	38
Glucose Syrup 63 DE	42
Water	37
Colour and Flavour	As required
Yield	100

Formula (A) produces a moderately firm jelly, whilst formula (B) gives a slightly more tender product.

(C)   Unbuffered Slow Set Pectins

	Parts by weight
Pectin	0·82
Citric Acid Monohydrate	0·28
Potassium Citrate	0·25
Sugar	51
Glucose Syrup	29
Water	40
Colour and Flavour	As required
Yield	100

The amount of citric acid monohydrate used will depend upon the type of pectin. For some types of unbuffered slow set apple pectins, 0·28 parts would be required, while for unbuffered slow set citrus pectin, 0·4 parts of citric acid should be used.

(D)   Unbuffered Slow Set Pectins (using 63 DE Glucose Syrup)

	Parts by weight
Pectin	0·82
Citric Acid Monohydrate	0·28
Potassium Citrate	0·25
Sugar	38
Glucose Syrup	42
Water	37
Colour and Flavour	As required
Yield	100

Methods for Continuous Production

For continuous production, it is necessary to first prepare a stable pectin solution. The pectins most suitable are slow set buffered and low methoxyl (buffered). It is essential to ensure complete solution before use. Failure to do so can result in weak gel formation and inefficient utilisation of the full gelling power. It is recommended that solutions are made up to a known concentration by weight, and advice should be taken from the pectin manufacturer as to the type and solubility of the buffer salt used.

PECTIN SOLUTION

	Parts by weight
Pectin	2
Sugar	10
Water	88

Method

1. Mix the pectin and sugar in the dry state.
2. Place water in mixing vessel and heat to 70°–77° C (158°–170° F).
3. Start the stirrer and add the pectin–sugar mixture to the water.
4. Heat to boiling point and stir for one minute.
5. Cool the solution to 50°–60° C (122°–140° F).

Note: Cooling is necessary to prevent degradation of the pectin. It can be omitted if the solution is to be used immediately.

This solution can be made up several times during the course of a day's production, and kept in bulk prior to mixing with the remaining ingredients. When making up the complete slurry before pumping to the continuous cooker, it is necessary to calculate the total soluble solids required in the finished product. The slurry should contain approximately the same percentage of soluble solids as in the finished product. The total amount of acid required should be metered into the solution after cooking. Any loss of inversion, caused by this procedure, can be compensated for by the addition of invert sugar to the slurry, or by an increased amount of 63 DE glucose syrup.

A suggested flow line is given below in schematic form:

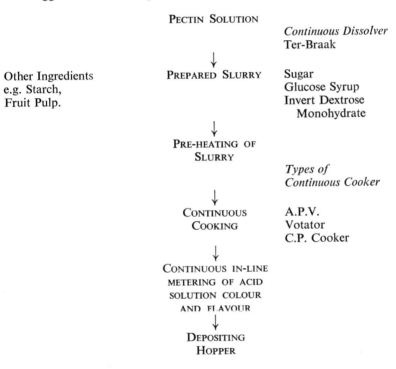

PECTIN SOLUTION

Continuous Dissolver
Ter-Braak

↓

Other Ingredients
e.g. Starch,
Fruit Pulp.

PREPARED SLURRY

Sugar
Glucose Syrup
Invert Dextrose
  Monohydrate

↓

PRE-HEATING OF
SLURRY

*Types of
Continuous Cooker*

↓

CONTINUOUS
COOKING

A.P.V.
Votator
C.P. Cooker

↓

CONTINUOUS IN-LINE
METERING OF ACID
SOLUTION COLOUR
AND FLAVOUR

↓

DEPOSITING
HOPPER

12.19 LOW METHOXYL PECTIN JELLIES

Low methoxyl pectins will form jellies over a wide range of pH (approximately 2·8–6·5) and soluble solids (10–80%). Their use in confectionery manufacture is almost entirely limited to those products with a soluble solids content of 70–80 where a somewhat bland and mild acidic taste is required. The texture of such products is, in general, somewhat softer and less elastic than those of the slow set pectin type. This texture can be considerably modified by the introduction of thin boiling starch. The formula given for

TABLE 61. Pectin Jelly: Faults and their Prevention

Fault	Cause	Action to Prevent Recurrence
Syneresis (weeping bleeding commonly called sweating)	High reducing sugars resulting from over-inversion.	Use glucose syrup instead of relying on in-process inversion. No more than 30% reducing sugar should be present in the jelly.
	Low pH caused by too much acid.	Check using pH meter. Value to be used depends upon type of pectin and acid added. Reduce amount of acid particularly that added at the start of boiling process.
	Insufficient pectin. Pectin not completely dissolved.	Increase pectin content and check the quality of the stored pectin. Check pectin solution visually. Increase amount of water in first stage of boiling.
	Low soluble solids.	Check using refractometer. Increase boiling temperature.
	Excessive boiling causing pectin breakdown.	Reduce the amount of water used.
	Too low temperature used during depositing causing premature set.	Speed up depositing. Reduce the batch size.
Crystallisation (dullness)	Dextrose crystallisation, resulting from too much inversion.	Check invert sugar content. Raise pH. Reduce acid level. decrease boiling time.
	Use of added Dextrose Monohydrate as a humectant.	Do not use dextrose, honey or high dextrose fruit pastes in the manufacture of pectin jellies. Increase glucose syrup.
	Sucrose crystallisation caused by low reducing sugars.	Increase inversion by reducing pH or extending boiling time.
Too firm set	Excessive pectin.	Reduce amount of pectin.
	High soluble solids content.	Check with refractometer, maximum soluble solids content should be no greater than 82%.
	Low pH.	Check acid content of any other ingredient added, e.g. pulp.

Fault	Cause	Remedy
	Wrong grade of pectin used. No buffer salt added.	Use slow set pectin. Setting can be delayed for 20 minutes or more by adding a buffer salt.
Discoloration of jellies	Wrong type of pectin. Excessive cooking time. Contaminations by metals. Too much buffer salt.	Use a citrus type for best colour. Cook no longer than 20 minutes. Eliminate source of metallic contamination. Maximum amount 10 oz (283 gr) per 100 lb (50 kg).
Cupping (hollow backs)	Low soluble solids content at depositing stage. High total solids content caused by excessive drying in starch.	Increase soluble solids content to minimum level of 75%. Reduce drying time and increase the soluble solids content of the deposited jelly.
Tough, chewy	High soluble solids content. Wrong grade of glucose syrup used.	Maximum limit should be 82%. Change type of glucose syrup to 63 DE grade.
Too rapid setting	Excessive acid. Wrong grade pectin used. No buffer salt used.	Reduce acid level, to give pH 3·2–3·6. Use a slow set grade. Check pectin contains buffer salt. If not add suitable type, e.g. potassium citrate. Reduce level if final set is satisfactory.
Mushy jelly	Premature gelation of pectin, caused by adding ingredients after boiling. Acid solution added too soon. Insufficient water in formula. Pumping at too low temperature.	Stop adding extra sugar, either near the end of boil or after. Add final acid solution after boil is completed. Increase water to obtain better solution of pectin. Do not pump or move solution when the temperature falls below 70° C (158° F).

turkish delight jelly will yield a product with a pH of approximately 5·0 and soluble solids content of 76%.

Part of the strength of this type of jelly is due to the effect upon pectin of the natural calcium in the dissolving water. If water with a high calcium content, i.e. very hard water, is used, it may be necessary to slightly reduce the amount of low methoxyl pectin. With very soft water no formula alterations are recommended, unless a very firm jelly is required. If a firm jelly is required an addition to the boiling mixture of up to 0·125 parts/100 parts jelly of a 10% solution of calcium chloride or an equivalent amount of other calcium salts should be made. As with slow set pectin jellies, depositing or spreading should be completed as quickly as possible in order to prevent any premature setting.

Diffiiulties arising from excessive levels of in-batch produced invert sugar is not normally a problem with turkish delight, due to the relatively high pH of this confection. However turkish delight batches should not be subjected to a long boiling period as this can result in a considerable degradation of the pectin.

PECTIN JELLY: TURKISH DELIGHT
(containing low methoxyl pectin and thin boiling starch)

	Parts by weight
Buffered Low Methoxyl Pectin	2
Sugar	42·5
Glucose Syrup 42 DE	45
Water	40
Thin Boiling Starch	3·5
Water for Starch Slurry	18
Colour and Flavour	As required
Yield	108

Method (batch production)
1. Mix pectin in dry state with 4 parts of the sugar.
2. Heat the water to 70° C (158° F) and add the pectin–sugar mixture, stirring continuously.
3. Bring the mixture to the boil and boil for one minute.
4. Slurry the starch in cold water, add slowly to the boiling mixture, maintaining boiling point.
5. Add the remainder of the sugar, together with the glucose syrup, boil to 107° C (225° F) to produce a total soluble solids content of 76%.
6. Add colour and flavour.
7. Deposit into starch moulds or spread onto a slab.

13

Liquorice and Cream Paste

13.1 LIQUORICE

Liquorice paste, usually referred to as liquorice, is a partially or wholly gelatinised starch paste which contains a range of sugars for sweetening and block liquorice juice as flavouring. The recipes used for producing liquorice paste vary particularly with regard to the desired eating texture. It can be produced using either open pan cooking or continuous cooking using scraped surface heat exchangers of the 'votator' type. Three recipes for liquorice are given in Table 62 overleaf.

13.2 METHODS FOR MANUFACTURING LIQUORICE PASTE

Method A—Continuous process

1. Place the glucose syrup and water in the jacketed disintegrator/agitator pan and add the brown sugar. Mix.
2. Raise the temperature to 40° C (104° F).
3. Break up the block juice and add to 1 gal of hot water; heat to dissolve and add to the premix.
4. Add any remaining ingredients and prepare a homogeneous slurry by recycling for 20 minutes.
5. Raise the temperature to 60° C (140° F) and recycle the mix for a further two minutes.
6. Pump into the votator unit at constant speed (machine setting is determined by the desired product texture).

Method B—Batch process

1. Place the slurry water in a stirring pan and add the wheat flour; blend.
2. Run the mix water into the cooking pan, heat to boiling and add the hydrol, brown sugar, salt and the block juice (previously dissolved in boiling water).
3. For liquorice sheet only, add the treacle, glucose syrup and molasses.
4. Continue heating and when boiling run in the starch slurry.

5. When all the starch slurry has been added, bring to the boil and cook for the specified period.
6. For liquorice novelties and plug only, the required weights of treacle glucose syrup and molasses should be added 30 minutes prior to the end of the cooking period.
7. On completion of the cook period, release heat and add the liquid caramel, aniseed flavouring, black colour and the prepared gelatine solution.
8. Mix until a constant shade is achieved.
9. Discharge the cooked mass and transport to the extruders.

Method C—BCH 'HK' flowline plant
1. Mix the liquid ingredients of an unmodified 'batch' recipe and transfer to the slurry premix unit.
2. Start the pan agitator and add any remaining 'solid' raw materials; recycle to prepare a homogeneous premix.

TABLE 62.   Recipes for Liquorice Paste

| | 'Open Pan' Batch | | |
| | *Sheet* | *Novelties* | *'Continuous Cooking' Sheet* |
Ingredient	*Parts by weight*	*Parts by weight*	*Parts by weight*
⎰ Slurry Water	50	50	—
⎱ Wheat Flour	150	150	125
Mix Water	130	160	80
Brown Sugar	125	100	60
Crude Treacle	75	150	140
Hydrol	25	—	25
Glucose Syrup			
(high DE grade)	12·5	12·5	10
⎰ Block Juice	20	25	18
⎱ Dissolving Water	15	20	10
Liquid Caramel	15	25	10
Hardened Palm			
Kernel Oil	2·5	2·5	2·5
Aniseed Oil	0·25	0·25	0·25
Black Colour	1	1	1
Salt	0·5	0·5	0·5
⎰ Water	5	5	—
⎱ Gelatine	5	5	—
GMS	0·5	0·5	0·5
Cooking Time, minutes	80	150	Pump speed and temperature should be controlled according to quality required.
Scrap addition— no more than:	25	50	25

Note: Red liquorice can be prepared by leaving out the liquid caramel and substituting golden syrup for treacle. Add 1 part of red colour to produce a bright red shade omitting the black colouring.

3. Turn on

    (*a*) the steam in the FM cooker,

    (*b*) the extractor fan to remove any evaporated water, and

    (*c*) the water flow in condenser unit positioned in the vapour vent.

4. Pump the premix into the cooker and commence cooking.
5. Observe the level of the condensed water collected in the measuring tank and the amperage reading. (Note—the amount of water condensed is indicative of the rise in solids content, while the rise in power consumption will indicate the progression of gelatinisation.)
6. As soon as the amount of condensed water has reached the calculated level to give the desired moisture content of the liquorice paste at the end of cooking turn off the steam, the fan and the cooling water.
7. Discharge the cooked paste on to a conveyor and transport to the extruder. Extrude at 70°–82° C (158°–180° F).
8. Pass the extruded sheet through a 40 ft cooling tunnel for $1\frac{1}{2}$–5 minutes (depending on shape) and guillotine or cut to size with rotary cutters.

13.3 PROPERTIES OF LIQUORICE PASTE

Processing procedures for the manufacture of liquorice paste result in the removal of moisture, the controlled gelatinisation of starch, and development of gloss. The second stage, the control of gelatinisation is the most important of these affecting directly or indirectly texture, the extrusion characteristics, gloss and the efficiency of removal of moisture. The level of gelatinisation desired will vary according to the type of product being produced. Liquorice sheet needs little gloss but requires a very short texture with little elasticity. Liquorice novelties should have a good gloss and a firmer texture which will resist breaking. Tubes of liquorice paste which are sold hollow or filled with cream paste should be firm and of high gloss.

The texture of liquorice paste should be similar to that of any other confectionery product in which it is placed in close association. Thus liquorice paste for 'sandwiches' should be of a similar bite to that of the layers of cream paste (French paste, see later).

The moisture content should be varied according to the type of product. Liquorice for sheet should be discharged from the batch cookers at 70–74% total solids, that for count or novelty lines should be cooked to a higher degree and contain 73–77%, and the liquorice paste produced using continuous processing methods should be discharged at a lower figure of 70–73%. To achieve the economic production of liquorice by the batch method, the cooking pots should be of at least a half ton capacity. This large batch size and higher heating costs have accelerated the adoption of continuous methods for the production of liquorice paste.

Gloss is directly related to gelatinisation. The greater the gelatinisation, the better the gloss. Loss of gloss may be caused through sugar crystallisation on the surface of the confection. When this is suspected the proportion of reducing sugars in the recipe should be increased. Where a lower level of gelatinisation is necessary to achieve a particular eating texture, synthetic glazes should be used to improve the surface appearance; see later in this chapter.

Texture, including both extensibility and elasticity, is related to the extent of starch gelatinisation that has taken place. It is affected by the choice of manufacturing conditions, process method used, residual water content and total sugar content.

13.4 COMPOSITION OF LIQUORICE

The most important ingredient in liquorice recipes is wheat flour which contributes most of the starch involved in gelatinisation. The colour and the presence of bran in the wheat flour are not of great importance. Gluten does not make a significant contribution to liquorice texture though that present should be elastic. Low grade 'hard' wheat flour which is high in protein should be used.

Gelatinisation temperatures recorded for wheat flour range from 60°–90° C (140°–194° F). Gelatinisation can be considerably inhibited by the presence of sugar and is largely suppressed when the sugar concentration exceeds 55%. This suppression can be used to control the level of gelatinisation. Liquorice being produced in sheet form for layering with cream paste (French paste, see later) to produce sandwiches in an 'allsort' selection, should have the wheat starch present in a partially gelatinised form. Novelties or count lines (liquorice shapes sold by number) being produced with liquorice paste should contain most of the wheat starch in a gelatinised form. Complete gelatinisation of the wheat starch is never achieved during liquorice manufacture.

To achieve the variation in gelatinisation needed to produce liquorice most suited for a particular type of confection, five factors should be balanced: (i) type and amount of wheat flour; (ii) proportion of water used in the slurry; (iii) proportion of water used with the sugar mix; (iv) concentration of sugars at the commencement of cooking; (v) length of boiling time.

The progress can be followed microscopically by observing the progressive swelling and bursting of the starch granules. This is best carried out under polarised light when the disappearance of the characteristic 'light' cross on the surface of the starch cell indicates that gelatinisation has taken place. A crude indication can be obtained by removing a portion of the liquorice and rolling between the palms of the hand. The shape and feel of the ball so produced is indicative of the stage reached.

The proportion of wheat flour included in liquorice recipes produced on the batch principle varies from 25–40%. The flour should first be slurried with water and recycled to obtain an even dispersion. It should then be pumped or gravity fed at a slow rate into the rest of the ingredients held in the cooking pots. The rate of addition should be sufficiently slow not to allow the batch to go off the boil. A crude rule is that a sheet liquorice recipe should contain 0·3 parts of water for every part of other ingredients while count lines should have 0·4 parts water. For continuous manufacture the premix should be prepared at 70% solids.

Cooking times should be varied according to the type of product. Sheet liquorice will only require approximately half the cooking time being used for count lines liquorice. Although cooking times of up to 5 hours are suggested for the batch production of 'count line' liquorice, this is too long and no more than 3 hours cooking should ever be required. Where necessary the mix water should be reduced to achieve the shorter boiling time. To accelerate the gelatinisation of wheat starch in count lines liquorice recipes, a proportion of the sugars should be held back from the initial mix and added towards the end of the cooking period. All liquorice pastes should contain some gelatinised flour otherwise the product will lack stand up properties and after drying become extremely brittle in texture. With increasing gelatinisation there is increasing elasticity.

The sugars used for the manufacture of liquorice should be full flavoured. Brown sugars of the types Australian Raw Pieces, No. 10, Barbados, etc. should be used in preference to refined white sugars. These sugars have the additional advantage of being cheaper. Checks should however be carried out to ensure that the crude sugars are of a satisfactory bacteriological purity. Liquid sugars of the type such as dark strong flavoured treacle or molasses should also be incorporated. Doctor sugars are present in these syrups but these need to be boosted by the addition of glucose syrup. Additions of 2–4% of high DE glucose syrup is preferred as the liquorice which is produced has a softer texture and improved moisture retention properties. Hydrol (crude dextrose solids) should also be incorporated to improve texture.

A small amount of vegetable fat such as hardened palm kernel oil (HPKO) (see Chapter 4) will improve both the bite of the liquorice paste and the extrusion properties. Fat may be added at a rate of 2–3% of the final batch weight. In addition a surfactant, such as glyceryl monostearate (GMS) or polyoxyethylene sorbitan monostearate (POE) should be incorporated when adding the fat to liquorice paste to improve the chewing properties, delay hardening while on store and improve the stripping away of the sheet from the extrusion boards. About 0·2–0·3% of surfactant by cooked batch weight should be added to the recipe.

Another ingredient which improves the quality is gelatine. Small additions of 0·2–0·4% of medium Bloom will act as a binder and greatly improve moisture retention by the paste. Clarity of the gelatine gel is unimportant and therefore cheap grades are acceptable. The presence of a small proportion of gelatine will reduce cracking which tends to occur while cutting to shape. Gelatine powder should be presoaked in its own weight of water for 30 minutes prior to use. Immediately prior to the addition of the cooked mass of liquorice paste, the gelatine solution should be heated to 60° C (140° F) to bring the raw material into solution. The gelatine solution should not be added with the other ingredients at the start of boiling, but after cooking has been discontinued.

Three flavourings should be used in liquorice paste: block liquorice juice, aniseed oil, and salt.

Block juice (see §7.12) should be used at a rate of 3% of the total cooked batch weight. The actual amount used will depend on the desired product quality set for the line. Liquorice juice can be bought in slab, spray dried or granulated form. The latter is more convenient to use and commands a higher price. Block juice must be broken into small pieces and soaked in three times its own weight of water before use. The liquorice juice should be brought into solution by boiling the mix, before being added to the remaining ingredients. Liquorice flavour can be enhanced by the incorporation of 0·03% aniseed oil and 0·1% common salt.

Without added colour, a cooked liquorice is brown and insipid in appearance. A permitted black colouring, such as refined carbon black, should be used; a check must be made to ensure compliance with local regulations; this applies too to any colouring in the added scrap.

13.5   PROCESSING LIQUORICE PASTE

In open pan cooking it is necessary that the paddle sweep of the mixer efficiently removes the paste from the walls of the cooker. Liquorice paste is a poor conductor of heat. Fairly low steam cooking pressures are adequate—60 lb/in².

Immediately after cooking and with the completion of mixing, the liquorice paste should be 'tinned off' into stacking containers. When stacking, sufficient space should be left to allow any expelled water vapour to be discharged. Roller conveyors should be provided to transfer these containers from the discharge chute of the cooker to the stacking areas.

Moisture checks on the cooked batch can be carried out using electrical or chemical moisture meters. The former require calibrating for each liquorice recipe and for varying test conditions.

Cooking times for open pan processing will depend on the type of pan in use, batch size, and amount of water present in the ingredient mix.

Batches prepared from recipes should be cooked for 1–2 hours and discharged at 70–74% solids. A batch of liquorice paste for count lines should be cooked for $2\frac{1}{2}$–4 hours and discharged at 73–77% solids.

Process times must be strictly controlled for products of consistent quality.

The use of a scraped heat exchanger of the 'votator' type is an economic way of continuously producing liquorice paste under closely defined conditions. The mechanically induced turbulance enables the equipment to handle highly viscous liquids. Design features of the 'votator' plant (see Fig. 31) include a central shaft holding a row of floating scraper blades which revolve inside a jacketed heat transfer cylinder. These blades remove the liquorice paste which is being held in the narrow space between the central shaft and the internal cylinder wall. A feed pump of the positive displacement type is needed to move the paste through the system. The speed of flow is dependent on the setting of the pump. Gelatinisation can be carried out under elevated pressure conditions. The inlet temperature is governed by the preheat setting of the liquorice paste mix which should be 65°–70° C (149°–158° F). Outlet temperatures can be controlled to suit the requirements for depositing.

Tubes for the scraped heat exchangers used for liquorice manufacture can be produced in mild steel, nickel or other metal types which have sufficient strength and which can be chromium plated.

Very little loss of moisture from the paste mix occurs during continuous processing using scraped heat exchangers because both cooking and cooling take place in a closed system. Some moisture is released on discharge to the atmosphere but this rarely exceeds more than 2–3% of the cooked batch weight. The liquorice paste for sheets should be discharged at the point just before the starch granules burst. This takes place when the cook temperature is between 140°–160° C (284°–320° F) with steam pressures of 100 lb/in². Flow time for the liquorice paste to pass through the unit should be controlled from 18–26 seconds. To yield a satisfactory product the premix solids content should be prepared at 68–70%. Higher solids contents will produce a premix which is difficult to pump and lacks gloss. The time–temperature relationship in scraped heat exchanger processing is critical to the effectiveness of cooking. Some loss of gloss occurs when comparable recipes are produced using continuous procedures, but this can be redressed by dipping the extruded paste through a glaze solution. Open pan recipes do not translate well to continuous cooking procedures. In particular, the proportion of flour should be reduced in these recipes.

All the valves that are used in connection with the cooking and transportation of liquorice paste should be treated with a polytetrafluroethylene (PTFE) impregnated stainless steel coating (such as 'Armourcote'—Fothergille Harvey Ltd). This also applies to those used for viscous raw materials such as treacle, glucose syrup and molasses.

The cooked liquorice paste should be extruded at 100°–120° C (212°–248° F). Before the liquorice is placed into the extruder, the hopper, scroll and die box should be preheated. A standard controlled extrusion temperature must be adopted if uniform extrusion thicknesses are to be achieved. Lower extrusion temperatures should be used when producing hollow liquorice goods. Extrusion can be carried out by multiple worm or screw feeds which are supplied with liquorice paste from a PTFE impregnated hopper head. The worm or screw compartment (scroll box) should be hinged to give easy access to the scrolls for cleaning. Worm or screw feeds should be capable of being operated at varying speeds to take account of differences in liquorice paste viscosity. Viscosity will rise rapidly for even small falls in temperature and the paste should be extruded as quickly as possible after manufacture. To speed extrusion, the heads and dies should be PTFE coated. This will improve release, give faster extrusion due to the lowering in friction and improved gloss. A larger die box will be needed when hollow goods are being produced. Extruders can be constructed in stainless steel or in other materials that have been chromium plated.

Extrusion bands can be made of PTFE coated fibre glass or in stainless steel. These bands may also need a coating of a thin smear of release agent. This can be applied from a revolving absorbent roller which is so arranged as to slightly touch the band. A suitable release agent for liquorice paste is one based on acetylated monoglycerides. Silicone treated parchment papers will give excellent release of the liquorice paste but are more expensive to use. Coated papers have some application as a standby for such time when production breakdowns have necessitated the stacking of the extruded liquorice sheet. The use of plastic films which have not been previously coated with release agent is not recommended due to the poor release properties they exhibit to liquorice paste. Liquorice extruded on water cooled steel bands will not require the same level of application of release agent.

Extrusion is more traditionally carried out on 3–4 ft long boards which are subsequently stacked for drying. The boards can be made in plywood or in laminate and should contain a $\frac{3}{4}$ in raising square positioned on the underside of the boards at each corner. Aluminium–magnesium alloy holding trays are available, which, though more expensive, are longer lasting and are less likely to cause splinters which may become incorporated in the paste. All types of board require the application of a release agent to assist in the stripping off of the extruded liquorice paste. Vegetable based release agents should not be used with wooden boards, due to the absorption into the wood with the later development of rancidity.

Liquorice paste should be cooled as quickly as possible after being run on to the band or on to boards. It can be passed through a dehumidifying tunnel in which a turbulent mass of cooled air is passed over the extruded liquorice. This air should be reactivated by passing through dehumidifying columns, chilled to $-5°$ C (23° F) and the relative humidity adjusted to 50%. Liquorice chilled in this way can be guillotined to shape immediately after leaving the chilling tunnels with little or no sticking taking place on the knives. A suitable band speed for liquorice manufacture is between 20–40 ft per minute.

Liquorice tubes can be extruded on similar equipment to that described for count lines but in this case air must be blown through the centre of the tube to prevent collapsing. The ends of the tubes must be pinched to stop collapsing during storage.

Stoving for liquorice goods should be carried out at 40°–50° C (104°–122° F). Good air circulation within the stoves is essential to achieve products with a consistent moisture content and standard 'bite'. If practicable, the stove atmosphere should be held at between 50–60% relative humidity. This will prevent case hardening which occurs in very dry atmospheres. The confections should be removed as soon as the moisture content has fallen to between 18–20%. This will take from 12–24 hours. Regular checking of the moisture content can be carried out using the calibrated moisture meters mentioned earlier. Liquorice novelties should contain less water than that left in liquorice intended for 'allsort' centres. A suitable moisture range for novelties is 16–18%.

It is advisable to maintain regular records for the moisture drying rates being achieved with the stoves and as soon as a falling away of performance is detected, arrangements should be made for the stripping down and servicing of these units. The commonest cause of variations in texture due to changing moisture contents is differing air velocity and temperature variations in confectionery stoves.

Continuous stoving can be carried out by passing the extruded sheet through drying tunnels operated at 50° C (122° F) and 50% relative humidity. The length of the tunnel is related to the desired moisture loss and the type of liquorice product being produced. Complex effects occur during stoving and it is probable that moisture is lost initially from an approximate one-eighth of an inch layer of liquorice below the surface. Any remaining moisture loss will then be by diffusion.

Liquorice should after stoving be conditioned for 1 day at 20° C (68° F) and 50% relative humidity. This conditioning period permits a redistribution of the varying levels of moisture between the surface and centre of the cooked paste.

Well gelatinised liquorice paste will have a high gloss after extrusion. The liquorice paste produced in scraped heat exchangers has not a sufficiently high sheen to be acceptable without additional glazing. Three acceptable methods for glazing liquorice paste are

(1) Passing through an alginate bath (ingredients in parts by weight):

PART A
Sodium alginate, low viscosity (e.g. Manucol DF, Alginate Industries Ltd, London) 18; water 500.

PART B

Sodium citrate 20; water 100.

PART C

Liquorice block 125; water 400.

PART D

Calcium chloride 25; water 1000.

Method

1. Prepare parts A to D.
2. Mix solutions A to C.
3. Immerse the liquorice in the mix.
4. Remove and dip in solution D.
5. Remove, drain and allow to dry.

(2) Spraying or dipping in a mixture of zein held in an alcoholic solution of an acetylated monoglyceride.

(3) Painting a glazing solution on to the extruded pieces.

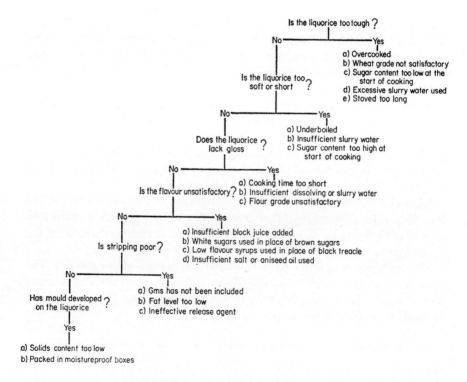

FIGURE 39. Check-list of liquorice faults.

The solution of glaze should be prepared as follows

	Parts by weight
Cane or Beet Sugar	10
Gum Arabic	10
Glucose Syrup	10
Block Liquorice	2
Water	25

Method

Mix the sugar and gum arabic and add to the water. Bring to the boil and add the crumbled block juice. Simmer and when all the ingredients have dissolved, add the glucose syrup. Allow to cool and skim. When needed, dilute with an equal weight of water.

Liquorice pieces can be packed in waxcoated glassine bags or in heat sealed regenerated cellulose acetate film. The type of film must permit a limited passage of water vapour. A too humid atmosphere in the pack may result in mould growth developing on the liquorice paste.

To maintain high quality, no more than 5% of liquorice scrap should be added to any one batch. Liquorice paste should never be considered as a means of disposing of scrap being produced within the manufacturing unit. A check list to identify the cause of liquorice faults is given in Fig. 39.

13.6   CREAM AND FRENCH PASTE

Cream or French paste is a blended, flavoured sugar and fat mix containing both a solid and a liquid phase. Recipes for this type of confection are given in Table 63 overleaf.

Method

1. Load the glucose syrup and invert sugar in a boiling pan and cook to 111° C (232° F).
2. Cool the cooked syrup to 90° C (194° F) and add the gelatine solution and hardened palm kernel oil; mix.
3. Load half the dry ingredients into a beating pan and add the syrup fraction; commence mixing.
4. When mixed add the remaining dry ingredients and the colouring and flavour; mix.
5. Discharge to the extrusion hoppers.

Note: An edible glue for sticking cream paste to liquorice paste can be prepared as follows

EDIBLE GLUE

	Parts by weight
Water	10
Cane or Beet Sugar	7
Gelatine (140 Bloom)	1
Batch Yield	18

Method

1. Dissolve the gelatine in hot water.
2. Add the cane or beet sugar and warm to dissolve.
3. Hold solution at 80° C (176° F).

13.7 PROCESSING CREAM PASTE

Cream paste can be delivered in batch quantities continuously using the Buss-Ko-Kneader and the BCH 'HK Flow line'. Both units provide precise control of manufacturing conditions and achieve consistency in paste quality. A major difficulty in developing a continuous method is in obtaining the necessary level of crystallisation of sugar that is developed

TABLE 63. Recipes for Cream and French Paste

Ingredient	Parts by weight		
	French Paste	Coconut Roll Paste	Cream Paste
Icing sugar	100	100	100
Glucose syrup (63 DE grade)	14	15	15
Invert sugar syrup 70%	8	15	9
Coconut flour	6		7
Dessicated coconut	—	10	—
Fine granulated sugar	5		—
Hardened palm kernel oil	3	3	4
Gelatine (160 Bloom)	1	2	1
Hot water	1	2	1
Glycerine	—	—	1
Colouring	(a) blue (b) brown (c) orange (d) pink (e) yellow	(a) pink (b) yellow	(a) brown (b) pink (c) yellow
Flavouring	0·1% of (a) geranium otto (e) lemon oil (c) lilac otto (d) rose otto	0·1% of (a) raspberry essence (b) lemon oil	(a) 2 parts of cocoa powder (b) 0·1% of raspberry essence (c) 0·1% of lemon oil

during the maturation period included in conventional batch production procedures.

The aim in the manufacture of cream paste should be maximum crystal formation as quickly as possible after the completion of mixing. Rapid crystallisation produces smaller crystals than those which are developed by a slow maturation period. Cream paste containing large sucrose crystals is coarser to the palate and has a low consumer acceptability. Crystallisation of sucrose can be accelerated by extruding the cream paste on to a cooled continuous stainless steel conveyor band. 'Shock crystallised' cream paste is less liable to stick to other surfaces than is paste extruded on to dusted wooden boards. If the recipe is incorrectly balanced so that the proportion of crystal phase is too high, the extruded sheet will crack during size reduction on the brake rollers. This can be overcome by lowering the viscosity of the mix through the syrup phase. To increase the syrup phase additional amounts of invert sugar should be added. Increasing the fat lowers the viscosity of the mix.

To achieve the maximum early crystallisation, the cooked syrup should be added to the dry ingredients at as low a temperature as is consistent with satisfactory working.

13.8 COMPOSITION OF CREAM PASTE

The moisture content of cream or French paste is between 4–5%, 0·5% of the moisture is present as bound water and will not be lost during drying. Equilibrium relative humidity values are dependent on the recipe being used but normally lie within the range 60–70%. Under the normal climatic conditions of the United Kingdom cream paste tends to dry out. It is particularly important in paste manufacture to work to high standards of accuracy in weighing. The water content of cream paste is critical for the achievement of storage properties and even small changes can significantly affect both shelf life and texture. The e r h value can be reduced to around 50% by the incorporation of glycerine or sorbitol. The use of these materials increases costs and will produce confections which have different handling characteristics. The proportion of syrup fraction, dependent on the recipe, is normally 20–30%.

The method used for manufacture can be to add either hot or cold syrup to the other ingredients; texture will vary accordingly. Small amounts of gelatine should be added to bind the water and reduce the danger from cracking during extrusion. The use of glycerine and/or sorbitol in cream paste recipes will produce a confection that has a softer textured and changed eating qualities. If caster sugar is used in preference to icing sugar, the paste produced will be more transparent.

Fat should be incorporated if good cutting properties are to be achieved; a suitable stable fat is hardened palm kernel oil with a melting point of

32°–33° C (90°–92° F), added at 3% of the final batch weight. If the paste is still too hard the amount of fat should be increased. Increasing the glucose syrup level will also soften the paste. Excessive use of these ingredients will give a paste which is difficult to work or has poor cutting characteristics when guillotined. In this case the recipe should be modified by increasing the amount of icing sugar added.

13.9 EXTRUSION OF CREAM PASTE

The paste should be passed through brake rollers and/or extrusion heads to produce the required thickness of sheeting. Most cream paste produced is not used alone but layered with other flavours or colours of cream paste or with liquorice paste.

To produce layered paste, the first extrusion should be made on to a cold stainless steel conveyor band. After passing some 10 feet along the band, a second layer should be added. When using this procedure there is no need to coat the liquorice paste with edible glue as the heat of the extruded sheet is sufficient to produce adhesion. Layered confectionery built up in the traditional manner from 4 foot lengths of liquorice and cream paste must be glued together with an edible adhesive mix of sugar and gelatine (recipe, see §13.6 above). The excessive use of glue may cause disfiguration on the confections, the slipping of layers during cutting and mould growth while on store. The application of glue is sometimes difficult when commercially oil based release agents have been used on the liquorice sheet or when the processing has developed a high level of gelatinisation causing it to become relatively impermeable.

The cream or French paste or layered mixture can be built by further extrusions on to the deposited paste following 10 foot of travel of the conveyor band. Once it has been extruded the cream paste should be quickly cooled to accelerate crystallisation. This can conveniently be carried out by passing the extruded material through a 40–50 ft cooling tunnel. At the mid-point of the tunnel, the temperature minimum should be 10° C (50° F). Discharge temperatures should not be lower than 16° C (61° F) if condensation from the air is to be avoided. Cutting using strip or rotary cutters can take place immediately after discharge from the cooling tunnel. Blast freezing promotes easy cutting but confections should be packed immediately.

The traditional method for extrusion is on to wooden, plastic-covered or metallic boards dusted with cornflour, or a 50:50 icing sugar/cornflour mix. The boards should be stacked to permit surface drying and maturation. The sheets should then be removed and built up into the desired type of layered confection, using edible glue. The equipment used in direct contact with the paste, in both the traditional and continuous processes, should be impregnated with PTFE to give good release.

13.10 LIQUORICE ALLSORTS

Liquorice allsorts are a traditional mix of liquorice and cream paste confections with some aniseed flavoured gelatine jellies. The mix is made up of six items which are

Single sandwich Two sheets of cream paste separated by a sheet of liquorice. The cream paste is produced in four colours white, pink, yellow and brown. Both of the cream paste layers are produced in the same colour.

Double sandwich Three sheets of cream paste separated by two sheets of liquorice. This confection is normally produced in white only.

Liquorice plug Extruded liquorice rod.

Liquorice roll Extruded hollow liquorice rod which is filled with white cream paste.

Coconut roll Cream paste which contains a higher level of coconut flour and which, after colouring yellow or red is wrapped round extruded liquorice rod. The roll is usually surface dipped into large coconut shreds. Some 6% by weight of coconut is retained on the rolls.

Nonpareil jelly A deposited aniseed flavoured (0·1%) gelatine jelly which has been coated with pink or blue coloured nonpareils.

TABLE 64. Dimensions of Confections in
Liquorice Allsort Selection

Confection	Description	Measurement in inches	Count/lb
Coconut Rolls	Extruded circular liquorice rod covered with cream paste.	*uncovered* $\frac{3}{8} \times \frac{3}{8}$ dia. *covered* $\frac{3}{8} \times \frac{7}{8}$ dia.	75
Plug	Extruded circular liquorice rod.	$\frac{7}{8} \times \frac{1}{2}$ dia.	140
Twist	Twisted extruded liquorice rod.	$\frac{7}{8} \times \frac{1}{2}$ dia.	140
Single Sandwich	Paste/liquorice/paste	$\frac{1}{8}$ layers, $\frac{3}{4}$ square	120
Double Sandwich	Paste/liquorice/paste/ liquorice/paste layers	$\frac{1}{8}$ layers, $\frac{5}{8}$ square	80

TABLE 65. Mix Ratio of Liquorice Allsorts Selection

Confection	Composition	
	Number	Weight, %
Nonpareil covered jellies	1	5
Liquorice plug	} 3	} 15
Liquorice roll		
Coconut rolls	3	20
Double sandwich	6	25
Single sandwich	10	35

TABLE 66.   Suggested Dimensions for Liquorice Novelty Goods

Name	Description	Approximate Weight, grammes	Measurement inches	Packing Instructions
Bootlaces	Circular rod	18	2 lengths each $18 \times \frac{1}{8}$ dia.	Fold in half and secure in centre
Nail Rod	Square rod	18	$6 \times \frac{1}{2} \times \frac{1}{2}$	
Plug Tobacco	Strip	18	$3 \times 1\frac{1}{4} \times \frac{1}{8}$	Plug tobacco label needed on each bar
Record	Stamped disc	60	4 dia. $\times \frac{1}{8}$	Glaze, place label in the centre
Red Hot Poker	Circular rod	19	$7 \times \frac{1}{2}$ dia.	1in end dipped in glue and red nonpareils
Telephone Cable	Circular rod	18	$30 \times \frac{1}{8}$ dia.	Fold in 6in lengths, clip in centre
Twists	Twisted rod	18	$6 \times \frac{1}{2}$ dia.	

Notes: (1) Hold on waxed sulphited boards; (2) Weight tolerance ± 5%.

The dimensions for items contained in liquorice allsorts are given in Table 64 and a satisfactory mix specification in Table 65. Single and double sandwiches are normally bulk mixed and added as make-up weight while the rolls, plug and nonpareils are counted into each selection box. Dimensions for liquorice novelty goods are given in Table 66.

Although counting by hand is the most widely used procedure for speciality allsorts, electronic counters such as those developed by Kerdon Ltd. are faster, more accurate and more hygienic. Packaging should protect against loss of moisture: clear moistureproof heat sealed bags held in cardboard printed boxes are most suitable.

14

Tablets, Lozenges and Extruded Paste

14.1 TABLETS

A tablet is a mixture of flavourings, lubricant, binding and base material which has been held under pressure so as to form a hard, cohesive confection which contains very little moisture. Tablets can be produced by wet granulation or by slugging procedures. Both methods are given below together with a basic recipe.

TABLETS

	Parts by weight
Icing Sugar	100
Stearic Acid	0·75
Isopropanol	1·25
Gelatine	0·75
Glucose Syrup	0·5
Water	4·0
Flavouring	0·125

Method: Wet Granulation
1. Dissolve the stearic acid in the isopropanol.
2. Dissolve the gelatine in the requisite amount of warm water and blend in the glucose syrup.
3. Place the icing sugar in the bowl of the mixer.
4. Add the liquid components and work into the batch.
5. Check that the mixture forms a ball when held in the hand.
6. If the mix is of a satisfactory consistency, granulate and pass through a suitable mesh (normally No. 6) to form a small granular mix (*See* Note 1).
7. Spread the crumbled dough on a tray and transfer to drying ovens.
8. Dry at 60° C (140° F) for 10 hours (*See* Note 2).
9. Transfer to a tumbler mixer and add the lubricant and flavouring. Mix.
10. Transfer to the tableting units and compress to shape.

286

Notes: (1) This can be carried out in oscillating extrusion or reciprocating granulators with large mesh sieves or in hammer mills. (2) Fluid air bed drying can be used at this stage to reduce drying time to 30 minutes.

14.2 SLUGGING

The use of a precompression stage to form free flowing granules called slugging is the preferred method when the mix contains components which are likely to pick up moisture from the atmosphere or when volatile components have to be added.

Method: Slugging
1. Prepare the dry mix as before and work in the binder solution.
2. Transfer to the tableting unit and compress into large tablets.
3. Break the tablets into granules of fairly uniform size.
4. Dry.
5. Add additional lubricant and compress to final tablet shape.

The granules should be less than one-tenth the size of the final tablet size [A. C. C. NEWMAN, A. AXON, SCI Symposium, Sept. 1960]. In both methods it is essential to produce powders which flow evenly into the compression dies. A starch hydrolyzate has recently become available which consists of 92% dextrose and 8% glucose syrup in granular form. This material takes up flavouring and colouring and is highly suited for tablet manufacture. The presence of too great a quantity of fine material in powder at this stage can give an abrasive mixture which will be detrimental to the manufacturing plant. This 'fine' material can result in a greater amount of air being entrapped in the tablet. There is always some air present within the tablets when sugar is used in the recipe. According to T. HIGIUCHI *et al.* [*J. Amer. Pharm. Assoc.*, 1952, *43*, 245] this entrapped air can range from 2-10% of the tablet volume. Incorporated air effects the speed of disintegration of the tablet. The presence of some fines can therefore be desirable but excessive quantities can lead to problems during manufacture.

14.3 TABLET COMPOSITION

Tablets will harden with age if the major base material in the recipe is icing sugar. Hardening also occurs with certain binding materials, particularly when gums such as gum acacia are the sole binder. Dextrose, which produces a tablet which has a pleasant cooling effect on the tongue, and lactose, can be used as alternative base materials. It is then essential to include a binder such as gelatine of the highest grade—at least 200 Bloom strength, preferably 230, food grade, added to the recipe at a rate of 2% of the final batch weight. Disintegration times of tablets are always lengthened when gelatine is used as a binder. Tablets containing gelatine exported to humid climates may develop mould growth. Solubilised starch can also be used for this purpose but in a considerably higher proportion. Guar gum has also been used. The damping liquid can be either water or, preferably, a 10% solution of low DE glucose syrup.

The use of dextrose as a substitute for sucrose will remove the need for the normal granulating process used for the production of compressed tablets. This is because the needle-shaped, crystalline form of dextrose monohydrate forms a tightly bound structure when held under compression. A simple formulation can be used. Attention, however, should be paid to efficient blending of the components. A typical formulation is:

TABLETS (USING DEXTROSE)

	Parts by weight
Granular Dextrose Monohydrate	98·5
Magnesium Stearate	0·6
Calcium Stearate	0·5
Powdered Flavour	0·3–0·4
Powdered Lake Colour	0·1

These components are carefully blended together and fed direct into the tableting machine.

The third major component of a tablet is a lubricant, to improve the quality of the mix or to improve the compression properties of the recipe ingredients. Talc is extremely useful, for this purpose, as are the calcium, magnesium and sodium salts of stearic acid. These salts give mixtures which have superior flow properties and which produce tablet surfaces which are amenable to forming clear impressions of decorative wording. Stearic acid can itself be used as a lubricant though the heat from the sealing units in use during packaging may cause slight melting of this material on the surface of the tablet. Glidants may also improve the flow properties of powders by absorbing surplus moisture or reducing friction between the individual particles. They are employed up to a 3% level and include such materials as modified starch, several types of silica and talc.

Powered tartaric acid is a better acidulant for use in tablet manufacture than powdered citric acid. Successful flavouring and colouring of tablets are difficult to achieve; added incorrectly they can cause speckling. Flavouring materials are best premixed with the starch, or in a proportion of the total quantity of sugar prior to being mixed into the full batch. The glucose syrup should be low in sulphur dioxide to prevent bleaching of the added colour. This apart, colouring is best dissolved and added, with any other liquid, at the mixing stage. It should not be forgotten that the quality of certain colours can be affected by the presence of acid flavourings.

14.4 Manufacture of Tablets

Tablets can be produced on single punched or on rotary multiple punching machines, the latter need less lubricant to give effective release. In both types of machines, the powdery or granular material is spread on to a die panel and allowed to fill up the die impression. Both the lower and upper punches are, at this stage, at the farthest point of their travel on their reciprocating action. Normally the power punch is then slightly raised and a sweeping motion takes off a thin layer of exposed powder. This action permits an equal loading of powder in all the dies. The lower punch then returns to the lowest point of travel and the actual compression cycle commences. Both the lower and upper punches close to give a constant compression rate of the powder. Following compression, the punches open and the formed tablets are ejected from the machine.

Punch dies are usually in stainless steel which has both strength and resistance to corrosion. It is easier to produce convex-shaped punches, but centres required for subsequent sugar panning will require the more expensive concave punches. The upper and lower punches should not be allowed to come into contact with one another, i.e. a tableting machine should never be run empty; the two punches hitting each other will result in the flattening of the faces with subsequent 'capping' occurring on the tablets. It is false economy to continue to use the punches for so long as to prevent their refurbishing. If punches become too worn, they are not suitable for regrinding. Tablets will stick and fail to be ejected when the punches lose their polished faces. A common failure is when the punches seize because some of the feed material clings to the die walls and is held on the punch sides. Erratic ejection of the tablet can occur through the walls of the dies becoming pitted. 'Capping' and 'lamination' may also arise from this cause.

'Capping' is the term used when the top of the tablet splits away from its side, at the point of join. A frequent cause is the excessive incorporation of air during the compression stage. 'Lamination' is the splitting into layers following the ejection of the tablet from the machine. It is caused by excessive dampness of the paste and the use of worn dies and punches.

Dies and punches should be washed in a warm solution of water containing a good detergent and after drying, they should be lightly greased, or oiled, prior to being stored.

Before a machine run is started the dies should be filled with the powder mix of the required weight. The machine stroke should then be set for the volume of material. Tablet weights will vary if consistent feed weights are not maintained. Neither the type of base material nor the speed of machine operation will affect tablet weight, but varying the granule size of feed material will do so. In general, the bigger the tablet size the less the danger of weight variations.

Compressibility becomes more difficult as the feed granule size falls. The smaller the granules. the greater the amount of lubricant that should be used in the recipe. When the tablet is wetted by the saliva in the mouth, a certain amount of heat is generated. This causes expansion of the entrapped air and the tablet commences to disintegrate. This effect can be moderated by reducing the level of entrapped air and in particular, by increasing the compression rate. Again, water in the saliva seeps through the fissures in the tablet and preferentially dissolves certain of the recipe components, causing a weakening of the structure and disintegration. Tablets which contain a proportion of corn and potato starch have quicker disintegration rates than those which do not. Alginate salts are useful in achieving the rapid breakdown of the tablet. The hardness of the tablet is dependent on the even flow of the material into the machine dies and correct compressibility rates.

The cause of common faults occurring in tablet manufacture is shown in Fig. 40.

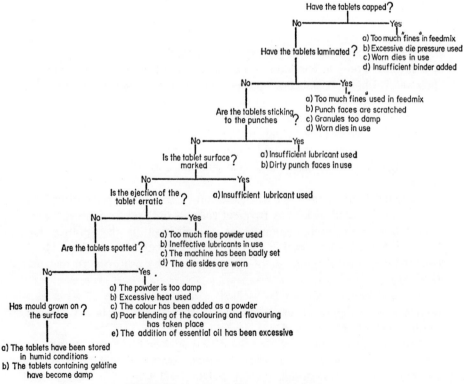

FIGURE 40. Check-list of tablet faults.

14.5 LOZENGES

A lozenge is a sugar dough which has been flavoured, cut to shape and subsequently dried to remove most of the added water. The dough normally contains a binder, usually a mixed solution of gum and gelatine, which is added to assist in the retention of shape.

LOZENGES

	Parts by weight
Icing Sugar	300
Gum Solution A	
Gum Arabic	4
Water	6
Gelatine Solution	
Gelatine (100 Bloom)	5
Water	3
Gum Solution B	
Gum Tragacanth	0·03
Water	0·5
Flavouring	2

Method (see Fig. 41(*a*))
1. Place the icing sugar in the mixer.
2. Prepare the gelatine mix with water which is no hotter than 80° C (176° F).
3. Add the gum solutions (prepared the previous day) to the gelatine mix. Strain the gum/gelatine solution and mix before use.
4. Blend the flavour into a proportion of the icing sugar and add to the remainder of the batch.
5. Add the gelatine/gum mix to the icing sugar.
6. Mix slowly and thoroughly for such time as is necessary for the particular version of mixer in use.
7. Discharge into containers and transfer to the feed hopper of the stamping unit.

Yield: 315.

Size: Large lozenges—200/lb (440/kg); Small lozenges—500/lb (1100/kg); Cachons—1000/lb (2200/kg).

Variants

Pan Room Centres	Add 10 parts of cornflour at stage 1—this will produce lozenges which are harder and less likely to break in the revolving pans.
Coloured and Scented Lozenges (Cachons)	Use 0·05 parts of colouring to produce the desired pastel shade and scent with 0·02 parts of violet, peach blossom, rose and lilac perfumes.
Medicated Lozenges	Use 1½ parts powdered tartaric acid added at stage 4, and 3 parts cough essence.

14.6   COMPOSITION OF LOZENGES

Smaller lonzenges require slightly less gum solution than is given in the recipe, which is for lozenges measuring $\frac{3}{4}$ in or more. As a general rule it can be taken that one part by weight of binder solution will be required for each 12 parts of other solids. A gelatine–dextrin mixture can be used as a substitute for gum solutions. Gelatine binder alone will produce a lozenge which becomes brittle while on store and will tend to break during packaging. Lozenges produced with gum arabic solutions alone are also more brittle than those containing in addition gum tragacanth, and tend to dry out at a more rapid rate.

The viscosity of both gum tragacanth and gum arabic solutions is affected by acid conditions (under pH 4) and the recipe weights should be adjusted accordingly when lozenges which are high in acid flavourings are to be produced. Gum tragacanth should be soaked in water for at least 12 hours prior to manufacture to achieve the maximum viscosity. In practice up to 90% of the swelling occurs within 2 hours; a shorter soak period can therefore be used provided a higher weight of gelatine has been added. Some gums, in particular gum tragacanth, are unstable in high temperature conditions; hot conditions should be avoided for dissolving and mixing. Gum arabic requires twice its own weight of soak water and once a solution has been prepared it should be used quickly to prevent bacterial breakdown. The solution is not stable and will tend to clump. This gum slowly deteriorates in the dry state and purchasing must be carefully controlled to avoid overstocking (not more than 3 months stock of gum should be held). Gum or gelatine solutions should not be kept for more than one day prior to use. All gum solutions should be strained before being added to the lozenge mix. The addition of two per cent glycerine to a lozenge recipe is useful in preventing excessive case hardening occurring while on store.

Commercial grade icing sugar is perfectly satisfactory for the production of lozenges. Generally the finer the particle size, the better the quality of the lozenge. The addition of a small amount of glucose syrup produces a finer paste but slows down the removal of moisture during stoving.

A considerable loss of flavour occurs during the manufacture of lozenges: some through mixing but primarily due to stoving. To counteract this it is necessary to use twice the normal quantity of flavouring added for other types of confectionery products. It is helpful to bind the flavouring with a small proportion of the total recipe weight of icing sugar prior to adding to the main mass. Flavouring materials should be added at the last possible moment compatible with efficient mixing.

Peppermint oils which have a high content of menthol are very suited for lozenge manufacture due to their penetrating flavour. Normal peppermint oils can be boosted by the addition of 0·1% menthol held in propylene glycol. The actual rate of usage of flavourings is very dependent on the type of plant available, but a reasonable addition would be 0·5–1·0% of the final batch weight. A small trace of blue colouring carefully added to 'naturally coloured' white lozenges intensifies the 'whiteness' of the lozenge.

14.7 PRODUCTION OF LOZENGES

Efficient mixing is the key to the satisfactory production of lozenges (Fig. 41(a). Z arm or similar powerfully armed, reverse action mixers are most suitable. Mixing times must be standardised to produce homogenised paste without excessive flavour loss. Low batch volumes which only partially fill the mixer can lead to process variations. Paste which is at the completion of mixing should retain the shape of the operative's fingers without expressing liquid, appearing sloppy or breaking.

The tendency of the lozenges to stick to the conveyor bands can be reduced by sprinkling with a food grade dusting powder. Externally release coated cutter blades will prevent paste build up. Each blade should be resharpened at the same time rather than attempts be made to sharpen

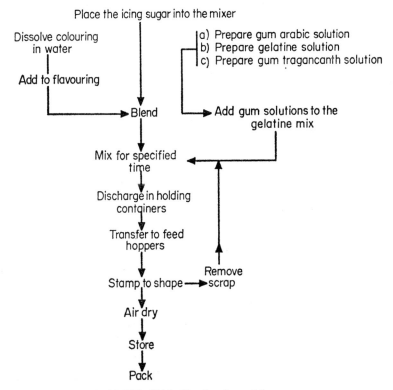

FIGURE 41(a). Production of lozenges.

individual blades when difficulties arise. Stamped lozenges should not be piled in more than one layer on the take-off trays. On leaving the stamping unit they should be air dried for at least 4 hours. The trays should then be inverted to reveal the underside of the lozenge and a further 4 hour air drying period given. Direct sunlight should be avoided during drying. A hot air stoving period of 23 hours at 35°–40° C (95°–104° F) will then be sufficient to harden off the lozenges for packing. Glazing can be achieved by lightly steaming with superheated steam and drying.

The web of paste from which the lozenges have been stamped, should be removed from the collecting trays at frequent intervals and re-used before excessive case hardening can occur. If done quickly it can be added back to the feed hopper. Should a delay occur, it must be added to a subsequent batch at the mixing stage with an assumed 10% loss in flavouring materials.

Fig. 41(b) indicates the common causes of faults which arise in the manufacture of lozenges.

14.8   SWEET CIGARETTES

This line based on lozenge paste is produced for the children's trade and consists of a flavoured sugar mixture containing starch added as binder.

SWEET CIGARETTES

	Parts by weight
Icing Sugar	100
Maize Starch	50
Glucose Syrup (high DE grade)	22
Gelatine Solution	
Gelatine (100 Bloom)	10
Water	20
Gum Solution	
Gum Arabic	1
Water	1
Hardened Palm Kernel Oil	4
Lemon Essence	0·5
Batch Yield	200

Method

1. Prepare the gelatine solution by slowly adding the requisite weight of gelatine powder to hot water held at 80° C (176° F). Stir until dissolved.

2. Prepare the gum arabic mix by slowly adding the gum arabic to hot water held at 80° C (176° F). Stir until dissolved.

3. Place the glucose syrup and fat in a small boiling pan and heat to 116° C (240° F) (alternatively pass the glucose syrup through a Farley type cooker and add the fat to the discharged syrup).

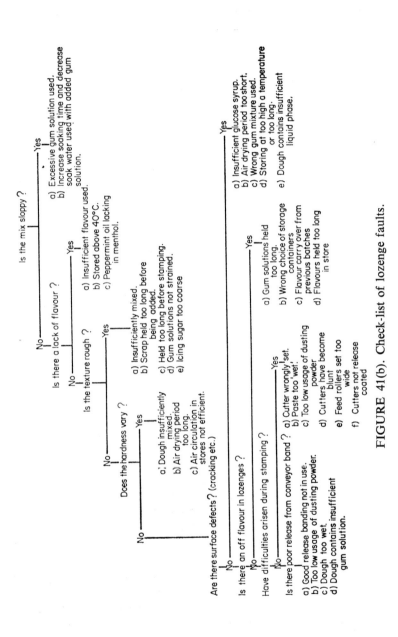

FIGURE 41(b). Check-list of lozenge faults.

4. Allow the syrup/fat mix to cool to 90° C (194° F) and then add to the icing sugar which is held in a Z arm or ribbon type mixer. Blend.

5. Add the gelatine mix held at 80° C (176° F) and the gum arabic solution also held at the same temperature.

6. Add portionwise the full weight of maize starch and flavouring.

7. Continue to mix for a further 5 minutes after visual examination has indicated that mixing has been achieved.

8. Discharge the paste and extrude from a cigarette forming unit as rods of $\frac{1}{4}$ in diameter (dust with maize starch as required to prevent sticking).

9. Take off the rods on to stacking boards.

10. Dry in stoves held at 35° C (95° F) for 18 hours.

11. Guillotine or saw the cigarettes into $2\frac{3}{4}$ in lengths returning any crumbled scrap into subsequent batches.

12. Collect together the cut cigarettes into wooden collecting troughs which have sides set at 80 degrees and allow the sweets to protrude for an eighth of an inch.

13. Tip the ends of the sweet cigarettes with a red colour solution, prepared by dissolving the colour in isopropanol solvent, and applied with a small absorbent paint roller of the expanded plastic solvent resistant variety.

14. Transfer the cigarettes to the packing station.

Notes on Method: (*a*) The count per lb of sweet cigarettes should be between 140–150. (*b*) Packing should be in groups of 5, 10 or 20 in preformed cardboard boxes, which hold a printed picture card, or in formed paper packs which are stuck down using an edible starch adhesive.

14.9 PRODUCTION CONTROL FOR SWEET CIGARETTES

The successful production of sweet cigarettes is dependent on the control of (i) the amount of syrup phase in the recipe; (ii) the drying period; (iii) storage of the packed confections. The temperature at which the syrup is added to the icing sugar must be consistent from batch to batch. To minimise the formation of invert sugar, any prepared syrup which contains sucrose must be held for as short a period as possible commensurate with normal production demands. It is extremely important to ensure that no operator error occurs when weighing out the 'liquid' raw materials. In particular small differences in the weight of the syrup mix added in the recipe will bring about significant changes in product texture and in the drying out properties.

Increasing the proportion of starch in the recipe will cheapen the product but is likely to cause more rapid hardening on store. Dextrose or high dextrose conversion products may be used to replace the icing sugar though the resultant product will not match the expected taste for sweet cigarettes. An interesting variant can be brought about by adding 5% coconut flour to mix. Gelatine need not be of high quality, 100 Bloom grade being satisfactory.

Drying should be carried out by circulating warm air at 35° C (95° F) through the stacked trays. The extruded paste must not be stacked near the hot steam discharge from boiling pans. Movement of the trays slowly through a hot air tunnel, immediately after extrusion, can reduce the total drying period. Cigarettes may soften just prior to packing, due to high air humidity; soft sweets can be given an additional light 2 hour stoving period to overcome this fault.

The purpose of stoving is to produce a surface crust on the sweet cigarettes to enable them to be packed. Once packed, redistribution of moisture takes place and the confections soften. After packing the e r h of the sweet cigarettes approaches 70%. At the time of extrusion the moisture content of the paste is 10–12%. Following drying the moisture level falls to 6–7%. Further excessive losses of water on store will result in deterioration. Overwraps of the bulk pack should not be highly moisture proof, as moisture evaporation or deposition can cause serious disfiguring of the appearance of the confection. Overstacking of the packed boxes of newly produced sweet cigarettes can cause flattening and breakages.

Cutting to shape can be carried out either by guillotine or by sawing. The guillotine blades rapidly become blunt if the paste is left too long before cutting. Continuous sawing is a useful method: the small round saw blades should be set on the spindle at the required distance of $2\frac{3}{4}$ in apart. Sawing increases dust removal problems, and increases the level of scrap by

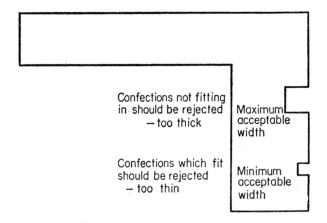

FIGURE 42. Go–no-go gauge.

3%. Size testing should be regularly carried out on the thickness of the extrusion, using a go–no-go gauge, Fig. 42.

Product quality of sweet cigarettes should be assessed on the basis of (i) overall appearance; (ii) cleanness of end cut; (iii) absence of dusting starch; (iv) application of colouring to tip; (v) brittleness of texture; (vi) smoothness of product; (vii) flavour quality.

15

Marshmallow and Nougat

15.1 MARSHMALLOW CONFECTIONS

Originally, marshmallow was produced in France under the name of *Pâte de Guimauve*, from the extract of the root of *Althaea officinalis*; the plant, which grows in marshy areas, is similar to the hollyhock. The roots produce a viscous juice and this was mixed with eggs and sugar and beaten to a light foam. Today the texture of 'marshmallow' is more tender and, with changes in retailing, it is necessary to produce a product with a longer shelf life. The whipping and gelling agent has also changed and gelatine is now normally used together with egg albumen. Alternatively, gum arabic or starch are added to improve body.

The two most important ingredients of marshmallow are air and moisture. Air is incorporated to increase the volume and improve the texture. The moisture in marshmallow products is one of the 'highest' of all confections and, this means, that there is a danger of mould growth. The high moisture content enables a large volume of air to be incorporated and also controls the viscosity of the product. Marshmallow is produced by an essentially cold process. The base syrup is prepared by boiling to a fixed concentration. Solutions of whipping agent should only be added after cooling this syrup to a temperature normally insufficient to sterilise the ingredients, and therefore very special attention should be paid to equipment and plant hygiene.

An extensive investigation on the influence of overrun, viscosity, elasticity and moisture has been made by P. J. TIEMSTRA [*Food Tech.*, 1964, (915) 125; (921), 131; (1084), 140].

Marshmallow products can be manufactured by using open planetary whisking machines at normal atmospheric pressure, or in horizontal beating machines. This method has however largely been replaced by batch or continuous mixers which operate under increased pressure. Air is generally incorporated by two basically different methods. In method (*a*), the one-step system, nearly all of the ingredients are dissolved and beaten together.

This procedure is for products containing a fairly high percentage—generally within the range 15–25%, of moisture. Method (*b*), the two-step system, is used where a low density is required combined with a high soluble solids content. The aerating materials are beaten to a foam and the rest of the ingredients added in the form of a boiled batch. Details of the various products with appropriate methods are given below.

Product	Process	Sp. Gravity	Total Soluble Solids %
Frappé	One step	0·35–0·50	70–80
Angel or Negro Kiss	Two step	0·17–0·25	75–80
Snowballs	Two step	0·25–0·35	75–82
Marshmallow	One step	0·35–0·45	75–82
Deposited Marshmallow	One step	0·45–0·50	76–82
Extruded Marshmallow	One step	0·25–0·35	75–80
Grained Marshmallow	One step	0·50–0·70	78–84
Nougat	Two step	0·80–0·90	82–92
Fondant Cream	Two step	0·60–0·85	88–94
Fruit Caramel	Two step	0·80–0·90	82–92

15.2   FRAPPÉ BASED ON EGG ALBUMEN, CONTAINING STARCH

	Parts by weight	
Sugar	50	
Glucose Syrup (63 DE)	250	
Water	11	
Starch (Thin Boiling)	8·75	} Mix to a suspension
Water	70·0	
Egg Albumen	4·5	} Prepare a solution
Water	9·0	

Method

1. Bring the sugar, glucose syrup and water to the boil.
2. Slowly add a suspension of the starch and cold water.
3. Continue cooking with stirring, until a temperature of 110° C (230° F) is reached.
4. Place in the mixing bowl and cool to a temperature of below 70° C (158° F) before adding the egg albumen solution.
5. Beat until the required density is obtained.

Note: It is possible, by cooking only 50% of the glucose syrup and adding the remainder after cooking, to speed up the cooling stage. This formula produces a simple, multi-purpose and stable frappé.

The basic syrup for marshmallow products consists of cane or beet sugar blended with high DE glucose syrup; the latter has good humectant whipping and moisture-holding properties. Sometimes a three sugar system is employed in which the third sugar is either invert sugar, dextrose monohydrate or sorbitol.

A typical specification for a high conversion 63 DE glucose syrup suitable for marshmallow manufacture is:

Baumé at 100° F	$43.2° \pm 0.2°$
Colour (optical density)	0·7 max
Heat Colour (optical density)	6·0 max
pH	4·7–5·0
Dextrose Equivalent (DE)	62–66%
Sulphur Dioxide	40 ppm max.
Iron	5 ppm max.
Copper	2 ppm max.
Total Solid (soluble) % w/w	81·6–82·4
Refractive Index at 20° C	1·4971–1·4993
Density at 20° C lb/Imp Gall	14·3
Viscosity (CPS) at 100° F	6000

Newer types of glucose syrups are continuously being developed and could find particular application for marshmallow type products. Of considerable interest are likely to be high laevulose syrups, which have high sweetness value and, compared to sugar at 15% concentration, equal relative sweetness.

A specification for this type of syrup is expected to be:

Total Solids (soluble) % w/w	80
Dextrose Equivalent (DE)	90
Dextrose	48
Laevulose	40

High and very high maltose syrups produced by enzymic processes which gives a high disaccharide (maltose) content are also of value. They have a lower sweetness than high dextrose syrup, being equal in this respect to regular types of glucose syrup, but possess a much lower viscosity and higher moisture retention than the regular 42 DE grades. They are of particular value where dextrose monohydrate is included in the formula in preventing the possibility of dextrose crystallisation. Typical specifications for a high maltose syrup suitable for marshmallow manufacture are:

	Maltose Syrup	
	High	Very High
Total Solids (soluble) % w/w	82	82
Dextrose Equivalent (DE)	38–42	40–44
Dextrose	8	2–3
Maltose	33	55–56
Higher Saccharides	60	41–42

It is possible to produce a marshmallow syrup containing glucose syrup as the only sweetener: this considerably shortens and simplifies the manufacturing process.

A number of additives for marshmallow recipes have been proposed for improving the whipping properties; obviating dusting of spray dried products and preventing heat damage. Two important modifiers are likely to be US Patent 2,933,397 in which egg whites are caused to produce a good foam in a shorter time by containing a small amount of an ester, e.g. acetic ester of glycerol. A further patent, US Patent 3,219,457 describes a method in which the incorporation of Okra Gum is used to reduce whipping time

L

and also increase the volume. It can also be combined with other additives, such as triethyl citrate, with a further decrease in whipping time; even the reduction of 70% is claimed.

Malto-dextrins are comparatively new ingredients for use in aerated products as partial replacements of gelatine and egg albumen. Sometimes called hydrolyzed cereal solids in the USA, they are free-flowing, highly soluble white powders, principally composed of higher saccharides (hexa-saccharides and above). They are specially useful for marshmallows in which carbohydrates are required which will not affect the overall sweetness. Certain grades of Malto-dextrins may be used as a carbohydrate filler to partially replace sugar thereby reducing the sweetness level. They can be used to replace up to 15% gelatine or 25% egg albumen in marshmallow manufacture.

15.3 GELATINE MARSHMALLOW

In marshmallow manufacture all gelatine should be soaked before use in at least 4 parts cold water for every 1 part of gelatine: more water may be used if the formula permits. The gelatine solution should be prepared at least 20 minutes before use. The presoaked gelatine can be added directly to the batch if the temperature of the syrup is above 60° C (140° F) and below 70° C (158° F). However, if the temperature is below 60° C (140° F) it should be dissolved by gently heating in a water jacketed mixing vessel until a clear solution is obtained. The temperature, however, should not rise above 60° C (140° F). Gelatine should be of the highest possible quality giving low viscosity solutions. A low grade gelatine normally produces a long elastic texture of poor colour. The recommended type of gelatine is high Bloom 200–250, which has a low viscosity and high gel strength. The normal amount used is about 2%.

In the manufacture of aerated products, high Bloom strength enables a lower percentage of gelatine to be used, which, in turn, reduces the viscosity. This permits a lower back pressure and discharge temperature. The rate of setting is generally quicker, which is necessary particularly for continuously extruded products.

The production methods for gelatine marshmallow can be divided into hot or cooked, and cold or uncooked.

SYRUPS FOR GELATINE MARSHMALLOW: HOT OR COOKED

| | Parts by weight | |
	A	B
Sugar	60	60
Glucose Syrup	40 (High DE)	40 (Regular DE)
Water	20	16
Invert Sugar	—	5
Pre-soaked Gelatine	2·75	2·25
Water	20·00	12

Method
1. Place sugar, glucose syrup, water and invert sugar in a steam jacketed boiling pan and boil to a temperature of 115° C (239° F).
2. Cool this syrup to 60° C (140° F).
3. Transfer to whipping machine and add the soaked gelatine.
4. Beat this mixture until light. The volume should be controlled batch by batch.

Note: The progress of beating should be checked at regular intervals by filling a beaker of known volume with marshmallow and weighing the contents.

The cold or uncooked method is most useful when producing products with a high moisture content and also when the crystal sugar percentage is low. In cases where a liquid sugar mixture is used, or a total sweetener component based on glucose syrup is employed, this cold or uncooked process is most applicable. Careful control should be exercised over the moisture content and control maintained by regular checks using a refractometer. Small differences in moisture percentage can cause many difficulties, particularly with respect to whipping time, yield of the batch and possibly fermentation of the finished product.

GELATINE MARSHMALLOW: COLD OR UNCOOKED

	Parts by weight
Sugar	315
Water	60
High DE Glucose Syrup	215
Gelatine (200–250 Bloom)	11·25
Water	60

Method
1. Place the cane or beet sugar, glucose syrup and water in a pan, warm and agitate until solution is obtained (at about 60° C (140° F)).
2. Dissolve the gelatine in hot water and add to the syrup.
3. Transfer to whipping machine and add the soaked gelatine.

15.4   CONTINUOUS PRODUCTION OF MARSHMALLOW USING GELATINE

The incorporation of air into the syrup by plantary beater at atmospheric pressure has largely been replaced by continuous processing in which air at higher pressure is beaten into the syrup; when the latter leaves the continuous processing unit, the air cells expand due to the reduction in pressure. The advantages are a continuous process with exact mechanical control over every variable, thus ensuring uniform quality and texture. An excellent example of such an aerator mixer is the Oakes continuous automatic beater mixer, which can be used to manufacture high quality marshmallows of varying types, mazetta, frappé, nougat and negro kiss. The feature of the Oakes mixer is the head or mixing chamber, Fig. 43. This consists of three parts—the rear stator, the rotor and front stator. The internal faces of the stators, and both faces of the rotor are fitted with concentric rows or blades. The two stators are bolted together and the rotor is mounted on a revolving shaft between the stators, the blades of the rotor mesh with the blades of the stators, in such a way that there is no contact of moving parts.

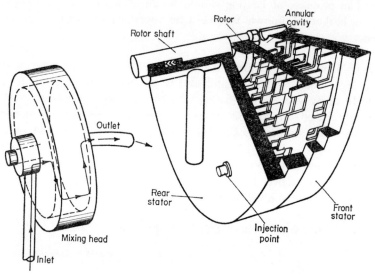

FIGURE 43. Oakes mixing head.

The sugar/glucose syrup, with added colloids, enters the mixing head at the centre of the rear stator, and flows between the blades of the rear stator and rotor to the outer circumference of the stator cavity. The mixture then flows between the blades of the front stator and rotor to the centre of the stator from which it is discharged. Prior to, or after the syrup mixture enters the mixing head, air is introduced under pressure into the syrup stream in the proportion required to produce the desired density; this is controlled by the adjustment of the flowmeter. At any given capacity, final density is inversely proportional to the quantity of admitted air. The syrup mixture to be aerated is delivered by pump through a pipe line, under pressure, to the mixing head and thence to the hopper of the depositor.

An air compressor driven by an electric motor fitted with automatic controls maintains the pressure on the volume of air required for a given production rate and density of the marshmallow. Nitrogen may be substituted for air to extend the shelf life of the product.

GELATINE MARSHMALLOW FOR CONTINUOUS PRODUCTION
by Oakes Equipment

	Parts by weight
High DE Glucose Syrup	430
Gelatine (230 Bloom)	15
Water	45

Method
1. Prepare the gelatine mix using hot water.
2. Heat the glucose syrup to 35° C (95° F).
3. Add the gelatine solution to the heated glucose syrup and mix.
4. Add the colour and flavour.
5. Transfer the prepared solution to the holding tank of the Oakes mixer, (total soluble solids content 75%).
6. Process the solution using a rotator speed of 280 and a back pressure of 40–50 lb/in², to obtain a density of around 0·3.

Note: A solution temperature of 30°–35° C (86°–95° F) should be maintained. Higher temperatures will necessitate a very high back pressure to obtain the desired density.

Marshmallows can also be continuously manufactured using Votator equipment. A pre-mix should be prepared by warming the mixture sufficiently to dissolve any solid sugar and whipping agent. If gelatine is used as the whipping agent, it must be soaked with its own weight of water for two hours prior to making up the mix. It should not be added to the solution at temperatures above 65° C (149° F). The pre-mix is then pumped to a Votator cooler, where it is aerated and cooled. Aeration is achieved by means of an air compressor or air bottle. The air inlet is fed into the product line just prior to its reaching the Votator cooler. Suitable air filters are installed. A fine control valve for the air can be adjusted according to the readings on the flowmeter. A back pressure valve is fitted to the product outlet. For a marshmallow used for depositing on wafers, the pre-mix should contain a minimum of 75% solids and be cooled to approximately 29° C (84° F). The high speed shaft is both an efficient beater, and a heat exchanger.

The Whizolator equipment (Fig. 44) for the manufacture of marshmallow (US Patent 2,424,950 and 2,536,340) is based on diffusion. The syrup is mixed with compressed air and by a system of jet mixing, atomising and dispersion under pressure, becomes aerated. The diffusing chamber is filled with ceramic balls, which produces a tortuous path for the mixed syrup. By using different sized diffusion heads, a greater or less tortuous path can be obtained, and by this means it is possible to aerate light marshmallow to heavy nougats. A low temperature can be used, so preventing possible heat damage to whipping agents. Of considerable advantage is that, apart from

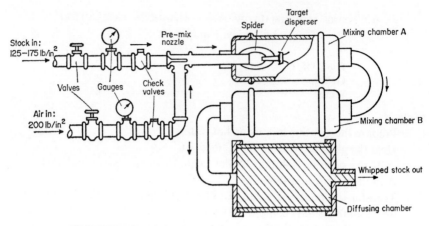

FIGURE 44. Whizolator for marshmallow production.

pumps, the equipment has no moving parts. Some recipes suitable for the Whizolator follow.

DEPOSITED MARSHMALLOW (GELATINE BASED)

	Parts by weight
Gelatine (225 Bloom)	2·75
Hot Water	23·00
Dissolve and add	
Glucose Syrup (42 DE grade)	44·50
Cane or Beet Sugar	50·00
Sorbitol (70% concentration)	6·50

Method

1. Heat the prepared mix to 57° C (135° F) and continue to stir until dissolved.
2. Pump through the Whizolator to the desired density (about 0·4–0·45).
3. Deposit in dry starch.

GRAINED MARSHMALLOW

	Parts by weight
Gelatine (225 Bloom)	2·0
Hot Water	24·5
Dissolve and add	
Glucose Syrup (42 DE grade)	28·00
Sorbitol (70% concentration)	10·50
Cane or Beet Sugar	70·00

Method

1. Heat the prepared mix to 70° C (158° F) and continue to stir until thoroughly dissolved.

2. Add colour and flavour and mix in.
3. Pump through the Whizolator to the desired density.
4. Deposit into warm starch, place into a hot stove to induce graining.

MARSHMALLOW TOPPING

		Parts by weight
(a)	Gelatine (225 Bloom)	1·25
	Water	6·00
(b)	Glucose Syrup (63 DE grade)	75·00
	Sorbitol Solution (70% concentration)	10·00
	Water	11·00

Method

1. Soak the gelatine in the water.
2. Add this solution to the solution (b).
3. Pump through the Whizolator to desired density.

Marshmallow can be manufactured in the Turbomat 1100 (Fig. 45), a continuous machine manufactured by Otto Hansel, which employs the Fauser system for the production of a wide range of depositable and extrudable foam, down to a minimum density of 0·16. The equipment consists of six basic features: A Piston metering pump for colloidal solution (albumen/gelatine solution). B Piston metering pump for syrup solution (sugar/glucose syrup). C Aerating unit for colloidal solution. D Compressed air to aerating unit. E Emulsifier. F Compressed air metered to the emulsifier.

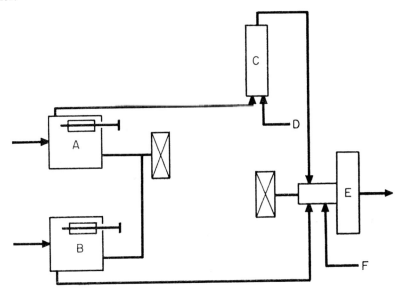

FIGURE 45. Turbomat arrangement for marshmallow production.

Two methods may be used with this equipment.

(a) *One stage method*. The premix containing sugar, glucose syrup, water, gelatine at pre-determined total solids, is fed to the aerating unit in a dissolved state. By adding compressed air, the first aeration takes place. From here the aerated solution moves continuously to the emulsifier, where more compressed air is added, and where the relevant emulsifier revolutions take place. The required specific gravity is thus obtained, which should come within the range 0·3–0·7.

(b) *Two stage method*. A boiled solution of sugar, glucose syrup and water is fed via a metering pump to the emulsifier direct. Parallel to this a metering pump feeds a solution containing the whipping agent to the aerating unit, where it is whipped into a foam by the addition of compressed air, in which stage it is transferred to the emulsifier, where a homogeneous mixing and emulsifying of foam and syrup solution takes place. The specific gravity obtained by this method is minimum 0·16–0·35.

The Eur-O-Matic foam beater (Rubatex NV) depends on compressed air being forced into the albumen sugar premix during its passage between a toothed stator and inner variable speed rotator. Partially treated foam is then passed to a static twist tube and then to a discharge tube whose outlet orifice is controlled by an automatic back pressure regulator.

15.5 EGG ALBUMEN MARSHMALLOW

(a) *Preparation of Egg Albumen Solution*

Egg Albumen	20
(Spray Dried Powder)	
Water	100

Method

1. Mix and whip to a firm peak.

The albumen solution is prepared in advance, but only sufficient prepared for one day's production. The solution should be stored in earthenware or glass containers. Metal vessels, apart from stainless steel, should be avoided. The albumen solution should be strained through a fine sieve before use. Albumen solutions are prone to microbiological spoilage and strict attention should be paid to preparation, storage and plant hygiene.

(b) *Preparation of Syrup*

Water	80
Sugar	200
Glucose Syrup High DE 63	240

Method
1. Place the ingredients in a jacketed pan and dissolve by stirring.
2. Heat to a temperature of 115°–119° C (239°–246° F).

(c) *Preparation of the Marshmallow*
1. Cool the syrup to below 93° C (200° F).
2. Pour the cooled syrup into the prepared egg albumen whip. (Note the syrup should be added slowly in a thin stream).
3. Continue whipping until the required density is obtained.
4. Process the prepared marshmallow mix by piping, extruding or depositing onto a band using a suitable depositing machine, such as the Oka or NID.

15.6   MODIFICATION OF RECIPES FOR CONTINUOUS PRODUCTION

Open pan recipes cannot be translated directly to continuous cooking methods, because marshmallow produced by atmospheric open-bowl beating loses moisture during manufacture. It is, therefore, necessary to compensate for this factor. Typical examples are given below for marshmallow and frappé formulations using Hyfoama DS (a modified milk protein whipping agent prepared by Lenderink and Co., N.V., Holland).

MARSHMALLOW: FORMULA ADAPTATION

Atmospheric Beating		*Pressure Beating*	
Water (hot)	10·0	Water (hot)	8·0
Gelatine	2·0	Gelatine	2·0
Whipping Agent Hyfoama DS	0·25	Whipping Agent Hyfoama DS	0·25
Sugar	28·0	Sugar	28·0
Water	10·0	Water	10·0
63 DE Glucose Syrup	12·0	63 DE Glucose Syrup	12·0
Boil to 111° C (232° F)		Boil to 111° C (232° F)	
Invert Sugar	12·0	Invert Sugar	12·0

All figures are parts by weight

FRAPPÉ: FORMULA ADAPTATION

Atmospheric Beating		*Pressure Beating*	
Part A			
Treated Milk Protein (Hyfoama DS)		Treated Milk Protein (Hyfoama DS)	
(Whipping Agent)	0·45	(Whipping Agent)	0·45
Water	6·0	Water	0·90
Powdered Sugar	10·0	Glucose	2·0
Part B			
Sugar	28·0	Sugar	38·0
Water	10·0	Water	12·0
Boil to 111° C (232° F)		Boil to 110° C (230° F)	
Part C			
Glucose	56·0	Glucose	54·0

Production Method

Atmospheric	*Pressure*
1. Mix Hyfoama, water and powdered sugar and beat to stiff foam.	1. Mix Hyfoama and water, add glucose.
2. Boil sugar and water to indicated temperature.	2. Boil sugar and water to indicated temperature.
3. Add glucose and add this mix to the whip.	3. Add glucose and place in bowl of pressure beater.
4. Continue beating until desired density is obtained.	4. Add whipping agent dispersion and beat under approx. 30 lb/in² for 3 minutes.

Continuous production of marshmallow topping using egg albumen

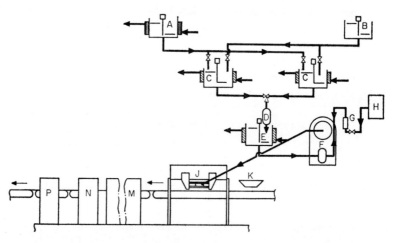

FIGURE 46. Continuous production of egg albumen marshmallow.

Continuous mixers can also be used for the production of products based on egg albumen. Fig. 46 shows a typical flow line for the manufacture of marshmallow snowballs, either in chocolate enrobed form, or coconut covered variety, employing Oakes equipment. The equipment consists of: A Syrup preparation tank. B Egg albumen preparation tank. C Premixing vessels. D Transfer pump. E Mixer reservoir vessel. F Continuous automatic mixer. G Flowrator. H Air compressor. J Depositor. K Starch sprinkler. L Starch recovery, M Skinning tunnel. N Chocolate enrober. P Coconut topping machine.

Egg albumen marshmallows can also be produced using the other continuous systems described under gelatine marshmallow (see §15.4).

Continuous production of Negro Kisses and similar articles

Products of this kind with a density down to around 0·2 can also be made using the Oakes equipment with a double headed synchronised positive displacement pump, which meters both egg albumen and heated syrup simultaneously. The egg albumen solution enters the rear stator of the mixing head wherein it is aerated; as the aerated albumen enters the front stator section, syrup at about 116° C (240° F) is injected through the periphery of the latter and blended into it. The unit is operated at a back pressure of approximately 60 lb/in².

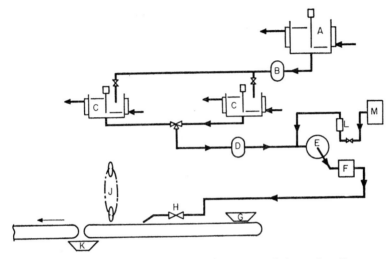

FIGURE 47. Continuous production of extruded marshmallow.

The principle of continuous extruded marshmallow production is illustrated in diagrammatic form in Fig. 47. The main units are provided by Oakes equipment and the Votator unit provides the necessary cooling. A Gelatine preparation tank. B Gelatine pump. C Syrup preparation tanks. D Transfer pump. E Oakes continuous automatic mixer. F Votator. G Starch sprinkler. H Multi-head extruder. J Rotary cutter. K Starch recovery. L Flowrator. M Air compressor.

Method of Production

Gelatine, of about 230 Bloom, is pumped to one or other of two syrup holding tanks, each temperature controlled and agitated, enabling the gelatine and the syrup to be blended. These tanks are used alternately, giving a continuous supply of mix. The latter is then pumped through the Oakes mixing head, at a back pressure of approximately 60 lb/in². The resultant aerated marshmallow passes through a Votator where the mix is continuously cooled and to an Oakes extrusion manifold, which extrudes the desired number of marshmallow strips on to a lightly starch-covered conveyor band. The strips can then be cut into the lengths, using a mechanical cutter as now widely used for the cutting of Swiss roll.

EXTRUDED MARSHMALLOWS

(a) Gelatine and Milk Protein Type	Parts by weight
Cane or Beet Sugar	240
Dextrose Monohydrate	160
Water	80
Glucose Syrup A	100
Glucose Syrup B (high maltose grade)	240
Water (hot)	48
Gelatine (230 Bloom)	16
Treated Milk Protein (Hyfoama DS)	2

Method
1. Boil sugar, dextrose monohydrate, water and glucose syrup A to 120° C (248° F).
2. Add glucose syrup B to the boiled syrup batch.
3. Dissolve the gelatine in hot water.
4. Add the 'Hyfoama' and disperse into the syrup batch, together with the gelatine solution.
5. Add the colour and flavour.

(b) Gelatine and Starch Based	Parts by weight
Sugar	100
Water	10
Glucose Syrup (63 DE grade)	95
Gelatine (230 Bloom)	2·50
Modified Starch	2·75

Method
1. Boil the sugar, starch and water 117° C (242° F), stirring constantly.
2. Add the glucose syrup and mix thoroughly together to reduce the temperature below 80° C (176° F).
3. Add the gelatine, dissolved into hot water, to the syrup batch, together with colour and flavour.
4. Continuously process the prepared syrup.

(c) Gelatine Based	Parts by weight
Sugar	50
Dextrose Monohydrate	5
Glucose Syrup (high maltose grade)	4·5
Gelatine (230 Bloom)	2·5
Water	19

Prepare as for first recipe.

TABLE 67. Deposited Marshmallow: Faults and their Prevention

Faults	Cause	Action to prevent Recurrence
Gritty texture	Sugar crystallisation or advanced graining	Increase glucose syrup content.
Off-odours	Microbiological spoilage	Egg albumen and gelatine solutions should not be prepared and stored in advance.
	Unsterilized equipment	Sterilize weekly.
	Build up in pipe lines particularly continuous plants.	Dismantle and clean pipe lines daily.
Off-flavours	Oxidation of ingredients.	Use Nitrogen in place of compressed air.
Starch crust	High moisture moulding starch	Maximum moisture in moulding starch should be 8%, recommended is 4–6%.
Starch crust	Low soluble solids of batch	Minimum total solids content should be 75%.
Poor setting or collapse	Temperature of moulding starch too high	Should be kept below the setting point of gelatine, recommended 27° C (81° F).
Poor setting or collapse	Drying at too high a temperature	Maintain at room temperature or below for setting or drying to form a thin crust.
Stickiness	Packing before crust has formed	Leave in starch 12 hours before packing.
Poor texture	Low Bloom strength gelatine	Recommended Bloom strength is 200–250.
Long cohesive	Wrong type of glucose syrup	High DE glucose syrups should be used.
	Soluble solids too low	Final moisture content should be around 20%.
Fermentation	Adding water whilst whipping to assist thinning	If required, use a sweetener syrup of over 70% soluble solids. Recommended to adjust temperature of syrup batch.
Fermentation	Low total soluble solids	Raise soluble solids to 70% preferably 75%.
	Low grade Gelatine	Check microbiological specification
	Unclean equipment	Wash equipment daily. Sterilise weekly.
	Packing in an airtight package	Seek advice of packaging manufacturer recommended pack–ridged cardboard box with semi-permeable overwrap.
	If two stage method involving frappé – prepared too far in advance and stored in a closed container	Prepare for one day's production only. Store in open stainless steel or polythene containers.

TABLE 68. Extruded Marshmallow – Faults and their Prevention

Faults	Cause	Action to Prevent Recurrence
Too tough	High percentage gelatine	Reduce gelatine to 1·5–2·5% level.
	Either too little or too much doctor	Regular 42 DE glucose syrup up to 50%. High 63 DE glucose syrup up to 100%.
	High viscosity syrup	Use up to 30% dextrose monohydrate.
	Loss of moisture during beating	Increase beating speed to reduce time.
	Atmospheric process	Reduce boiling temperature of syrup.
	Loss of moisture continuous process	Recalculate formula to obtain higher percentage moisture in final syrup before beating by (a) reduce boiling temperature of syrup solution; (b) increase water addition for soaking gelatine.
Poor foam	Incorrect type of Gelatine used	Select acid pigskin type or special whipping varieties.
	High viscosity syrup	Re-adjust (a) temperature
		(b) glucose syrup to 63 DE
		(c) add dextrose monohydrate
	Insufficient water left during whipping process	Reduce total solid of syrup prior to beating. More likely in albumen types than gelatine. Additional beating after reaching peak results in foam collapse.
	Overbeating	*Atmospheric process*
		(a) increase speed of beater.
		(b) reduce quantity of mixture.
	Underbeating	*Continuous process*
		(a) increase back pressure.
		(b) increase volume of air.
		(c) lower temperature of syrup pre-mix.

Fault	Cause	Remedy
		(d) increase rotator or whisk speed. (e) if vessel type, increase pressure.
Off colour	High pH	A pH higher than 6 is not desirable. Yellowing can occur above this figure.
	Low grade gelatine	Use a gelatine which gives low colour in solution. Also test after heating to 60° C (140° F) for one hour.
	Albumen type soaking in metal containers	Soak in unbreakable glass pottery or stainless steel containers.
Shrinking	Syrup added too hot to albumen solution	Add albumen solution to syrup under 65° C (149° F).
	Gelatine type continuous production foam extruded too hot	Extrude for products to be chocolate covered at 38° C (100° F). Hot chocolate enrobed maximum 60° C (140° F).
	Back pressure too high	Keep back pressure under 80 lb/in^2
	High percentage gelatine used	Reduce gelatine to 1·5–2·5%.
Long texture		
Stretchy	Gelatine of too low Bloom strength	Use higher strength. Recommend Bloom strength 200–250
Fermentation	Low total soluble solids	Keep total soluble solids content above 70% absolute minimum. Recommended above 75%. Check microbiological specification.
	Low grade gelatine	
	Unclean equipment	Wash equipment daily. Sterilise weekly.
	Packing in an airtight package	Seek advice of packaging manufacturer. Pack recommended ridged cardboard box with semi-permeable overwrap.
	If two stage method involving frappé – prepared too far in advance and stored in a closed container	Prepare for one day's production only. Store in open stainless steel or polythene containers.

15.7 NOUGAT

Nougat type confections are considered to have originated in the Montelimar region of France, the original recipe consisting of egg whites, honey, together with chopped nuts, usually almonds.

Today nougat in its varied forms is produced in many countries. It is basically a high-boiled syrup, containing fat, to which is added a frappé. The frappé can be manufactured using egg albumen, gelatine, Hyfoama (§6.10), soya protein or in combinations with starch, gum arabic or agar.

Hardened vegetable oil is added, mainly to act as a lubricant and to facilitate cutting. It also helps to reduce stickiness. Many other ingredients can be incorporated—for example, cherries, different varieties of nuts, preserved fruits, and milk powder.

The temperature to which the syrup is boiled determines the texture and hardness of the confection.

Physical characteristics of a nougat can be influenced by changes in the following: (a) The volume or percentage of air incorporated. (b) The composition of the continuous syrup phase controlled by the relative proportions of sweeteners present. (c) The boiling point of the syrup portion. (d) The percentage of sugar crystals present.

In the production of short or grained nougat, for example, fondant or icing sugar is mixed in at the end of the process to produce the graining effect.

At a given moisture content, the higher the percentage of cane or beet sugar (sucrose) in the recipe, the higher will be the amount of graining. A chewy nougat should not grain and therefore it requires a low moisture content, together with a lower sugar ratio in the total sweeteners.

After cane or beet sugar, glucose syrup is the second major constituent. For chewy non-grained, non-chocolate enrobed confections, including fruit caramels, the use of a low DE 36–38 or high Maltose type glucose syrup will maintain a high viscosity in the syrup phase and help prevent stickiness and cold flow. For non-enrobed short textured and grained nougat, a 42 DE glucose syrup will produce a slightly more tender product, with increased moisture retention. For confections which are chocolate covered and are of a tender soft texture, a high 63 DE glucose syrup will provide considerably more moisture retention with reduced drying out during storage.

Dextrose Monohydrate and invert sugar can also be used for moisture retention, but this is not recommended as these sugars reduce the viscosity of the syrup phase, which can be the cause of cold flow and excessive stickiness. Invert sugars can also be formed during the syrup boiling process, due to inversion. This possibility can be reduced by keeping the boiling process as short as possible. The preparation of the syrup is best conducted using a continuous evaporation or vacuum process.

The type of whipping agent and its concentration is of prime importance. Traditional nougats are produced using egg albumen. However, gelatine can be used successfully. The replacement of egg albumen is common practice and whipping agents based on milk protein, such as Hyfoama and soya protein, can be used, with the main advantage of being stable at high temperatures.

15.8 Nougat using Egg Albumen

	Parts by weight
Sugar	40
Water	10
Glucose Syrup (36–38 DE or high maltose grade)	34
Spray-Dried Egg Albumen	0·75
Water	3·0
Hardened Vegetable Oil	0·75

Method
1. Dissolve the spray dried egg albumen in water.
2. Transfer this solution to a whisking machine and whip to maximum volume.
3. When the solution has been prepared, replace the whisk on the machine by a beater (or transfer to a nougat beating machine).
4. Dissolve the sugar in water completely.
5. Add glucose syrup and boil to a temperature of between 130°–140° C (266°–284° F), depending upon the degree of hardness required.
6. Melt any fat in the cooked syrup at this stage.
7. Pour the cooked syrup, containing the fat, slowly onto the whipped egg albumen solution.
8. Beat the batch until the required volume is obtained.
9. Mix in colour and flavour.
10. Transfer to cooling slabs or discharge to extrusion hoppers.

15.9 Nougat using Gelatine

	Parts by weight
Sugar	44·0
Glucose Syrup (36–38 DE grade or high maltose grade)	44·0
Water	0·8
Gelatine (180 Bloom)	2·0
Water	4·0
Hardened Palm Kernel Oil	0·8

Method
1. Dissolve the gelatine in twice its weight of water maintaining a temperature of 60° C (140° F).

2. Place the sugar and water in a steam jacketed pan and heat until dissolved.
3. Add glucose syrup, boil to a temperature of between 130°–138° C (266°–280° F), (depending upon the texture required).
4. Place the boiled batch into the bowl of a vertical planetary mixer.
5. Add the gelatine solution and commence beating to maximum required volume.
6. Melt the fat and add slowly to the batch, together with any flavour and colour.
7. Transfer the batch to prepared cooling slabs or rice paper lined trays, and spread to the required thickness, or discharge to extrusion hoppers.

15.10 NOUGAT USING A VERTICAL PLANETARY MIXER

(capacity required around 25 galls or 110 litres; parts by weight)

	Hard Short Nougat	Fruit Caramel	Short Soft Centre	Honey Nougat Centre
Treated Milk Protein (Hyfoama DS)	0·1	0·1	0·075	0·1
Water	1·5	1·5	1·5	0·6
Icing Sugar	2·5	2·5	2·5	—
Honey	—	—	—	5·0
Sugar	13·5	11·0	8·0	14·0
Glucose Syrup (36–38 DE grade)	17·5	18·0	10·0	14·0
Water	4·5	3·5	2·5	5·0
Skim Milk Powder	—	—	2·0	—
Icing Sugar	1·75	—	0·5	—
Fondant	—	—	—	1·5
Fat	—	0·6	1·0	—
Boiling Temperature	136° C (277° F)	131° C (268° F)	131° C (268° F)	131° C (268° F)

Method
1. Mix Hyfoama with water, add icing sugar.
2. Beat together in the mixer, using a whisk, until maximum volume is obtained.
3. Replace the whisk with a beater.
4. Add the boiled syrup slowly on slow speed.
5. After the incorporation of the boiled syrup add additional ingredients, including fat.
6. Continue mixing carefully to obtain a smooth consistency.
7. Transfer to cooling slabs or extruders.

15.11 Nougat using Pressure Beating

(capacity required—around 25 gall or 110 litres; parts by weight)

	Hard Short Nougat	Fruit Caramel	Soft Short Nougat Centre	Honey Nougat Centre
Sugar	24·0	20·0	16·0	21·0
Water	8·0	7·0	5·0	7·0
Glucose Syrup	26·0	26·0	14·5	21·0
Honey	—	—	—	7·5
Treated Milk Protein (Hyfoama DS)	0·150	0·150	0·120	0·150
Water	0·225	0·225	0·180	0·225
Glucose Syrup (36–38 DE grade)	0·625	0·625	0·450	0·625
Skim Milk Powder	—	—	3·0	—
Icing Sugar	2·5	—	0·75	—
Fondant	—	—	—	2·5
Fat	—	1·0	1·5	—
Boiling Temperature	125° C (257° F)	123° C (253° F)	120° C (248° F)	132° C (270° F)

Method

1. Preheat bowl of pressure beater 65° C (149° F).
2. Pour in the boiled syrup.
3. Prepare Hyfoama, water and glucose syrup dispersion.
4. Add to boiled syrup on slow speed.
5. For honey nougat, add honey at this stage.
6. Bring machine to operational pressure (50 lb/in^2).
7. Vent to expel water vapour, return to operational pressure.
8. Change to high speed for predetermined time (three minutes).
9. Stop mixer, allowing compressor to run to facilitate pressure discharge.
10. Discharge through bottom opening valve and pipe of suitable diameter into secondary mixer.
11. Add additional ingredients, including fat, on slow speed.
12. Mix to a smooth texture.
13. Transfer to cooling slabs or extruders.

15.12   Nougat using Malto-dextrins

	Chewy	Short	Grained
	(parts by weight in each case)		
Syrup			
Cane or Beet Sugar	38·82	30·85	42·00
Glucose Syrup	37·38	29·90	21·00
Water (sufficient to dissolve cane or beet sugar)			
Boiling Temperature	124° C (255° F)	124° C (255° F)	138° C (280° F)
Frappé			
Powdered Egg Albumen	0·83	0·88	0·90
Malto-Dextrin	0·83	0·67	0·90
Glucose Syrup	10·31	29·90	19·40
Water	8·50	4·00	9·20
Fat	3·33	3·80	3·60
Colour-Flavour	3·33	3·80	3·60
Cocoa Powder	—	—	1·50*
Icing Sugar	—	—	1·50

* For grained batch add cocoa powder and icing sugar, with melted fat.

Method (Using a vertical mixing machine at atmospheric pressure)

1. Prepare the syrup batch by dissolving the sugars and boiling to requisite temperature.
2. Prepare the frappé by mixing the egg albumen and malto-dextrin and dissolving in the water.
3. Place this frappé solution into a mixing bowl add glucose syrup, beat for 1 minute medium speed, followed by six minutes fast speed.
4. Reduce to a slow speed, add the boiled syrup.
5. At end of mixing, add melted fat at 110°–120° C (230°–248° F) with minimum of mixing.
6. Pour onto slab, allow to cool.

The diagrammatic layout for the batch production of nougat using the presswhip, manufactured by Ter Braak, is given in Fig. 48 and Photo 6. The stages are: A Sugar, water and glucose syrup are weighed in the correct proportion and pumped to the cooker. B The syrup is cooked to the required moisture content. C The syrup is then gravity-fed into the bowl of the pressure beater. D The solution of the whipping agents is also fed into the pressure beater at the same time, and beating is carried out for a predetermined time and pressure. The aerated batch is then emptied into the slow speed horizontal mixer. E In this horizontal mixer, ingredients such as fats, nuts, or, in the case of a grained product, powdered sugar, are added and the batch discharged by tilting.

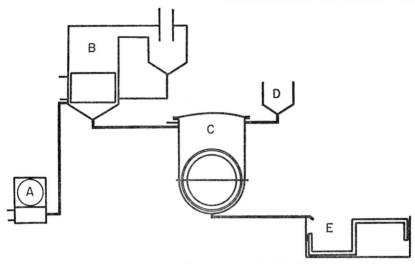

FIGURE 48. Batch production of nougat by Ter Braak presswhip.

15.13   CONTINUOUS PRODUCTION OF NOUGAT

This can be achieved by using a continuous, in-line aerator, such as the Oakes, combined with continuous cooking equipment, a metering pump for the whipping agent dispersion and liquid and dry feeders for additional ingredients. Fig. 49 illustrates the process of continuous production by pressure beating. In the pre-mixer 1 sugar and glucose syrup are weighed and continuously fed into the boiler 2. The boiled batch is again continuously fed by means of positive displacement pump 6 into the mixing head 5. At the same time, whipping agent solution, prepared in tank 3 is metered in by means of pump 4. The sugars–whipping agent mix is aerated under pressure 7. The batch leaving the mixer is discharged into the continuous secondary mixer 8, where auxiliary ingredients are added 9.

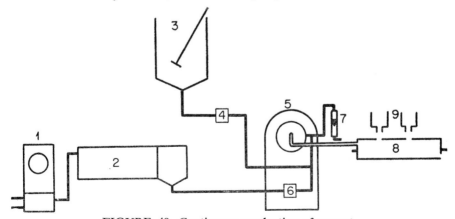

FIGURE 49. Continuous production of nougat.

TABLE 69. Nougat: Faults and their Prevention

Fault	Cause	Action to Prevent Recurrence
Waxy taste	Beating in hot kettle	Do not beat in the hot kettle (egg albumen coagulates). Add syrup below 93° C (200° F).
Lack of fluffiness	Beating	Do not overbeat. Get a stronger beater.
	Inadequate egg albumen	Increase egg albumen.
	Quality of egg albumen	Never over-purchase egg albumen.
	Continuous process	Increase air pressure or back pressure.
Discoloura-tion	Contamination of egg albumen	Prepare and store egg albumen solutions only in glass or earthen-ware.
Stickiness	Insufficient dissolving water	Use 2 parts by wt. of water to every 1 part albumen.
	Excessive glucose.	Reduce glucose syrup.
	Boiling temp. too low	Increase boiling temperature of syrup batch.
	Method of adding boiled batch	Wait until syrup boil is under 93° C (200° F) before adding to albumen.
	Excessive inversion	Lower the acid content if any.
	Use of honey	Reduce proportion in batch.
	Excessive inversion	Reduce boiling time.
Loss of foam	Mixing in warm kettle	Allow to cool or mix in separate container.
	Too rapid pouring	Pour the hot syrup in a slow but steady stream.
	Sugar boil too hot	Add syrup when the temperature is under 93° C (200° F).
	Oily flavour	Use essences when possible.
	Poor mixing	Fat in particular must be comple-tely dispersed.
	Overbeating	Continue only as long as to achieve the volume required.
	Addition of fat	Use plastic butter.
Lack of shape	Poor aeration	See 'loss of foam' and 'lack of fluffiness'.
	Undercooked	Increase boiling temperature of syrup batch.
	Cold process.	Use a hot method.
Breaking Graining	Boiled too high	Lower boiling temperature.
	Overbeating	Do not overbeat.
	Insufficient doctor	Increase glucose syrup.
	Adding low cook to high boiled syrup	Always add the high boil to the the frappé.
	Sugar graining	Replace some sugar by glucose syrup or use lower DE syrup.
Cold flow	Excessive inversion	Minimise formation of invert sugar.

Fault	Cause	Action to Prevent Recurrence
	High DE glucose syrup	Use a low DE glucose syrup.
	Warm storage	Store at lower temperature.
Hygroscopic	Sticky texture	Reduce formation of invert sugar. Use a low DE glucose syrup.
	Sticky surface	Check air humidity. Use high quality wrapping paper.
Moist	Excessive moisture retention	Boil to higher temperature. Use low DE glucose syrup. Do not add dextrose monohydrate or invert sugars.

16

Other Confectionery Types

16.1 PANNING

Panning is the process of building up in a controlled manner a sugar or chocolate coating on confectionery centres. The sugar coating can be 'hard' and contain cane or beet sugar only, or 'soft' when glucose syrup is also present. The differences are listed below.

TABLE 70. Differences between 'Hard' and 'Soft' Panning

	'Hard' Panning	*'Soft' Panning*
Composition of syrup charge:	cane or beet sugar	cane or beet sugar and glucose syrup
Inner surface finish of the pan:	smooth	roughened
Accuracy in building up shape of centre:	well-defined	ill-defined
Pan size to be used:	large diameter	small diameter
Speed in building up coating:	slow	rapid

The equipment required to set up a pan room is as follows:

Rotating Copper Pans	– usually 3 ft 6 in diameter, which can be set to rotate at between 15 to 35 rev/min
Hot and Cold Air Supply	– from movable nozzles above the pans
Sugar Syrup Boiling Pans	– 100 lb (45 kg) capacity
Measuring Containers	– for adding charges of syrup
Polishing Pan	– rotating copper; kept only for polishing
Storage Trays	
Weighing Scales	– small and large types for checking progress of panning and for weighing ingredients
Flavour Measure	
Sifting Sieves	
Screened off Drying/Storage Area	

Panning is a slow process which involves small batch sizes; but one operator can look after five or six pans, or with the automatic spray units described later, up to ten. One of the small sugar syrup boiling pans will be required for every three rotating pans.

324

The speed of the revolving pans depends on the size of the goods. Small sized pan goods require high speeds to produce an even coating while large panned goods need slower speeds. The lowest speed is that for large nuts, 15 rev/min. Nonpareils (coated sugar grains or 'hundreds and thousands') require speeds of 30–35 rev/min. Variable speed motor units are available, though for most purposes it is better to keep separate banks of pans operating at different speeds for particular types of goods.

Although an air supply to the pans is not essential, it greatly improves the effectiveness of panning by giving rapid drying, removing dust and cooling the frictional heat which is set up in the centres. A suitable temperature range for the hot air supply is 35°–65° C (95°–149° F) at a velocity of 1000–1500 ft/min. The temperature of the drying air should be kept in balance with the air velocity: an increase in one should be accompanied by a decrease in the other. The discharged goods should be stacked on perforated trays to allow the passage of cooling air.

16.2 HARD PAN WORK

This is based on the regular addition of a high sucrose concentration syrup to the centres. Before this is commenced, the centres should be prepared to receive the charge. With nuts, where oil seepage can be a problem, the sealant coating should be a gum arabic—wheat flour mixture. Other products such as nonpareils (hundreds and thousands) require no such sealant. The method is illustrated by the following procedure for nonpareils. Two terms used are specific to pan work: *Wetting* describes the charge of syrup added to the pan, *engrossing* the process of building up the centres.

NONPAREILS

1. Choose a medium grained, dust free sugar and dry overnight in a warm room at 25° C (77° F).
2. Load sufficient sugar into a pan into which is directed a hot air stream at 40° C (104° F). The final yield can be calculated on the basis that each part of sugar will require 0·4 parts cornflour and 20 parts syrup by weight.
3. Add a 10–15% wetting (based on centre weight) of 61% engrossing syrup prepared from cane or beet sugar (33° Baumé).
4. Dust with cornflour and run the wetted goods until dry (indicated by rising dust).
5. Repeat with a 64% concentration syrup (34°–35° Baumé).
6. Repeat the engrossing process until twice the weight of centres has been added as syrup.
7. Discontinue the cornflour dusting.
8. Remove the centres and sieve.

9. Return the goods to the pan and continue engrossing until 20 times the original weight of centres has been added as syrup. The goods should be removed periodically and sieved to remove any clumped pieces. (As the volume increases it will become necessary to split the centres into different pans.)
10. The final wetting should be made with 0·3% (by weight) charges of 59·2% engrossing syrup (32° Baumé).
11. When the centre has been built up to a satisfactory level, give three further wettings with 55% engrossing syrup (30° Baumé).
12. Sieve to remove clumps.

Colouring should be added with the last five wettings but flavouring matter should be added throughout engrossing. A small trace of blue colour added to 'white' pan goods produces a brighter appearance.

Each charge of syrup should be dried before any further additions. Cornflour sprinkled on the goods immediately after wetting will reduce sticking, but the amount must be treated with caution, as excessive use results in balling up in the pan. A small block of smooth wood placed in the pan helps prevent clumping.

For most types of pan work, the build-up of the syrup can be checked by weighing a fixed amount and counting the number of pieces. The relationship between centre weight, actual weight and desired weight is an accurate indication of progress. This is not practicable with nonpareils whose count per pound is around 70 000. In later sections of this chapter, the relationship between the centre and coated weight per pound of a range of panned goods is suggested.

The smaller the panned pieces the greater is the need for frequent sieving to remove waste. Increasing the size of the centre enables a larger charge of high concentration syrup to be used. Pitted surface colours on hard panned goods arise from a rough surface finish caused by too rapid drying or too high a sugar concentration in the syrup. Roughness may be corrected by engrossing with a thinner syrup. Colours must always be added with the dilute syrup. A better coloured product is given by slowly increasing the colour strength of the syrup rather than adding all the colour with one or two charges of syrup. To improve gloss the final charge of colour should not be allowed to completely dry in the pan.

Almonds are engrossed in a similar way to that described for nonpareils. In this case, the centres should be sealed before engrossing is commenced. The nuts should be dried at 40° C (104° F) for 8 hours and then loaded into the pans. If the drying is omitted, the shell may well crack during panning. A sealing coat of 50% gum arabic solution with a wheat flour dusting should then be given. More flour and gum arabic solution should be added until a smooth coating is achieved. A coating syrup of 66·9% cane or beet sugar (36° Baumé) should be added between the additions of the gum solution, to prevent oil seepage from the centre onto the sugar shell.

The sugar coating can be built up on the coated almond centres using successively (a) 61% cane or beet sugar syrup (33° Baumé), (b) 66·9% cane or beet sugar syrup (36° Baumé), (c) 61% cane or beet sugar syrup (33° Baumé). The relationship between degrees Baumé of a sugar solution and concentration is given in Table 71.

Cold air should be used in preference to hot air in sugared almond manufacture. In calculating yield, one part by weight of nuts will take two to four parts of sugar coating. A typical recipe would be 50 parts almonds, 15 parts wheat flour, 6 parts gum arabic solution (50%) and 125 parts cane or beet sugar held in 70 parts of water. The amount of perfume flavouring of a type such as otto of rose, for such a batch, will be as little as 0·001% ($\frac{1}{8}$ oz/200 lb or 3–4 ml/90 kg). For convenience in use, the ottos should be diluted with acceptable food solvents.

Other centres suitable for hard panning are small circular mint lozenges (centres 500/lb, panned to 150), liquorice sticks or torpedoes (centres 1000/lb, panned to 400/lb), chocolate beans (centres 400/lb, panned to 330/lb), high-boiled drops (500/lb, panned to 150/lb). Chewing gum and bubble gum pieces should be sugar panned to give a 25% coating. The panned chewing and bubble gum can be lightly coated with shellac in isopropanol to give added moisture protection.

Several automatic panning systems are available which double the number of pans that can be looked after by one operator. In the Steinberg spraying process (Photo 7; Gerhard Steinberg KG) the sugar is automatically dissolved in a stainless steel pressure vessel fitted with a stirrer. An organic additive is used at this stage to prevent the supersaturated syrup from crystallising. The prepared syrup is delivered to the jacketed spray head through a heated conveyor line. A fine spray of the syrup is directed onto the centres held in revolving pans. In a typical process cycle, the operating sequence is spray (60 sec)/pause (30 sec)/dry (120 sec).

The Boonton automatic coating system consists of coating pans, moisture sensing probes, blower unit, electronic control panel and jacketed spray nozzles. A typical panning cycle using this equipment is spray, pause, blow, pause, spray. Cycle times can be varied from 0–60 sec.

In the Driamet system, the raw materials are loaded into a reservoir pan, a controlled amount of water added through a previously set regulator valve and the turbomixer started. The prepared syrup is then piped through a sieve to the spray heads. The predetermined quantity of syrup is volumetrically measured and sprayed onto the centres which are held in revolving pans. The delivery cycle is controlled by charges in resistance caused through variations in relative humidity in the air above the coated centres. The wetting charges are automatically increased as the surface area of the centres.

TABLE 71.   Relation between Degrees Baumé and Sucrose Concentration of
Sugar Solutions held at 20° C (68° F)

Degrees Baumé at 20° C	Sucrose %	Degrees Baumé at 20° C	Sucrose %
1	1·8	21	38·2
2	3·6	22	40·1
3	5·4	23	41·9
4	7·2	24	43·8
5	9·0	25	45·7
6	10·8	26	47·6
7	12·6	27	49·5
8	14·4	28	51·4
9	16·2	29	53·3
10	18·0	30	55·0
11	19·8	31	57·1
12	21·6	32	59·2
13	23·5	33	61·0
14	25·3	34	63·0
15	27·1	35	64·9
16	29·0	36	66·9
17	30·8	37	68·9
18	32·6	38	70·9
19	34·5	39	72·9
20	36·4	40	74·9

In the Graco tablet system, a stream of sugar liquor is sprayed at head output pressures of 800–300 lb/in² (42–211 kg/cm²) to create a high velocity fluid stream. The shape of the spray tip has been found to be extremely important in controlling the spray pattern. A fine spray is essential to ensure that the coating builds up in an even way. Controlled spraying methods eliminate heavy and erratic coating and improve drying time. The output pressure in the Graco system is achieved using a reciprocating double action fluid pump. Timers are used to achieve consistent on–off spraying cycles. Spray nozzles are constructed from tungsten carbide and other parts of the equipment from stainless steel or polytetrafluroethylene coated metals.

16.3   POLISHING

Pans for this purpose should be kept free from dust and away from the humid conditions of the pan room. Beeswax should be run in a clean pan as a preliminary to polishing. This coating of beeswax, or hardened paraffin oil or canauba wax, is used to shine the hard pan goods. Cold air should be blown into the pan during polishing. Only small weights of coated goods should be polished at any one time. A thick coating of wax on the sweets will be obtained if the coating on the pan is allowed to become too soft.

During polishing small amounts of talc should be added to increase the shine. Excessive running of coated goods in the polishing pans will give an uneven coat. Polishing pans should not be washed after use, any dust or fragments being removed using a small hand vacuum cleaner.

If the coating flakes after sugar panning has been carried out using automatic spray equipment, it may be due to one of two causes: the incorrect setting of the pressure head on the sprays, or the spray mist. Blistering is normally due to the incorrect setting of the spray (pause) dry cycle; it is entrapped sugar syrup which causes this fault. The moisture present works outwards during storage and damages the sugar shell. Too rapid coating during engrossing will also produce an uneven finish. Slow drying may frequently be traced to the use of drying air which has a high relative humidity.

A common fault in hard panning is the speckling or spotting of the colour. This may be due to the too rapid introduction of the colour wettings or by polishing before the coating has had time to dry off. Time intervals between syrup additions should be 10 minutes or more. Attempts to shorten the panning time by increasing pan speed, air temperature or air flow will inevitably lead to failure. The wettings should be spread over the whole of the centres rather than concentrated on sweets in one part of the pan. Engrossing syrup should be free from crystallisation at the time of adding to the centres. Split centres are most frequently due to coating cold centres with a hot syrup. Where a particular centre is susceptable to this fault it should be first run dry in a warm pan. The development of stickiness on the surface of panned goods is frequently due to a high mineral ash content in the cane or beet sugar.

16.4   SILVER COATING

This is achieved by the addition of silver dust or leaf to the panned centres, a normal rate being around 0·5% of the final batch weight. The process is also known as silvering or gilding. Its main use is in the production of small silver dragées for cake decoration; these dragées are called in some areas 'rifle shot'.

Silvering should be carried out in a revolving glass lined pan operated at 35–40 rev/min. The process is not easy and the margin between success and failure very small.

The sugar crystal boule (or centre) should be first held in a container to which has been added a small amount of mixed gelatine, gum arabic and acetic acid wetting solution, prepared from 50 parts by weight of gelatine in 50 parts water, 50 parts gum arabic in 100 parts water and 4 parts glacial acetic acid. After mixing, the solution should be sieved and stored in amber-coloured bottles to exclude light. Care must be taken not to overwet the centres with this solution. The moistened centres should be transferred to the glass pans and coating commenced. The silver dust or leaf should have previously been added to these pans. No drying air should be used in silver coating. The time taken to build up an adequate silver finish is 4–24 hours depending on the size of centres.

The coated dragées should be held in sealed containers for one day and then polished or glazed by running for a short period in a glass lined pan operating at 50 rev/min, by revolving in a beeswax or carnauba (see also §4.16) coated pan, or by glazing with a mixture of shellac in isopropanol. Some operators recommend the use of a small trace of edible yellow colouring in the shellac glaze to improve reflectance. Colouring can be carried out by spraying on edible colours held in isopropanol, followed by shellac glazing. The causes of darkening of silver dragées are three: (i) storing near other confections or raw materials containing sulphur dioxide as preservative; (ii) using gelatine which has a high preservative content; (iii) storing in direct sunlight.

16.5   CHOCOLATE COATING

Chocolate coating is similar to hard panning, requiring a sealing coat on oily centres; a solution containing equal parts of gum arabic solution (50% $\frac{w}{w}$) glucose syrup and cane or beet sugar which has been tinted with brown colour can be used. The pans should be operated at 20 rev/min and held at 16° C (61° F) for plain chocolate and 14° C (57° F) for milk chocolate. Plain chocolate for coating should contain approximately 32% fat, and milk chocolate 28–29% fat. The chocolate should be added at 50° C (122° F). Chocolate additions should be cycled: charge/pause/dry. Any air used should be directed away from the centres onto the far side of the pan.

Chocolate panning can be carried out automatically using the systems described earlier for sugar panning. In addition, the EFCA spray gun can be used. The supply of chocolate to the spray heads is best carried out under pressure.

Polishing of chocolate panned goods may be carried out by the careful addition of small amounts of a solution of 4 parts gum arabic (50%), 6 parts water and 1 part glucose syrup. During polishing the coated centres should be kept revolving at 20 rev/min at a temperature of 16° C (61° F).

16.6   SOFT PANNING

The choice between hard and soft panning (§16.1) is dependent on the bite of the centre. A soft centre requires a soft panned coat. This cannot be used where it is necessary for the product appearance to closely resemble that of the centre. Soft panned work tends to be rounded and ball-like in appearance. Suggested build up levels for soft panned confections are given in Table 72.

TABLE 72. Soft Panned Confections

Description	Children's Assorted (Dolly Mixture Components)	Jelly Beans	Coconut Dessert
Type of centre:	French paste squares	Gelatine half moon jellies	Coconut paste centres
Count/lb of centre:	1000	200	160
Count/lb when coated:	600	100	80

For soft panning an engrossing syrup should contain 2 parts of glucose syrup to every part water. A small weight of centres should be placed in the revolving roughened surface pan and run cold at 20 rev/min. Small charges of syrup should be added to the centres and fine castor sugar sprinkled on until they dry. This process should be repeated until a sufficient coating has been achieved. Any colour or flavouring should be added to the syrup. Speckling, in preparing 'birds eggs', can be obtained by flicking a colour solution onto the panned goods using the bristle end of a brush. The final wettings should be dried with icing sugar in place of castor

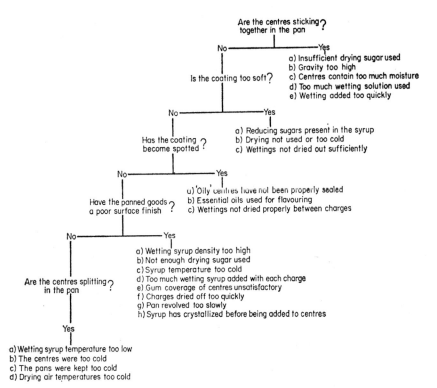

FIGURE 50. Check-list of sugar-panned goods faults.

sugar. It is necessary to halt the process at two or three stages during soft pan engrossing and transfer the partially coated centres onto trays so as to allow them to dry for 2 or 3 hours. Soft pan work is particularly susceptible to marking and any trays used should therefore be lined with greaseproof parchment paper or similar material. After coating has been completed the soft panned work should be dried in dust free rooms for 2 days at 20° C (68° F).

Glazing can be carried out by coating in 64·9% cane or beet sugar syrup (35° Baumé). A small amount of talc should be added as soon as this sugar coating has dried. Gloss may also be developed by coating with carnauba wax, beeswax or similar hard composition wax.

Typical usage rates for soft panning are 100 parts centre, $3\frac{1}{2}$ parts water, 7 parts glucose syrup, 90 parts caster sugar, 0·125 parts flavouring.

The causes of faults occurring during panning are shown in Fig. 50.

16.7   CHEWING GUM

Chewing gum can be prepared either as panned pieces or in stick form. The confection is composed mainly of mixed natural and synthetic gums and resins together with various sugar and flavouring materials.

The natural gums most commonly in use are chicle and jelutong—pontianak. These are used alone or more normally as a mixed gum base. Gutta siak, leche capsi, perillo, nispero tinu and pine tree resins have also been used for the base. All the above gums are claimed to pass through the digestive system of the body unaffected. Synthetic materials can be used, the most important being the vinyl esters. Polyvinyl acetate (PVA), frequently used, is a colourless, odourless and tasteless thermoplastic with a specific gravity of 1·189. It is soluble in alcohol. Butadiene styrene rubber, isobutylene—isoprene copolymer (butyl rubber) and polyisobutylene can be used in gum base manufacture; these polymers are non-toxic and have a slightly higher specific gravity. Butadiene styrene rubbers will undergo a

CHEWING GUM

	Parts by weight
Gum Base	16
Icing Sugar	40
Dextrose	10
Glucose Syrup 42 DE	24
Sorbitol Syrup (70% concentration)	4
Calcium Carbonate	1
Maize Starch	2
Glycerine	1
Hydrogenated Palm Kernel Oil	1
Soyabean Lecithin	0·5
Flavouring Colouring	0·5

change in texture when heated to 28° C (82° F) and by 55° C (131° F) have a rubber-like consistency. Polyvinylacetate will only break down at over 130° C (266° F). Chemical modification of PVA can produce a considerably more brittle texture. Plasticisers which may be used with the synthetic gum bases include glycerine esters of hydrogenated or polymerised resin, lanolin, and potassium and sodium stearates.

Method

This can be considered in two parts: preparation of gum base and blending and extrusion. Gum base is tedious to manufacture and for most confectioners it is preferable to buy in the requisite blend from a specialist manufacturer.

(A) *Preparation of Gum Base*
1. Grind the constituent gums and resins to a low piece size.
2. Spread the gum pieces on wire mesh trays.
3. Pass warm air at 35° C (95° F) through the trays to drive off the excess moisture.
4. Transfer the required weight of gum(s) to a steam heated mixing pan—raise the temperature to 90° C (194° F).
5. When the melt temperature has been reached, add an equal weight of warm water and knead for 150 minutes.
6. Bleach with weak caustic soda solution.
7. Wash with hot water for a period of 8 hours, draining and changing the water on at least three occasions.
8. Repeat the drying process detailed in stages 2 and 3.
9. Return the gum to the mixer and raise the temperature to 100° C (212° F).
10. Add the other waxy resins and synthetic gum components.
11. Blow the gum mix through a fine sieve into a centrifuge of the Sharples or Delavel type (this can be done using positive air pressure).
12. Spin to remove all the water insolubles.
13. Run through vacuum straining units into moulds.
14. Allow to set and remove, dusting the block with maize starch.

(B) *Production of Chewing Gum*
1. Load the specified weight of gum base into a heavy duty steam heated Z arm mixer/kneader.
2. Turn on the heat and melt the gums and waxes at a temperature of 90°–95° C (194°–203° F).
3. Commence the kneading action.
4. When the gum mix has softened add the specified recipe weight of icing sugar, warmed glucose syrup, sorbitol syrup and dextrose.
5. Mix for 90 minutes maintaining a temperature of 80° C (176° F).

M

6. Stop the mixer and add the specified weight of flavouring and colouring.
7. Continue the mixing process for a further 30 minutes.
8. On completion of mixing, discharge and extrude through sizing rollers to a 2 in thick sheet.
9. Guillotine into 10 lb (5 kg) blocks, pass through a cooling tunnel and cool to 20° C (68° F).
10. Condition for 24 hours by holding in air at 20° C (68° F) and a humidity of 50%.
11. Place the block into a kneading unit and knead for 30 minutes at 120° C (248° F).
12. Transfer the kneaded mass to an extrusion hopper and extrude at 50° C (122° F) through staggered reducing rollers.
13. Pass through transverse and longitudinal scoring rollers and cut to shape.

Notes: (*a*) A 50:50 icing sugar:cornflour mix can be used to prevent sticking—alternative dusting agents are talc or under short storage conditions, proprietory fat based release agents. (*b*) The strips should be conditioned overnight at 20° C (68° F) and 50% relative humidity before packing. (*c*) A cheap form of chewing gum can be produced by heating the glucose syrup to 100° C (212° F) and then adding the other ingredients in a heavy duty mixer—extrusion takes place in the manner described above.

A considerable number of alternative materials have been suggested for chewing gum base. In the thirty year period from 1931–1961 over 80 different additives have been patented and many more tried out in manufacturers' laboratories.

The main bulk of chewing gum is made up of sugar. Icing sugar of a low particle size should be used in preference to the more coarse grades. Chewing gum should contain a syrup phase and this can be achieved by the addition of glucose syrup of low or medium DE, the proportion of sucrose to glucose syrup being about 3–4:1. High glucose content chewing gums can be prepared, but tend to have a reduced shelf life. The use of invert sugar syrup as a partial or total replacement of glucose syrup is practicable but it is accompanied by a loss in keeping quality. A small proportion of sorbitol is useful as a humectant thereby preventing case hardening. The substitution of up to 15% of the icing sugar content by dextrose produces an interesting variant that has different texture properties. About 1–2% of refined hydrogenated vegetable oil will assist lubrication during chewing. Starch can be added as a filler, as can calcium carbonate, which latter is said usefully to neutralise mouth acids [L. S. FOSDICK, *J. Dental Res.*, 1948, *27*, 235–241]. Talc, when permitted under local food regulations, improves the rolling out of manufactured gum prior to stamping.

Other ingredients are permitted antioxidants, such as BHA, and emulsifiers such as lecithin, glyceryl monostearate and the sucrose esters. These compounds act as plasticisers and improve the softness of the chew. Propylene glycol and glycerine have the same purpose.

The major flavouring for chewing gum is spearmint and to a lesser degree peppermint. Generally, it can be said that cheap flavourings taste 'cheap' and it is not unusual when using these for an unexpected off flavour to develop on store, from interaction with components in the mixed gum base. Mixed fruit or 'tutti fruiti' flavourings have found some acceptance. A useful flavouring can be blended by mixing lemon, lime and tangerine oils with isopropanol in the proportion of 25:10:10:55. Alternative flavourings are sweet birch, aniseed and liquorice. A small trace of vanillin will produce a pleasing and reasonably long lasting background flavour.

A suitable size for the sticks of chewing gum is 70 mm by 19–20 mm with a thickness of 1·8–2·0 mm. Produced to these dimensions each stick will weigh 3–3·25 gr, giving a retail pack of 5 or 6 pieces weighing, with wrapping, around 20 gr. They should be wrapped in foil-wax paper laminates and held by an outer printed paper wrapper. An efficient end seal on the stick wrappers is essential to prevent moisture ingress.

For subsequent panning, chewing gum centres are best produced at a size of 450–500 pieces/lb (1000–1100 pieces/kg). After panning, these should weigh between 250 and 275/lb (550–600/kg), the chewing gum centre constituting around 55% of the total weight. For panning, chewing gum recipes should be increased in gum base content. The centres so produced can be panned by conventional techniques drying with dust free cold air. After the conditioning period (stage 13 in the recipe) the centres should be coated with a thin seal of gum arabic to which has been added a maize starch dusting; this must completely dry before panning is started. The sugar panned gums, after thorough drying, are glazed by running the coated centres in a wax impregnated canvas lined pan, or in slightly warmed pans to which has been added wax and talc. The wax should be a mix of 90% beeswax and 10% carnauba wax; the latter giving a harder polish.

Panned pieces pick up less moisture from the atmosphere than uncoated sticks. They are packed in small boxes for loose sale or, more commonly, in groups of five in waxed glassine or foil-wax paper laminates, wrapped with printed paper. Both stick and panned piece packs are best held in stiff cardboard boxes wrapped in transparent cellulose acetate sheet.

Shelf life under normal conditions is two years or more. Any sweating can be attributable to five causes: (a) lack of conditioning of the gum during manufacture; (b) manufacturing to uneven moisture contents; (c) the use of too high a level of glucose or invert sugar syrup; (d) unsatisfactory packaging; (e) storage in adverse conditions.

A gritty texture is normally due to the use of icing sugar of too high a particle size; graining to an incorrect balance of sucrose to glucose syrup

solids. Shrinkage, the other major defect, is caused through unsatisfactory
conditioning treatment during processing, or from insufficient kneading.

16.8 SUGARLESS CHEWING GUM (devised by Atlas Food Laboratories)

	suggested usage, %	range, %
Gum Base	25·0	25–26
Sorbitol (70% Solution)	17·0	16–17
Crystalline Sorbitol	36·0	36–40
Mannitol	18·6	14·5–17·1
Glycerine	0·5	0·5
Artificial Sweetener	0·5–1·5	0·5–1·5
Flavour	1·5	1·5

The latitude to vary the composition and still produce a satisfactory
sugarless chewing gum is restricted: small changes in one component can
affect both texture and keeping properties.

Method
1. Feed the gum base into a horizontal blade mixer and heat with steam
   for 5 minutes at 60° C (140° F).
2. When the base has softened (usually no longer than 5 minutes at
   55°–60° C (131°–140° F), add the sorbitol (70% solution) and glycerine. Turn on the mixer and cut off the steam.
3. Begin adding crystalline sorbitol and mannitol a third at a time, making
   the additions only when the preceding addition has been thoroughly
   incorporated.
4. Mix all the ingredients until the mixture is homogeneous, about 6–8
   minutes will be needed to complete stages 3 and 4.
5. Add flavour in two parts, again allowing the first to be thoroughly
   incorporated before adding the second.
6. Remove the gum from the mixer as soon as the flavours are incorporated: a good indication is a dry surface appearance. The gum
   temperature at this stage should be 45°–50° C (113°–122° F). If lower,
   the gum mix will be difficult to roll and size.

Notes: (1) The gum is then processed in the manner used for normal chewing gum, i.e. extrusion, followed by sizing rollers, cutting and wrapping.
(2) Dusting at all stages should be carried out using mannitol.

16.9 BUBBLE GUM

Producing a gum which will, on chewing, produce bubbles is mainly
dependent on the choice of gum base. This should be primarily jelutong
with appropriate resins and plasticisers. The proportion of gum base: icing

sugar:glucose syrup solids should be $1:1\cdot5:1\frac{1}{2}$. Bubbles will only be produced when all the grained sugar has been dissolved in the mouth.

BUBBLE GUM

	Parts by weight
Gum Base	100
Glucose Syrup (63 DE)	200
Icing Sugar	800
Glycerine	5
Colour to desired shade	

1. Melt the gum base at 50° C (122° F).
2. Slowly mix in the other ingredients.
3. Extrude into 1 in thickness sheet.
4. Reduce the sheet to 0·03 in thickness and cut into squares with 12 in sides.
5. Stack on starch dusted trays and condition for 24 hours at 50% relative humidity and 20° C (68° F).

16.10   MARZIPAN AND PERSIPAN

Marzipan is prepared from mixed sugars and almonds while persipan includes blanched debittered apricot and peach kernels as the nut fraction. In both products there is a syrup phase, a dispersed oil phase and mixed solid phase consisting of fine sugar crystals and nut fragments. The recipe ratios and method are similar for both confections.

MARZIPAN

	Parts by weight
Cane or Beet Sugar	100
Glucose Syrup	8
Blanched Sweet Almonds	40
Blanched Bitter Almonds	1·5
Glycerine	1
Sorbic Acid	0·2
50% Egg Albumen Solution	1

Method
1. Break down the nuts into small fragments.
2. Mix in nearly half the sugar (a Unimix can be used, see §12.1).
3. Pass the blend through a three roller refiner.
4. Roast the resulting paste at 80°–85° C (176°–185° F) for 20 minutes.
5. Mix in the remaining sugar.
6. Roll and stamp to size.
7. Cool in a temperature controlled room held at 20° C (68° F).

In the compilation of the recipe for such a product, six factors relating cost, quality and shelf life must be balanced: (a) proportions of nuts used; (b) particle size of the almonds; (c) crystal size of the sugar; (d) proportions of syrup and solid phases; (e) residual water content and (f) amount of preservatives necessary to achieve shelf life.

The generally agreed standard for marzipan in the UK is that the manu-factured product should contain at least 25% ground almonds (23·5% on a dry basis) and that of the remainder, 75% should be sugar. Both sweet and bitter almonds are available; but only 1% of the total nut weight should be bitter almonds. This sufficiently improves the flavour without excessively raising the prussic acid level (see Chapter 6).

If the almonds are to be stored they should be sprayed on arrival at the factory with insecticides to prevent infestation; and prior to use, should be sieved on vibrators to remove any broken pieces or shell. After blanching they should be sorted, using compressed air to blow off any discoloured almonds, and finally passed through metal detectors before being weighed out for use.

Refining, to reduce the nut fragment size, is expensive both in machine costs and time and small manufacturers can circumnavigate this part of the process by purchasing raw mass. This is a blend of almonds and sugar finely ground (typically 75% almonds to 25% sugar). It is then only neces-sary to add additional sugars and preservatives to produce the marzipan.

Marzipan made from cane and beet sugar and ground almonds has different keeping qualities from that prepared by grinding together almonds and cane or beet sugar, the latter being more likely to oil on store. A film of acetoglycerides on the surface helps preserve marzipan from mould growth, although some penetrates into the mass.

The proportion of cane or beet sugar to glucose syrup is dependent on the desired stiffness of the marzipan. A suitable ratio would be 1 part of glucose syrup to 15 parts of cane or beet sugar. Analysis of a typical com-mercial marzipan shows:

		%
Moisture	8	
Cane or Beet Sugar	62	
Nuts	26	
Oil		16
Protein		6
Glucose Syrup Solids	3	
Others (invert sugar, preservatives, etc.)	1	

This product has a syrup phase of 27% and a solids phase of 73%. The proportion of moisture left in the batch contributes significantly to the amount of syrup phase: an increase of 1% in moisture increases the syrup phase to 31%. The higher the amount of almonds, the higher will be the amount of syrup phase necessary to achieve a desirable consistency. It is dangerous however to produce marzipan containing 10% or more moisture. According to VON SCHELHORN [*Verpackungs Rundschau*, 1961, 12, (7), 53–4] the equilibrium relative humidity (e r h) of marzipan is 83–88%.

Marzipan has therefore a tendency to dry out on store. This can be counteracted by adding about 1% by weight of glycerine or sorbitol. Excessive use of glycerine will result in a pasty taste.

Increasing the glucose syrup fraction or adding a small amount of invert sugar syrup will also reduce drying out.

Small amounts of almond oil can also be added to improve texture, but seepage of oil on to the surface will occur if the marzipan is excessively heated during roasting.

Rancidity sometimes detectable after storage may be due to poor quality nuts, but more often to the development of yeasts and moulds. This is usually prevented by the roasting treatment during manufacture, but it is essential that the product is packed promptly and certainly never allowed to stand overnight. It should not be packed hot, nor should excessive head-space be left within the pack: for long store, packing in vacuum evacuated sealed tins is advisable. Cracks developing in the marzipan have been found by R. BLASCHKE-HELIMESSEN and G. TEUSCHEL [*Nährung* 1970, 14, (4), 249–67] to be due to the growth of *Saccharomyces rouxii*, which has also been detected by S. WINDISCH [*Gordian*, 1969, (3), 115–6, 9]. Bad attacks can be controlled by the disinfection of the plant with formalin.

To inhibit such contaminants, normal procedure should be to incorporate 0·1% sorbic acid in the recipe. BLASCHKE-HELIMESSEN and TEUSCHEL (loc cit) have found that sodium benzoate is ineffective for this purpose; but 0·05% of acetic acid in the presence of 0·3% sodium acetate buffer has an inhibitory effect.

17

Calculating Sugar Confectionery and Chocolate Recipes

17.1 CALCULATION OF RECIPES FROM ANALYTICAL RESULTS

In Table 73, the first factor f^d represents the ratio of dry solids weight to the 'wet' or delivered weight. The second factor f^* is $1/100$ of the ratio of delivered weight to solid matter. For example, a high-boiled sweet may be required which contains 30% glucose syrup solids so as to match the analysis of a competitor's product. Analytical results relate to dry weight; more than 30 parts of glucose syrup will be needed in every 100 parts of recipe ingredients to take account of its moisture (18%). The weight required will be $1/0.820$ times greater (i.e. $\times 1.22$). For a 100 unit batch, the calculation is:

$$100 \times \tfrac{30}{100} \times 1.22 \text{ units of Glucose Syrup high DE}$$

If we divide the 1.22 by the 100, giving 0.0122, the f^* factor, this is simplified to

Total final batch weight $\times$ analysis percentage $\times$ f* factor which can be represented by

$$B \times p \times f^*$$

Five stages are involved in developing a matching recipe from the results of a chemical analysis. These are:

(a) Decide the required cooked batch weight B

(b) Calculate the individual weight of each component, using

$$\text{Raw Material Weight} = B \times p \times f^* \tag{1}$$

(c) Assess whether extra water is needed (see Table 74). If required, its total weight in a recipe should be equivalent to one-half the weight of the cane or beet sugar content (sucrose).

(d) Calculate the weight of water required (to convert lb weight of water to gallons, divide by 10).

TABLE 73. Factors for Relating 'Dry Ingredient Weights' to 'Weights as Delivered' (§17.2)

Raw Material	Factor f^a	Factor $f*$	Raw Material	Factor f^a	Factor $f*$
Agar Agar	0·840	0·0119	Gum		
Block Liquorice Juice	0·813	0·0123	Arabic	0·901	0·0111
Butter	0·862	0·0116	Tragacanth	0·901	0·0111
Chocolate	0·990	0·0101	Honey	0·820	0·0122
Chocolate Crumb	0·990	0·0101	Invert Sugar (72%)	0·720	0·0139
Citric Acid, Hydrate	0·917	0·0109	Lecithin	0·990	0·0101
Cocoa Butter	0·100	0·0100	Milk Condensed (FC)	0·730	0·0137
Cocoa Liquor	0·100	0·0100	Milk Powder	0·971	0·0103
Cornflour	0·877	0·0114	Nuts	0·980	0·0102
Dates	0·752	0·0133	Sorbitol (70%)	0·700	0·0143
Dextrose Hydrate	0·909	0·0110	Soya Flour	0·926	0·0108
Fats	0·100	0·0100	Starch	0·893	0·0112
Fruit Pulp	0·015	0·1666	Sugar		
Gelatine	0·877	0·0114	Brown	0·971	0·0103
Glucose Syrup			Cane or Beet	0·100	0·0100
Low DE	0·806	0·0124	Icing	0·100	0·0100
Regular	0·813	0·0123	Lactose	0·100	0·0100
High DE	0·820	0·0122	Tartaric Acid	0·990	0·0101
Maltose	0·833	0·0120	Treacle	0·820	0·0122
Enzyme	0·833	0·0120	Wheat Flour	0·862	0·0116
Golden Syrup	0·833	0·0120	Whey, Condensed, (FC)	0·752	0·0133

TABLE 74. Need for Added Water in Confectionery Recipes

Water needed with sugars	*Not normally needed*
Boiled Sweets	Butterscotch
Butter Casing	Caramels
Creams	Chocolate
Fondant	Cream Paste
Jelly Goods	French Paste
Liquorice	Lozenge
	Tablets
	Toffees

$$\text{Added Water, parts by wt.} = \left\{ \frac{Ts - 2W}{2} \right\} \times \frac{B}{100} \tag{2}$$

where B = anticipated batch weight
Ts = sucrose content, %
W = water content, %

(e) Consider the grade of glucose syrup most likely to have been used in manufacture. Table 75 will be helpful in this context.

TABLE 75. Grades of Glucose Syrup most suited for Sugar Confections

Low DE	*Regular*	*High DE*	*Enzyme*
Rock	Butterscotch	Cream Paste	Cream Paste
Some Boiled Sweets	Caramels	Creams	Creams
	Liquorice	Fondant	Fondant
	Toffees	Table Jellies	
	Turkish Delight	Turkish Delight	

The following example will illustrate the use of this method for calculating a recipe which will match a given analysis.

Butter Casing Analysis

		%
Total Solids		96·2
Moisture	3·8	
Sucrose	60·0	
Glucose Syrup Solids	28·0	
Fat	8·2	

(a) Required batch weight B, say 100 parts

(b)

Components	$B \times p \times f*$	*Weight of Raw Material*
Sucrose	$100 \times 60·0 \times 0·0100 =$	60·0 parts
Glucose Syrup	$100 \times 28·0 \times 0·0123 =$	34·4 parts
Butter	$100 \times 8·2 \times 0·0116 =$	9·5 parts

(c,d) Water

$$\frac{Ts - 2W}{2} \times \frac{B}{100} \tag{2}$$

$$= \frac{60 - 7 \cdot 6}{2} \times \frac{100}{100}$$

$$= 26 \cdot 2 \text{ parts by weight}$$

(if in lb, this will be 2·6 gal)

(*e*)   Grade of Glucose Syrup: Regular

Hence recipe:

	Parts by weight
Sugar	60
Glucose Syrup, 43DE	34
Butter	9·5
Water	26

17.2   EFFECT OF INVERSION

Under normal processing conditions without the addition of a doctor such as cream of tartar, the level of in-batch inversion is small—rarely exceeding 3%. In calculating a matching recipe it is reasonable to assume, when low quantities of invert sugar are present, that it has not been added as a separate ingredient but arises from the inversion of cane or beet sugar. Any invert sugar reported should be converted into the original weight of sugar using the following formulae

$$\begin{array}{l} \text{Weight of Sugar inverted} \\ \text{during processing} \end{array} \quad = 0 \cdot 0095 \ I \times B \qquad\qquad (3)$$

where $I = \%$ invert sugar

B = required batch weight

If on analysis a boiled sweet sample is found to contain 1·4% invert sugar and the desired batch weight is 60 units, then the equivalent amount of cane or beet sugar that has been converted during processing is $0 \cdot 0095 \times 60 \times 1 \cdot 4$, i.e. 0·8 units.

17.3   EFFECT OF MILK SOLIDS

The determination of the original weight of full cream sweetened condensed milk used in a confectionery recipe is based on the analytical determination of milk solids not fat content. The weight of milk to be added can be calculated as follows

$$\text{Added Milk (ams)} = 3 \cdot 32 \times \text{Milk Solids not Fat} \qquad\qquad (4)$$

The milk solids content includes a number of component materials which contribute to the reported value; these include sucrose and butterfat. The weight of these components can be calculated using the following

Sucrose present in Milk	$= 0 \cdot 575 \times$ ams	(5)
Butterfat present in Milk	$= 0 \cdot 125 \times$ ams	(6)

(*a*) Once these values have been derived, formulae can be rewritten to derive the added sugar and fat.

Added Sugar, % $= S - 0.575 \times$ ams   (7)
Added Fat, % $= F - 0.575 \times$ ams   (8)

where S = sucrose %
F = fat, %

(*b*) Similar values can be calculated for full cream unsweetened condensed milk and these revised figures are as follows:

Added Milk (ams) % $= 1.38 \times$ Milk Solids not Fat   (9)
Butterfat present in the Milk, % $= 0.28 \times$ ams   (10)

(*c*) Comparative figures for skimmed condensed milks are given below:

Sweetened Skimmed Condensed Milk
Added Milk Solids (ams), % $= 2.75 \times$ Milk Solids not Fat   (11)
Sucrose present in the Milk, % $= 0.64 \times$ ams   (12)
Unsweetened Skimmed Condensed Milk
Added Milk Solids (ams), % $= 1.03 \times$ Milk Solids not Fat   (13)

(*d*) If dried milk is used the revised values are:

Full Cream
Added Milk (ams), % $= 1.38 \times$ Milk Solids not Fat   (14)
Skimmed
Added Milk (ams), % $= 1.016 \times$ Milk Solids not Fat   (15)

17.4   EFFECT OF MOISTURE LOSS ON JELLY GOODS

Most jelly goods lose moisture through stoving. Account should be taken of this loss when calculating out a matching recipe. The development of batch weight is best carried out using information on the average loss from stoving with particular equipment over specified times and under known processing conditions. If these conditions are not known, formula (16) given below can be used

Revised Batch Weight
(assuming high moisture loss) $= B \times \dfrac{TS + 2.5}{TS}$ (16)

where B = required batch weight and
TS = determined total solids content

Ingredient weights, other than the weight of water, should be calculated using the original batch value amended for the moisture loss likely to have taken place through stoving.

17.5   REPLACEMENT WEIGHT OF SCRAP SYRUP

The weight of scrap syrup to be added as a replacement for sugar is given by

Weight of Scrap to be Added $= \dfrac{d \times r}{(s)}$ (17)

where d = dry sugar solids weight of ingredients in original syrup

r = fixed percentage replacement level of scrap syrup

(s) = % sugar solids content of scrap syrup

Sugar for Boiled Sweet Manufacture

	Parts by weight
Cane or Beet Sugar	440
Glucose Syrup	220
Water	330

Scrap Syrup Composition

	%
Total Solids	70·0
Sucrose	30·0
Glucose Syrup Solids	30·0
Invert Sugar	10·0

Replacement level for Scrap Syrup — 10%

Weight of Scrap Syrup to be added $= \dfrac{d \times r}{(s)}$ (17)

$$= \frac{660 \times 10 \cdot 0}{70 \cdot 0} = 94 \cdot 3 \text{ parts}$$

Usage rounded off to 194 parts

Composition of Scrap Syrup $= B \times p \times f^*$ (1)

Sucrose $= 194 \times 30 \times 0 \cdot 0100 = 28$ parts

Glucose Syrup $= 194 \times 40 \times 0 \cdot 0123 = 46$ parts

Revised recipe (rounded off)	*Parts by weight*
Sugar	410
Glucose Syrup	175
Water	310
Scrap Syrup	95

17.6 CALCULATION OF PROBABLE ANALYTICAL COMPOSITION FROM THE CONFECTIONERY RECIPE

The stages to be used in this calculation are as follows:

(a) Convert all recipe weights into dry component weights, i.e. the weight of solid matter present in the ingredient. This is carried out as follows using the factors given in Table 74.

$$Dry \ Weight = Original \ Weight \times f^d \qquad (18)$$

(b) Summate the dry weights.

(c) Calculate the batch yield either using the boiling temperature calculation given later in §17.9 or from the expected or known total solids content of the confection. Total solids contents can be estimated from information given in Table 5 (see §1.1).

$$Expected\ Batch\ Yield = \frac{100 \times Total\ dry\ weights}{Total\ Solids\ Content} \tag{19}$$

(d) Derive the weights of the individual components in the raw materials from

$$Individual\ Component\ Weight = Raw\ Material\ Weight \times F_R \tag{20}$$

The factors F_R are given in Table 76.

(e) Calculate the analytical composition of the sugar confection as follows:

$$Component\ \% = \frac{Total\ Weight\ of\ Individual\ Components \times 100}{Expected\ Batch\ Yield} \tag{21}$$

(f) Check that the summation of the individual percentage composition agrees with the expected total solids content. Take care that components of milk solids (lactose, protein, etc.) and glucose syrup and invert sugar solids (reducing sugars) are not included in the total when carrying out this check.

(g) The reducing sugar content can be calculated by adding all the dextrose, lactose, invert sugar and that part of the glucose syrup which has reducing properties. The figures for the reducing sugar content of glucose syrup are as follows:

Low DE	=	$0.35 \times G_C$
Regular DE	=	$0.43 \times G_C$
High DE	=	$0.63 \times G_C$

where G_C = glucose syrup solids

The following example illustrates the method of calculation

BUTTERSCOTCH

	Parts by weight
Sugar	72
Glucose Syrup	30
Butter	10
Lecithin	0.375

Stage	Calculation	Sugar	Glucose Solids	Butter	Lecithin	
(a)	Dry weights (formula 18)	72×1·00 = 72	30×0·82 = 24·6	10·0×0·86 = 8·6	0·375×1·0 = 0·375	(Table 74)
(b)	Summation					105·6
(c)	Batch Yield	(see Table 5, §1·1 for total solids content)				$\frac{105\cdot6\times100}{96\cdot5}$ = 109·4
(d)	Sucrose					72
	Glucose Syrup					24·6
	Fat (including lecithin)					8·975

TABLE 76. Composition Factors (F_R) for Common Confectionery Raw Materials

Ingredient	Sucrose	Invert Sugar	Glucose Syrup Solids	Reducing Sugars	Protein	Fat	Acidity
Block Liquorice Juice	0·080			0·08			
Butter				0·005	0·005	0·81	
Chocolate							
Plain	0·42				0·045	0·35	
Milk	0·41			0·09	0·08	0·33	
Chocolate Crumb	0·54			0·14		0·14	
Citric Acid							0·91
Cocoa Liquor					0·005	0·54	
Cornflour							
Fruit Pulp				0·085			0·01
Gelatine					0·84		0·006
Golden Syrup	0·32	0·45					
Glucose Syrup							
Low DE			0·81	0·29			
Regular			0·82	0·34			
High DE			0·83	0·52			
Honey	0·06			0·77	0·015		0·01
Invert Sugar (70%)				0·70			
Milk Condensed (Full Cream)	0·42			0·14	0·09	0·09	
Milk Powder (Full Cream)				0·36	0·29	0·27	
Nuts						0·66	
Soya Flour				0·20	0·43	0·20	
Sugar, Brown	0·94			0·025			
Treacle	0·40			0·35			
Wheat Flour					0·14		
Whey, Condensed	0·39			0·27	0·06	0·005	

(e) Analysis % $\dfrac{72 \times 100}{109\cdot4}$ $\dfrac{24\cdot6 \times 100}{109\cdot4}$ $\dfrac{8\cdot975 \times 100}{109\cdot4}$

	%
Sucrose %	65·8
Glucose syrup solids %	22·5
Fat %	8·2
Moisture %	3·5

(g) Reducing Sugars $\dfrac{24\cdot6 \times 0\cdot43 \times 100}{109\cdot4}$ Reducing sugars %   9·7

17.7   CALCULATION OF SYRUP AND CRYSTAL PHASE

The calculation of syrup and crystal phases in a sugar confection can conveniently be carried out using the formula derived by C. L. HINTON [*Manufacturing Confectioner*, June 1958]. That is:

$$L = 2\cdot95M + 65R \qquad (22)$$

where L = syrup or liquid phase
M = moisture content
$$R = \frac{\text{glucose syrup solids} + \text{invert sugar solids}}{\text{total sugar solids}}$$

The solids composition of the syrup fraction can then be calculated using

$$\text{Component \%} = \frac{\text{Component Weight} \times 100}{\text{Total Component Weights}} \qquad (23)$$

The method for calculating syrup phase is illustrated by the following example for a fondant:

	%	
Total Solids		88·0
Moisture	12·0	
Sucrose	74·0	
Glucose Syrup Solids	11·0	
Invert Sugar	3·0	

Syrup Phase

Syrup Phase, %
$= 2\cdot95M + 65R$ (see 22)   (22)
$= 2\cdot95 \times 12\cdot0 + \dfrac{(11\cdot0 + 3\cdot0)}{88\cdot0} \, 65$
$= 35\cdot4 + (0\cdot159 \times 65)$
$= 35\cdot4 + 10\cdot3 = 45\cdot7$

Crystal Phase % $= 100 - 45\cdot7 = 54\cdot3$

This formula gives good results for 'all sugar' confections. It must be modified to take account of the presence of other raw materials which partially bind moisture present in a sweet. Ingredients such as gelatine and starch reduce the amount of water available to form the syrup phase. The amount of bound water can be estimated as follows:

Bound Water $=$ Component $(C) \times 0.14$ (24)
     where C $=$ percent, 'binder'
Free Water $(F) =$ Moisture, as determined $- 0.14C$ (25)

The value calculated for free water should be substituted for the moisture figure in the formula developed by Hinton for determining the syrup phase.

$$L = 2.95F + 65R \qquad (26)$$

17.8   SUGAR CONTENT OF THE SYRUP PHASE

A method for the calculation of the sugar content of the syrup phase has been devised by J. W. GROVER [*J. Soc. Chem. Ind.*, 1947, *66*, 201–205]. This formula has been modified according to the revised solubility values now known for sucrose.

Sucrose Content of Syrup Phase (S)
$$= 2.039 - 0.34 (g+i+sb) + 0.04 (g+i+sb) \qquad (27)$$
     where g, i and sb are the various weights of glucose syrup solids, invert sugar and sorbitol.

The method of calculating the syrup composition is as follows:

(a) Determine the weights of the various sugars (not sucrose) using

$$\frac{\text{Weight of individual Sugars per gramme of water present in the syrup phase}}{} = \frac{\% \text{ sugar component}}{\% \text{ free water}} \qquad (28)$$

(b) Substitute the calculated values in Grover's formula (27) and calculate the amount of sucrose in the syrup phase.

(c) List the weights of sucrose, glucose syrup solids, invert sugar per gramme of water in the syrup phase.

(d) Total the individual weights and calculate percent composition.

An example of the use of this method is given below for a sample of fondant (for analysis see §17.7).

Component	%		Weight of sugar g/g water
Water	12·0		
Sucrose in syrup phase	76·0	$\dfrac{74\cdot0 - 54\cdot3}{12\cdot0}$	1·642
Glucose Syrup Solids (g)	11·0	$\dfrac{11\cdot0}{12\cdot0}$	0·917
Invert Sugar (i)	11·0	$\dfrac{3\cdot0}{12\cdot0}$	0·250

$$S = 2 \cdot 039 - 0 \cdot 34(0 \cdot 917 + 0 \cdot 250) + 0 \cdot 04(0 \cdot 917 + 0 \cdot 250)^2$$
$$= 2 \cdot 039 - 0 \cdot 34 \times 1 \cdot 167 + 0 \cdot 04 \times 1 \cdot 167^2$$
$$= 2 \cdot 039 - 0 \cdot 40 + 0 \cdot 054$$
$$= 1 \cdot 693$$

Syrup Composition, (weight)

Sucrose	1·642
Glucose Syrup Solids	0·917
Invert Sugar	0·250
Water	1·000
Total	3·809

Syrup Composition, (per cent)

	%
Sucrose	43·1
Glucose Syrup Solids	24·1
Invert Sugar	6·6
Moisture	26·2

17.9   CALCULATION OF BOILING TEMPERATURE

Boiling a recipe mix to a fixed temperature under standard conditions will give a confection that has a constant total solids content. The effect of varying the cooking temperatures on composition and the effect of varying composition on the boiling properties can be calculated. The boiling temperatures for a range of sucrose syrups is given in Table 77.

In calculating boiling temperatures, the following steps should be taken:

(a) Assume that the sugar present is sucrose only and calculate the boiling temperature from Table 78.

(b) Calculate the 'equivalent sucrose concentration' of the glucose syrup ingredients using

$$ESC = Sc \times F_G \qquad (29)$$
where ESC = equivalent sugar concentration
Sc = sucrose concentration
F_G = factor for glucose syrup taken from Table 78

(c) Calculate the relevant boiling temperature from the information given in Table 79.

(d) Calculate the equivalent concentration of sucrose which would give the same boiling properties as the invert sugar.

$$ESC = Sc \times F_I \qquad (30)$$
where F_I = factor for invert sugar given in Table 78

(e) Portion out the various boiling effects according to the composition of the confection.

TABLE 77.   Boiling Points of Sucrose (Cane or Beet Sugar) Solutions

Sucrose Concentration (Sc) %	Boiling Point °C	°F
40	101·4	214·5
50	101·9	215·5
60	103·0	217·5
70	105·5	222
75	108·3	227
80	111·1	232
85	116·1	241
90	122·2	252
95	130·0	266

The following example illustrates the method of calculating boiling temperatures

Analysis of Syrup	%	
Total Solids		88·4
Moisture	11·6	
Sucrose	72·2	
Glucose Syrup Solids	16·2	

Step	Composition of Syrup	Concentration %	Boiling Temperature °C	Rate of Change of Temperature with Sucrose Concentration	Calculation	Calculated Boiling Temperature °C
(a)	All Sucrose	85·0	116·1	5·1° C/5% or		
		90·0	122·2	1·02° C/1%		
		88·4			116·1+ (3·4 × 1·02)	119·6
(b,c)	All Glucose	80·0 × 1·07 = 85·6	111·1	5·0/5% or		
		85·0 × 1·05 = 89·8	116·1	1·00/1%		
		88·4			111·1 + (2·8 × 1·00)	113·9 (29)
(e)	As Analysed	Contribution of Sucrose = 119·6 × (72·2÷88·4) = 97·7			+	118·8
		Contribution of Glucose Syrup	= 113·9 × (16·2÷88·4) = 20·9			

17.10   CALCULATION OF CHOCOLATE RECIPES

Method for Dried Milk

The stages in the calculation of chocolate recipes using dried milk are as follows:

(a)   Calculate the *milk solids not fat* value by multiplying % lactose by 1·82.   (*31*

(b)   Calculate the *fat free, dry cocoa solids* value from
fat free dry cocoa solids = 100·0−(sucrose, % + total fat, % + milk solids not fat, % + moisture, %).
(*32*)

TABLE 78. Factors Relating Concentration of Glucose Syrup (Gc) and Invert Sugar (Ic) to the Boiling Temperature of Sucrose Solutions

Sugar Concentration	Invert Sugar	Glucose Syrup Factors (FG)			
		Low DE	Regular	High DE	Enzyme
60	0·94	1·21	1·18	1·15	1·13
70	0·95	1·17	1·14	1·12	1·09
75	0·96	1·11	1·08	1·06	1·03
80	0·96	1·09	1·07	1·05	1·03
85	0·96	1·06	1·05	1·04	1·02
90	0·97	1·03	1·03	1·02	1·01
95	0·98	1·01	1·02	1·01	1·00

(c)   Write out analysis so as to list
      Sucrose
      Total Fat
      Milk Solids not Fat
      Fat free, Dry Cocoa Solids
      Moisture

(d)   Calculate the *butterfat* value by multiplying the lactose value by 0·69 (or by multiplying the milk solids not fat value by 0·38). (33)

(e)   Determine the *total milk solids* by totalling the milk solids not fat and the butterfat. (34)

(f)   Determine the *total cocoa butter* using cocoa butter = total fat content − (summation of all fats other than cocoa butter). (35)

(g)   Calculate the *cocoa butter present in the cocoa liquor* from cocoa butter in liquor = fat free, dry cocoa solids × 1·18. (36)

(h)   Determine the *added cocoa butter* using added cocoa butter = total cocoa butter content − cocoa butter in liquor. (37)

(i)   Determine the *cocoa liquor* by multiplying the fat free, dry cocoa solids by 2·17. (38)

(j)   Write out the analysis so as to list
      Sucrose
      Cocoa Liquor
      Added Cocoa Butter
      Milk Solids

(k)   Calculate recipe weights by the method given in Formula 1 using $B \times p \times f$* (§17.2).

Method for Milk Crumb carry out stages (a), (b), (c) then:

(l)   Calculate the amount of *milk crumb* by multiplying the milk solids not fat by 3·85. (39)

(m)   Determine the contribution of the *major components in milk crumb* as follows:

	%	
Sucrose	= 0·535 × mc	(40)
Cocoa Butter	= 0·050 × mc	(41)
Fat free, Dry Cocoa	= 0·045 × mc	(42)
Milk Fat	= 0·100 × mc	(43)

where *mc* = per cent milk crumb
(Note that moisture and milk fat solids not fat are given by 0·010 *mc* and 0·26 *mc* respectively).

(n)   Determine the *cocoa solids present in the cocoa liquor* using cocoa solids in liquor = cocoa solids as determined − cocoa solids in crumb (see §17·10b). (44)

(o)   Calculate the amount of *cocoa liquor* by multiplying the cocoa solids in liquor (n) by 2.17. (45)

(p)   Determine the *cocoa butter* in the liquor using cocoa butter in liquor = cocoa liquor (o) − cocoa solids in liquor (n) (46)

(q)   Determine the *added sugar* using added sugar = sucrose as determined − sucrose in milk crumb (47)

354 SUGAR CONFECTIONERY AND CHOCOLATE MANUFACTURE

TABLE 79. Chocolate Calculations

PLAIN CHOCOLATE

Step	Analysis			
	Moisture		0.7%	
	Fat free dry cocoa solids		12.9%	
	Cocoa butter		34.4%	
	Sucrose		52.0%	
	Other fats		Absent	
(u) Cocoa Liquor		12.9×2.17		28.0%
(v) Cocoa Butter in the Liquor		$28.0 - 12.9$		15.1%
(w) Added Cocoa Butter		$34.4 - 15.1$		19.3%
(x) Revised Analysis	Sucrose		52.0%	
	Cocoa liquor		28.0%	
	Added cocoa butter		19.3%	
(y) Individual Component (assume 560 lb batch)	Sucrose	560×0.52	293 lb sugar	
	Cocoa liquor	560×0.28	158 lb cocoa liquor	
	Cocoa butter	560×0.193	109 lb cocoa butter	

MILK CHOCOLATE PRODUCED FROM MILK CRUMB

	Analysis			
	Moisture		0.6%	
	Sucrose		45.1%	
	Lactose		8.3%	
	Total fat		34.3%	
	No foreign fats detected other than milk fat			
(a) Milk Solids, not fat		8.3×1.82		15.1%
Fat free, Dry Cocoa Solids		$100 - (45.1 + 34.3 + 15.1 + 0.6)$		4.9%

(b) Revised Analysis

Sucrose	45·1%
Total fat	34·3%
Milk solids not fat	15·1%
Fat free, dry cocoa solids	4·9%
Moisture	0·6%

(l) Milk Crumb $\quad 15·1 \times 3·85 \quad$ 58·1%

(m) Individual Components of Milk Crumb

Sucrose	$0·535 \times 58·1$	31·1%
Cocoa butter	$0·050 \times 58·1$	2·9%
Fat free dry cocoa	$0·045 \times 58·1$	2·6%
Milk fat	$0·100 \times 58·1$	5·8%

(n) Cocoa Solids in Cocoa Liquor $\quad 4·9 - 2·6 \quad$ 2·3%

(o) Cocoa Liquor $\quad 2·3 \times 2·17 \quad$ 5·0%

(p) Cocoa Butter in Liquor $\quad 5·0 - 2·3 \quad$ 2·7%

(q) Added Cocoa Butter $\quad 34·3 - (2·7 + 2·9 + 5·8) \quad$ 22·9%

(r) Added Sugar $\quad 45·1 - 31·1 \quad$ 14·0%

(s) Revised Analysis

Milk crumb	58·1%
Added cocoa butter	22·9%
Added sugar	14·0%
Cocoa liquor	5·0%

(k) Batch Yield $\quad$ assume 560 lb

Milk Crumb	$560 \times 0·581$	325 lb
Cocoa Butter	$560 \times 0·229$	128 lb
Sugar	$560 \times 0·140$	79 lb
Cocoa Liquor	$560 \times 0·050$	28 lb

(r)   Determine the *added cocoa butter* using added cocoa butter = total fat as determined (c) — (cocoa butter in liquor (p)+cocoa butter in milk crumb (m)+milk fat (m))   (48)

(s)   Write out the analysis so as to list
           Milk Crumb, %
           Added Cocoa Butter, %
           Added Sugar, %

(t)   Calculate the individual components as in (k)

Method for Plain Chocolate

(u)   Calculate the *cocoa liquor* by multiplying the fat free, dry cocoa solids (b) by 2·17   (49)

(v)   Determine the *cocoa butter in the cocoa liquor* using cocoa butter in cocoa liquor = cocoa liquor — fat free dry cocoa solids   (50)

(w)   Determine the *added cocoa butter* using added cocoa butter = total cocoa butter (f) — cocoa butter in liquor (p)   (51)

(x)   Write out the analysis so as to list
           Sucrose
           Cocoa Liquor
           Added Cocoa Butter

(y)   Calculate the weight of individual components as described in (k)

Note: The final stage should include the calculation of foreign fats if detected in the analysis.

Table 79 illustrates the methods above described, using lb units and assuming a batch-weight of 560 lb (users of metric units are referred to the Conversion Tables at the end of the book).

17.11   COUNT (NUMBER OF CONFECTIONS) PER UNIT WEIGHT

Avoirdupois:

$$\text{Count/lb} = \text{No. of sweets in test sample} \times \frac{16}{\text{weight in oz}} \qquad (52)$$

Count/lb, from metric measurements:
$$= \text{No. of sweets in test sample} \ \frac{454}{\text{weight in grammes}} \qquad (53)$$

Count/centigramme, from avoirdupois measurements:
$$= \text{No. of sweets in test sample} \ \frac{3·53}{\text{weight in oz}} \qquad (54)$$

$$\text{Count/unit weight of centres} = \frac{(\text{Count/unit weight of confections}) \times 100}{\% \text{ of centre in confection}} \qquad (55)$$

17.12 DETERMINATION OF EQUILIBRIUM RELATIVE HUMIDITY (ERH)

Of a number of methods suggested for this purpose, that developed by R. S. NORRISH at the British Food Manufacturing Research Association is both convenient and rapid. It employs the nomogram shown in Fig. 51. [R. S. NORRISH, *Conf. Prod.*, 1964, (*10*), 769, 771, 808.] The stages are:

(*a*) For each component sugar, calculate the weight of sugar in the syrup phase per unit of water, as follows:
Sugar/g water = % sugar component/% free water.

(*b*) Mark these unit weights on the respective scales, both the left hand set and the lower set.

(*c*) On left-hand set, join the points on scale A and scale B and produce the line to the blank scale C.

(*d*) From the point of contact on C draw a line through the point on scale D and produce to meet blank scale E. Continue this procedure until the line meets the XY axis. (If a component is absent the line should go through 0 on its scale.)

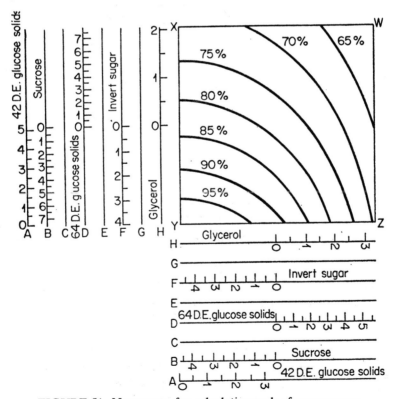

FIGURE 51. Nomogram for calculating e r h of sugar syrups.

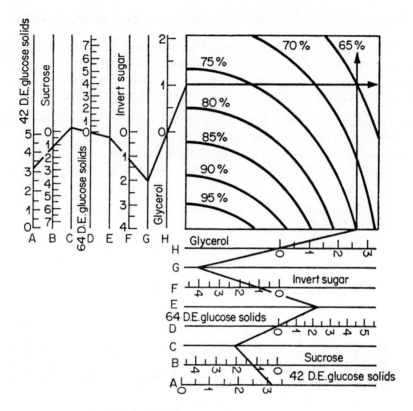

FIGURE 52. Nomogram of cream paste sample.

(e) Proceed in the same way for the lower set of scales, from scale A up to the YZ axis.

(f) Draw a horizontal line from the point of contact on the XY axis and a vertical line from that on the YZ axis. The intersection indicates the e r h percentage according to the curves.

Note that the invert sugar scale should be used for dextrose, fructose, sorbitol and gelatine. Fig. 52 shows the lines drawn for a cream paste sample with 3·16 g 42 DE glucose syrup solids/g water, 1·24 g sucrose/g water, 1·11 g invert sugar/g water and 0·19 g gelatine/g water in the syrup phase.

In J. W. GROVER's method, [*J. Soc. Chem. Ind.*, 1947, *66*, 201–5] the weight/g water for each component is converted to a sucrose weight of equivalent effect by a conversion factor q (Table 80) and the resulting equivalent sucrose mixture is related to an e r h value (Table 81).

TABLE 80. Vapour Pressure; Conversion Factors to Sucrose Equivalent

Raw Material	Conv. Factor (q)
Glucose Syrup, Starch, Gums, Pectins	0·8
Sucrose, Lactose	1·0
Invert Sugar, Gelatine, Casein, Sorbitol	1·3
Tartaric Acid, Citric Acid and their Salts	2·5
Glycerol	4·0
Sodium Chloride	9·0

Using the same example as above, for cream paste, the weights of the ingredients per gramme of water will be converted thus:

Glucose Syrup Solids	$3·16 \times 0·8 = 2·53$
Sucrose	$1·24 \times 1·00 = 1·24$
Invert Sugar	$1·11 \times 1·3 = 1·44$
Gelatine	$0·19 \times 1·3 = 0·25$
Summation Es	5·46

The e r h value taken from Table 81 is 62·6%.

TABLE 81. Equilibrium Relative Humidities corresponding to Equivalent Sucrose Concentrations

Equiv. sucrose conc.	Relative humidity %	Equiv. sucrose conc.	Relative humidity %
2·0	85·8	4·4	68·6
2·1	85·0	4·5	68·0
2·2	84·2	4·6	67·4
2·3	83·4	4·7	66·8
2·4	82·5	4·8	66·2
2·5	81·7	4·9	65·6
2·6	80·8	5·0	65·1
2·7	80·0	5·2	64·1
2·8	79·2	5·4	63·1
2·9	78·4	5·6	62·3
3·0	77·7	5·8	61·5
3·1	77·0	6·0	60·7
3·2	76·3	6·2	59·9
3·3	75·6	6·4	59·0
3·4	74·9	6·6	58·0
3·5	74·2	6·8	57·1
3·6	73·5	7·0	56·3
3·7	72·9	7·2	55·4
3·8	72·3	7·4	54·6
3·9	71·6	7·6	53·9
4·0	71·0	7·8	53·3
4·1	70·4	8·0	52·7
4·2	69·8	8·5	51·2
4·3	69·2	9·0	49·9

18

General Reference Tables

TABLE 82. Units and Conversion Factors

The UK 'imperial' units (of which those for weight are sometimes also called 'avoirdupois') is also used in USA with a few exceptions notably those set out below. This Table includes only those units of relevance to the confectionery industry; and only to a degree of accuracy sufficient for its purposes.

Data on the many hundreds of different units in use throughout the world can be found in Naft and da Sola: International Conversion Tables (London: Cassell; New York: Duell, Sloane and Pearce).

See Table 83 for examples of conversion calculations.

Imperial/US	*Metric*	*Metric*	*Imperial/US*
	WEIGHT		
1 ounce (oz) = 16 drams (dr)	= 28·35 grammes (g)	1 gramme	= 0·353 ounce
1 pound (lb) = 16 oz	= 0·4536 kilogrammes (kg)	1 kilogramme	= 2·2046 pounds
1 stone = 14 lb	= 6·350 kg		
1 hundredweight (cwt) = 112 lb	= 50·80 kg		
1 ton (long) = 2240 lb	= 1016·05 kg or 1·016 tonne	1 tonne (t) = 1000 kg	= 0·984 long ton or 1·1023 short ton
1 ton (short: US) = 2000 lb	= 907·19 kg or 0·907 tonne		
	CAPACITY		
1 fluid ounce (fl oz) = 0·961 US fl oz	= 28·41 cubic cm (cm³)	1 litre (l) = 1000 cm³	= 1·76 pint or 0·22 imp gal
1 pint = 20 fl oz	= 0·568 litre (l)		
1 gallon (imp) = 8 pints = 1·201 US gal	= 4·55 litres		
1 gallon US = 0·833 imp gal	= 3·79 litres	**1 litre**	= 0·264 US gal
	LENGTH, AREA AND VOLUME		
1 inch (in)	= 25·40 millimetres (mm)	1 metre (m) = 1000 mm	= 1·094 yd
1 yard (yd) = 36 in	= 0·914 metre	1 millimetre	= 0·0394 in

TABLE 82.—*contd.*

1 square in	$= 645 \cdot 2$ mm^2	1 cm^2	$= 0 \cdot 155$ in^2
1 square foot	$= 0 \cdot 0929$ m^2	1 m^2	$= 1 \cdot 196$ yd^2
1 cubic in	$= 16 \cdot 39$ cm^3	1 cm^3	$= 0 \cdot 061$ in^3
1 cubic foot	$= 0 \cdot 0283$ m^3	1 m^3	$= 1 \cdot 308$ yd^3

OTHER IMPERIAL UNITS AND EQUIVALENTS

1 gallon (imperial) of water weighs 10 lb	1 cubic foot of water weighs 62·55 lb
4 gills = 1 pint (capacity)	7000 grains = 256 drams = 1 lb (weight)
1 cal = 4·1868J	1hp = 745·7W

TABLE 86.   Temperature Conversion: °C and °F

Centigrade	Fahrenheit	Centigrade	Fahrenheit	Centigrade	Fahrenheit
−12·2	10	25	77	79·4	175
−10	14	26	78·8	80	176
−9·5	15	26·6	80	82·2	180
−6·6	20	27	80·6	85	185
−5	23	28	82·4	87·7	190
−3·8	25	29	84·2	90	194
−1·1	30	29·4	85	90·5	195
0	32	30	86	93·3	200
1	33·8	31	87·8	95	203
1·6	35	32	89·6	96·1	205
2	35·6	32·2	90	98·8	210
3	37·4	33	91·4	100	212
4	39·2	34	93·2	101·7	215
4·4	40	35	95	104·4	220
5	41	36	96·8	105	221
6	42·8	37	98·6	107·2	225
7	44·6	37·7	100	110	230
7·2	45	38	100·4	112·8	235
8	46·4	39	102·2	115	239
9	48·2	40	104	115·6	240
10	50	40·5	105	118·4	245
11	51·8	43·3	110	120	248
12	53·6	45	113	121·1	250
12·7	55	46·1	115	123·9	255
13	55·4	48·8	120	125	257
14	57·2	50	122	126·7	260
15	59	51·6	125	129·5	265
15·5	60	54·4	130	130	266
16	60·8	55	131	132·2	270
17	62·6	57·2	135	135	275
18	64·4	60	140	137·8	280
18·3	65	62·7	145	140	284
19	66·2	65	149	140·6	285
20	68	65·5	150	143·4	290
21	69·8	68·3	155	145	293
21·1	70	70	158	146·1	295
22	71·6	71·1	160	148·9	300
23	73·4	73·8	165	150	302
23·8	75	75	167	151·7	305
24	75·2	76·6	170	154·5	310

TABLE 83. Example of Conversion of Units

Syrup for use in Boiled Sweet Manufacture

Ingredient	Recipe A			Recipe B		
	Avoirdupois Weight	*Calculation*	*Metric Value*	*Metric Weight*	*Calculation*	*Avoirdupois Value*
Cane Sugar	240 lb	240×0.4536	109 kg	100 kg	100×2.2046	220 lb
Glucose Syrup	160 lb	160×0.4536	73 kg	50 kg	50×2.2046	110 lb
Water	14 gal	$14 \times 10 \times 4.536$	63·5 l	50 l	50×0.22	11 gal

TABLE 84. Specific Gravity (Water=1) of some Confectionery Products

Product	Sp. Gravity
Caramels	1·38
Cream Paste	1·26
High Boilings	1·49
Liquorice Paste	1·35

TABLE 85. Specific Heats (Water=1) of some Confectionery Ingredients

Ingredient	Sp. Heat
Fat	0·48–0·51
Flour	0·42
Sugar	0·32
Sugar Solution, 65% at 20° C (68°F)	0·63

TABLE 87. Equivalent Rises in Temperature Scales, above Freezing Point

Rise in Centigrade degs.	1	2	3	4	5	6	7	8	9
Rise in Fahrenheit degs.	1·8	3·6	5·4	7·2	9	10·8	12·6	14·4	16·2
Rise in Fahrenheit degs.	1	2	3	4	5	6	7	8	9
Rise in Centigrade degs.	0·6	1·1	1·7	2·2	2·8	3·3	3·9	4·4	5·0

TABLE 88. Storage Space Requirements of some Ingredients

Ingredient	Weight in lb occupying 1 ft^3	Weight in kg occupying 1 m^3
Chocolate	78–85	1250–1360
Cocoa Beans	30–40	480–640
Flour	30–40	480–640
Glucose Syrup	85–90	1360–1440
Salt	45–50	720–800
Sugar Crystals	47–65	750–1040
Starch	90–100	1440–1600

19

Glossary

BALLING	Formation, when sieving a powder, of balls which cannot pass through the mesh.
BAUMÉ SCALE	A scale, devised for convenient hydrometer reading, which can be related to concentrations of sugar solutions (see §16.2).
BLANCH, to	To clean away the skin of nuts by scalding with hot water.
BLOCKING (of powder)	Compression of a powder so as to produce a non-flowing mass.
BLOOM	*See* Fat or Sugar Bloom.
BLOOM GRADE	Measure of the strength of a jelly determined on a Bloom gelometer.
BRAKE	Twin adjustable rollers used to reduce the thickness of confectionery products.
BRIX SCALE	A scale with the same purpose as the Baumé (above).
BUFFER	Salt used to minimise small changes in acidity, and acidity arising from the addition of other ingredients.
CANDY, to	To preserve fruits by immersing them in syrup thereby increasing their sugar content.
CARAMEL (in boiling)	A stage reached during the boiling of sugar syrup, see §1.2.
CHEW, the	The 'mouth feel' of a confection during mastication.
CONFECTIONER'S GLUCOSE	A defunct term for glucose syrup.
CRACK	Stage in boiling sugar syrup; see §1.2.

DRESS, to	To restore a piece of equipment, such as a roller, or an ingredient, such as starch, to its original specification.
DROP	Variety of high-boiled sweet produced on a drop roller.
DUSTING	Coating confections with icing sugar, fine sugar crystals or anti stick powders.
DOCTOR (SUGAR)	A sugar ingredient which represses the crystallisation of sucrose by raising total saturation concentration.
EXTRA HARD CRACK	Stage in boiling sugar syrup; see §1.2.
ENGROSSING	In panning, the building up of a sugar coat on centres.
ENROBE, to	To cover a confectionery centre with a coating of chocolate.
FAT	Term for a greasy look to a confection, due to excessive inversion of sucrose during boiling.
FAT BLOOM	Development of unstable fat crystals on the surface of chocolate.
FEATHER	Stage in boiling sugar syrup; see §1.2.
FLOW	Term used generally for flow behaviour of a confection.
FOAM	Beaten mixture of a whipping agent in water.
FORMERS	Series of horizontal rollers arranged to form boiled sugar syrup into a thin rope.
FRAPPÉ	Whipped mixture of foaming agent in sugar syrup.
FUDGE (fudging)	Unplanned crystallisation of sugar in a confection.
GEL, to	To form a jelly.
GELLING AGENT	A material which promotes gelling.
GLASS	An amorphous 'rigid liquid' arising when cooling takes place so rapidly that crystallisation does not occur.
GLAZE, to	To coat a confection with a solution which, on drying, produces a high gloss.
GLU	A corruption of term 'glucose syrup'.
GRAINING	Unplanned crystallisation of sugar in a confection.

N

GREASY	See FAT.
HARD CRACK	Stage in boiling sugar syrup; see §1.2.
INVERSION	Breakdown of sucrose into its two constituent sugars.
INVERT SUGAR	Mixture of approximately equal parts of dextrose and laevulose.
KETTLE	Steam jacketed warming or boiling pan.
LARGE BALL	
LARGE PEARL	Stages in boiling of sugar syrup; see §1.2.
LARGE THREAD	
LEACHING (of sugars)	Transfer of sugar or starch from one confectionery type into another.
LEAKAGE	Seepage of syrup from a coated confection.
LIGHT CRACK	Stage in boiling sugar syrup; see §1.2.
LIQUID SUGAR	Commercial mixture of sugars offered in syrup form.
MASSECUITE	Mixture of boiled syrup and sugar crystals.
MEDIUM CRACK	Stage in boiling sugar syrup; see §1.2.
MOGUL	Machine for depositing confectionery mixtures into impressions formed in starch or in rubber mats.
'ON THE TURN'	Change of a boiled sugar mass from the plastic to the glassy state.
PEARL	A stage reached during the boiling of sugar syrup.
PLASTIC STATE	The semi-labile state of high-boiled sugar syrup during cooling, see §1.2.
PRESS CAKE	Compressed cocoa powder after removal of cocoa butter.
PULLING	Repeated folding of high-boiled sugar syrup, carried out on the revolving arms of a pulling machine.
ROPE	Rod of cooked sugar syrup produced on a forming machine.
SAND, to	To coat confections with icing sugar or fine sugar crystals.
SEEDING	Addition of a small amount of crystals ('seed')

to a supersaturated syrup to promote crystallisation.

SMALL BALL	Stages in boiling sugar syrup; see §1.2.
SMALL PEARL	
SNAP	Breaking characteristics of a confection.
SOUFFLÉ	Stage in boiling sugar syrup; see §1.2.
SUGAR BLOOM	Development of fine sugar clusters on the surface of chocolate.
SWEAT (bleeding)	Appearance of droplets of moisture or sugar syrup on the surface of a confection.
TEMPER, to	To process chocolate so that any crystallisation of fat occurs in a stable modification.
THREAD	Stage in boiling sugar syrup; see §1.2.
TRAY OFF	To remove confections on to a holding tray.
WEEPING	Same as 'sweat'.
WETTING	Charge of syrup added during sugar panning.
WHIP	To beat a syrup mixture so that air becomes entrapped.
WHIPPING AGENT	Product which promotes the formation of stable whips and foams.

Appendix

Manufacturer's Name on Imported Plant	U.K. Representatives
Aasted	J. W. Greer Co. Ltd., Sittingbourne.
ASIMA	Emmerich (London) Ltd., London E18.
Barth	Bramigk & Co. Ltd., London E3.
Bauermeister	Bramigk & Co. Ltd., London E3.
Bindler	Norman Bartleet Ltd., London W14.
Carle and Montanari	Cornwall Products Ltd., London W1.
Dänger	Bramigk & Co. Ltd., London E3.
Dumoulin	Bramigk & Co. Ltd., London E3.
Eur-O-Matic	Norman Bartleet Ltd., London W14.
Hamac Hansella	Robert Bosch Packaging Machinery (UK) Ltd., London W3.
Henkel	Norman Bartleet Ltd., London W14.
Heuze Malevez and Simon	Norman Bartleet Ltd., London W14.
HMS	Norman Bartleet Ltd., London W14.
Jensen	Bramigk & Co. Ltd., London E3.
Kampert/Bodderas	Bramigk & Co. Ltd., London E3.
Kreuter	Bramigk & Co. Ltd., London E3.
Lehmann	F. Jahn & Co. Ltd., London N1.
Mikrovaek	Bramigk & Co. Ltd., London E3.
Nalder & Nalder	Norman Bartleet Ltd., London W14.
NID	Norman Bartleet Ltd., London W14.
Nuovafirmia	Raglen Packaging Ltd., Southall.
Petzholdt	Emmerich (London) Ltd., London E18.
Rasch	Norman Bartleet Ltd., London W14.
Schroter	Clifford Coupe Ltd., Kingston upon Thames.
Seragnoli	Wrapping Machines Ltd., London NW1.
Smith & Sons	Clifford Coupe Ltd., Kingston upon Thames.
Steinberg	F. Jahn & Co. Ltd., London N1.
Ter Braak	Bramigk & Co. Ltd., London E3.

[*Situation as at August 1972.*]

Index